Computational Complexity and Statistical Physics

Lecture Notes Volumes

Swarm Intelligence: From Natural to Artificial Systems, 1999
 Eric Bonabeau, Marco Dorigo, and Guy Theraulaz

Modeling Extinction, 2002
 Mark E. J. Newman and Richard Palmer

Proceedings Volumes

Scaling in Biology, 2000
 James H. Brown and Geoffrey B. West, editors

Dynamics in Human and Primate Societies, 2000
 Timothy A. Kohler and George J. Gumerman, editors

*Design Principles for the Immune System and Other Distributed
Autonomous Systems*, 2001
 Lee A. Segel and Irun Cohen, editors

*Integrating Geographic Information Systems and Agent-Based
Modeling Techniques*, 2001
 H. Randy Gimblett, editor

*Evolutionary Dynamics: Exploring the Interplay of Selection, Accident,
Neutrality, and Function*, 2003
 James P. Crutchfield and Peter Schuster, editors

New Constructions in Cellular Automata, 2003
 David Griffeath and Cristopher Moore, editors

Nonextensive Entropy—Interdisciplinary Applications, 2004
 Murray Gell-Mann and Constantino Tsallis, editors

Perspectives on Adaptation in Natural and Artificial Systems, 2005
 Lashon Booker, Stephanie Forrest, Melanie Mitchell, and Rick Riolo, editors

*Robust Design: A Repertoire of Biological, Ecological, and Engineering
Case Studies*, 2005
 Erica Jen, editor

The Internet as a Large-Scale, Complex System, 2005
 Kihong Park and Walter Willinger, editors

The Economy as an Evolving Complex System III, 2005
 Lawrence E. Blume and Steven N. Durlauf, editors

Ecological Networks: Linking Structure to Dynamics in Food Webs, 2005
 Mercedes Pascual and Jennifer Dunne, editors

Computational Complexity and Statistical Physics, 2005
 Allon G. Percus, Gabriel Istrate, and Cristopher Moore, editors

Computational Complexity and Statistical Physics

Editors

Allon G. Percus
Institute for Pure and Applied Mathematics, UCLA &
Los Alamos National Laboratory

Gabriel Istrate
Los Alamos National Laboratory

Cristopher Moore
University of New Mexico & Santa Fe Institute

Santa Fe Institute
Studies in the Sciences of Complexity

OXFORD
UNIVERSITY PRESS

2006

OXFORD
UNIVERSITY PRESS

Oxford University Press, Inc., publishes works that further
Oxford University's objective of excellence
in research, scholarship, and education.

Oxford   New York
Auckland   Cape Town   Dar es Salaam   Hong Kong   Karachi
Kuala Lumpur   Madrid   Melbourne   Mexico City   Nairobi
New Delhi   Shanghai   Taipei   Toronto

With offices in
Argentina   Austria   Brazil   Chile   Czech Republic   France   Greece
Guatemala   Hungary   Italy   Japan   Poland   Portugal   Singapore
South Korea   Switzerland   Thailand   Turkey   Ukraine   Vietnam

Copyright © 2006 by Oxford University Press, Inc.

Published by Oxford University Press, Inc.
198 Madison Avenue, New York, New York 10016

www.oup.com

Oxford is a registered trademark of Oxford University Press

Library of Congress Cataloging-in-Publication Data
Computational complexity and statistical physics / edited by Allon Percus,
Gabriel Istrate, and Cristopher Moore.
p. cm. — (The Santa Fe Institute studies in the sciences of complexity)
Includes bibliographical references and index.
ISBN-13 978-0-19-517737-4; 978-0-19-517738-1 (pbk.)
ISBN 0-19-517737-1; 0-19-517738-X (pbk.)
1. Computational complexity. 2. Combinatorial analysis. 3. Statistical physics.
4. Phase transformations (Statistical physics) I. Percus, Allon. II. Istrate, Gabriel.
III. Moore, Cristopher. IV. Proceedings volume in the Santa Fe Institute studies
in the sciences of complexity.
QA267.7.C683 2005
511.3'52—dc22   2005047785

Printed in the United States of America
on acid-free paper

About the Santa Fe Institute

The *Santa Fe Institute* (SFI) is a private, independent, multidisciplinary research and education center, founded in 1984. Since its founding, SFI has devoted itself to creating a new kind of scientific research community, pursuing emerging science. Operating as a small, visiting institution, SFI seeks to catalyze new collaborative, multidisciplinary projects that break down the barriers between the traditional disciplines, to spread its ideas and methodologies to other individuals, and to encourage the practical applications of its results.

All titles from the *Santa Fe Institute Studies in the Sciences of Complexity* series carry this imprint which is based on a Mimbres pottery design (circa A.D. 950–1150), drawn by Betsy Jones. The design was selected because the radiating feathers are evocative of the outreach of the Santa Fe Institute Program to many disciplines and institutions.

Contributors List

Alfredo Braunstein, *International School for Advanced Studies, via Beirut 9, I-34100 Trieste, Italy; e-mail: abraunst@sissa.it*

Simona Cocco, *École Normale Supérieure, Laboratoire de Physique Statistique, 24 rue Lhomond, F-75231 Paris Cedex 05; e-mail: cocco@lps.ens.fr*

Demetrios Demopoulos, *Rice University, Department of Computer Science, Duncan Hall, 3099, Mail Stop 132, Houston, TX 77251; e-mail: demopoul@cs.rice.edu*

Hasan Guclu, *Rensselaer Polytechnic Institute, Department of Physics, Applied Physics and Astronomy, 110 8th Street, Troy, NY 12180; e-mail: gucluh@rpi.edu*

Tad Hogg, *HP Labs, MS 1139, 1501 Page Mill Road, Palo Alto, CA 94304; e-mail: tad.hogg@hp.com*

Harry B. Hunt, III, *University at Albany–SUNY, Department of Computer Science, Albany, NY 12222; e-mail: hunt@cs.albany.edu*

Gabriel Istrate, *Los Alamos National Laboratory, Basic and Applied Simulation Science (CCS-5), MS M997, Los Alamos, NM 87545; e-mail: istrate@lanl.gov*

Gil Kalai, *Hebrew University of Jerusalem, Institute of Mathematics, Givat Ram, Jerusalem 91904, Israel; and Yale University, Department of Computer Science and Mathematics Department, New Haven, CT 06520; e-mail: kalai@math.huji.il*

Alexis Kaporis, *University of Patras, Department of Computer Engineering and Informatics, University Campus, Patras GR-26504, Greece; e-mail: kaporis@ceid.upatras.gr*

Lefteris Kirousis, *University of Patras, Department of Computer Engineering and Informatics, University Campus, Patras GR-26504, Greece; e-mail: kirousis@ceid.upatras.gr*

Sigismund Kobe, *Institut für Theoretische Physik, Technische Universität Dresden, D-01062 Dresden, Germany; e-mail: kobe@theory.phy.tu-dresden.de*

György Korniss, *Rensselaer Polytechic Institute, Department of Physics, Applied Physics, and Astronomy, 110 8th Street, Troy, NY 12180-3590; e-mail: korniss@rpi.edu*

Jarek Krawczyk, *Institut für Theoretische Physik, Technische Universität Dresden, D-01062 Dresden, Germany; and ARC Centre of Excellence for Mathematics and Statistics of Complex Systems, The University of Melbourne, Parkville, Victoria 3010, Australia; e-mail: j.krawczyk@ms.unimelb.edu.au*

Madhav Marathe, *Virginia Bio-Informatics Institute and Department of Computer Science, Virginia Tech, Blacksburg, VA 24061; e-mail: marathe@vt.edu*

Stephan Mertens, *Institut für Theoretische Physik, Universitätsplatz 2, D-39108 Magdeburg, Germany; e-mail: stephan.mertens@physik.uni-magdeburg.de*

Marc Mézard, *Laboratoire de Physique Théorique et Modéles Statistiques, Université Paris-Sud, F-91405 Orsay, France; e-mail: mezard@lptms.u-psud.fr*

Rémi Monasson, *École Normale Supérieure, Laboratoire de Physique Théorique, 24 rue Lhomond, F-75231 Paris Cedex 05, France; e-mail: monasson@lpt.ens.fr*

Andrea Montanari, *École Normale Supérieure, Laboratoire de Physique Théorique, 24 rue Lhomond, F-75231 Paris Cedex 05, France; e-mail: montanari@lpt.ens.fr*

Cristopher Moore, *University of New Mexico, Department of Computer Science and Department of Physics and Astronomy, Farris Engineering Center, Albuquerque, NM 87131; and Santa Fe Institute, 1399 Hyde Park Road, Santa Fe, NM 87501; e-mail: moore@cs.unm.edu*

Mark A. Novotny, *Mississippi State University, ERC Center for Computational Sciences and Department of Physics and Astronomy, Mississippi State, MS 39762; e-mail: novotny@msstate.edu*

Allon Percus, *University of California, Los Angeles, Institute for Pure and Applied Mathematics, 460 Portola Plaza, Los Angeles, CA 90095; and Los Alamos National Laboratory, Computer and Computational Sciences, MS B256, Los Alamos, NM 87545; e-mail: percus@ipam.ucla.edu*

Christian M. Reidys, *Los Alamos National Laboratory, Basic and Applied Simulation Science (CCS-5), MS M997, Los Alamos, NM 87545; e-mail: duck@santafe.edu*

Daniel J. Rosenkrantz, *University at Albany–SUNY, Department of Computer Science, Albany, NY 12222; e-mail: djr@cs.albany.edu*

Shmuel Safra, *Tel Aviv University, School of Mathematical Sciences, Ramat Aviv, Tel Aviv 69978, Israel; and Princeton University, Institute for Advanced Studies, School of Mathematics, 1 Einstein Drive, Princeton, NJ 08540; e-mail: safra@tau.ac.il*

Guilhem Semerjian, *École Normale Supérieure, Laboratoire de Physique Théorique, 24 rue Lhomond, F-75231 Paris Cedex 05, France; e-mail: guilhem@lpt.ens.fr*

Yannis C. Stamatiou, *University of Ioannina, Mathematics Department, P.O. Box 1186, 45110 Ioannina, Greece; e-mail: istamat@cc.uoi.gr*

Richard E. Stearns, *University at Albany–SUNY, Department of Computer Science, Albany, NY 12222; e-mail: res@cs.albany.edu*

Zoltan Toroczkai, *Los Alamos National Laboratory, Theoretical Division and CNLS, MS B258, Los Alamos, NM 87545; e-mail: toro@lanl.gov*

Moshe Y. Vardi, *Rice University, Department of Computer Science, Mail Stop 132, Houston, TX 77251; e-mail: vardi@cs.rice.edu*

Martin Weigt, *Institute for Scientific Interchange, Viale S. Severo 65, I-10133 Torino, Italy; e-mail: weigt@isiosf.isi.it*

Riccardo Zecchina, *The Abdus Salam International Centre for Theoretical Physics, Strada Costiera 11, I-34100 Trieste, Italy; e-mail: zecchina@ictp.trieste.it*

Michele Zito, *University of Liverpool, Department of Computer Science, Liverpool L69 3BX. United Kingdom; e-mail: michele@csc.liv.ac.uk*

Contents

PART 3: IDENTIFYING THE THRESHOLD

PART 4: EXTENSIONS AND APPLICATIONS

Preface

By its very nature, computational complexity seeks a precise characterization of problems and the means required to solve them. Statistical physics tolerates—even exploits—uncertainty in a problem's description. And yet, a great scientific success story of the past ten years has been the way in which each of these fields has contributed to the other. Physicists have productively applied concepts developed in condensed matter theory to reshape our understanding of solving hard computational problems and to develop better algorithms. Theoretical computer scientists have contributed methods of analysis to statistical physics models that put physicists' predictions on a rigorous footing and help understand the detailed structure of physical systems.

With this as background, we organized a workshop in September 2001, in Santa Fe, New Mexico, entitled *Computational Complexity and Statistical Physics*. The stated aim was to "provide an interdisciplinary forum for the exchange of ideas, enabling a better understanding of the state-of-the-art, and more ambitiously, charting the course towards a theory of critical phenomena in algorithmic problems." Much of this sounds rather generic. But at the time,

Computational Complexity and Statistical Physics, edited by
Allon G. Percus, Gabriel Istrate, and Cristopher Moore, Oxford University Press.

few venues enabled the contributing scientific communities to interact. We were struck by how well they interacted, and how much progress was subsequently made towards what we called the more ambitious goal: developing a theoretical understanding of how phase transitions impact algorithms.

The Santa Fe workshop was followed by a workshop on *Phase Transitions and Algorithmic Complexity* in June 2002, at the Institute for Pure and Applied Mathematics, UCLA. At both of these meetings, we put out a call for chapter submissions to a peer-reviewed, edited volume. The volume was intended not as a conference proceedings *per se*, but rather as an overview of an emerging field. To this end, we requested that submissions be at a level where they could be appreciated by an interdisciplinary audience, and we particularly encouraged review papers giving a broad perspective.

We were excited by the enthusiasm with which leading researchers responded. The excitement turned to delight when we read the submissions. We asked one or more anonymous referees to review each submission, and we edited the resulting chapters for thematic, stylistic, and notational cohesion, in close consultation with authors. While much hard work has gone into this volume, from the editors' point of view it has been a labor of love. We hope that the outcome is a volume with both timely and timeless qualities, serving as a reference for years to come.

This book consists of four parts. *Fundamentals* provides background to current research in the field. *Statistical Physics and Algorithms* presents physical methods of analysis and their impact on performance of algorithms. *Identifying the Threshold* outlines the probabilistic and numerical methods used by computer scientists to understand the phase structure of combinatorial problems. *Extensions and Applications*, finally, gives a number of broader views of the impact of computational complexity on statistical physics and vice-versa. We have aimed to ensure that all parts of the book can be appreciated by researchers who are *not* experts in the field. We mean it to be accessible to motivated graduate students, and to highly motivated undergraduates as well.

We owe a large debt of gratitude to the many people who have helped make this book possible, and who have exercised extraordinary patience in waiting for it to see the light of day. Our thanks go, first of all, to the authors, as well as to the anonymous referees. We are grateful to the Santa Fe Institute and Oxford University Press for having agreed to publish this book, and for having good-naturedly accommodated our complex scheduling needs. Above all, we thank the Santa Fe Institute's publication's office—Della Ulibarri, production manager, Laura Ware, publications assistant, and Ronda K. Butler-Villa, director of publications—without whose support and extremely hard work this volume would never have made it into print. We also gratefully acknowledge the assistance provided by Roderick Garcia and Andi Sutherland in making the 2001 Santa Fe workshop such a success. Additional financial support for this project and the original workshops was provided by the Laboratory-Directed Research and Development program and the Center for Nonlinear Studies at Los Alamos National Laboratory, the Institute for Pure and Applied Mathematics at UCLA, the Intelligent Information Systems Institute at Cornell University, Microsoft Research, and the National Science Foundation. We deeply appreciate their generous funding. Finally, our families have been the source of inspiration, joy, and every imaginable form of support. For them, we reserve our deepest and most universal thanks.

Los Angeles and Santa Fe, September 2005

Allon G. Percus
Institute for Pure and Applied Mathematics, UCLA &
Los Alamos National Laboratory

Gabriel Istrate
Los Alamos National Laboratory

Cristopher Moore
University of New Mexico & Santa Fe Institute

Part 1: Fundamentals

CHAPTER 1

Introduction: Where Statistical Physics Meets Computation

Allon G. Percus
Gabriel Istrate
Cristopher Moore

1 BACKGROUND

Computer science and physics have been closely linked since the birth of modern computing. This book is about that link. John von Neumann's original design for digital computing in the 1940s was motivated by applications in ballistics and hydrodynamics, and his model still underlies today's hardware architectures. Within several years of the invention of the first digital computers, the Monte Carlo method was developed, putting these devices to work simulating natural processes using the principles of statistical physics. It is difficult to imagine how computing might have evolved without the physical insights that nurtured it. It is impossible to imagine how physics would have evolved without computation.

While digital computers quickly became indispensable, a true theoretical understanding of the efficiency of the computation process did not occur until twenty years later. In 1965, Hartmanis and Stearns [227] as well as Edmonds [139, 140] articulated the notion of computational complexity, categorizing algorithms according to how rapidly their time and space requirements grow with input

Computational Complexity and Statistical Physics, edited by
Allon G. Percus, Gabriel Istrate, and Cristopher Moore, Oxford University Press.

size. The qualitative distinctions that computational complexity draws between algorithms form the foundation of theoretical computer science. Chief among these distinctions is that of polynomial versus exponential time.

A combinatorial problem belongs in the complexity class P (*polynomial time*) if there exists an algorithm guaranteeing a solution in a computation time, or number of elementary steps of the algorithm, that grows at most polynomially with input size. Loosely speaking, such problems are considered computationally *feasible*. An example might be sorting a list of n numbers: even a particularly naive and inefficient algorithm for this will run in a number of steps that grows as $O(n^2)$, and so sorting is in the class P. A problem belongs in the complexity class NP (*non-deterministic polynomial time*) if it is merely possible to test, in polynomial time, whether a specific presumed solution is correct. Of course, $P \subseteq NP$: for any problem whose solution can be found in polynomial time, one can surely verify the validity of a presumed solution in polynomial time.

However, finding a needle in a haystack involves a great deal more than just verifying that an object is a needle. For many problems in NP, even our best attempts at finding a solution have yielded algorithms that require exponential time. A famous example is the traveling salesman problem of finding a tour with n cities, such that the tour's total length is less than a fixed constant. One can readily confirm whether a proposed solution meets the desired criteria, but there is no known polynomial-time algorithm for locating a solution among the $n!$ possible orders in which we could visit the cities. Thus, some problems in NP appear to be computationally hard or *intractable*. To the extent possible, we would like to categorize which NP problems are also in P, and which are not.

In the early 1970s, Cook [109] and Karp [299] took a large step towards such a categorization with the notions of NP-hardness and NP-completeness. A problem $\mathcal{A}$ is NP-hard if any NP problem can be converted or *reduced* to it in polynomial time: if there were a polynomial-time algorithm for $\mathcal{A}$, all NP problems could be solved in polynomial time. A problem is NP-complete if it is both NP-hard and itself in NP. NP-complete problems are therefore the hardest among NP problems. If any of them could be solved by a polynomial-time algorithm, that would immediately imply $P = NP$. It is widely believed that this is not the case. Finding a solution in an exponentially large search space seems intrinsically harder than checking a proposed solution. But proving or disproving that $P = NP$ remains an open question to this day, and is unquestionably the central unsolved problem in theoretical computer science [124].

Cook's main result was a proof that the problem of *satisfiability*, or deciding whether or not a propositional formula in Boolean logic can be satisfied, is NP-complete. Having established satisfiability as the founding NP-complete problem, one may then prove that other problems are NP-complete by showing that satisfiability can be reduced to them. This is indeed what Karp did, for a host of well-known combinatorial problems including graph coloring, vertex cover, number partitioning, and the traveling salesman problem. Since that time, many thousands of other problems have been proven NP-complete, ranging over an astonishing variety of problem domains, from industrial resource allocation to predicting how proteins fold. It appears highly unlikely that there are algorithms that can guarantee a solution to any of these problems in polynomial time.

The crucial term, however, is "guarantee." Computational complexity theory deals with the universal quantifier: can one solve the problem in polynomial time, for all possible instances of the problem? This is a worst-case notion. Computer scientists sometimes imagine a fictitious adversary who designs instances that are as hard as possible, deliberately trying to make our algorithms fail. But in many cases, we would be satisfied with a weaker guarantee. What if the problem is NP-complete, but for many types of instances it can still be solved in polynomial time? What if the hard instances are actually rather rare, and in practice the problem can almost always be solved in polynomial time? It did not case take researchers very long to discover that this is exactly what happens for certain forms of the satisfiability problem [167, 203].

Here is where physics comes back into the picture. Physicists are used to problems given to them by nature, not designed by a malicious adversary. To physicists, nature can be astonishingly benevolent, often admitting beautiful and elegant solutions to its problems. While computer science has to work in some contexts where there really is an adversary—for instance, in cryptography—perhaps real-world instances of NP-complete problems are more like natural systems than maliciously designed ones.

There is another crucial cultural difference between computer science and physics. While computer scientists think of problem instances as given with complete specificity, statistical physicists try to study the *macroscopic* properties of a system and avoid explicit consideration of its microscopic details. The canonical nineteenth century example is Boltzmann's unification of thermodynamics with Newtonian dynamics, showing how bulk properties such as temperature and pressure emerge from the statistical behavior of atoms in a gas. This approach necessarily implies averaging over the local properties of individual atoms in order to obtain a broad statistical description, explaining how the system "typically" behaves at an appropriate level of resolution.

Kirkpatrick, Gelatt, and Vecchi [320] exploited the relation between computationally hard combinatorial problems and the principles of statistical physics in their 1983 paper introducing the simulated annealing method. The idea was as follows. Finding the solution to a combinatorial optimization problem, such as the shortest possible traveling salesman tour, is formally equivalent to finding the *ground state*, or lowest-energy state, of a physical system in thermal equilibrium. In both cases there is an objective function to be minimized, consisting of contributions from all the components of the system: the tour length is the sum of all link lengths in the tour, and the energy is the sum of the interaction energies among all atoms in the system. In statistical mechanics, given a certain physical temperature τ (measured in units of energy), the probability of the system finding itself in a specific state C with energy $E(C)$ is proportional to the

Boltzmann factor:

$$\mathbf{Pr}[C] \propto e^{-E(C)/\tau}. \tag{1}$$

In the *zero-temperature* limit $\tau \to 0$, this probability is concentrated at the ground state. The third law of thermodynamics tells us that achieving $\tau = 0$ is a physical impossibility, but by *annealing* a system, or cooling it slowly enough, one may at least come close to reaching the ground state. The computational analogy for a combinatorial optimization problem is to pick as a starting point some valid solution—not necessarily the optimal one—along with some starting value of the temperature parameter τ, and iteratively update this solution by a Monte Carlo process that mimics thermal fluctuations. One then slowly reduces τ over the course of the simulation, in the hope of descending upon the solution that minimizes the objective function.

Simulated annealing offered a very practical recipe for finding solutions to NP-hard problems that are optimal or near-optimal. But the analogy it suggested opened the way to a far broader view of the connections between statistical physics and theoretical computer science. The key insight involves considering computational problems whose inputs are random combinatorial structures: for instance, satisfiability over suitably generated random formulas, or graph coloring over a particular random graph ensemble. As Kirkpatrick et al. noted in their paper [320], this view is entirely appropriate for problems with large input size n. The asymptotic limit $n \to \infty$ is analogous to the thermodynamic limit in statistical physics, where the law of large numbers should apply and relative fluctuations around the average case should go to zero. When this occurs, the system is said to be *self-averaging*. Of course, asymptotic analysis is no stranger to complexity theory either. When one speaks of an algorithm that runs in polynomial time, one refers to the way running time scales with n in precisely the same limit $n \to \infty$.

While statistical physicists initially studied models on regular lattices, such as the Ising model of magnetism, they subsequently considered *disordered* models in which the parameters or topology of the interactions vary randomly from site to site. One model of particular interest has been that of *spin glasses* [396], generalizations of the Ising model that describe how glassy materials behave. It was noticed early on that finding the ground state of a spin glass is an NP-hard combinatorial optimization problem. Inspired by this analogy, researchers became increasingly interested in applying techniques from spin glasses to other combinatorial problems. This resulted in some important successes. Using the replica method, which we outline later in this chapter, Mézard and Parisi [394] provided a closed-form analytical prediction for the optimal value of the objective function in the minimum-weight matching problem, over an ensemble of random weights in the asymptotic limit. They subsequently extended this analysis to the traveling salesman problem [393], giving numerical estimates for the asymptotic optimal tour length that later studies have largely confirmed [282, 348, 434].

2 PHASE TRANSITIONS

Let us return to the issue of worst-case versus average-case complexity, as that leads us to one of the primary subjects of this book. In 1991, a paper by Cheeseman, Kanefsky, and Taylor appeared in the artificial intelligence literature, entitled "Where the *really* hard problems are" [91]. The paper pointed out two empirical properties taking place in random instances of several NP-complete problems, including satisfiability and graph coloring.

- With an appropriate parametrization of the ensemble, there is a sharp phase boundary separating different problem instances. In the case of satisfiability, when the density α of logical constraints in the formula (specifically: the number of clauses per variable) lies below a certain critical value α_c, the formula is almost certainly satisfiable. This is shown by the solid curve in figure 1. When $\alpha > \alpha_c$, the formula is almost certainly unsatisfiable. Furthermore, the threshold becomes increasingly sharp as the problem size n increases. Such a phase boundary had in fact been predicted several years earlier, by Huberman and Hogg [264], in the context of artificial intelligence applications.
- These problems are relatively easy to solve as long as the input instance is clearly in one phase or the other. The hard instances are those near the boundary between the two regions: that is where search algorithms require the largest running time to find a solution, or determine that there is none. Increasing the control parameter α gives rise to an "easy-hard-easy" pattern, as one moves from the underconstrained region, across the critical threshold, and into the overconstrained region. This is shown by the broken curve in figure 1.

To a statistical physicist this looks conspicuously like a *phase transition*. As some macroscopic parameter crosses a critical threshold, the system undergoes a sudden change in its properties. The canonical example is when water freezes; when the temperature crosses the freezing point, the global behavior changes drastically even though the local interactions between water molecules stay the same. Furthermore, phase transitions are associated with the phenomenon of *critical slowing-down*, where relaxation times diverge and the system can take very long to reach equilibrium. Phase transitions have been a major area of study in mathematical physics since years before the introduction of computational complexity theory [80, 159, 285]. There is a well-developed theory of critical phenomena for modeling and analyzing the system's properties, particularly the types of nonanalyticities that appear at the critical point and how various quantities scale in its vicinity.

The study of phase transitions also has a distinguished history in graph theory. In their 1959 paper, Erdős and Rényi [148] proved that over an ensemble of random graphs with n vertices, for large n the global structure of the graph changes dramatically when the mean degree is increased from slightly below 1 to slightly above 1. Below the threshold, connected clusters of vertices are very

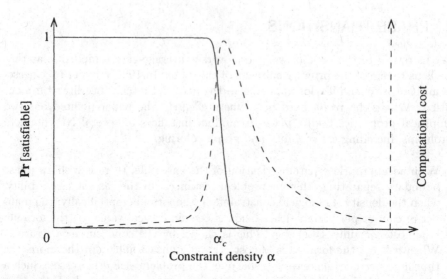

FIGURE 1 Schematic representation of phase transition in satisfiability. Solid curve denotes probability that a formula is satisfiable, falling rapidly from 1 to 0 at the threshold. Broken curve denotes computational cost for determining satisfiability, and displays easy-hard-easy pattern as constraint density is increased across the threshold.

small, and with high probability the largest one has size only $O(\log n)$. At the threshold, however, there is an abrupt change, and above the threshold a *giant component* of size $O(n)$ emerges. The probability that the graph possesses a giant component is governed by a *zero-one law*, jumping discontinuously from zero to one at the threshold.

Whether referred to as phase transitions, sharp thresholds, or zero-one laws, these phenomena are hardly anomalous. As discussed in chapter 2, one might argue that in view of the law of large numbers, when the size of the problem gets large enough, the probability distribution of an event over independent random inputs should become very sharply peaked. If one tosses a coin many times, and the coin is even very slightly biased, with high probability the results of the overall experiment will closely reflect the bias. If the coin comes up heads with probability p, and p is an adjustable parameter, then if one were to increase p from $1/2 - \epsilon$ to $1/2 + \epsilon$ the chances of seeing more heads than tails would jump abruptly from very low to very high. As the number n of coin tosses goes to infinity, this threshold becomes sharp. Admittedly, the example of coin tossing is trivial. But it motivates why one should not be altogether surprised if, say, the minimum fraction of constraints violated in a Boolean formula becomes sharply concentrated about its mean for large formulas. The critical value α_c of the constraint density would then be the value at which this fraction reaches zero and the formula becomes satisfiable.

To the extent that threshold phenomena in computationally hard problems mirror phase transitions as studied in statistical physics and graph theory, much existing work can be carried over to the realm of computer science. That is what Kirkpatrick and Selman did in 1994 [319], in their paper analyzing the satisfiability phase transition. Using the statistical physics techniques of finite-size scaling, they provided numerical estimates of several fundamental properties of the transition, including the control parameter's critical value and the *critical exponent* characterizing how quickly the critical window narrows with increasing problem size. The hope was that an improved understanding of phase transitions in this context would lead to an improved understanding of which instance classes of an NP-hard problem are truly hard, what *makes* them hard, and how one might design algorithms appropriately.

This hope is well on its way to being fulfilled. Over the past decade, the goal of understanding and exploiting the relationship between phase transitions and average-case complexity has mobilized computer scientists, mathematicians, and physicists alike. A flurry of activity has resulted, encompassing conjectures, theoretical insights, and numerical as well as rigorous results. These form the subject of the upcoming chapters, and fall into two broad and occasionally commingled categories: methods of analysis from statistical physics used to investigate algorithmic behavior near the threshold, and probabilistic techniques used to prove properties of the threshold. The first category contains recent work [406] inspired by the statistical mechanics of the satisfiability problem, exploring the connection between the precise nature of the phase transition and the problem's average-case complexity. It also includes the more detailed view of phase structure discussed in chapter 3, originating from spin glass theory, and resulting in algorithmic methods such as the *survey propagation* algorithm described in chapter 4. The second category contains a host of new results in probabilistic analysis. Examples include an exact mathematical characterization of the phase transition [67] for a specific variant of satisfiability (albeit one in P), as well as bounds on the location of the critical threshold for the NP-complete variant 3-SAT, discussed in chapter 7.

3   BASIC MODELS

The satisfiability problem will occupy our attention for much of this book. It has become the combinatorial model of choice for investigating threshold behavior, due to its fundamental role in NP-completeness, its practical applicability in artificial intelligence, and its simple formulation. In this section we define satisfiability, as well as two more model problems, graph coloring and the spin glass. Other combinatorial problems that have attracted the attention of physicists, such as vertex cover and number partitioning, will be described in depth in subsequent chapters of the volume.

3.1 SATISFIABILITY (SAT)

Consider n Boolean variables $x_1, \ldots, x_n$, where each x_i can be assigned the value TRUE or FALSE. Define a logical *formula* $\phi(x_1, \ldots, x_n)$ as a Boolean function of these variables, composed of the logical operators AND, OR, and NOT. The satisfiability problem is to determine whether there is a truth assignment for these variables such that $\phi(x_1, \ldots, x_n) = $ TRUE.

Any Boolean formula can be rewritten in *conjunctive normal form* (CNF), defined as follows. Let a *literal* be either a variable x_i or its complement $\overline{x_i} =$ NOT x_i. Let a *clause* be the *disjunction*, i.e., the OR, of a set of literals. A CNF formula is then the *conjunction*, i.e., the AND, of a set of clauses. Thus a possible CNF formula might be

$$\phi = (x_3 \text{ OR } \overline{x_2} \text{ OR } x_5) \text{ AND } (\overline{x_1} \text{ OR } x_2) \text{ AND } (x_3 \text{ OR } x_4 \text{ OR } \overline{x_5} \text{ OR } \overline{x_6}). \quad (2)$$

In this particular formula, the clauses do not all have the same length (number of literals). When they do, and when the length is k, the formula is said to be k-CNF. Satisfiability on k-CNF formulas is a frequently discussed version of the problem, and is known as k-SAT.

It is possible to rewrite any CNF formula, and thus any Boolean formula, in 3-CNF form. For instance, by introducing two new variables z_1 and z_2, eq. (2) can be rewritten as

$$\phi = (x_3 \text{ OR } \overline{x_2} \text{ OR } x_5) \text{ AND } (\overline{x_1} \text{ OR } x_2 \text{ OR } z_1) \text{ AND } (\overline{x_1} \text{ OR } x_2 \text{ OR } \overline{z_1})$$
$$\text{AND } (x_3 \text{ OR } x_4 \text{ OR } z_2) \text{ AND } (\overline{x_5} \text{ OR } \overline{x_6} \text{ OR } \overline{z_2}).$$

Satisfiability is known to be NP-complete. It is relatively straightforward to transform any CNF formula into a 3-CNF formula in a number of steps that is polynomial in n, using the method above. It follows that 3-SAT, and more generally k-SAT for any $k \geq 3$, is NP-complete. By contrast, 2-SAT is in the complexity class P, and it is *not* generally possible to transform a CNF formula into a 2-CNF formula!

All of these forms of SAT are *decision problems*. The goal is to answer the yes/no question of whether the formula is satisfiable. But there is also an analogous optimization problem, MAX-SAT: find a truth assignment that *maximizes* the number of satisfied clauses. Since it is not clear how to verify that a proposed truth assignment is optimal, it is common to define an NP version of this problem in which we ask whether it is possible to satisfy more than a certain number of clauses. Interestingly, this version of MAX-2-SAT, the optimization problem corresponding to 2-SAT, is NP-complete in spite of the fact that 2-SAT is solvable in polynomial time.

If we wish to construct *random k*-SAT instances with n variables and m clauses, a natural way to do so is as follows. Construct each clause by choosing k variables randomly and negating each one with probability $1/2$. The *clause density* is then $\alpha = m/n$; note that we take the limits $m, n \to \infty$ simultaneously so that α is held constant.

The *satisfiability threshold conjecture* states that there is a critical α_c separating the underconstrained phase from the overconstrained phase. Specifically, it is believed that for each $k \geq 3$, there is a *sharp threshold* α_c with the following property: given any $\epsilon > 0$, in the limit $n \to \infty$ the probability that a random k-SAT formula is satisfiable tends to 1 if $\alpha < (1-\epsilon)\alpha_c$ and to 0 if $\alpha > (1+\epsilon)\alpha_c$. For $k = 2$, this is known to be true, and the threshold is exactly $\alpha_c = 1$. For $k = 3$, it has not yet been rigorously proven that a sharp threshold exists; but assuming it does, numerical evidence and arguments from statistical physics suggest that $\alpha_c \approx 4.27$ [395].

3.2 GRAPH COLORING (COL)

Consider a graph with n vertices and edges connecting certain pairs of vertices. The graph coloring problem is to assign colors to vertices so that no edge connects two vertices of the same color. When our palette is limited to q colors, the problem is known as q-COL.

Analogously to SAT, 3-COL is NP-complete whereas 2-COL can be solved in polynomial time. The optimization problem corresponding to the decision problem is to find the color assignment that minimizes the number of violated edges, connecting vertices of the same color. This is best described by a picture: figure 2 shows an example of a 3-COL assignment that results in two violated edges.

Now construct graphs randomly, so that an edge connects any given pair of the n vertices with probability p. This is the famous $\mathcal{G}_{n,p}$ ensemble of random graphs studied by Erdős and Rényi [148]. The mean degree of such a graph is $\alpha = p(n-1) \simeq pn$ in the limit $n \to \infty$. Just as there is a sharp threshold at $\alpha = 1$ where the giant component emerges, we believe that for any $q \geq 3$, q-COL has a sharp threshold where the probability of q-colorability drops abruptly from 1 to 0. Recent numerical estimates for the 3-COL threshold location give $\alpha_c \approx 4.69$ or 4.70 [59, 412].

3.3 SPIN GLASSES

Computer scientists typically describe problems using *hard constraints*, where for instance every clause must be satisfied or every edge must have endpoints of different colors. Physicists, on the other hand, often describe systems in terms of an energy function or *Hamiltonian*. To map one onto the other, we may as-

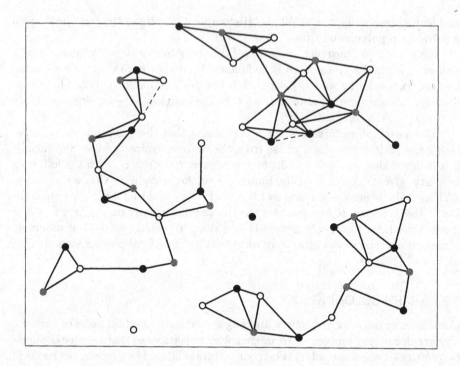

FIGURE 2   3-COL assignment in a graph, with two edge violations. Colors assigned to vertices are represented by filled circles, shaded circles and empty circles. Dashed lines denote violated edges in the graph, connecting a pair of vertices of the same color.

sign a positive energy contribution to each violated constraint; then the system's ground-state energy will be zero if and only if it is possible to satisfy all constraints. This mapping has been especially fruitful in the case of the spin glass Hamiltonian, a central topic of research among statistical physicists over the past two decades. Arguably, the spin glass model is as fundamental to the physics of disordered systems as satisfiability is to computational complexity.

Before discussing the spin glass, let us define the simpler *Ising model*, which uses the language of spins to provide a basic explanation of the physical phenomenon of ferromagnetism. Consider n binary variables $s_1, \ldots, s_n$, where any s_i can be assigned the value $+1$ or -1. Physically, these variables represent the quantum mechanical *spin* state of a spin-1/2 particle. We call $s_i = +1$ "up" and $s_i = -1$ "down." The energy associated with interactions between particles is given by the Ising Hamiltonian

$$E_{\text{Ising}} = -J \sum_{\langle i,j \rangle} s_i \, s_j$$

where the notation $\langle i, j \rangle$ represents all pairs of particles i and j that are nearest neighbors on a square lattice. Recall that at a given temperature τ, the probability of the system adopting a specific configuration C of the spin variables is given by the Boltzmann factor, eq. (1). In the thermodynamic limit ($n \to \infty$), and for positive J, there is a phase transition at the *Curie temperature* τ_c. For $\tau > \tau_c$ there is no overall magnetization: there are as many up spins as down spins, and distant sites are independent of one another. But for $\tau < \tau_c$, the system becomes spontaneously magnetized, and the majority of spins align with one another. At $\tau = 0$ the system adopts a ground-state configuration, minimizing E_{Ising} by having all spins s_i taking on the same value: either up or down.

The Ising model is clearly an idealization or "toy model" of magnetic materials: in particular, it assumes that spins are arranged in a square lattice and only interact with their nearest neighbors. However, physicists have found that while the transition temperature τ_c depends on the details of a materials' topology and interactions, the *type* of transition does not. In particular, the critical exponents describing how correlations, relaxation times, and magnetizations scale near the phase transition depend only on the dimension of the lattice, and not, for instance, on whether it is triangular versus square, or on whether interactions extend to neighbors several steps away. This fortunate fact means, first of all, that the Ising model is a far more effective description of real ferromagnetic materials, such as iron, than we might have originally thought. Second of all, it inspires physicists to think of systems as being grouped into *universality classes* that abstract away their details and capture the qualitative aspects of their behavior. Such a qualitative classification is not altogether dissimilar to that of computational complexity theory, in which constraint satisfaction problems are generically NP-complete and only a few special cases are in P.

While the Ising model displays a nontrivial phase structure, as a combinatorial optimization problem it is uninteresting. But now, imagine that the material being modeled is not entirely homogeneous and that interactions are not only between lattice neighbors. Furthermore, imagine that not all interactions are ferromagnetic, encouraging spins to align in the same direction; some are also antiferromagnetic, encouraging them to align in opposite directions. The Hamiltonian generalizes to

$$E = -\sum_{i<j} J_{ij}\, s_i\, s_j\,, \tag{3}$$

where the coupling constants J_{ij} can be positive, negative or zero. Equation (3) describes the Hamiltonian for the spin glass, so named because magnetic materials modeled in this way, such as copper-manganese alloys, can have a "glassy" phase displaying short-range order but long-range disorder.

Finding the ground state of a spin glass is, in general, an NP-hard problem [31]. Like the models we have considered up until now, it is appropriate to consider the spin glass over an ensemble of random inputs. Physically, this makes sense: glasses are distinguished by the randomness of the disorder spread through them, as distinct from the ordered structure of a crystalline solid. Thus, the theory of spin glasses has focused on studying these materials when the coupling constants J_{ij} are chosen randomly. One analytically tractable ensemble, introduced by Sherrington and Kirkpatrick in 1975 [474], considers J_{ij} for each unordered pair i, j to be chosen independently from a Gaussian distribution with mean zero. Another ensemble, the Edwards-Anderson $\pm J$ spin glass [141], considers J_{ij} to be nonzero only when i and j are lattice neighbors—as in the Ising model—in which case it is chosen from $+J_0$ or $-J_0$ with equal probability.

The basic problem we have posed for the spin glass is an optimization problem rather than a decision problem. Of course, the model is related in a formal sense to combinatorial problems that are well-studied outside of the physics community. For instance, a straightforward transformation of eq. (3) shows that finding the ground state of a spin glass is equivalent to the classic graph-theoretic problem of weighted MAX-CUT [31]. In this problem, the vertices of a weighted graph must be partitioned into two sets, while maximizing the sum of the weights along all edges that connect vertices in opposite sets.

Moreover, the NP-complete problems we have presented earlier can be captured by variants of the spin glass Hamiltonian. Consider first graph coloring. One may generalize the basic Ising model to the *Potts* model, where spins s_i are not binary but can take on any one of q values, or colors, in $\{1, \ldots, q\}$. The Potts Hamiltonian is then

$$E_{\text{Potts}} = -J \sum_{\langle i,j \rangle} \delta(s_i, s_j),$$

where the Kronecker δ function gives 1 when $s_i = s_j$ and 0 otherwise. This model can be extended from a lattice to an arbitrary graph. If J is negative, the Potts model is antiferromagnetic and adjacent spins try to have different colors; since the energy is J times the number of violated edges, the ground-state energy is zero if and only if the graph is q-colorable.

Now consider satisfiability. For each Boolean variable x_i, define a corresponding spin $s_i = +1$ if $x_i = \text{TRUE}$, and $s_i = -1$ if $x_i = \text{FALSE}$. Define the clause matrix W such that $W_{ji} = +1$ if clause j includes literal x_i, $W_{ji} = -1$ if clause j includes literal $\overline{x_i}$, and $W_{ji} = 0$ otherwise. It follows that for k-CNF formulas, the indicator expression

$$V_j = \frac{1}{2^k} \prod_{i=1}^{n} (1 - W_{ji} s_i)$$

takes on the value 0 when clause j is satisfied and 1 when it is violated. The number of violated clauses is then given by

$$E_{k\text{-SAT}} = \sum_{j=1}^{m} V_j = \frac{1}{2^k} \sum_{j=1}^{m} \prod_{i=1}^{n} (1 - W_{ji} s_i). \tag{4}$$

Minimizing the number of violated clauses is the same as maximizing the number of satisfied clauses, so finding the ground state of this "k-SAT Hamiltonian" is equivalent to solving the MAX-k-SAT problem. The ground-state energy is zero if and only if the formula is satisfiable. The main difference between eq. (4) and the spin glass Hamiltonian of eq. (3) is that now there are interactions between groups of k spins, rather than just between pairs. Fortunately, models of this type are well known in statistical physics.

In satisfiability and graph coloring, we might be tempted to focus simply on finding a solution or confirming that none exists. Indeed, this is traditionally how computer scientists have framed such problems. But the analogy with spin glasses reveals that the system's behavior is far richer than that: the transition from satisfiability to unsatisfiability is only a part of the picture. As we will see in the next section, the *order parameter* relevant to the transition is not only the probability that a solution exists, but is in fact an entire probability distribution describing the solution structure. Certain techniques developed for spin glasses lend themselves particularly well to the study of k-SAT [405], leading to both analytical insights and new algorithms.

4   THE VIEW FROM STATISTICAL PHYSICS

The chapters of this volume discuss diverse methods of analysis that researchers have brought to bear on combinatorial problems, drawn from computer science, mathematics, and physics. In this section, we give a glimpse of how statistical physicists study the structure of these problems, focusing in particular on the replica method.

The replica method is a powerful analytical approach developed in spin glass theory and recently applied to a variety of NP-hard problems. We do not attempt to cover the technical details involved in the replica method; rather, we outline the method in the hope of demonstrating how analyzing the physics of the problem can provide valuable insight. Our discussion serves as background to much of the material in this book. In illustrating the replica method and related approaches, we use k-SAT as a model problem and follow the language of Martin et al. [382].

Consider a physical system in thermal equilibrium at temperature τ. As we have seen in eq. (1), the probability of being at a specific state C is proportional to the Boltzmann factor $\exp(-E(C)/\tau)$. Normalizing this gives

$$\mathbf{Pr}[C] = \frac{e^{-E(C)/\tau}}{Z}, \qquad \text{where } Z = \sum_C e^{-E(C)/\tau}.$$

But the quantity Z, called the *partition function*, is far more than a mere normalizing constant: it embodies a considerable amount of information about the system. Z is a generating function from which one can directly obtain many thermodynamic quantities of interest. For instance, the thermally-averaged energy of the system,

$$\langle E \rangle = \sum_C E(C) \, \mathbf{Pr}[C] = \frac{1}{Z} \sum_C E(C) e^{-E(C)/\tau} ,$$

is given by Z and its first derivative:

$$\langle E \rangle = \frac{\tau^2}{Z} \frac{dZ}{d\tau} .$$

In principle, the ground-state energy E_{GS} is then found by taking the limit $\tau \to 0$. There, one can show that $\langle E \rangle$ approaches $-\tau \log Z$.

   This is all for a given *realization* of the system, meaning a given setting of the couplings J_{ij} in a spin glass, or a given instance of graph coloring or k-SAT. We want to work over an ensemble of random instances. In the case of k-SAT, in order to study the problem's phase behavior for clause density α near α_c, we need to understand the distribution of the random variable E_{GS} over the ensemble. Notably, if we denote by $\overline{E_{GS}}$ the average over random instances at a given α—not to be confused with the thermal average above—then a typical instance will be satisfiable if $\overline{E_{GS}} = 0$ and unsatisfiable if $\overline{E_{GS}} > 0$.

   Using the k-SAT Hamiltonian in eq. (4), $\overline{E_{GS}}$ for $m = \alpha n$ clauses can be written as

$$\overline{E_{GS}} = \min_{s_1,\ldots,s_n} \frac{1}{2^k} \sum_{j=1}^{\alpha n} \prod_{i=1}^{n} (1 - W_{ji} s_i) .$$

Since this form does not clearly lend itself to analysis, let us make use of the partition function. We know that

$$\overline{E_{GS}} = - \lim_{\tau \to 0} \tau \, \overline{\log Z}$$

where

$$Z = \sum_{s_1,\ldots,s_n} \exp \left(-\frac{1}{\tau} \frac{1}{2^k} \sum_{j=1}^{\alpha n} \prod_{i=1}^{n} (1 - W_{ji} s_i) \right) .$$

Calculating the ensemble average of the logarithm of a function is difficult if not impossible. However, note that the logarithm satisfies the property

$$\log Z = \lim_{r \to 0} \frac{Z^r - 1}{r} ,$$

so

$$\overline{E_{GS}} = - \lim_{\tau \to 0} \lim_{r \to 0} \tau \frac{\overline{Z^r} - 1}{r} .$$

   We now introduce the replica trick: proceed as if r were a positive integer, and calculate the rth moment of the partition function. Then, after doing so, perform an analytic continuation to real r and finally take the limit $r \to 0$. Proceeding in this way,

$$\overline{Z^r} = \overline{\left[\sum_{s_1,\ldots,s_n} \exp\left(-\frac{1}{\tau}\frac{1}{2^k} \sum_{j=1}^{\alpha n} \prod_{i=1}^{n}(1 - W_{ji}s_i) \right) \right]^r}$$

$$= \sum_{s_1^1,\ldots,s_n^1} \cdots \sum_{s_1^r,\ldots,s_n^r} \overline{\prod_{j=1}^{\alpha n} \exp\left(-\sum_{a=1}^{r}\frac{1}{\tau}\frac{1}{2^k} \prod_{i=1}^{n}(1 - W_{ji}s_i^a) \right)}.$$

We can interpret the leading sums as being over the states of r copies, or *replicas*, of the system, all with the same random realization. Thus, for integer r, the rth moment $\overline{Z^r}$ is the average partition function for the r replicas.

Although it is much easier to calculate $\overline{Z^r}$ than $\overline{\log Z}$, it is by no means easy. Furthermore, even if we can calculate $\overline{Z^r}$ for all integer r, its analytic continuation may or may not make sense in the limit $r \to 0$. One can argue that for finite n, given all moments of Z, one can perfectly reconstruct its probability distribution and, therefore, justify the existence and uniqueness of the analytic continuation. Unfortunately, we are interested in the $n \to \infty$ limit where this argument does not hold. It is remarkable that in spite of the lack of rigorous justification, the replica method has been extremely successful in predicting effects later confirmed by other theoretical approaches and by numerical experiments.

After a certain amount of algebraic manipulation [382], writing $\overline{Z^r}$ in the limit $n \to \infty$ leads to a saddle-point integral. In order to write this integral, we introduce the notation $\vec{\sigma}$ to represent an r-dimensional binary vector, $\vec{\sigma} \in \{-1,1\}^r$, with components $\sigma^1,\ldots,\sigma^r$ over the r replicas. We furthermore introduce $\vec{u}$ to represent a real-valued 2^r-dimensional vector with components $\{u_{\vec{\sigma}} : \vec{\sigma} \in \{-1,1\}^r\}$, in turn, over the 2^r possible values of $\vec{\sigma}$. Then,

$$\overline{Z^r} = \int \prod_{\vec{\sigma}} du_{\vec{\sigma}} \, \delta\left(\sum_{\vec{\sigma}} u_{\vec{\sigma}} - 1 \right) e^{nF(\vec{u})}, \text{ where}$$

$$F(\vec{u}) = \alpha \log\left[\sum_{\vec{\sigma}_1,\ldots,\vec{\sigma}_k} u_{\vec{\sigma}_1} \cdots u_{\vec{\sigma}_k} \exp\left(-\frac{1}{\tau} \sum_{a=1}^{r} \prod_{l=1}^{k} \frac{1 + \sigma_l^a}{2} \right) \right] - \sum_{\vec{\sigma}} u_{\vec{\sigma}} \log u_{\vec{\sigma}}.$$

In the replica formalism, $u_{\vec{\sigma}}$ has a physical interpretation as the fraction of spin indices i with the sequence of values $s_i^a = \sigma^a$ over the replicas $a \in \{1,\ldots,r\}$. Note that $u_{\vec{\sigma}}$ is constrained by the Dirac δ-function, representing a normalization condition. Counting the 2^r dimensions of $\vec{u}$ and the one constraint, $\overline{Z^r}$ is an integral over a space of $2^r - 1$ dimensions.

The saddle-point approximation for this integral gives $\overline{Z^r} \sim \exp(nF_{\max})$ in the large n limit, where F is maximized over all $\vec{u}$. F is symmetric under any permutation $\pi(a)$ of the replicas: as long as a certain vector $\vec{u}^*$ maximizes F, so too does any vector $\vec{u}$ where $u_{\sigma^1,\ldots,\sigma^r} = u^*_{\sigma^{\pi(1)},\ldots,\sigma^{\pi(r)}}$ for all $\vec{\sigma}$, i.e., $\vec{u}^*$

with its components reshuffled. If, furthermore, F has a *unique* maximum, then $u^*_{\sigma^1,\dots,\sigma^r} = u^*_{\sigma^{\pi(1)},\dots,\sigma^{\pi(r)}}$ for all $\vec{\sigma}$, and we may restrict our space to vectors $\vec{u}$ that are themselves invariant under permutation. For a given $u_{\vec{\sigma}}$, we need only consider how many components of $\vec{\sigma}$ have the value 1 and how many have the value -1.

The assumption of a unique maximum for F is known as *replica symmetry*. Under such an assumption, we can write $u_{\vec{\sigma}}$ in the form

$$u_{\vec{\sigma}} = \int_{-1}^{1} d\mu \, P(\mu) \prod_{a=1}^{r} \frac{1 + \mu\sigma^a}{2}, \tag{5}$$

which may be inserted into the equation for $F(\vec{u})$. We can now perform the analytic continuation of r to the real numbers and take the limit $r \to 0$. The result is a functional equation for $F[P(\mu)]$. Using Lagrange multipliers we optimize F over the function space of $P(\mu)$, leading to a self-consistent integral equation for $P(\mu)$. What is the meaning of $P(\mu)$ when $\tau \to 0$? Let μ_i be the magnetization, or average value of a given variable s_i over all possible ground-state configurations. It turns out that if the assumption of replica symmetry is correct, $P(\mu)$ gives the distribution of magnetizations μ_i. Thus, $P(\mu)$ is simply the probability density for a variable's value averaged over the ground states.

The self-consistent equation for $P(\mu)$ admits a family of solutions. All of these share an important qualitative feature in the $\tau \to 0$ limit. For α below a fixed α_c ($\alpha_c = 1$ for 2-SAT, $\alpha_c \approx 4.6$ for 3-SAT), $P(-1) = P(1) = 0$, meaning that the expected fraction of variables completely "frozen" to a value of TRUE or FALSE over all optimal assignments is zero. For $\alpha > \alpha_c$, however, the form of $P(\mu)$ changes and the distribution starts having nonzero weight at $\mu = \pm 1$: a "backbone" emerges, in which certain variables are constrained to be TRUE or FALSE. $P(\mu)$ is, therefore, not only a function, but also an order parameter that signals a phase boundary.

In calculating $\overline{Z^r} \sim \exp(nF_{\max})$ under the assumption of replica symmetry, one finds that the structural change in $P(\mu)$ is mirrored by a structural change in $\overline{E_{GS}}$. For $\alpha < \alpha_c$, $\overline{E_{GS}} = 0$, whereas for $\alpha > \alpha_c$, $\overline{E_{GS}} > 0$. The latter is certainly not surprising: if a finite fraction of the variables could be frozen to specific values over all satisfying assignments, the addition of a single new clause would with finite probability lead to a violation. Interestingly, though, the nature of the transition in $P(\mu)$ is different for 2-SAT and for 3-SAT [406]. In the case of 2-SAT, there is a continuous transition. At $\alpha = \alpha_c$, $P(\pm 1) = 0$ and then increases continuously with increasing α. In the case of 3-SAT, there is a discontinuous transition. Already at $\alpha = \alpha_c$, a nonzero backbone spontaneously emerges with $P(\pm 1) > 0$.

The replica symmetric (RS) solution is a very convenient one, and helps provide a valuable physical understanding of the phase structure. But it only tells part of the story. The manner in which the various limits are taken lacks mathematical rigor, and there is no guarantee that replica symmetry holds: F

may not have a unique maximum. Indeed, while the RS solution is exact for 2-SAT, it does not give the correct threshold location for 3-SAT. Empirically, we know that α_c is closer to 4.27 than to 4.6. We do not yet know how to provide a firm mathematical foundation for the replica method, but we can, on the other hand, improve upon the RS solution by explicitly introducing a form of *replica symmetry breaking* (RSB) into $F(\vec{u})$ [56].

The intuition for RSB is as follows. Consider two different optimal assignments for a 3-SAT instance, and look at the relative Hamming distance d between them: the fraction of variables that are set to TRUE in one configuration but FALSE in the other. A consequence of the RS assumption and eq. (5) is that, for large n, over the space of optimal configuration pairs the Hamming distance distribution $p(d)$ is sharply peaked at a single value

$$d_{RS} = \frac{1}{2} - \frac{1}{2} \int_{-1}^{1} \mu^2 P(\mu)\, d\mu\,.$$

Under RSB, however, one allows $p(d)$ to take on a non-trivial structure. The simplest form of RSB, called "one-step replica symmetry breaking," assumes that the distribution has two sharp peaks. One might imagine optimal assignments being contained within clusters, so that any pair within a given cluster is separated by Hamming distance d_0, but pairs from different clusters are separated by Hamming distance d_1. More complex forms of RSB impose multiple peaks in $p(d)$, corresponding to a hierarchical construction of clusters within clusters. The limiting case of this is the *full RSB* scheme, introduced by Parisi for the Sherrington-Kirkpatrick spin glass [396], where $p(d)$ is a continuum.

For 3-SAT, one-step RSB appears to be sufficient. The resulting analysis [56, 395] suggests a more subtle phase diagram than the one seen in figure 1. For α below $\alpha_{RSB} \approx 3.92$, the RS solution appears to be correct. The distribution $p(d)$ only displays a single peak, at d_{RS}, and with high probability instances are satisfiable. In this "easy satisfiable" phase, one is very likely to find a satisfying assignment with minimal computational effort. At α_{RSB}, the system undergoes a replica symmetry breaking transition, and for $\alpha_{RSB} < \alpha < \alpha_c$, $p(d)$ displays both peaks d_0 and d_1. This is the "hard satisfiable" phase, where with high probability instances are satisfiable, but the satisfying assignments are separated into clusters, creating many local optima and making it difficult to find a solution. Finally, at α_c, the system becomes overconstrained, and enters the unsatisfiable phase where satisfying assignments are unlikely to exist.

This clustering picture is one of the topics of chapter 3. The most successful approach for analyzing it is based on the *cavity method*, which uses techniques closely related to the replica method but not identical. In addition to providing a refined understanding of the k-SAT phase structure, the cavity method results in a prediction for the threshold location that is believed to be exact: $\alpha_c \approx 4.27$ for $k = 3$. Even more significantly, the method gives rise to an efficient algorithmic procedure for finding satisfying assignments in the hard satisfiable phase. The procedure, known as *survey propagation*, is discussed and analyzed in chapter 4. It is a perfect example of how improved insights into critical phenomena in combinatorial problems can lead to direct improvements in algorithmic performance.

5   THE VIEW FROM COMPUTER SCIENCE

Theoretical tools from the physics community, such as the replica method, have been instrumental in improving our understanding of the fundamentals of computing. At the same time, advances in theoretical computer science—both from a probabilistic and from an algorithmic perspective—have expanded the frontiers of mathematical physics. One clear difference between these two approaches is in the methods of analysis. But another very fundamental cultural difference involves the questions that are asked. Statistical physicists have been deeply interested in understanding the structure of computational problems and algorithms, characterizing critical behavior through appropriate order parameters and critical exponents. Theoretical computer scientists have focused on proving threshold properties with the aim of obtaining increasingly tight bounds on algorithmic performance. One of the great successes of the past decade has been the interaction between these two groups. Let us now highlight some of the main results that have come from the computer science community, and how these have motivated further results among physicists.

Two key challenges related to the phase transition in satisfiability are proving that a unique sharp threshold exists for random k-SAT, and identifying its location. For $k \geq 3$, both of these remain open problems. Friedgut [182] has shown that there exists a *function* $\alpha_c(n)$ such that the threshold becomes arbitrarily sharp about $\alpha_c(n)$ in the large n limit. However, it has not been proven that $\alpha_c(n)$ converges to a constant α_c as $n \to \infty$, in spite of overwhelming belief and a large body of experimental and nonrigorous evidence such as the survey propagation method mentioned above. Much effort has, therefore, been devoted to establishing upper and lower bounds on the threshold location, discussed at length in chapter 7. For $k = 3$, the best lower bound [223, 295] and upper bound [132] to date give $3.52 < \alpha_c < 4.506$, still leaving a considerable gap. For large k, the best lower bounds [3, 4] and upper bound [167] give $\alpha_c = (1 - o(1))2^k \log k$, confirming nonrigorous results from the replica method [405] and survey propagation [395].

The case of $k = 2$ is quite different. As mentioned above, random 2-SAT is known to have a sharp threshold at $\alpha_c \doteq 1$ [94, 202]. Moreover, a lot is now understood about this transition [67], including exact values for the critical exponents that characterize the sharpness of the threshold. This has put on a firm mathematical footing the original 1994 numerical study of Kirkpatrick and Selman [319], at least for $k = 2$. In addition, Bollobás et al. [67] have proven an essential property concerning the nature of the 2-SAT transition: an order parameter called the *spine* goes to zero continuously as α approaches α_c from above. Since the spine is an upper bound on the backbone mentioned above, a corollary of this result is that the replica prediction of a continuous backbone transition at the 2-SAT threshold is correct.

Rigorous results have been obtained for a number of other variants of satisfiability. One example is the problem of *1-in-k* satisfiability, a form of k-SAT where a clause is satisfied only if *exactly* one literal in the clause is TRUE. For $k \geq 3$, 1-in-k-SAT has been shown [7] to have a sharp threshold at $\alpha_c = 1/\binom{k}{2}$. Interestingly, even though 1-in-k-SAT is NP-complete, what makes the precise threshold value possible to obtain here is the structural similarity of the problem to 2-SAT. Just as in 2-SAT, if one maps the formula to a hypergraph, unsatisfiability emerges as a direct consequence of contradictory cycles of implications. Another example of satisfiability—albeit not an NP-complete one—with a rigorously determined threshold is the XORSAT problem. Here, the logical XOR operator, or *exclusive or*, replaces the OR operator in a CNF formula. This is equivalent to solving a linear system of equations modulo 2, and is solvable in polynomial time by Gaussian elimination. The problem has attracted the interest of statistical physicists as being a form of SAT that is particularly amenable to analysis via the replica method. A one-step RSB calculation [445] predicts a threshold location of $\alpha_c \approx 0.918$ for 3-XORSAT. Recent work in theoretical computer science [131] has shown rigorously that the replica prediction is indeed exact, justifying not only the numerical results of the replica method but also the physical picture that it provides. In particular, this work has proven the existence of a hard satisfiable phase like the one proposed for 3-SAT, where solutions exist but are grouped into clusters with large Hamming distances between them.

Finally, several connections have been suggested between the nature of the phase transition and the complexity of various classes of algorithms. Recall that in 2-SAT, the backbone order parameter marking the transition is continuous (though nonanalytic) across the threshold, whereas in 3-SAT, the replica method indicates that it is discontinuous. Now consider a broad class of resolution algorithms that work by successively assigning values to variables and backtracking to an earlier assignment when a constraint is violated. This class of algorithms, known as Davis-Putnam or DPLL [117, 118], is described in chapter 3. To analyze the relation between the continuity of the order parameter and the complexity of DPLL algorithms on random formulas at the transition, Monasson et al. [406] have considered the problem $(2 + p)$-SAT, for real $p \in [0, 1]$, that interpolates between 2-SAT and 3-SAT. Random instances of $(2 + p)$-SAT with constraint density α are generated by drawing $\alpha(1 - p)n$ random clauses of length 2 and αpn random clauses of length 3. Based on the replica method, the transition appears continuous for p close to zero but becomes discontinuous when p exceeds a critical value $p_0 = 2/5$. At the same p_0, the complexity of DPLL algorithms seems to change from polynomial to exponential.

Recent results in the computer science literature have both supported this picture and helped clarify its limitations. It has been confirmed [8] that for $p \in$

[0, 2/5], the threshold behavior of $(2 + p)$-SAT resembles that of random 2-SAT, and the location of the threshold is simply the constraint density at which the 2-CNF component of the random formula becomes unsatisfiable. Furthermore, the spine order parameter that was proven continuous for the 2-SAT threshold [67] has indeed been shown to be discontinuous for k-SAT when $k \geq 3$ [273]. This is a weaker result than showing that the backbone is discontinuous, and hence does not in itself confirm the replica prediction, but motivates considering the spine as the order parameter of interest. The connection with the complexity of DPLL algorithms closely involves the study of *proof complexity*, of key interest in automated theorem proving: one attempts to bound the number of steps needed to confirm or refute a proposition. A combination of old and new work in proof complexity [9, 95, 273] shows that a discontinuity in the k-SAT spine directly correlates with exponential resolution complexity, meaning that verifying the unsatisfiability of a formula takes DPLL an exponential number of steps. Conversely, a continuous spine implies that the resolution complexity must be smaller than any exponential—as for instance in 2-SAT and 1-in-k-SAT, where contradictions are verified in $O(n)$ steps. These results can be extended from k-SAT to more general constraint satisfaction problems [401], and lead to the hope that a better understanding of a problem's resolution complexity might help identify the threshold location.

6   OUTLINE OF THE VOLUME

In this introductory chapter, we have sketched some of the models, methods of analysis, and results at the intersection of complexity theory and statistical mechanics. These have given rise to the rich set of scientific interactions that form the subject of this book as a whole. Our broad aim is to provide the reader with an appreciation of how physical approaches have contributed to the study of computationally hard problems, and how advances in probabilistic and algorithmic techniques have made the connection such a fruitful one. To this end, the volume draws on contributions from authors in the computer science, mathematics, and physics communities—roughly in equal measure, and often in close collaboration. We hope to make apparent how the constituent disciplines have worked together to create a new and flourishing field of research. Among the products of these research efforts have been new algorithmic methods, new combinatorics, and new physics.

Our main focus here is on phase transitions and threshold phenomena in the context of random combinatorial structures. The book is composed of four parts:

- **Part 1: Fundamentals.** This part includes two chapters, introducing the reader to the basic combinatorial and physical concepts of the volume. The present chapter has given the essential background. Chapter 2 provides a deeper view of the mathematical foundations of threshold phenomena. The authors explain the origins of sharp thresholds, and guide the reader through an explicit description of how they relate to complexity theory and mathematical physics, as well as applications in other fields of science such as economics. They highlight a number of important open problems that are echoed in subsequent chapters.

- **Part 2: Statistical Physics and Algorithms.** The four chapters of this part are devoted to the role of physical analysis in computational problems as well as the use of algorithmic methods in understanding the structure of physical problems. Chapter 3 studies the dynamics of DPLL and local search algorithms, showing how both the critical threshold and a different "dynamical" transition affect algorithmic complexity. Chapter 4 presents the algorithmic framework of survey propagation, describes the theory, and applies it to satisfiability and graph coloring. Chapter 5 discusses number partitioning, analyzing the phase transition by exploiting its similarities to a tractable physical problem. Chapter 6 considers the spin glass model, and shows how a well-studied algorithmic method can lead to a physical understanding of the dynamics of glassy systems.

- **Part 3: Identifying the Threshold.** This part contains three chapters that demonstrate the probabilistic and numerical techniques used to argue for the existence of thresholds, as well as to identify their location. Chapter 7 reviews recent improvements on upper bounds for α_c in the case of k-SAT, illustrating the methods by which these bounds have been derived. Chapter 8 presents a powerful methodology for proving conditional randomness that enables the analysis of search heuristics and leads to improved lower bounds on α_c. Chapter 9 discusses the phase transition for a form of satisfiability called HornSAT, using numerical finite-size scaling techniques together with related analytical models to investigate the nature of the threshold.

- **Part 4: Extensions and Applications.** The final part of the volume contains four chapters that connect the foregoing discussion to a range of applications extending far beyond model problems. Chapter 10 considers phase transitions in the context of quantum computing, and shows how the behavior of quantum search algorithms relates to problem structure. Chapter 11 relates computational complexity to physical models of surface growth, analyzing the scalability of parallel simulation processes by means of techniques from statistical mechanics. Chapter 12 introduces a biological motivation, investigating a model of RNA folding by way of random graph analysis and the threshold where a giant component emerges. Chapter 13 extends the concept of typical-case complexity beyond ensembles of random instances: the chapter proposes a framework in which realistic instances of a problem can be considered, and provokes thoughts on future directions for computational complexity.

The entire collection of chapters is intended to form a cohesive volume, rather than simply a set of technical articles. The chapters have been arranged to form a logical and pedagogical progression, although they may also be appreciated individually and do not necessarily have to be read in order.

A major challenge in editing a volume of this kind is anticipating the audience and adjusting the level of discussion to this audience. We expect our subject to interest a wide range of researchers in computer science, mathematics, and physics. Given the different scientific cultures and backgrounds, it is an ambitious exercise to make statistical physics understandable to computer scientists and computer science understandable to physicists. Nevertheless, we have worked hard to strike the right balance between phenomenology and theory. Wherever possible, we have standardized notation and terminology across the entire volume. We assume only basic literacy in the research tools of discrete mathematics and physics.

Of course, the intersection of computational complexity and statistical physics is vast. It is impossible to do it justice in a single volume. By focusing primarily on threshold phenomena, we necessarily omit other important and exciting research topics, such as the probabilistic analysis of Markov chain algorithms and the study of network dynamics. Nevertheless, we hope that this volume will serve both as a reference on an emerging cross-disciplinary field, and as a snapshot of the state of the field at this point in time.

CHAPTER 2

Threshold Phenomena and Influence: Perspectives from Mathematics, Computer Science, and Economics

Gil Kalai
Shmuel Safra

1 INTRODUCTION

Threshold phenomena refer to settings in which the probability for an event to occur changes rapidly as some underlying parameter varies. Threshold phenomena play an important role in probability theory and statistics, physics, and computer science, and are related to issues studied in economics and political science. Quite a few questions that come up naturally in those fields translate to proving that some event indeed exhibits a threshold phenomenon, and then finding the location of the transition and how rapid the change is. The notions of sharp thresholds and phase transitions originated in physics, and many of the mathematical ideas for their study came from mathematical physics. In this chapter, however, we will mainly discuss connections to other fields.

A simple yet illuminating example that demonstrates the sharp threshold phenomenon is Condorcet's jury theorem, which can be described as follows. Say one is running an election process, where the results are determined by simple majority, between two candidates, Alice and Bob. If every voter votes

Computational Complexity and Statistical Physics, edited by
Allon G. Percus, Gabriel Istrate, and Cristopher Moore, Oxford University Press.

for Alice with probability $p > 1/2$ and for Bob with probability $1 - p$, and if the probabilities for each voter to vote either way are independent of the other votes, then as the number of voters tends to infinity the probability of Alice getting elected tends to 1. The probability of Alice getting elected is a monotone function of p, and when there are many voters it rapidly changes from being very close to 0 when $p < 1/2$ to being very close to 1 when $p > 1/2$.

The reason usually given for the interest of Condorcet's jury theorem to economics and political science [535] is that it can be interpreted as saying that even if agents receive very poor (yet independent) signals, indicating which of two choices is correct, majority voting nevertheless results in the correct decision being taken with high probability, as long as there are enough agents, and the agents vote according to their signal. This is referred to in economics as *asymptotically complete aggregation of information*.

Condorcet's jury theorem is a simple consequence of the weak law of large numbers. The central limit theorem implies that the "threshold interval" is of length proportional to $1/\sqrt{n}$. Some extensions, however, are much more difficult. When we consider general economic or political situations, the aggregation of agents' votes may be much more complicated than a simple majority. The individual signal (or signals) may be more complicated than a single bit of information, the distribution of signals among agents can be more general and, in particular, agents' signals may depend on each other. On top of that, voters may vote strategically by taking into account the possible actions of others in addition to their own signal, and distinct voters may have different goals and interests, not only different information. In addition, the number of candidates may be larger than two, resulting in a whole set of new phenomena.

Let us now briefly mention two other areas in which threshold behavior emerges. The study of random graphs as a separate area of research was initiated in the seminal paper of Erdős and Rényi [148] from 1959. Consider a random graph $G(n,p)$ on n vertices where every edge among the $\binom{n}{2}$ possible edges appears with probability p. Erdős and Rényi proved a sharp threshold property for various graph properties. For example, for every $\epsilon > 0$, if $p = (1 + \epsilon) \log n / n$ the graph is connected with probability tending to 1 as n tends to infinity, while for $p = (1 - \epsilon) \log n / n$ the probability that the graph will be connected tends to zero. Since the time of their work, extensive studies of specific random graph properties have been carried out and, in recent years, results concerning the threshold behavior of general graph properties have been found. For a general understanding of the threshold properties of graphs, *symmetry* plays a crucial role: when we talk about properties of graphs we implicitly assume that those properties depend only on the isomorphism type of the graphs, and not on the labeling of vertices. This fact introduces substantial symmetry to the model. We will discuss how to exploit this symmetry.

Next, we mention complexity theory. Threshold phenomena play a role, both conceptual and technical, in various aspects of computational complexity theory. One of the major developments in complexity theory in the last two decades is the emerging understanding of the complexity of approximating optimization problems. Here is an important example: for a graph G let $m(G)$ be the maximum number of edges between two disjoint sets of vertices of G. MAX-CUT, the problem of dividing the vertices of a given input graph into two parts so as to maximize the number of edges between the parts, is known to be NP-hard. However, simply finding a partition such that the number of edges between the two parts is at least $m(G)/2$ is easy. The emerging yet unproven picture for this problem is that if we wish to find a partition of the vertices with at least $cm(G)$ edges between the parts, then there is a critical value c_0 such that the problem is easy (a randomized polynomial-time algorithm solves it) for $c < c_0$, and hard (likely NP-hard) for $c > c_0$. For MAX-CUT, the critical value $c_0 = 0.878567\ldots$ is reached by the famous Goemans-Williamson algorithm [200] based on semidefinite programming. More generally, for many other problems we can expect a sharp threshold between the region where approximation is easy and the region where approximation is hard. In addition, the study of threshold phenomena and other related properties of Boolean functions is an important technical tool in understanding the hardness of approximation.

Another connection with complexity theory occurs in the area of circuit complexity. It turns out that Boolean functions in very "low" complexity classes necessarily exhibit coarse threshold behavior. For example, the majority function that exhibits a very sharp threshold behavior cannot be represented by a bounded-depth Boolean circuit of small size. This insight is related to another major success of complexity theory: lower bounds for the size of bounded-depth circuits.

Let us now explicitly define the basic mathematical object that is the subject of our considerations. A *Boolean function* is a function $f(x_1, x_2, \ldots, x_n)$ where each variable x_i is a Boolean variable, taking the value 0 or 1. The value of f is also 0 or 1. A Boolean function f is monotone if $f(y_1, y_2, \ldots, y_n) \geq f(x_1, x_2, \ldots, x_n)$ when $y_i \geq x_i$ for every i. Some basic examples of Boolean functions are named after the voting method they describe. For an odd integer n, the *majoritys* function $M(x_1, x_2, \ldots, x_n)$ equals 1 if and only if $x_1 + x_2 + \ldots + x_n > n/2$. The *dictatorship* function is $f(x_1, x_2, \ldots, x_n) = x_i$ for some i. *Juntas* refer to the class of Boolean functions that depend on a bounded number of variables, namely functions that disregard the value of almost all variables except for a few, whose number is independent of n.

Now consider the probability $\mu_p(f)$ that $f(x_1, x_2, \ldots, x_n) = 1$, when the probability that $x_i = 1$ is p, independently for $i = 1, 2, \ldots, n$, just as we had earlier for the election between Alice and Bob. When f is a monotone Boolean function, the function $\mu_p(f)$ is a monotone real function of p. Given a real number $1/2 > \epsilon > 0$, the *threshold interval* depending on ϵ is the interval $[p_1, p_2]$ where $\mu_{p_1}(f) = \epsilon$ and $\mu_{p_2}(f) = 1 - \epsilon$. Understanding the length of this threshold interval is one of our central objectives.

Before we describe this chapter's sections it is worth noting that the notion of a sharp threshold is an asymptotic property and therefore applies to a sequence of

Boolean functions when the number of variables becomes large. Giving explicit, realistic, and useful estimates is an important goal. In the election example above, the central limit theorem provides explicit, realistic, and useful estimates. In more involved settings, however, this task can be quite difficult.

The main messages of this chapter can be summarized as follows:

- The threshold behavior of a system is intimately related to combinatorial notions of "influence" and "pivotality" (section 2).
- Sharp thresholds are common. We can expect a sharp threshold unless there are good reasons not to (section 3 and 5.3).
- A basic mathematical tool in understanding threshold behavior is Fourier analysis of Boolean functions (section 4).
- Higher symmetry leads (in a subtle way) to sharper threshold behavior (section 5.2).
- Sharp thresholds occur unless the property can be described "locally" (section 5.3).
- Systems whose description belongs to a very low complexity class have rather coarse (not sharp) threshold behavior (section 6.1).
- In various optimization problems, when we seek approximate solutions, there is a sharp transition between goals that are algorithmically easy and those that are computationally intractable (section 6.3).

In section 2 we introduce the notions of pivotality and influence and discuss *Russo's lemma*, which relates these notions to threshold behavior. In section 3 we describe basic results concerning influences and threshold behavior of Boolean functions. In section 4 we discuss a major mathematical tool required for the study of threshold phenomena and influences: Fourier analysis of Boolean functions. In section 5 we discuss the connection to random graphs and hypergraphs and to the k-SAT problem. In section 6 we discuss the connections to computational complexity. Section 7 is devoted to the related phenomenon of noise sensitivity. Section 8 discusses connections with the model of percolation. Section 9 discusses an example from social science: a result by Feddersen and Pesendorfer that exhibits a situation of self-organized criticality. Section 10 concludes with some of the main open problems and challenges.

2   PIVOTALITY, INFLUENCE, POWER, AND THE THRESHOLD INTERVAL

In this section we describe the n-dimensional hypercube, and define the notions of "pivotal" variables and influence for Boolean functions. We state Russo's fundamental lemma connecting influences and thresholds.

2.1 THE DISCRETE CUBE

Let $\Omega_n = \{0,1\}^n$ denote the discrete n-dimensional cube, namely, the set of 0-1 vectors with n entries. A Boolean function is a map from Ω_n to $\{0,1\}$. Boolean functions on Ω_n are of course in one-to-one correspondence with subsets of Ω_n. Elements in Ω_n are themselves in one-to-one correspondence with subsets of $[n] = \{1,2,\ldots,n\}$. Boolean functions appear under different names in many areas of science.

We will equip Ω_n with a metric, namely a distance function, and a probability measure. For $x,y \in \Omega_n$ the Hamming distance $d(x,y)$ is defined by

$$d(x,y) = |\{i : x_i \neq y_i\}|. \tag{1}$$

Denote by $\Omega_n(p)$ the discrete cube endowed with the product probability measure μ_p, where $\mu_p(\{x : x_j = 1\}) = p$. In other words,

$$\mu_p(x_1, x_2, \ldots, x_n) = p^k(1-p)^{n-k}, \tag{2}$$

where $k = x_1 + x_2 + \cdots + x_n$.

2.2 PIVOTALITY AND INFLUENCE OF VARIABLES

Consider a Boolean function $f(x_1, x_2, \ldots, x_n)$ and the associated event $A \subset \Omega_n(p)$, such that $f = \chi_A$, namely that f is the indicator function of A. For $x = (x_1, x_2, \ldots, x_n) \in \Omega_n$ we say that the kth variable is *pivotal* if flipping the value of x_k changes the value of f. Formally, let

$$\sigma_k(x_1, \ldots, x_{k-1}, x_k, x_{k+1}, \ldots, x_n) = (x_1, \ldots, x_{k-1}, 1 - x_k, x_{k+1}, \ldots, x_n) \tag{3}$$

and define the kth variable to be pivotal at x if

$$f(\sigma_k(x)) \neq f(x). \tag{4}$$

The *influence* of the kth variable on a Boolean function f, denoted by $I_k^p(f)$, is the probability that the kth variable is pivotal, that is,

$$I_k^p(f) = \mu_p\Big(\{x : f(\sigma_k(x)) \neq f(x)\}\Big). \tag{5}$$

The influence of a variable in a Boolean function and more general notions of influences were introduced by Ben-Or and Linial [46] in the context of "collective coin-flipping."

The total influence $I^p(f)$ is the sum of the individual influences.

$$I^p(f) = \sum_{k=1}^{n} I_k^p(f). \tag{6}$$

We omit the superscript p for $p = 1/2$. For a monotone Boolean function thought of as an election method, $I_k(f)$ $(= I_k^{1/2}(f))$ is referred to as the Banzhaf power index of voter k. The quantity

$$\phi_k(f) = \int_0^1 I_k^p(f)dp, \tag{7}$$

is called the Shapley-Shubik power index of voter k.

The mathematical study (under different names) of pivotal agents and influences is quite basic in percolation theory and statistical physics, as well as in probability theory and statistics, reliability theory, distributed computing, complexity theory, game theory, mechanism design and auction theory, other areas of theoretical economics, and political science.

2.3   RUSSO'S LEMMA AND THRESHOLD INTERVALS

A Boolean function f is monotone if its value does not decrease when we flip the value of any variable from 0 to 1. For a monotone Boolean function $f \subset \Omega_n$, let $\mu_p(f)$ be the probability that $f(x_1, \ldots, x_n) = 1$ with respect to the product measure μ_p. Note that $\mu_p(f)$ is a monotone function of p. Russo's fundamental lemma [210, 450] asserts that

$$\frac{d\mu_p(f)}{dp} = I^p(f). \tag{8}$$

Suppose now that f is a non-constant monotone Boolean function. Given a small real number $\epsilon > 0$, let p_1 be the unique real number in $[0, 1]$ such that $\mu_{p_1}(f) = \epsilon$ and let p_2 be the unique real number such that $\mu_{p_2}(f) = 1 - \epsilon$. The interval $[p_1, p_2]$ is called a *threshold interval* and its length $p_2 - p_1$ is denoted by $t_\epsilon(f)$. Denote by p_c the value satisfying $\mu_{p_c}(f) = 1/2$, and call it the critical probability of the event A.

By Russo's lemma, a large total influence around the critical probability implies a short threshold interval.

Remark: Let us now exhibit the notions introduced here using a simple example. We will return to this example to demonstrate several issues discussed in the chapter. Let M_3 represent the majority function on three variables. Thus, $M_3(x_1, x_2, x_3) = 1$ if $x_1 + x_2 + x_3 \geq 2$ and $M_3(x_1, x_2, x_3) = 0$ otherwise. Clearly, $\mu(M_3) = 1/2$. This follows from the fact that M_3 is an *odd* Boolean function, namely one that satisfies the relation

$$f(1 - x_1, 1 - x_2, \ldots, 1 - x_n) = 1 - f(x_1, x_2, \ldots, x_n). \tag{9}$$

A simple calculation gives, for general p,

$$\mu_p(M_3) = p^3 + 3p^2(1 - p). \tag{10}$$

As for the influence of the variables, we obtain $I_k(M_3) = 1/2$ and $I_k^p(M_3) = 2p(1-p)^2 + 2p^2(1-p)$ for $k = 1,2,3$. Therefore, $I(M_3) = 3/2$ and $I^p(M_3) = 6(p(1-p))$, which is indeed equal to $d\mu_p(M_3)/dp$.

3 BASIC RESULTS ON INFLUENCES AND THRESHOLD BEHAVIOR OF BOOLEAN FUNCTIONS

Some basic facts on influences and the corresponding results on threshold intervals are as follows. Dictatorships and juntas have small total influence, and thus coarse thresholds. Conversely, when the critical probability is 1/2, a coarse threshold implies that the function "looks like" a junta. These results are formalized as follows.

3.1 THE TOTAL INFLUENCE CANNOT BE OVERLY SMALL

Theorem 3.1. *For every Boolean function* f,

$$I(f) \geq 2\mu(f) \log_2(1/\mu(f)). \tag{11}$$

In particular, if $\mu_{1/2}(f) = 1/2$ then $I(f) \geq 1$ and equality holds if and only if f is a dictatorship, namely $f(x_1, \ldots, x_n) = x_i$ for some i, or an "antidictatorship," $f(x_1, \ldots, x_n) = 1 - x_i$ for some i. Inequality (11) has its origins in the works of Loomis and Whitney [364], Harper [225], Bernstein [50], Hart [226], and others. It is of great importance in many mathematical contexts. Inequality (11) is often referred to as the *edge-isoperimetric inequality*. It can be regarded as an isoperimetric relation for subsets of the discrete cube, analogous to the famous Euclidean isoperimetric relations. This analogy goes a long way, and we will return to it in section 5.4. Ledoux's book [357] is an excellent source for the related phenomenon of "measure concentration."

An upper bound for the length of the threshold interval can be derived from the bounds on the sum of influences combined with Russo's lemma.

Theorem 3.2 (Bollobás and Thomason [66]). *For every monotone Boolean function* f,

$$t_\epsilon(f) = O(\min(p_c, 1 - p_c)). \tag{12}$$

Two brief remarks are in order. First, note that for a function $f(x_1, x_2, \ldots, x_n)$ we can consider the "dual" function defined by

$$g(x_1, x_2, \ldots, x_n) = f(1 - x_1, 1 - x_2, \ldots, 1 - x_n). \tag{13}$$

Then it is easily seen that

$$\mu_p(g) = 1 - \mu_{1-p}(f). \tag{14}$$

Due to this duality we may, without loss of generality, restrict ourselves to the case where $p_c(f) \leq 1/2$, which will simplify several of the statements below. Second, note that another way to state the Bollobás and Thomason result is that for every Boolean function f and every $\epsilon > 0$ there exists a value $c(\epsilon)$ such that $t_\epsilon(f)/p_c(f) \leq c(\epsilon)$.

Theorem 3.2 is the basis for the following definition: we say that a sequence (f_n) of Boolean functions has a *sharp threshold* if for every $\epsilon > 0$,

$$t_\epsilon(f_n) = o(\min(p_c, 1 - p_c)). \tag{15}$$

Otherwise, we say that the sequence demonstrates a *coarse threshold* behavior. When the critical probabilities for the functions f_n are bounded away from 0 and 1 then having a sharp threshold simply means that for every $\epsilon > 0$, $t_\epsilon(f_n) = o(1)$.

3.2 SIMPLE MAJORITY MAXIMIZES THE TOTAL INFLUENCE OF MONOTONE BOOLEAN FUNCTIONS

Let n be an odd integer. Denote by M_n a simple majority function on n variables.

Proposition 3.3. *Let f be a monotone Boolean function over n variables, n odd, and with $p_c(f) = 1/2$. Then for every p, $0 < p < 1$,*

$$I^p(f) \leq I^p(M_n). \tag{16}$$

See, for example, lemma 6.1 of Friedgut and Kalai [178] and Chayes et al. [90]. By Russo's lemma it follows that:

Proposition 3.4. *Let f be a monotone Boolean function over n variables, n odd, and with $p_c(f) = 1/2$. Then, for every $p > 1/2$, $\mu_p(M_n) \geq \mu_p(f)$.*

3.3 NOT ALL INDIVIDUAL INFLUENCES CAN BE SMALL

Theorem 3.5 (Kahn-Kalai-Linial [287]). *There exists a universal constant K such that for every Boolean function f,*

$$\max_k I_k(f) \geq K \min(\mu(f), 1 - \mu(f)) \log n/n. \tag{17}$$

This theorem answered a question posed by Ben-Or and Linial [46], who gave an example of a Boolean function f with $\mu(f) = 1/2$ and $I_k(f) = \Theta(\log n/n)$. Note that theorem 3.5 implies that when all individual influences are the same, that is, when A is invariant under the induced action from a transitive permutation group on $[n]$, then the total influence is at least $K \min(\mu(f), 1 - \mu(f)) \log n$. An extension for arbitrary product probability spaces was found by Bourgain, Kahn, Kalai, Katznelson, and Linial [75]. Talagrand [499] extended the result of Kahn, Kalai, and Linial in various directions and applied these results for studying threshold behavior. Talagrand also presented a very useful extension for arbitrary real functions on the discrete cube. Talagrand's extension for the product measure μ_p is stated as follows:

Theorem 3.6 (Talagrand [499]). *There exists a universal constant K such that for every Boolean function f,*

$$\sum_{k=1}^{n} \frac{I_k^p(f)}{\log 1/I_k^p(f)} \geq K \frac{\mu_p(f)(1 - \mu_p(f))}{\log 2/(p(1-p))}. \tag{18}$$

The next result describes Boolean functions with a small total influence.

Theorem 3.7 (Friedgut [175]). *Let f be a monotone Boolean function. For every $0 < z \leq 1/2$, $a \geq 1$ and $\gamma > 0$, there exists a value $C = C(z, a, \gamma)$ such that if $z \leq p \leq 1 - z$ and $I^p(f) \leq a$, then there is a monotone Boolean function g depending on at most C variables, such that*

$$\mu_p\Big(\{x \in \Omega_n : f(x) \neq g(x)\}\Big) \leq \gamma. \tag{19}$$

Theorem 3.7 asserts that if the critical probability is bounded away from 0 and 1 and the threshold is coarse, then for most values of p in the threshold interval, f can be approximated by a junta with respect to the probability measure μ_p. Note that when p tends to zero with increasing n, the size of the junta is no longer bounded; when p tends to zero as a fractional power of $1/n$, the theorem carries no information. We will return to this important range of parameters later.

Likewise, if no one influence is unduly large, then the threshold is sharp, as demonstrated by the following.

Theorem 3.8 (Russo-Talagrand-Friedgut-Kalai). *Let f be a Boolean function. For every $0 < z \leq 1/2$, $\epsilon > 0$ and $\gamma > 0$, there exist values $\delta_i = \delta_i(z, \epsilon, \gamma) > 0$, $i = 1, 2, 3$ such that if $z \leq p_c(f) \leq 1 - z$, then any of the following conditions implies that*

$$t_\epsilon(f) < \gamma.$$

1. *For every k, $1 \leq k \leq n$, and for every p, $0 < p < 1$, $I_k^p(f) \leq \delta_1$ [178, 449, 499].*
2. *For every k, $1 \leq k \leq n$, and for p such that $\epsilon < \mu_p(f) < 1 - \epsilon$ (e.g., $p = p_c(f)$), $I_k^p(f) < \delta_2$ [291].*
3. *For every k, $1 \leq k \leq n$, the Shapley-Shubik power index $\phi_k(f) \leq \delta_3$ [291].*

Part 1 of the theorem was proven by Russo [449]. A sharp version was proven by Talagrand [499] and Friedgut and Kalai [178] based on the Kahn-Kalai-Linial theorem and its extensions.

Parts 2 and 3 are based on Friedgut's result and some additional observations, and are derived in Kalai [291], but the values of δ_2, δ_3 are rather weak (doubly logarithmic in γ). It would be interesting to find better bounds. Part 3 in the theorem above is, in fact, a characterization:

Theorem 3.9. *Let (f_n) be a sequence of monotone Boolean functions. For every $\epsilon > 0$,*

$$\lim_{n \to \infty} t_\epsilon(f_n) = 0$$

if and only if the maximal Shapley-Shubik power index for f_n tends to zero [291].

4   FOURIER ANALYSIS OF BOOLEAN FUNCTIONS

In this section we describe an important mathematical tool in the study of threshold phenomena and in various related areas. The material described here is not essential for reading most of the remaining sections, and so the reader who wishes to skip this section may safely do so. But as the topic is central to many of the mathematical results presented in the chapter, we feel it is important to familiarize the reader with it at this early stage.

4.1   ALL THE WAY TO PARSEVAL

Let Ω_n denote the set of 0-1 vectors $(x_1, \ldots, x_n)$ of length n. Let $L_2(\Omega_n)$ denote the space of real functions on Ω_n, endowed with the inner product

$$\langle f, g \rangle = \sum_{(x_1, x_2, \ldots, x_n) \in \Omega_n} 2^{-n} f(x_1, \ldots, x_n) g(x_1, \ldots, x_n). \tag{20}$$

The inner product space $L_2(\Omega_n)$ is 2^n-dimensional. The L_2-norm of f is defined by

$$\|f\|_2^2 = \langle f, f \rangle = \sum_{(x_1, x_2, \ldots, x_n) \in \Omega_n} 2^{-n} f^2(x_1, x_2, \ldots, x_n). \tag{21}$$

Note that if f is a Boolean function, then $f^2(x)$ is either 0 or 1 and therefore $\|f\|_2^2 = \sum_{(x_1, \ldots, x_n) \in \Omega_n} 2^{-n} f^2(x)$ is simply the probability $\mu(f)$ that $f = 1$ (with respect to the uniform probability distribution on Ω_n). If the Boolean function f is odd, i.e., satisfying relation (9), then $\|f\|_2^2 = 1/2$.

For a subset S of $[n]$ consider the function

$$u_S(x_1, x_2, \ldots, x_n) = (-1)^{\sum_{i \in S} x_i}. \tag{22}$$

It is not difficult to verify that the 2^n functions u_S for all subsets S form an orthonormal basis for the space of real functions on Ω_n.

For a function $f \in L_2(\Omega_n)$, the Fourier-Walsh coefficient $\hat{f}(S)$ of f is

$$\hat{f}(S) = \langle f, u_S \rangle. \tag{23}$$

Since the functions u_S form an orthogonal basis, it follows that

$$\langle f, g \rangle = \sum_{S \subset [n]} \hat{f}(S)\hat{g}(S). \tag{24}$$

In particular,

$$\|f\|_2^2 = \sum_{S \subset [n]} \hat{f}^2(S). \tag{25}$$

This last relation is called Parseval's formula.

Remark: To demonstrate the notions introduced here we return to our example. Let M_3 represent the majority function on three variables. The Fourier coefficients of M_3 are easy to compute: $\hat{M}_3(\varnothing) = \sum(1/8)M_3(x) = 1/2$. In general, if f is a Boolean function then $\hat{f}(\varnothing)$ is the probability that $f(x) = 1$ and when f is an odd Boolean function, $\hat{f}(\varnothing) = 1/2$. Next, $\hat{M}_3(\{1\}) = 1/8(M_3(0,1,1) - M_3(1,0,1) - M_3(1,1,0) - M_3(1,1,1)) = (1-3)/8$ and thus $\hat{M}_3(\{j\}) = -1/4$, for $j = 1,2,3$. Next, $\hat{M}_3(S) = 0$ when $|S| = 2$ and finally $\hat{M}_3(\{1,2,3\}) = 1/8(M_3(1,1,0) + M_3(1,0,1) + M_3(0,1,1) - f(1,1,1)) = 1/4$.

4.2 THE RELATION WITH INFLUENCES

It is surprising how far one can get with the simple base-change of the Fourier-Walsh transform and Parseval's formula. The relation between influences and Fourier coefficients is given by the following expressions, whose proof is elementary:

$$I_k(f) = 4 \sum_{S:k \in S} \hat{f}^2(S). \tag{26}$$

$$I(f) = 4 \sum_{S \subset [n]} \hat{f}^2(S)|S|. \tag{27}$$

If f is monotone we also have $I_k(f) = -2\hat{f}(\{k\})$.

The following notation is useful:

$$W_k(f) = \sum_{S:|S|=k} \hat{f}^2(S), \tag{28}$$

allowing us to rewrite relation (27) as $I(f) = 4\sum_{k \geq 0} kW_k(f)$.

To practice these notions, observe that $\hat{f}(\varnothing) = \|f\|_2^2 = \mu(f)$, so from Parseval's formula, $\sum_{S \subset [n], S \neq \varnothing} \hat{f}^2(S) = \mu(f)(1 - \mu(f))$. It follows from eq. (27) that

$$I(f) \geq 4\mu(f)(1 - \mu(f)).\tag{29}$$

If one considers a Boolean function f where $\mu(f) = 1/2$, $I(f) \geq 1$. This is an important special case of the edge-isoperimetric inequality (11).

Remark: Indeed, for our example M_3 we have

$$3/2 = I(M_3) = 4 \sum_{S \subset [n]} \hat{M}_3^2(S)|S| = 4(3(1/16) + (1/16)3).$$

4.3   BERNOULLI MEASURES

When we consider the probability distribution μ_p, we have to define the inner product by

$$\langle f, g \rangle = \sum_{(x_1, x_2, \ldots, x_n) \in \Omega_n} f(x_1, \ldots, x_n)g(x_1, \ldots, x_n)\mu_p(x_1, \ldots, x_n).\tag{30}$$

We need an appropriate generalization for the Walsh-Fourier orthonormal basis for general Bernoulli probability measures μ_p. Those are given by

$$u_S^p(x_1, x_2, \ldots, x_n) = \left(-\sqrt{\frac{1-p}{p}}\right)^{\sum_{i \in S} x_i} \left(\sqrt{\frac{p}{1-p}}\right)^{n - \sum_{i \in S} x_i}.\tag{31}$$

Let p be a fixed real number, $0 < p < 1$. Every real function f on Ω_n can be expanded to

$$f = \sum_{S \subset [n]} \hat{f}(S; p)u_S^p,$$

where

$$\hat{f}(S; p) = \sum_{x \in \Omega_n} f(x)u_S^p(x)\mu_p(x).$$

The relations with influences also extend as follows:

$$p(1-p)I_k^p(f) = \sum_{S : k \in S} \hat{f}^2(S; p),\tag{32}$$

$$I^p(f) = \frac{1}{p}\frac{1}{1-p} \sum_{S \subset [n]} \hat{f}^2(S)|S|.\tag{33}$$

Exercise: Compute the coefficients $\hat{M}_3(S, p)$ and verify eq. (33) for the case of M_3.

4.4   THE BONAMI-GROSS-BECKNER RELATION

The reader who did not skip this whole section may still wish to skip this subsection. We will consider here a technical inequality that will not be explicitly mentioned again in the chapter, but nevertheless underlies many of the proofs and results. There are many ways of viewing the inequality, and its remarkable effectiveness remains somewhat mysterious. We will present the simplest application of it that we know.

For a real function $f : \Omega_n \to \mathcal{R}$, $f = \sum \hat{f}(S)u_S$, define the L_w-norm of a function f to be

$$\|f\|_w = \left(\sum_{x \in \Omega_n} 2^{-n} |f(x)|^w \right)^{1/w}. \tag{34}$$

Note that, due to the normalization coefficient 2^{-n} in the definition, if $1 \leq v < w$ then

$$\|f\|_v \leq \|f\|_w. \tag{35}$$

Next define the operator

$$T_\rho(f) = \sum_{S \subset [n]} \hat{f}(S)\rho^{|S|}u_S, \tag{36}$$

so that

$$\|T_\rho(f)\|_2^2 = \sum_{S \subset [n]} \hat{f}^2(S)\rho^{2|S|}. \tag{37}$$

The Bonami-Gross-Beckner (BGB) inequality [40, 68, 213] asserts that for every real function f on Ω_n,

$$\|T_\rho(f)\|_2 \leq \|f\|_{1+\rho^2}. \tag{38}$$

Because this inequality involves two different norms, it is referred to as *hypercontractive* [212]. The inequality can be regarded as an extension of the Khintchine inequality [311], which states that the different L_w-norms of functions of the form $\sum_k \alpha_k u_{\{k\}}$ differ only by absolute multiplicative constants. Beckner used this inequality in the early 1970s to handle classical problems in harmonic analysis. The work was influenced by earlier hypercontractive inequalities by Nelson and others, originating in the mathematical study of quantum field theory [213, 413].

Here is a quick and sketchy argument giving a flavor of the use of the BGB inequality. Note that for a Boolean function f and every $w \geq 1$,

$$\|f\|_w^w = \mu(f). \tag{39}$$

Let $0 < \rho < 1$. Now, if a large portion of the L_2-norm of f is concentrated at "low frequencies" $|S|$, then $\|T_\rho(f)\|_2$ will not be too much smaller than $\|f\|_2$. The BGB inequality implies that in this case, $\|f\|_{1+\rho^2}$ cannot be too much smaller than $\|f\|_2$ either. This fact, however, cannot coexist with eq. (39) if $\mu(f)$ is sufficiently small.

More formally, suppose that $\mu(f) = s \leq 1/2$, and we will try to give lower bounds for $I(f)$. In section 4.2 we derived from Parseval's formula that $I(f) \geq 4(s-s^2)$. The edge-isoperimetric inequality (eq. (11)) asserts that $I(f) \geq 2s\log_2(1/s)$. Let us try to understand the appearance of $\log_2(1/s)$. Take $\rho = 1/2$ and thus $1 + \rho^2 = 5/4$. The BGB inequality and eq. (39) give

$$ \sum \frac{\hat{f}^2(S)}{2^{2|S|}} \leq \|f\|_{5/4}^2 = s^{1+3/5} . $$

Noting that $2^{2|S|} < 1/\sqrt{s}$ for $0 < |S| < \log_2(1/s)/4$,

$$ \sum_{0<|S|<\log(1/s)/4} \hat{f}^2(S) \leq \sqrt{s}s^{3/5} \leq K\sqrt{s(1-s)} $$

for some constant $K < 1$, since $s \leq 1/2$. This implies that a finite fraction of the L_2 norm of f is concentrated at Fourier coefficients $\hat{f}(S)$ where $|S| \geq K'\log(1/s)$. It then follows from the discussion in section 4.2 that $I(f) \geq K''(\mu(f)(1-\mu(f))\log(1/\mu(f))$. Up to a multiplicative constant this gives the fundamental edge-isoperimetric relation (eq. (11)), but the information on Fourier coefficients, while not sharp, is even stronger.

An extension of the BGB inequality for general p can be found in Talagrand [499]. The recent remarkable notion of Orlitz hypercontractivity [35] appears to be very promising for further applications.

REMARKS

- The Fourier coefficients of Boolean functions are tailor-made to deal with the total influence that by Russo's lemma gives the "local" threshold behavior. However, to understand the behavior in the entire threshold interval, a further understanding of the relation between the behavior at different points is required. For a global understanding of influences over the entire threshold interval, the quantities $\int_0^1 \hat{f}(S,p)dp$ may play a role: it would be interesting to study them.
- This section is only a taste of a rather young field of Fourier analysis of Boolean functions which has many connections, extensions, applications, and problems. We hope to be able to give a fuller treatment elsewhere.

5 FROM ERDŐS AND RÉNYI TO FRIEDGUT: RANDOM GRAPHS AND THE K-SAT PROBLEM

5.1 GRAPH PROPERTIES AND BOOLEAN FUNCTIONS

Another origin for the study of threshold phenomena in mathematics is random graph theory and, particularly the seminal works by Erdős and Rényi [148]. Some good references on random graphs are Alon and Spencer [17], Bollobás [62], and Janson et al. [279].

Consider a graph $G = (V, E)$, where V is the set of vertices and E is the set of edges. Let $x_1, x_2, \ldots, x_{|E|}$ be Boolean variables corresponding to the edges of G. An assignment of the values 0 and 1 to the variables x_i corresponds to a subgraph $H \subseteq G$, where $H = (V, E')$ and $e \in E'$ if and only if $x_e = 1$. We will mostly consider the case where G is the complete graph, namely, $E = \binom{V}{2}$.

This basic Boolean representation of subgraphs (or substructures for other structures) is very important. A graph property P is a property of graphs that does not depend on the labeling of the vertices. In other words, P depends only on the isomorphism type of G. The property is monotone if when a graph H satisfies it, every graph G on the same vertex set obtained by adding edges to H also satisfies the property. Examples include: "the graph is connected," "the graph is not planar" (a graph is planar if it can be drawn in the plane without crossings), "the graph contains a triangle," and "the graph contains a Hamiltonian cycle." Understanding the threshold behavior of monotone graph properties for random graphs was the main motivation behind the theorem of Bollobás and Thomason ([66], theorem 3.2). Their result applies to arbitrary monotone Boolean functions, so it does not rely on the symmetry that Boolean functions representing graph properties have.

Theorem 5.1 (Friedgut and Kalai [178]). *For every monotone property P of graphs, there exists a constant C such that*

$$t_\epsilon(P) \leq C \log(1/\epsilon)/\log n. \tag{40}$$

Theorem 5.1, which answered a question suggested by Nati Linial, is a simple consequence of the Kahn-Kalai-Linial theorem and its extensions combined with Russo's lemma. The crucial observation is that all influences of variables are equal for Boolean properties defined by graph properties. As a matter of fact, this continues to be true for Boolean functions f describing random subgraphs of an arbitrary edge-transitive graph.[1] All influences being equal implies that the total influence $I^p(f)$ is at least as large as $K \min(\mu_p(f), 1 - \mu_p(f)) \log n$. By Russo's lemma, this gives the required result.

---

[1] A graph is edge-transitive if for every two edges e and e' there is an automorphism of the graph that maps e to e'.

Friedgut and Kalai [178] raised several questions that were addressed in later works:

- What is the relation between the group of symmetries of a Boolean function and its threshold behavior?
- What would guarantee a sharp threshold when the critical probability p_c tends to zero with increasing n?
- What is the relation between influences, the threshold behavior, and other isoperimetric properties of f?

We will describe in some detail the work of Bourgain and Kalai [74] on the first question and the works of Friedgut [177] and Bourgain [73] on the second. The last question was addressed by several papers of Talagrand [495, 496, 497] and also Benjamini et al. [45], though we will not elaborate on it here.

Let us make one comment at this point. When we consider the Fourier coefficients $\hat{f}(S)$ of a Boolean function representing a graph property, then the set S, which can be regarded as a subset of the variables, also represents a graph. As mentioned above, being a graph property implies large symmetry for the original Boolean function: it is invariant under permutations of the variables that correspond to permutations of the vertices of the graph. The same is true for the Fourier coefficients: the Fourier coefficient $\hat{f}(S)$ depends only on the isomorphism type of the graph described by the set S. This is a crucial observation for the results that follow.

5.2 THRESHOLD UNDER SYMMETRY

We now describe a measure of symmetry that is related to the threshold behavior. The key intuition is that the more symmetry we have, the sharper the threshold behavior we observe. The measure of symmetry is based on the size of orbits.

A graph property for graphs with n' vertices is described by a Boolean function on $n = \binom{n'}{2}$ variables. Such Boolean functions are invariant under the induced action of the symmetric group $S_{n'}$ on the vertices, namely the group of all permutations of the vertices, acting on the edges. (Note that the variables of f correspond to the n edges of the complete graph on n' vertices.) In the previous section we used this symmetry to argue that all individual influences are the same. Here we would like to exploit further the specific symmetry in the situation at hand.

Bourgain and Kalai [74] studied the effect of symmetry on the threshold interval, leading to the following result:

Theorem 5.2 (Bourgain and Kalai). *For every monotone property P of graphs with n' vertices, and every $\tau > 0$, there exists a value $C(\tau)$ such that*

$$t_\epsilon(P) \leq C(\tau) \log(1/\epsilon)/(\log n')^{2-\tau}. \tag{41}$$

It is conjectured that the theorem continues to hold for $\tau = 0$. Let Γ be a group of permutations of $[n]$. Thus Γ is a subgroup of the group of all $n!$ permutations of $[n]$. The group Γ acts on Ω_n as follows:

$$\pi(x_1, x_2, \ldots, x_n) = (x_{\pi(1)}, x_{\pi(2)}, \ldots, x_{\pi(n)}),$$

for $\pi \in \Gamma$. A Boolean function is Γ-invariant if $f(\pi(x)) = f(x)$ for every $x \in \Omega_n$ and every $\pi \in \Gamma$. We would like to understand the influences and threshold behavior of Boolean functions that are Γ-invariant.

We now describe certain parameters of Γ that depend on the size of the orbits in the action of Γ on subsets of $[n]$. Divide the discrete hypercube Ω_n into layers: write Ω_n^m for the vectors in Ω_n with exactly m 1's. For a group Γ of permutations of $[n]$, let $T(m)$ denote the number of orbits in the induced action of Γ on Ω_n^m and let $B(m)$ be the smallest size of an orbit of Γ acting on Ω_n^m. For graph properties, $T(m)$ is the number of isomorphism types of graphs with n' vertices and m edges, and $B(m)$ is the minimum number of (labeled) graphs with n' vertices and m edges that are isomorphic to a specific graph H. The number of graphs isomorphic to H is $n'!/|\text{Aut}(H)|$, where $\text{Aut}(H)$ denotes the automorphism group of H.

When we consider graph properties for graphs with n' vertices, $B(m)$ grows as $\left(\frac{n'}{\sqrt{m}}\right)$. To see this, note that when $m = \binom{s}{2}$ for some $s \leq n'$, graphs H with the fewest isomorphic copies (hence with the largest automorphism groups) are complete graphs on s vertices, leading to $B(m) = \binom{n'}{s}$.

Define the parameter $\kappa(\Gamma)$ as follows:

$$\kappa(\Gamma) = \min\{m : B(m) < 2^m\}. \tag{42}$$

Since greater symmetry leads to smaller $B(m)$, $\kappa(\Gamma)$ measures the "size" of the group of symmetries.

Define also for $\tau > 0$:

$$\kappa_\tau(\Gamma) = \min\{m : B(m) < 2^{m^\tau}\}. \tag{43}$$

Bourgain and Kalai showed that for every $\tau > 0$ the total influence $I^p(f)$ of a Γ-invariant Boolean function f satisfies the inequality

$$I^p(f) \geq K(\tau)\kappa_\tau(\Gamma)\min(\mu_p(f), 1 - \mu_p(f)), \tag{44}$$

where $K(\tau)$ is a positive function of τ. It can be shown that this reduces to Theorem 5.2 when we specialize to graph properties, emphasizing that the symmetry implied by Γ-invariance leads directly to a sharp threshold.

Bourgain and Kalai also gave examples of Γ-invariant functions f_n such that $\mu(f_n)$ is bounded away from 0 and 1 and $I(f_n) = \Theta(\kappa(f_n))$. Based on this result and results on primitive permutation groups (that require the classification of finite simple groups), it is possible to classify the coarsest threshold behavior for Γ-invariant Boolean functions, when Γ is a primitive permutation group. Welcome results here would include sharper lower bounds for the influences and, for example, proving a lower bound of $K \log^2 n \mu(f)(1 - \mu(f))$ on the influence of Boolean functions that describe graph properties. See Bourgain and Kalai [74] for further details.

5.3   THRESHOLD BEHAVIOR FOR SMALL CRITICAL PROBABILITIES

Theorem 3.7 addressed the consequences of a coarse threshold when p is bounded away from 0. In this section we state theorems by Friedgut [177] and by Bourgain [73] on the sharpness of thresholds (as defined by eq. (15)), that apply when the critical probability p_c tends to zero. These theorems yield sharp threshold results for graph properties when p_c tends to zero. Recall that theorem 5.2 asserts that a sharp threshold is guaranteed for graph properties when the critical probability is bounded away from 0 and 1.

Given a family $\mathcal{G}$ of graphs, let $g_{\mathcal{G}}$ be the Boolean function describing the graph property: "The graph contains a subgraph H, where $H \in \mathcal{G}$." For a graph H, $e(H)$ denotes the number of edges in H.

Theorem 5.3 (Friedgut [177]). *Let f represent a monotone graph property. For every $a \geq 1$ and $\gamma > 0$, there exists a value $C = C(a, \gamma)$ such that if $I^p(f) < a$, then there is a family $\mathcal{G}$ of graphs such that*

$$e(H) \leq C \text{ for every } H \in \mathcal{G}$$

and

$$\mu_p \Big(\{ x : f(x) \neq g_{\mathcal{G}}(x) \} \Big) \leq \gamma. \tag{45}$$

The interpretation of the theorem is that a coarse threshold implies that the function has "local" behavior.

Friedgut's proof relies on symmetry and the statement extends to hypergraphs and similar structures. The crucial property appears to be that the number of orbits of sets of a given size, or $T(m)$ in the notation of the previous section, has a uniform upper bound. (For graphs this reads: For a fixed nonnegative integer m, the number of isomorphism types of graphs with n' vertices and m edges is uniformly bounded.)

Friedgut conjectured that his theorem can be extended to arbitrary Boolean functions. For a collection $\mathcal{G}$ of subsets of $[n]$ (which without loss of generality we assume to be an antichain of sets, so it does not contain two sets Q and R with $Q \subset R$) let $g_{\mathcal{G}}(x_1, x_2, \ldots, x_n)$ be defined as follows: $g_{\mathcal{G}}(x_1, x_2, \ldots, x_n) = 1$ if and only if for some $S \in \mathcal{G}$, $x_i = 1$ for every $i \in S$. The sets S in $\mathcal{G}$ are called minterms for the function $g_{\mathcal{G}}$. Of course, every Boolean function can be represented in such a way.

Conjecture 5.4 (Friedgut). *Let f be a monotone Boolean function. For every $a \geq 1$ and $\gamma > 0$, there is a value $C = C(a, \gamma)$ such that if $I^p(f) < a$, then there is a family $\mathcal{G}$ of subsets of $[n]$ such that*

$$|S| \leq C \text{ for every } S \in \mathcal{G}$$

and

$$\mu_p\Big(\{x : f(x) \neq g_{\mathcal{G}}(x)\}\Big) \leq \gamma.$$

In other words, Friedgut's conjecture asserts that a Boolean function with low influence can be approximated by a Boolean function with small minterms.

A theorem towards this conjecture which is very useful for applications is:

Theorem 5.5 (Bourgain [73]). *Let f be a monotone Boolean function. For every $a \geq 1$, there is a value $\delta = \delta(a) > 0$ such that if $I^p(f) < a$ then there is a set S of variables, $|S| < 10a$, such that*

$$\mu_p(f(x)|x_i = 1 \text{ for every } i \in S) \geq (1 + \delta)\mu_p(f).$$

Both Friedgut's and Bourgain's theorems are very useful for proving sharp threshold behavior in many cases. We will mention one example that was studied in Friedgut's original paper, and is central to this volume. We refer the reader to Friedgut's recent survey article [176] for many other examples. This survey article also describes various handy formulations of theorems 5.3 and 5.5.

The 3-SAT problem. This problem has been discussed at length in chapter 1. Consider n Boolean variables, $x_1, \ldots, x_n$. A "literal" z_i is either x_i or $\overline{x_i}$. A clause c is an expression of the form $(z_i \vee z_j \vee z_k)$ where the symbol $\vee$ represents the logical OR and $1 \leq i < j < k \leq n$. A 3-CNF formula with m clauses is a formula of the form $(c_1 \wedge c_2 \wedge \cdots \wedge c_m)$, where the symbol $\wedge$ represents the logical AND. A random formula of length m is obtained by choosing c_i uniformly at random among the possible $8\binom{n}{3}$ possible clauses. A closely related model is obtained by choosing each one of the possible $8\binom{n}{3}$ clauses at random with probability p. (See chapter 7 for further discussion of the differences between these ensembles.) A formula is satisfiable if we can assign truth values to the variables so that the Boolean value of the entire formula is TRUE. The larger m is, the more difficult it is. Using a slight extension of Theorem 5.3, Friedgut proved that there is a threshold $\alpha_c(n)$ such that for every $\epsilon > 0$, a random formula with $(\alpha_c(n) + \epsilon)n$ clauses is satisfiable with probability tending to 0 (as n tends to infinity) while a random formula with $(\alpha_c(n) - \epsilon)n$ clauses is satisfiable with probability tending to 1. It is still an outstanding problem to show that $\alpha_c(n)$ can be replaced by a constant α_c in the large n limit, meaning that the location of the critical probability does not oscillate.

Recent advances concerning the location of the critical value for the k-SAT problem are discussed in chapter 7.

5.4 MARGULIS' THEOREM

Margulis [381] found in 1974 a remarkable condition guaranteeing a sharp threshold for Boolean functions, and applied it to study random subgraphs of highly connected graphs. His paper also contains an earlier proof of Russo's lemma. The theorem later improved by Talagrand [498] gives another general method for proving threshold behavior.

Let f be a monotone Boolean function. For $x \in \Omega_n$ let

$$h(x) = |\{y \in \Omega_n : d(x,y) = 1, f(y) \neq f(x)\}|, \tag{46}$$

with the Hamming distance $d(x,y)$ as defined in eq. (1). Thus, $h(x)$ counts the number of neighbors of x for which the value of f changes, which is the number of pivotal variables at x. Note that the total influence is then given by

$$I^p(f) = \sum_{x \in \Omega_n} \mu_p(x) h(x). \tag{47}$$

Define $h_+(x) = h(x)$ if $f(x) = 1$ and $h_+(x) = 0$ if $f(x) = 0$. Since every pair x, y with $f(x) \neq f(y)$ has precisely one element where f attains the value one, one finds

$$pI^p(f) = \sum_{x \in \Omega_n} \mu_p(x) h_+(x).$$

Theorem 5.6 (Talagrand [498]).

$$\sum_{x \in \Omega_n} \mu_p(x) \sqrt{h_+(x)} \geq \mu_p(f)(1 - \mu_p(f)) \frac{\sqrt{2}\min(p, 1-p)}{\sqrt{p(1-p)}}.$$

Suppose (for simplicity) that $p_c(f)$ is bounded away from 0 and 1. Suppose also that if $h_+(x) > 0$ then $h_+(x) \geq k$. This implies that

$$I^p(f) = (1/p)\mu_p(x) \sum_{x \in \Omega_n} h_+(x) \geq \sqrt{k} \sum_{x \in \Omega_n} \mu_p(x) \sqrt{h_+(x)}.$$

It then follows from theorem 5.6 that

$$I^p(f) \geq C\sqrt{k}.$$

By Russo's lemma the length of the threshold interval is $O(1/\sqrt{k})$.

Here is Margulis' original application. Let G be a k-connected graph, that is, at least k vertices must be deleted from G for it to no longer be connected. Consider a random spanning subgraph H where an edge of G is taken to be absent from H with probability p. We assume that H has n edges and let f be the Boolean function that represents the property: "H is not connected." Margulis proved that the threshold interval for connectivity is of length $O(1/\sqrt{k})$. The reason is that if H is not connected, but it is possible to make H connected by adding back a single edge of G (so that $h_+(x) > 0$), then H must have precisely two connected components. Since G is k-connected, there are at least k edges in $G \backslash H$ such that adding any of them to H yields a connected graph. It thus follows that if $h_+(x) > 0$ then $h_+(x) \geq k$.

5.5 FURTHER CONNECTIONS AND PROBLEMS

- **The giant component.** Both Talagrand's strengthening of Margulis' theorem and Friedgut's theorem give the sharp threshold of graph connectivity as a special case. This is nice, but a serious criticism would be that the more interesting phase transition relating to connectivity occurs earlier, when p is around $1/n$. The value $1/n$ is the critical probability of the emergence of the "giant component" [17, 147, 279]. It would be desirable to understand even the basic facts concerning the giant component in the context of general threshold phenomena, discrete isoperimetry, and Fourier analysis.

- **Graph invariants.** We have discussed a monotone graph property, or more generally a monotone Boolean function, and varied the parameter p. A different scenario would be to consider a parameter of graphs or a function defined on the discrete cube and study its distribution for a fixed p. We can consider, for example, the chromatic number, the clique number, the size of the maximal component, etc. The probabilistic properties of monotone functions on the discrete cube, and especially those which come from interesting graph parameters are of great interest. Discrete isoperimetric relations play a central role in this study. But direct relations with threshold results and with Fourier analysis are sparse.

- **Hereditary properties.** We could also consider non-monotone properties. A property of graphs (on n vertices) described by a Boolean function f is *hereditary* if there is a collection $\mathcal{H}$ of graphs such that $f = 1$ if the graph contains a subgraph H from $\mathcal{H}$ as an *induced* subgraph. Alon and Kalai asked for which hereditary properties is it the case that the measure of the set of p's for which $\epsilon < \mu_p(f) < 1 - \epsilon$ tends to 0 as n tends to infinity. Since f need not be monotone, this set will not necessarily be an interval. Of course, monotone properties are hereditary.

- **Influence of Boolean functions with tiny measure.** Another criticism would be that we concentrate on the secondary problem of threshold behavior while neglecting the primary problem of finding the location of the critical probability. Indeed, finding the critical probability of particular properties of random structures is a large and beautiful field, and is the subject of later chapters of this book. We comment that there are a very few cases where knowing that the threshold is sharp helps in estimating its location, since it is sufficient to show that the property is satisfied with a probability that is small but bounded away from zero. The analogy with physical models suggests that the threshold behavior, like certain critical exponents for models of statistical physics, may exhibit more "universal" behavior than the location of the critical probability.

Finally, recent work of Kahn and Kalai [286] suggests that for a large class of problems, good estimates on the location of critical probabilities can follow from understanding the behavior of the function $t_\epsilon(f)$ when ϵ itself is a function that tends to zero with increasing n. Such an understanding can be derived from some conjectures, quite similar to theorems 5.3, 5.5 and conjecture 5.4, about influences of Boolean functions when $\mu_p(f)$ tends to zero with increasing n.

6   THRESHOLD BEHAVIOR AND COMPLEXITY

In this section we will discuss two areas where threshold phenomena and complexity theory are related. First we will describe results on bounded depth circuits, a very basic notion in computational complexity. Second we will describe the connection to the area of "hardness of approximation."

6.1   BOUNDED DEPTH BOOLEAN CIRCUIT

The important complexity class AC^0 of Boolean functions consists of those that can be expressed by Boolean circuits of polynomial size (in the number of variables) and bounded depth. Although functions belonging to AC^0 are of very low complexity, the class is an important one. Here we show that such functions must have a coarse threshold behavior.

A Boolean circuit is a directed acyclic graph with $2n$ sources, each corresponding to a variable x_i or its negation $\overline{x_i}$, and one sink representing the output of the computation. The intermediate vertices are called gates and can represent the Boolean operations AND and OR. The size of a Boolean circuit is the number of vertices including all sources, gates, and sink. The depth is the maximum length of a directed path.

Boppana [69] proved that if a Boolean function f is expressed by a depth-c circuit of size N, then

$$I(f) \leq C_1 \log^{c-1} N . \tag{48}$$

Earlier, Linial, Mansour, and Nisan [362] proved that for Boolean functions that can be expressed by Boolean circuits of polynomial (or quasi-polynomial) size and bounded depth, the Fourier coefficient sum $W_k(f)$ defined in equation (28) decays exponentially with k when k is larger than poly-logarithmic in the number of variables. This result relies on the fundamental Håstad switching lemma [17, 232], and a more precise result was recently given by Håstad [234]. It appears that all these results and their proofs apply to the probability measure $\mu_p(f)$ when p is bounded away from 0 and 1.

Remark: A *monotone circuit* is one where all the gates are monotone increasing in the inputs, that is, there are no NOT gates. The Håstad lemma for monotone Boolean circuits is easier, and was already proven much earlier by Boppana [70].

It can be conjectured that the only reason for a small total influence, and hence for a coarse threshold behavior, comes from bounded depth small circuits. Here, *small* means a slowly growing function of n. For that to be the case, an inequality that is roughly the reverse of eq. (48) must also hold. The following conjecture is a particularly bold version of the statement:

Conjecture 6.1 (Reverse Håstad). *Let f be a monotone Boolean function. For every $\epsilon > 0$ there is a value $K = K(\epsilon) > 0$ and another function g expressible as a Boolean circuit of size N and depth c, such that*

$$\log^{c-1} N < KI(f),$$

and

$$\mu\{x : f(x) \neq g(x)\} < \epsilon.$$

Remarks:

- As discussed in the previous chapter, a large number of papers in recent years have suggested a bold and far-reaching statistical physics approach to fundamental questions in complexity. These papers regard classical optimization problems as zero-temperature cases of statistical physics systems. The approach further proposes that the complexity of problems may be related to the type of phase transition of the physical system. In addition, statistical physics suggests both a way of thinking and heuristic mathematical machinery for dealing with these problems. This approach has met with some skepticism within the complexity theory community, and evidence for its usefulness is still tentative. The results by Håstad, Linial-Mansour-Nisan, and Boppana can be interpreted as going in the direction suggested by physicists. Of course, when we deal with complexity classes beyond AC^0, caution is still advised.
- Connections between influences and the model of decision trees can be found in Friedgut et al. [179] and O'Donnell et al. [418].

6.2   HARDNESS OF APPROXIMATION AND PCP

Given an optimization problem, what is the complexity of finding an approximation to an optimal solution? Sometimes approximation is intractable and sometimes it is easy. The theory of probabilistically checkable proofs (PCP) is a powerful tool for studying approximation. Technical results pertaining to sharp threshold phenomena are important for showing that certain approximation problems are difficult.

The PCP theorem concerns *constraint satisfaction problems* (sometimes referred to as label-cover problems) of various types, and is the main tool in proving

NP-hardness for approximation problems. As examples, consider the following two computational problems:

Vertex cover (VC): Given a graph G, find the smallest set of vertices whose complement is an independent set.

MAX-CUT: Given a graph G, find a partition of its vertices that maximizes the number of edges between the two sets of the partition.

Coming up with the optimal solution for these problems is known to be NP-hard [299]. The next best option is to approximate the optimal solution. In the case of VC, that means coming up with an appropriate set that may not be the smallest, but whose size is larger by at most some fixed *approximation factor*. Approximating MAX-CUT requires coming up with a partition that may not maximize the cut size, but gives a cut whose size is within a fixed approximation factor of the maximum.

Proving that such problems are NP-hard requires extending the Cook-Levin [109, 360] characterization of NP, which in simple terms states that SAT is NP-complete. One has to show that even approximating SAT is NP-hard, in the following sense.

A *constraint satisfaction problem* (CSP) involves a set of variables and constraints over the assignment to those variables. Let X and Y be two sets of (not necessarily Boolean) variables, whose range is R_X and R_Y respectively. R_X and R_Y are two fixed sets independent of the sizes of X and Y. For some pairs of variables (x, y) where $x \in X$ and $y \in Y$, there is a *constraint* $\phi_{x,y} \subset R_X \times R_Y$, specifying the values of x and y that satisfy it. The constraints imposed on the variables are local, in the sense that they only involve one variable in X and one in Y. Let us further assume that all constraints have the *projection* property: for each constraint $\phi_{x,y}$, for every $a \in R_X$ there is only one $b \in R_Y$ so that both satisfy $\phi_{x,y}$. Our objective is to find an assignment for all variables $x \in X$ and $y \in Y$ such that no constraint will be violated.

A very general version of the PCP theorem is as follows:

Theorem 6.2 (PCP [20, 21, 438]). *Given a CSP Φ as defined above, there exists a constant $\delta > 0$ such that it is NP-hard to exclude either of the following alternatives:*

- *There is a variable assignment satisfying all the constraints $\phi \in \Phi$.*
- *There is no variable assignment satisfying even a fraction $|R_X|^{-\delta}$ of the constraints $\phi \in \Phi$.*

Note that if we had an approximation algorithm determining whether or not there is an assignment satisfying at least an ϵ fraction of the constraints, this algorithm would necessarily rule out one of the two alternatives. Namely, given a CSP instance, if the algorithm satisfies an ϵ fraction of the entire set of constraints, the second alternative is ruled out, while if it satisfies less than an ϵ fraction of the constraints, the first alternative is ruled out. Therefore, the corresponding approximation problem is NP-hard.

A general scheme for proving hardness of approximation was developed in Arora et al. [21], Arora and Safra [20], Bellare et al. [43], Dinur and Safra [125], and Håstad [233, 235]. Let us demonstrate this scheme on the VC problem from above. We consider a basic combinatorial construction in which sufficiently large independent sets—or equivalently, small vertex covers—are represented by juntas. We then sketch a reduction of CSP to VC, such that juntas lead to variable assignments satisfying an ϵ fraction of the constraints. By the PCP theorem, this implies that approximating VC is NP-hard.

We proceed as follows. First, consider the graph $G_I^{[n]}$, whose vertex set Ω_n is the set of all binary vectors $\{0,1\}^n$ of length n. One may think of these vertices as all possible input vectors to a function over n Boolean variables. In $G_I^{[n]}$, two vertices v and u are adjacent if there is no $i \in [n]$ so that $v_i = u_i = 1$. This is referred to as the *non-intersection* graph, and it is the complement of the *intersection* graph (where two vectors are adjacent if the sets of indices where they are 1 have non-empty intersection), which has been investigated extensively. It is easy to see that no independent set in $G_I^{[n]}$ contains more than half of the vertices. This upper bound corresponds to an independent set that for some index i takes all vectors whose ith entry is 1. Such an independent set is the pre-image of a dictatorship Boolean function. What other large independent sets can one find in $G_I^{[n]}$?

The pre-image of the majority function (or any other odd monotone Boolean function) is also an independent set in the non-intersection graph, as any two vectors with more than half of their indices being 1 must have an index in which both are 1. For odd n that independent set matches the upper bound. To apply the PCP theorem we will need to "eliminate" independent sets, such as the majority function, that are not close to juntas.

For this purpose, one may impose a different distribution on the vertices of $G_I^{[n]}$ that will rule out such examples. One can assign weights to the vertices of $G_I^{[n]}$ according to μ_p, for some p smaller than $1/2$, weighting independent sets as the sum of their vertices' weight. In that case, dictatorships' weights are p, while majority's weight tends to 0 as n tends to infinity.

What about independent sets that are smaller than those corresponding to dictatorships, but still within some constant factor of that size? It turns out that for $p < 1/2$ any independent set of non-negligible weight must correspond in some sense to a junta. The following result relies on Friedgut's theorem 3.7 and Russo's lemma.

Theorem 6.3 (Dinur and Safra [125]). *Let W be a locally maximal independent set in $G_I^{[n]}$ (thus, every vertex $x \in G_I^{[n]}$ is either in W or is adjacent to a vertex* in W), and let f be a Boolean function where $f(x) = 1$ if $x \in W$ and $f(x) = 0$ if $x \notin W$. For every $0 < p < 1/2$, $\gamma > 0$ and $\epsilon > 0$, there exists a value $q \in [p, p+\gamma]$, a value $C(\gamma, \epsilon) \leq 2^{O(1/\gamma\epsilon)}$ and another Boolean function g depending on at most C variables, such that

$$\mu_q\Big(\{x \in \Omega_n : f(x) \neq g(x)\}\Big) \leq \epsilon.$$

Note that if we let $J \subseteq [n]$ denote the C variables that g depends on, the pre-image $g^{-1}(1)$ represents a set of vectors over J that constitutes an independent set over G_I^J.

We now sketch the reduction from the CSP instance Φ above to VC. One constructs a graph G_Φ as follows. G_Φ consists of one copy of $G_I^{R_X}$ for every variable $x \in X$, and one copy of $G_I^{R_Y}$ for every variable $y \in Y$. Additional edges, representing constraints, are then added to connect the copies. The effect of these edges is that large independent sets reflect consistent assignments of Φ: in particular, if there is an assignment satisfying all constraints, then the set of vertices made up of the dictatorships in each copy forms an independent set in G_Φ. Theorem 6.3 guarantees that any independent set in G_Φ corresponds to juntas in many of the copies of G_I in G_Φ, so a sufficiently large independent set allows one to design an assignment that satisfies at least an ϵ fraction of Φ. This excludes the second alternative in the PCP theorem. Consequently, finding whether or not such a large independent set exists must be NP-hard.

We now describe another powerful form of PCP. Consider a further restricted CSP variant. Above we required the constraints to satisfy the projection property, meaning that for any constraint $\phi_{x,y}$, the value for x, $a \in R_X$, determines a unique value for y so that both satisfy $\phi_{x,y}$. What if we require in addition that the value for y uniquely determines the value of x?

Given a CSP instance satisfying this *uniqueness* property, one can efficiently figure out whether there is an assignment satisfying all constraints. Nevertheless, one may consider the following problem which was recently studied extensively by Khot.

Unique game [312]. Given a CSP instance Φ that conforms to the uniqueness property, decide whether one of the following alternatives can be exlcuded:

- There exists an assignment satisfying at least a fraction $1 - \epsilon$ of the constraints $\phi \in \Phi$
- No assignment satisfies even a fraction ϵ of Φ.

For $\epsilon > 0$, the complexity of this problem is still wide open. No polynomial algorithm is known for it; neither is it known to be NP-hard. (Khot himself conjectures that the problem is NP-hard.) Placing this problem within the known complexity classes is an exciting open question. The motivation for this problem, and the reason it is so interesting, is that it is often possible to relate the hardness of approximation problems to that of the unique game problem. We will give examples in the next section.

6.3   THE SHARP THRESHOLD BETWEEN EASY AND HARD PROBLEMS

In the previous section we briefly discussed PCP and indicated how technical results for threshold phenomena are used. There is another threshold aspect to the story. It turns out that for various optimization problems, when we try to approximate the solution, there is a sharp threshold between cases that are very easy to solve and cases in which the problem is NP-hard. This insight and the methodology for observing such phenomena are fairly recent, and a deeper understanding of the issues involved may lead both to improved approximation algorithms and to tighter hardness results. (We do not see a clear connection between the two appearances of sharp thresholds in this story.) Harmonic analysis of Boolean functions has already proven to be a powerful tool for such considerations.

Here are some results concerning sharp transitions between easy and hard computational problems:

- MAX-3-LIN(2): Given a set of linear equations over $\mathbb{Z}_2$ (integers modulo 2), assign variables in such a way as to satisfy as many of them as possible. Satisfying half of the equations is easy—by just taking a random assignment—and this "algorithm" can be derandomized easily. However, for all $\epsilon > 0$, it is NP-hard to distinguish instances where $1/2 + \epsilon$ of the equations are satisfied and instances where $1 - \epsilon$ of the equations are satisfied [235].
- MAX-3-SAT: A similar problem—only instead of equations one has ORs over three literals each. A fraction 7/8 of the constraints are expected to be satisfied by a random assignment, yet distinguishing between $7/8 + \epsilon$ and 1 is NP-hard [235].
- SET-COVER: Given a collection of subsets of $[n]$, find the smallest number of sets from the collection such that their union is $[n]$. A $\log n$ approximation (one that uses at most $\log n$ times as many sets as actually necessary) is simple to obtain, but nothing better can be achieved unless NP-complete problems with input size n have a deterministic algorithm with running time $n^{O(\log \log n)}$ [153, 439].

When we consider reductions to the unique game problem, further results can be proven.

- MIN-2-SAT-DELETION: The instance is a formula in 2-CNF form, that is, a conjunction of clauses, each one consisting of 2 literals connected by OR. The goal is to delete as few of the clauses as possible, such that the remaining instance is completely satisfiable. Approximation within any constant factor (finding a solution that deletes at most a constant times as many clauses as actually necessary) is as hard as the unique game problem [312].

- VERTEX COVER: Given an undirected graph, find the minimal number of nodes that touch all edges. A 2-approximation, namely covering the edges by at most twice the number of nodes needed, is quite easy—for example, by taking both ends of each as yet uncovered edge. Any better approximation is as hard as the unique game problem [313].
- MAX-CUT: Find a 2-partition of the nodes of a given graph such that there are as many edges as possible between the two parts. We will return to this problem in the next section.

Remarks:

1. Other interesting cases of threshold behavior in complexity theory concern fault-tolerant computations, both for classical notions of computation and for quantum computation.
2. A recent paper by Khot and Vishnoi [314] presents a remarkable connection between Fourier analysis on the discrete cube, unique games, and classical embedding problems for metric spaces.

7 NOISE SENSITIVITY

Motivated by mathematical physics, Benjamini, Kalai, and Schramm [45] have studied low levels of noise in the signals—or viewed differently, to small errors in the counting of votes. Their assumption is that there is a probability $\epsilon > 0$ of a mistake in counting a given vote and these probabilities are independent. Simple majority tends to be quite stable in the presence of noise. Two-level majority like the U.S. electoral system is less stable and multi-tier council democracy is quite sensitive to noise. This study is also closely related to works by Tsirelson, Vershik and Schramm [460, 505, 506]. For an attempt to apply the notion of noise sensitivity in finance, see Akahori [12].

For a Boolean function f and $\omega > 0$, consider the following scenario. First choose voter signals $x_1, x_2, \ldots, x_n$ randomly such that $x_i = 1$ with probability p, independently for $i = 1, 2, \ldots, n$. Let $S = f(x_1, x_2, \ldots, x_n)$. Next let $y_i = x_i$ with probability $1 - \omega$ and $y_i = 1 - x_i$ with probability ω, independently for $i = 1, 2, \ldots, n$. Let $T = f(y_1, y_2, \ldots, y_n)$. Define $C_\omega(f)$ to be the correlation between S and T.

Let $p, 0 < p < 1$, be fixed. A sequence $(f_n)_{n=1,2,\ldots}$ of Boolean functions such that $\mu_p(f_n)$ is bounded away from 0 and 1 is called *asymptotically noise-sensitive* if, for every $t > 0$,

$$\lim_{n \to \infty} C_\omega(f_n) = 0. \tag{49}$$

We will now define the complementary notion of noise stability. A class $\mathcal{F}$ of Boolean functions is *uniformly noise-stable* if for every $f \in \mathcal{F}$ and every $s > 0$ there exists a value $\omega = \omega(s) > 0$ such that $C_\omega(f) \geq 1 - s$.

A basic result concerning noise sensitivity is that the class of simple and weighted majority functions f such that $\mu_p(f)$ is bounded away from 0 and 1 is noise-stable. A sharp version was recently demonstrated by Peres [435]. Note that when the individual influences tend to 0, the property is a consequence of the central limit theorem.

The main result of Benjamini et al. [45] is a sort of converse of this. It asserts the following:

Theorem 7.1. *For every sequence* (f_n) *of monotone Boolean functions such that* $\mu_p(f_n)$ *is bounded away from 0 and 1 and* (f_n) *is not asymptotically noise-sensitive, there exists a weighted majority function* g *such that the correlation between* (f_n) *and* g *is bounded away from zero.*

The basic relation between noise sensitivity and influences is that for a sequence (f_n) of asymptotically noise-sensitive monotone Boolean functions, $\lim I^p(f_n) = \infty$. Therefore, if f is noise-sensitive in its threshold interval, it must have a sharp threshold behavior. On the other hand, in this case the threshold interval is of length $\Omega(1/\sqrt{n})$.

In this chapter, we have described several results where, in order to demonstrate a sharp threshold behavior, we exhibited a large total influence. In some of these results the proofs actually give the stronger property of noise sensitivity.

The following four remarks will further demonstrate the relevance of noise sensitivity:

1. **The connection with Fourier coefficients.** A simple but important result from Benjamini et al. [45] asserts

Theorem 7.2. *For every sequence* (f_n) *of Boolean functions such that* $\mu(f_n)$ *is bounded away from 0 and 1,* (f_n) *is asymptotically noise-sensitive if and only if for every* $k > 0$

$$\lim_{n \to \infty} \sum_{i=1}^{k} W_i(f_n) = 0 \, . \tag{50}$$

Thus, f is noise-sensitive if and only if most of the L_2-norm of f is concentrated at "high frequencies." By the same token, noise stability is equivalent to the statement that most of the L_2-norm of f is concentrated at "low frequencies."

Theorem 7.3. *A class $\mathcal{F}$ of Boolean functions is uniformly noise-stable if and only if for every $f \in \mathcal{F}$ and every $\epsilon > 0$ there exists a value k such that*

$$\sum_{i \geq k} W_i(f) < \epsilon. \tag{51}$$

2. **The majority-is-stablest conjecture.** What are the Boolean functions most stable under noise? It was conjectured by several authors that under several conditions that exclude individual variables having a large influence, majority is (asymptotically) most stable to noise. This conjecture has recently been proven by Mossel, O'Donnell, and Oleszkiewicz [410].
   We define a sequence (f_n) of Boolean functions to have a *diminishing individual influence* if

$$\lim_{n \to \infty} \max\{I_k(f_n) : 1 \leq k \leq n\} = 0. \tag{52}$$

Theorem 7.4 (Mossel-O'Donnell-Oleszkiewicz [410]). *For every sequence (f_n) of Boolean functions with diminishing individual influence,*

$$C_\omega(f_n) \leq (1 - o(1)) \left(1 - \frac{2}{\pi} \arccos(1 - 2\omega) \right). \tag{53}$$

The fact that the right-hand side gives the precise asymptotic description of the noise stability of the majority function is a nineteenth-century result by Sheppard.

3. **MAX-CUT.** Khot, Kindler, Mossel, and O'Donnell [315] showed that the majority-is-stablest theorem (which at the time was a conjecture that they posed) implies a sharp threshold for approximating MAX-CUT based on the unique game problem. The famous Goemans-Williamson algorithm based on semidefinite programming achieves the ratio $\alpha = .878567\ldots$ Khot, Kindler, Mossel, and O'Donnell showed that assuming the majority-is-stablest theorem, anything better is as hard as the unique game problem.

4. **Monotone threshold circuits.** Threshold circuits form an important class of circuits that are more general than Boolean circuits, since they allow weighted majority gates. Contrary to the situation for Boolean circuits, it is not the case that functions expressible by constant depth threshold circuits have coarse threshold behavior, as is evident from the majority of such circuits. But there is a far-reaching conjecture [45] regarding their stability to noise that is analogous to the theorems by Boppana, Linial-Mansour-Nisan, and Håstad mentioned in the previous section:

Conjecture 7.5. *Consider the class $\mathcal{F}$ of monotone Boolean functions f that are expressed by monotone depth-c threshold circuits of size $N(f)$. Then, for* *every $f \in \mathcal{F}$ and every $\epsilon > 0$ there is a value $K = K(\epsilon)$ such that*

$$\sum_{k > K \log^{c-1} N(f)} W_k(f) < \epsilon. \qquad (54)$$

Equation (51) shows that a noise-stable Boolean function can be well approximated by a low depth threshold circuit, but we do not know whether, when the function is monotone, this can be achieved by a monotone threshold circuit.

Finally, let us note an important criticism arising from works by Schramm and Tsirelson [460, 505]. These demonstrate that Boolean functions are too restricted for various problems and applications concerning noise sensitivity, and indicate that "binary trees" (in the form used in basic probability theory) rather than "cubes" are the correct mathematical framework. That more general setting allows the study, for example, of "correlated" random walks and Brownian motions. It suggests that the extensive investigation of Boolean functions, based on the discrete cube, may be complemented by investigations based on binary trees. This point of view may reflect on other topics studied in this chapter.

8 PERCOLATION

We have mentioned in the introduction that the area in which threshold behavior was originally studied is physics. In this section we will discuss the model of percolation.

Consider the graph G of an m by $m+1$ planar rectangular grid. The vertices of G are thus points of the form $(i, j) : 1 \leq i \leq m, 1 \leq j \leq m+1$, and two vertices are adjacent in the graph G if they agree in one coordinate and differ by one in the other coordinate. Questions concerning percolation in the plane (usually on the infinite grid) are very important. Russo's lemma was proven in the context of percolation, and Kesten proved a sharp threshold result on the way to proving his famous result [306] on critical probabilities for planar percolation. (For a simple proof of Kesten's theorem and an extension to Voronoi percolation, see the recent papers by Bollobás and Riordan [64, 65].)

Choose every edge in G to be "open" with probability p. What is the probability of an open path from the left side of the rectangle to the right side? Is there a sharp threshold? We can ask and immediately answer the analogous question on the torus when we identify the left and right sides of the rectangle and the top and bottom sides, or even just for a cylinder when we identify only the left and right sides. When we look for a path homotopic to the horizontal path from $(0,0)$ to $(0, m+1)$, a sharp threshold follows from the proof of theorem 5.1.

The total influence of the Boolean function f described by "left-right" percolation on the $m + 1$ by m grid is a basic notion in percolation theory. It is conjectured that $I(f) \simeq m^{3/4} \simeq n^{3/8}$, where n is the number of variables. This conjecture was verified for one of the variants of planar percolation (site percolation on the triangular grid) based on the works of Smirnov [479], and Lawler, Schramm, and Werner [355].

Basic Problem: For a Boolean function f with $\mu(f)$ bounded away from 0 and 1, find sufficient conditions to guarantee that for some $\alpha, \beta > 0$, $n^\alpha < I(f) < n^{1/2-\beta}$.

It was shown by Kesten [307, 308] that this property holds for the crossing event for planar percolation. Why does the total influence for percolation behave as a power of n? We can expect that the reason lies in some symmetry like the one considered in theorem 5.2 of Bourgain and Kalai. However, two facts are worth noting. The first is that the present formulation of Theorem 5.2 is not sufficiently strong to yield lower bounds of the form $I(f) > n^\alpha$. The second is that the Boolean function we described does not admit many symmetries. What it does seem to have is "approximate" symmetries. We expect that as the grid becomes finer, there will be some "limit object" (the scaling limit) reflecting an approximate symmetry of our functions under continuous maps of the square to itself. Such a symmetry is expected in any dimension. In two dimensions, it is expected that the limit object is symmetric under conformal maps. This was proven by Smirnov [479] for site percolation on the triangular grid. Noise sensitivity for the crossing event was proved in Benjamini et al. [45] and Schramm and Steif [459] recently proved a very strong form of it.

We now briefly discuss several related issues:

1. **First passage percolation.** Let f be a Boolean function. Consider a real function g defined on the discrete cube. Let $y_1, y_2, \ldots, y_n$ be independent, identically distributed random variables. Define

$$g(x_1, x_2, \ldots, x_n) = \min \left\{ \sum x_1 y_1 + x_2 y_2 + + x_n y_n : f(x_1, x_2, \ldots, x_n) = 1 \right\}.$$
$$(55)$$

Understanding the behavior of the function g is of interest in percolation theory. In this context f is the Boolean function that describes the existence of a path of open edges between two points on the grid. Curiously, the same model is related to questions raised in mechanism design in economics theory. Influences and methods used to study them apply very nicely to the study of first passage percolation [44].

2. **Models with dependence.**   One of the major research challenges is to extend the results described in this chapter to models where the probability distribution is not a product distribution. Important cases are the Ising and the more general Potts and random cluster models, as well as models based on random walks of various types. The random cluster model is a model of random subgraphs of a graph G with n edges, where one has a real parameter

$q > 0$. The probability of a spanning graph H with k edges is proportional to

$$p^k(1-p)^{n-k}q^c,$$

where c is the number of connected components of H. This model thus defines a two-parameter probability distribution on random subgraphs. The challenge is to find useful discrete isoperimetric theory and useful harmonic analysis for these probability distributions that will allow us to extend some of the general theorems described in this chapter. Very recently, Graham and Grimmett [207] have made a breakthrough in this area, extending the Kahn-Kalai-Linial theorem and deducing sharp threshold theorems for measures of the random-cluster type.

3. **The Fourier coefficients.** The Fourier coefficients of the crossing (and other) events for percolation are indexed by subgraphs of the grid. The Fourier transform gives a distribution on such subgraphs which is very interesting.

9 ECONOMICS AND VOTING: AN EXAMPLE OF SELF-ORGANIZED CRITICALITY

Let us now return to the Condorcet jury theorem from section 1. A key assumption in the theorem is that each agent votes according to his or her signal. There is recent interesting literature on the case where voters vote *strategically* based on their signals. Suppose that every voter wishes to minimize the probability of mistakes, where we may assign different weights to mistakes in the two directions. Feddersen and Pesendorfer [152] considered the example of juries, where a much larger weight is typically given to an innocent person being convicted than to a guilty one being acquitted. Suppose that in order to convict, one needs two thirds of the votes. Suppose furthermore that each juror k receives a Boolean signal s_k such that if the defendant is guilty then $s_k = 1$ with probability $p > 1/2$ and if the defendant is innocent then $s_k = 1$ with probability $1 - p$. (We assume these signals are independent.) Now, if jurors vote according to their signals, then when $p = 0.51$ and the number of jurors is large, they will hardly ever convict.

Feddersen and Pesendorfer considered the case where jurors vote strategically, using mixed (randomized) strategies. The surprising conclusion is that in such a situation, ever with a high threshold for conviction and a weak signal, the probability of either convicting an innocent defendant or acquitting a guilty one tends to zero as the number of jurors grows, even if the signal is weak. The one case where this does not hold is where unanimity among all jurors is required. Feddersen and Pesendorfer's result and analysis is based on the notion of Nash equilibrium. Nash equilibrium in this case gives us a nice example of "self-organized criticality." The behavior at the critical point is significant even when the voting method is biased from the beginning.

For the reader who is not familiar with game theory, some explanation is in order. To start with, every member of the jury has four pure strategies for how to act, given the signal he or she receives: act according to the signal, act opposite to the signal, acquit regardless of the signal, and convict regardless of the signal. A mixed strategy means a strategy involving randomization, so the outcome is probabilistic. In our case, a mixed strategy for juror k would be: upon receiving a signal to acquit, acquit with probability α_k and convict with probability $1 - \alpha_k$; upon receiving a signal to convict, acquit with probability β_k and convict with probability $1 - \beta_k$. We assume that each juror knows the signal s_k he or she has received, but not the signals or strategies of the other voters, and the jurors vote in a secret ballot. Furthermore, we assume that the signal strength p is known to all.

Each juror now votes in such a way as to maximize his or her own perceived "payoff," defined as follows. Jurors want to minimize the probability of a wrong decision, and it is considered worse to convict an innocent defendant than to acquit a guilty defendant. So if the jury reaches the right decision, the payoff for each juror is zero. If the jury acquits a guilty defendant, the payoff for each juror is $-q$, where $q \in (0, 0.5)$. If the jury convicts an innocent defendant, the payoff for each juror is $q - 1$. Note that the payoff function is the same for all jurors, and depends only on the collective decision of the jury. Given a sequence of mixed strategies, one for each juror, and based on an equal prior probability of innocence and guilt, a juror can estimate the posterior probability that the defendant is guilty as well as the expected payoff. In game theory, the Nash equilibrium point is a sequence of mixed strategies such that no player can expect a gain in payoff by deviating from his or her strategy as long as none of the other players deviates.

When we consider general voting methods and not only majority rules, it can be shown that "asymptotically complete aggregation of information" is intimately related to having a sharp threshold [451]. In particular, if there is a sharp threshold, then there is always a Nash equilibrium point for which the probability of mistakes tends to zero as the number of voters grows.

Fedderson and Pesendorfer's result is related to the question of why we care about critical behavior to start with. Why is it so often the case that shortly before an election between two candidates, both of them appear to have a significant chance of being elected? How come the probabilities we can assign to the choices of each individual voter do not "sum up" to a decisive collective outcome? This seems especially surprising in view of the sharp threshold phenomenon. Fedderson and Pesendorfer's result suggests that the strategic behavior of voters can push the situation towards criticality. Another explanation would challenge the independence of the signals received by the voters.

There are other relations between threshold phenomena and economics and social choice theory. We have already seen in theorem 3.9 that having a sharp threshold for a sequence of monotone Boolean functions is equivalent to having a diminishing Shapley-Shubik power index. A famous result in social choice theory is Arrow's impossibility theorem [22] concerning election methods when there are three or more candidates. Condorcet's famous "paradox" demonstrates that given three candidates A, B, and C, the majority rule may result in the society preferring A to B, B to C, and C to A. Arrow's Impossibility Theorem is an extension of Condorcet's paradox, and states that under certain general conditions such non-transitive social preferences cannot be avoided under *any* non-dictatorial voting method. Relations between threshold phenomena and Arrow-type theorems are described in Kalai [288, 289].

As in the percolation discussion in section 8, a further problem in the context of economics is to understand matters under more realistic probabilistic assumptions, moving away from product distributions. This poses interesting conceptual and technical problems. Haggstrom, Kalai, and Mossel [222] studied aggregation of information in models with dependence. Another challenge in the economic arena is to study threshold phenomena (aggregation of information) and related notions such as noise sensitivity for more complex models.

10 CONCLUSIONS AND OPEN PROBLEMS

Threshold phenomena and related concepts such as pivotality, influence, and noise sensitivity are important in many areas of mathematics, science, and engineering. We have described some mathematical advances in the understanding of threshold behavior and related phenomena, as well as various applications and connections, and some open problems. The underlying mathematical concepts are similar in different disciplines. However, bridging the different points of view, methodologies, and interpretations is a major challenge. The subequent chapters of this book address this challenge from the perspectives of physics and computer science.

Over the course of this chapter, we have highlighted some important open problems. These include proving Friedgut's conjecture 5.4 and finding sharper versions of Bourgain and Kalai's theorem 5.2.[2] A less explicit but nevertheless important problem is to explain the emergence of power laws in the threshold interval, where the width of the interval behaves as $n^{-\beta}$ where $\beta > 0$ is a real number.

A fundamental challenge is to relate the threshold behavior to the threshold's location, and to find methods to exclude the possibility of oscillating critical probabilities. We have mentioned this issue in the context of the k-SAT problem. It is equally of interest for many other problems as well.

Another important challenge is to find methods to deal with the influence of events of small probability. This is related to a detailed understanding of how the function $\mu_p(f)$ behaves, and especially to the analysis of large deviations of the threshold behavior. In this chapter we have dealt mainly with $t_\epsilon(f)$ when ϵ is

---

[2]Falik and Samorodnitsky [150] have very recently found a new proof of the Kahn-Kalai-Linial theorem based on an extension of the edge-isoperimetric inequality. Their methods may be relevant to some of the problems that we have mentioned.

fixed. It is of great interest to understand dependence on ϵ. The precise behavior of the function $\mu_p(f)$ in the threshold interval and the situation when ϵ itself is very small and expressed as a function of n are both very interesting topics. Kahn and Kalai [286] have proposed far-reaching conjectures concerning the influence $I^p(f)$ of Boolean functions f when $\mu_p(f)$ is a function of n and tends to 0 with increasing n. Additionally, they have studied possible applications towards finding the location of the critical probability.

It would also be interesting to study threshold behavior and influences when we replace the Boolean cube $\{0, 1\}^n$ by Σ^n when Σ is a finite alphabet with more than two letters. We expect, in that case, that for symmetric monotone functions the transition will occur in small "membranes" [290]. There is interesting related work concerning powers of arbitrary graphs by Alon, Dinur, Friedgut, and Sudakov [18]. There are various other generalizations of Boolean functions. Some can be found in Ben-Or and Linial's original paper [46] on collective coin flipping and are waiting to be explored further. Another important generalization is to functions of the form

$$f : \{0, 1\}^n \rightarrow \{0, 1\}^m. \tag{56}$$

These are of great importance in mathematics (e.g., error-correcting codes) and computer science (e.g., extractors).

Finally, it is worth repeating a problem already mentioned in several contexts: studying threshold behavior and related notions of noise sensitivity and Fourier analysis for various models, with non-product probability distributions, namely, when the assumption of probability independence is dropped.

ACKNOWLEDGMENTS

Research supported in part by an NSF grant and by an ISF bikura grant. We thank Allon Percus without whose encouragement and help this chapter would not have been written, and are thankful to many friends and colleagues including Noga Alon, Itai Benjamini, Irit Dinur, Ehud Friedgut, Jeff Kahn, Guy Kindler, Nati Linial, Elchanan Mossel, Ryan O'Donnell, Yuval Peres, Oded Schramm, and Boris Tsirelson for inspiring discussions and helpful remarks.

Part 2: Statistical Physics and Algorithms

CHAPTER 3

Analyzing Search Algorithms with Physical Methods

Simona Cocco
Rémi Monasson
Andrea Montanari
Guilhem Semerjian

1 INTRODUCTION

The computational effort needed to deal with large combinatorial structures varies considerably with the task to be performed and the resolution procedure used [425]. The worst-case complexity of a decision or optimization problem is defined as the time required by the best algorithm to treat any possible input to the problem. For instance, the worst-case complexity of the problem of sorting a list of n numbers scales as $n \log n$: there exist several algorithms that can order any list in at most $\sim n \log n$ elementary operations, and none with asymptotically fewer operations. Unfortunately, the worst-case complexities of many important computational problems, called NP-complete, are not known. Partitioning a list of n numbers in two sets with equal partial sums is one among hundreds of known NP-complete problems. It is a fundamental conjecture of theoretical computer science that there exists no algorithm capable of partitioning any list of length n, or of solving any other NP-complete problem with inputs of size n, in a time bounded by a polynomial of n. Therefore, when trying to solve such a

Computational Complexity and Statistical Physics, edited by
Allon G. Percus, Gabriel Istrate, and Cristopher Moore, Oxford University Press.

problem exactly, one necessarily uses algorithms that may take exponential time on some inputs. Quantifying how "frequent" these hard inputs are for a given algorithm is the question answered by the analysis of algorithms. We will present an overview of recent work by physicists to address this point, and more precisely to characterize the average performance—hereafter simply called *complexity*—of a given algorithm over a distribution of inputs to a computational problem.

The history of algorithm analysis by physical methods and ideas is at least as old as the use of computers by physicists. One well-established chapter in this history is the analysis of Monte Carlo sampling algorithms for statistical mechanics models. It is well known that phase transitions, that is, abrupt changes in the physical properties of the model, can imply a dramatic increase in the time necessary for the sampling procedure. This phenomenon is commonly known as critical slowing down. The physicist's insight comes from the analogy between the dynamics of algorithms and the physical dynamics of the system. That analogy is quite natural: in fact many algorithms mimic the physical dynamics.

A very new idea is, instead, to abstract from physically motivated problems and use ideas from statistical mechanics to analyze the dynamics of algorithms. There are many reasons to consider the analysis of algorithms and statistical physics as close relatives. In both cases one would like to understand the asymptotic behavior of dynamical processes acting on configuration spaces that are exponentially large in the size of the problem. The differences between the two disciplines lie mainly in the methods—and, we are tempted to say, the style—of investigation. Theoretical computer science derives rigorous results based on probability theory. However, these results are sometimes too weak for a complete characterization of the algorithm. Physicists instead provide heuristic results based on intuitively sensible approximations. These approximations are eventually validated by a comparison with numerical experiments. In some lucky cases, approximate results are exact in the asymptotic limit of large problem size: estimates are turned into conjectures which are left for future rigorous derivations.

Perhaps more interesting than stylistic differences is the "point of view" that physics brings. Let us highlight two consequences of this point of view.

First, a particular importance is attributed to *complexity phase transitions*, in other words, abrupt changes in the resolution complexity as some parameter defining the input distribution is varied [177, 254]. We shall consider two examples in the next sections:

1. Random satisfiability of Boolean constraints (SAT). In k-SAT one is given an instance, namely a set of m logical constraints (clauses) among n Boolean variables $x_i, \ldots, x_n$, and wants to find a truth assignment for the variables that fulfills all the constraints. Each clause is the disjunction (logical **OR**) of k literals, a literal being one of the n variables or its negation. An example of a 3-SAT clause might be $(x_1 \vee x_{17} \vee \overline{x_{31}})$. Random k-SAT is the k-SAT problem supplied with a distribution of inputs uniform over all instances having fixed

values of n and m. The limit of interest is $n, m \to \infty$ at fixed ratio $\alpha = m/n$ of clauses per variable [196, 400].

2. Vertex cover of random graphs (VC). An input instance of the VC decision problem consists of a graph G with n vertices and m edges, and an integer number X. The problem is to find a way of distributing X covering marks over the vertices in such a way that every edge of the graph is covered: that is, at least one of its ending vertices is marked. A possible distribution of inputs is provided by drawing random graphs G à la Erdős-Rényi, that is, with uniform probability among all the graphs having n vertices and m edges. The limit of interest is $n, m \to \infty$ at fixed mean degree $c = 2m/n$.

The algorithms for random SAT and VC we shall consider in the next sections undergo a complexity phase transition as the input parameter π ($= \alpha$ for SAT, c for VC) crosses some critical threshold π_c. Typically, resolution of a randomly drawn instance requires linear time below the threshold $\pi < \pi_c$ and exponential time above $\pi > \pi_c$. The observation that the most difficult instances are located near the phase boundary confirms the relevance of the phase-transition phenomenon.

Second, a key role is played by the intrinsic (algorithm-independent) properties of the instance under study. The intuition is that, underlying the dramatic slowing down of a particular algorithm, a *qualitative* change occurs in some structural property of the problem, that is, the geometry of the space of solutions. While there is no general understanding of this question, we can further specify the statements above case-by-case. Let us consider, for instance, a local search algorithm for a combinatorial optimization problem. If the algorithm never increases the value of the cost, or energy function $E(C)$ where C is the configuration (assignment) of variables to be optimized over, the number and geometry of the local minima of $E(C)$ will be crucial for the understanding of the dynamics of the algorithm. This example is illustrated in section 3.3. The "dynamical" behavior of a particular algorithm is not necessarily related to any "static" property of the instance, but this approach is nevertheless of great interest because it could conceivably provide us with "universal" results. Some properties of the instance, for example, may imply the ineffectiveness of an entire class of algorithms.

While in this chapter we mainly study the performance of search algorithms applied to hard combinatorial problems such as SAT and VC, we also consider easy—that is, polynomial—problems as benchmarks for these algorithms. The reason is that we want to understand if the average hardness of resolution for an NP-complete problem with a given distribution of instances and a given algorithm truly reflects the intrinsic hardness of the combinatorial problem, or is simply due to the algorithm's lack of efficiency. The benchmark problem we shall consider is random XORSAT, a version of satisfiability that is much simpler than SAT from a computational complexity point of view [112]. The essential difference with SAT is that a clause is said to be satisfied if the exclusive, rather than inclusive, disjunction of its literals is TRUE: logical OR is replaced by XOR.

XORSAT may be recast as a linear algebra problem, where a set of m equations involving n Boolean variables must be satisfied modulo 2, and is, therefore, solvable in polynomial time by methods such as Gaussian elimination. Nevertheless, it is legitimate to investigate the performance of general search algorithms for this kind of polynomial computational problem. In particular, we shall see that some algorithms requiring exponential time to solve random SAT instances behave badly on random XORSAT instances too. A related question we shall focus on in section 3.2 is decoding, which in some cases may also be expressed as the resolution of a set of Boolean equations.

The chapter is organized as follows. Section 2.1 gives an overview of backtracking search algorithms, which, roughly speaking, work in the space of instances. We explain the general ideas and then illustrate them on random SAT (sec. 2.2) and VC (sec. 2.3). In section 2.4 we consider the fluctuations in running times of these algorithms and analyze the possibility of exploiting these fluctuations in random restart strategies. In section 3 we turn to local search algorithms, which work in the space of configurations. We review the analysis of such algorithms for decoding problems (sec. 3.2), random XORSAT (sec. 3.3), and SAT (sec. 3.4). Finally, we suggest some possible future developments in the field.

2   ANALYSIS OF THE DAVIS-PUTNAM-LOVELAND-LOGEMAN SEARCH PROCEDURE

2.1   OVERVIEW OF THE ALGORITHM AND PHYSICAL CONCEPTS

In this section, we briefly describe the Davis-Putnam-Loveland-Logemann (DPLL) procedure [118, 220]. A decision problem can be formulated as a constraint satisfaction problem, where variables must be assigned so as to fulfill the required constraints. For simplicity, we suppose here that variables may take a finite set of values with cardinality v, that is, $v = 2$ for SAT or VC. DPLL is an exhaustive search procedure operating by trial and error, the sequence of which can be represented graphically by a search tree (fig. 1). The tree is defined as follows:

1. A splitting node in the tree corresponds to a variable being selected, by a heuristic method to be specified.
2. An outgoing branch (edge) codes for the value of the variable and the logical implications of this choice upon constraints and variables not yet assigned. Clearly, a splitting node gives birth to v branches at most.
3. Implications can lead to:
    3.1 a solution (**S** in fig. 1) satisfying all constraints, terminating the search process

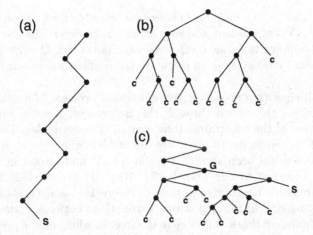

FIGURE 1 Types of search trees generated by the DPLL solving procedure for variables taking $v = 2$ values at most. Splitting nodes (black dots) stand for the selection of variable made by a heuristic, and edges between nodes denote the implications of assigning a value to the variable. (a) *simple branch:* the algorithm easily finds a solution **S** without any backtracking. (b) *dense tree:* in the absence of a solution, the algorithm repeatedly encounters contradictions **C** and builds a "bushy" tree, with many branches of various lengths, before stopping. (c) *mixed case, branch + tree:* if many contradictions **C** arise before reaching a solution, the resulting search tree can be decomposed in a single branch followed by a dense tree. The junction **G** is the highest backtracking node reached back by DPLL.

3.2 a violated constraint, in which case the branch ends in a contradiction (**C** in fig. 1), the last choice is modified (backtracking on the tree) and the procedure goes on along a new branch (repeat at step 2 above)

3.3 a state where some constraints remain and further assumptions on the variables have to be made (repeat at step 1 above)

A computer-independent measure of computational complexity is the number of operations necessary to solve the instance. This reflects the resolution time, and is given by the size Q of the search tree: the number of splitting nodes it contains. Performance can be improved by designing sophisticated heuristic rules for choosing variables in step 1 above. Q is a stochastic variable that depends on the instance under consideration and on the choices made by the variable assignment procedure. Its average value,[1] $\bar{Q}$, is a function of the input distribution

[1]More precisely, we are interested in the median value. The mean and median coincide in the absence of large fluctuations, but even in the presence of large fluctuations the median behavior can be reconstructed from the mean complexity of a search subtree. We will see this in section 2.2.3.

parameters π, that is, the ratio α of clauses per variable for SAT, or the average degree c for the VC of random graphs. Our aim is to determine the values of π for which the complexity is linear, $\bar{Q} = \gamma n$ or exponential, $\bar{Q} = 2^{n\,\omega}$, in the size n of the instance. We also wish to calculate the coefficients γ, ω as functions of π.

The DPLL algorithm gives rise to a dynamical process. The initial instance is modified during the search through the assignment of some variables and the simplification of the constraints that contain these variables. Therefore, the parameters of the input distribution are modified as the algorithm runs. This dynamical process has been studied rigorously and understood in the case of a search tree reducing to one branch (fig. 1(a)) [1, 88, 89, 182, 294]. Study of trees with massive backtracking, that is, figure 1(b) and (c), is much more difficult. Backtracking introduces strong correlations between nodes visited by DPLL at very different times, but close in the tree. In addition, the process is non-Markovian in that instances attached to each node are committed to memory, to allow the search to resume after a backtracking step.

The study of the operation of DPLL is based on the following, elementary observation. Since instances are modified when treated by DPLL, a description of their statistical properties requires not only the defining parameter (or parameters) π of the input distribution, but also additional parameters π' characterizing the progress of the algorithm. Our task therefore consists of:

1. identifying these extra parameters π', a point considered in greater mathematical depth in chapter 8;
2. deriving the phase diagram of this new, extended distribution π, π' to identify, in π, π' space, the critical surface separating instances having a solution with high probability (the satisfiability, or SAT phase) from instances having generally no solution (the UNSAT phase), see figure 2;
3. tracking the evolution of an instance under resolution with time t (number of steps of the algorithm), that is, the trajectory of its characteristic parameters $\pi(t), \pi'(t)$ in the phase diagram.

Whether this trajectory remains confined to one of the two phases or crosses the boundary in between them has dramatic consequences on the resolution complexity. We find three typical behaviors, depicted in figure 2:

1. *Lower (easy) SAT*. If the initial instance has a solution and the trajectory remains in the SAT phase, the instance is easily satisfiable: resolution is linear with high probability and there is almost no backtracking (fig. 1(a)).[2] The trajectory coordinates $\pi(t), \pi'(t)$ of the instance during resolution obey a set

---

[2]This statement is correct for SAT and VC but is not true for the graph coloring problem on random graphs [409]. For graph coloring, linear resolution takes place with a finite probability, though not tending to one when the size of the instance goes to infinity.

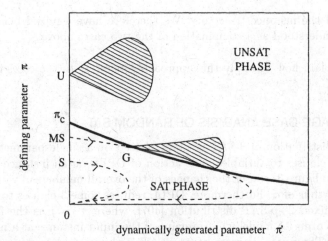

FIGURE 2 Schematic representation of the resolution trajectories in the SAT phase (branch trajectories symbolized by dashed lines) and UNSAT phase (tree trajectories represented by shaded regions). For simplicity we have considered the case where both π and π' are scalar rather than vector parameters. The vertical axis is the defining parameter π for the instance distribution. Instances are almost always satisfiable (SAT) if $\pi < \pi_c$, unsatisfiable (UNSAT) if $\pi > \pi_c$. Under the action of DPLL, the distribution of instances is modified and requires another parameter π' to be characterized (horizontal axis). Here, π' is equal to zero prior to any action of DPLL. For non-zero values of π', the critical value of the defining parameter π changes: the bold line $\pi_c(\pi')$ defines a boundary separating typically SAT from typically UNSAT instances. For satisfiable and easy instances **S**, DPLL goes along a branch trajectory in a linear time. For unsatisfiable instances **U**, DPLL takes an exponential time to go through the tree trajectory. For the mixed case of hard satisfiable instances **MS**, a branch trajectory crosses the boundary separating the two phases at point **G** (corresponding to junction in fig. 1(c)), leading to the exploration of UNSAT subtrees before a solution is finally found.

of coupled ordinary differential equations, accounting for the changes in the distribution parameters under DPLL.

2. *UNSAT.* If the initial instance has no solution, then solving the instance—by finding a proof of unsatisfiability—takes exponentially large time and makes use of massive backtracking (fig. 1(b)). Analysis of the search tree is much more complicated than in the linear regime, and requires a partial differential equation that gives information on the population of branches with parameters π, π' throughout the growth of the search tree.

3. *Upper (hard) SAT.* In some intermediary regime, instances are satisfiable but hard: finding a solution one requires an exponentially long time (fig. 1(c)). This may be related to the crossing of the boundary between SAT and UNSAT

phases of the instance trajectory. We therefore have a mixed behavior that can be understood as a combination of the two cases above.

We now explain how to apply this approach concretely to the cases of random SAT and VC.

2.2   AVERAGE-CASE ANALYSIS OF RANDOM SAT

The input distribution of 3-SAT is characterized by a single parameter $\pi = \alpha$, the ratio of clauses to variables. The action of DPLL on an instance of 3-SAT, illustrated in figure 3, causes the changes of the overall numbers of variables and clauses, and thus of α. Furthermore, DPLL reduces some 3-clauses to 2-clauses. We use a mixed 2+p-SAT distribution [407], where $\pi' = p$ is the fraction of 3-clauses, in order to model what remains of the input instance at a node of the search tree. The phase diagram of 2+p-SAT is the natural space in which the DPLL dynamics takes place. An input 3-SAT instance with ratio α shows up on the right vertical boundary of figure 4 as a point of coordinates $(p = 1, \alpha)$. Under the action of DPLL, the representative point moves away from the 3-SAT vertical axis and follows a trajectory in the (p, α) plane. Using experiments and methods from statistical mechanics [407] as well as rigorous calculations [8], the threshold line $\alpha_c(p)$ separating SAT from UNSAT phases may be estimated with the results shown in figure 4. For $p \leq p_0 = 2/5$, that is, left of point $\mathbf{T}$, the threshold line is given by $\alpha_c(p) = 1/(1 - p)$. Above p_0, no exact expression for $\alpha_c(p)$ is known.

In this section, we show that the trajectory location in the phase diagram allows a precise understanding of the search tree structure and of complexity as a function of the parameter α of the instance to be solved (inset of fig. 4). In addition, we present an approximate calculation of trajectories accounting for the case of massive backtracking, for UNSAT instances as well as slightly below the threshold in the SAT phase. Our approach is based on a non-rigorous extension of works by Chao and Franco, who first studied the action of DPLL (without backtracking) on easy satisfiable instances [88, 89] as a way of obtaining lower bounds on the threshold α_c. See Achlioptas [1] for a recent review.

DPLL requires a mechanism for selecting variables at splitting nodes. We consider two heuristics [88, 89] for doing this:

1. *Unit Clause (UC):* pick a literal at random among a unit clause if any, or pick any unset variable at random otherwise; and
2. *Generalized Unit Clause (GUC) heuristic:* pick a literal at random among the shortest available clauses.

Let us emphasize that the idea of trajectory is made possible thanks to an important statistical property of these heuristics, namely that they induce no bias or correlation in the instance distribution [89]. Such a statistical "invariance"

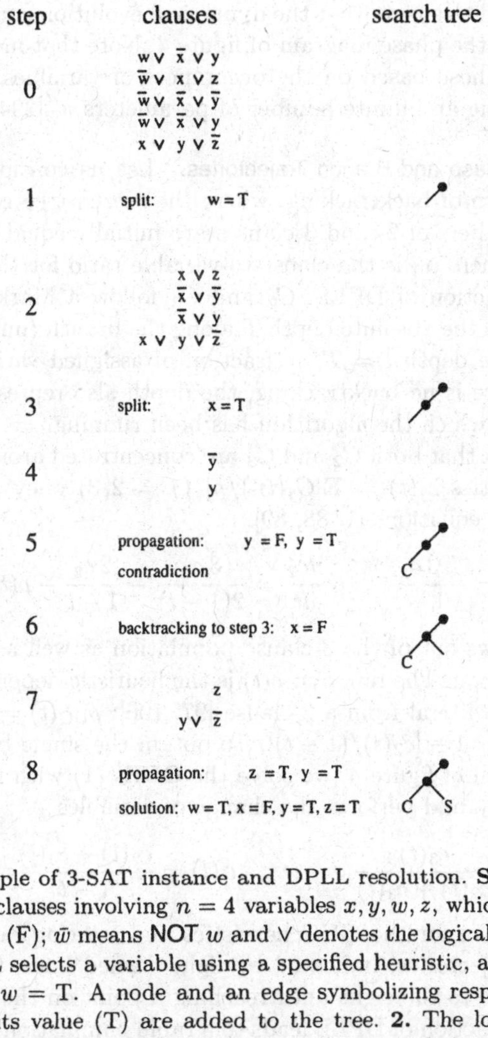

step	clauses	search tree
0	$w \vee \bar{x} \vee y$ $\bar{w} \vee x \vee z$ $\bar{w} \vee \bar{x} \vee \bar{y}$ $\bar{w} \vee \bar{x} \vee y$ $x \vee y \vee \bar{z}$	
1	split: $w = T$	
2	$x \vee z$ $\bar{x} \vee \bar{y}$ $\bar{x} \vee y$ $x \vee y \vee \bar{z}$	
3	split: $x = T$	
4	$\bar{y}$ y	
5	propagation: $y = F, \ y = T$ contradiction	
6	backtracking to step 3: $x = F$	
7	z $y \vee \bar{z}$	
8	propagation: $z = T, \ y = T$ solution: $w = T, x = F, y = T, z = T$	

FIGURE 3 Example of 3-SAT instance and DPLL resolution. **Step 0.** The instance consists of $m = 5$ clauses involving $n = 4$ variables x, y, w, z, which can be assigned to TRUE (T) or FALSE (F); $\bar{w}$ means NOT w and $\vee$ denotes the logical OR. The search tree is empty. **1.** DPLL selects a variable using a specified heuristic, and assigns a value to the variable, e.g., $w = T$. A node and an edge symbolizing respectively the variable selected (w) and its value (T) are added to the tree. **2.** The logical implications of the last choice are extracted: clauses containing w are satisfied and eliminated, clauses including $\bar{w}$ are simplified and the remaining ones are left unchanged. If no unit clause (with a single variable) is present, a new variable has to be selected. **3.** Splitting takes over. Another node and another edge are added to the tree. **4.** Same as step 2 but now unit clauses are present. The variables they contain have to be fixed accordingly. **5.** Propagation of the unit clauses results in a contradiction. The current branch dies out and gets marked with **C. 6.** DPLL backtracks to the last split variable (x), inverts it (F) and creates a new edge. **7.** Same as step 4. **8.** Propagation of the unit clauses eliminates all the clauses. A solution **S** is found and the instance is satisfiable. For an unsatisfiable instance, unsatisfiability is proven when backtracking (see step 6) is not possible anymore since all split variables have already been inverted. In this case, all the nodes in the final search tree have two descendant edges and all branches terminate in a contradiction **C.**

(see ch. 8) is required to ensure that the dynamical evolution generated by DPLL remains confined to the phase diagram of figure 4. Note that more sophisticated heuristics, that is, those based on the occurences of variables in the instance, could require tracking an infinite number of parameters π' [294, 521].

2.2.1 Lower SAT Phase and Branch Trajectories.

Let us consider the action of DPLL in the absence of backtracking, where the search tree is a single branch (fig. 1(a)). The numbers of 2- and 3-clauses are initially equal to $C_2 = 0, C_3 = \alpha_0 n$ respectively, where α_0 is the clause-to-variable ratio for the instance to be solved. Under the action of DPLL, C_2 and C_3 follow a Markovian stochastic evolution process, as the absolute depth T along the branch (number of assigned variables) or relative depth $t = T/n$ (fraction of assigned variables) increases. Note that since there is no backtracking, the depth also represents the time or number of steps for which the algorithm has been running.

It may be shown that both C_2 and C_3 are concentrated around their average values, whose densities $c_j(t) = \mathbf{E}[C_j(tn)/n]$ $(j = 2, 3)$ obey a set of coupled ordinary differential equations [1, 88, 89],

$$\frac{dc_3}{dt} = -\frac{3\,c_3}{1-t}, \qquad \frac{dc_2}{dt} = \frac{3\,c_3}{2(1-t)} - \frac{2\,c_2}{1-t} - \rho(t), \tag{1}$$

representing the flows out of the 3-clause population as well as into and out of the 2-clause population. The function $\rho(t)$ is the heuristic-dependent probability that DPLL selects a literal from a 2-clause [97, 100]: $\rho_{\mathrm{UC}}(t) = 0$, and provided $\alpha_0 > 2/3$, $\rho_{\mathrm{GUC}}(t) = 1 - [c_2(t)/(1-t)]$. To obtain the single branch trajectory in the phase diagram of figure 4, we solve the ODEs (1) with initial conditions $c_2(0) = 0, c_3(0) = \alpha_0$, and perform the change of variables

$$p(t) = \frac{c_3(t)}{c_2(t) + c_3(t)} \qquad , \qquad \alpha(t) = \frac{c_2(t) + c_3(t)}{1-t} \qquad . \tag{2}$$

Results are shown for the GUC heuristics and starting ratios $\alpha_0 = 2$ and 2.8 in figure 4. Trajectories, indicated by light dashed lines, first head to the left and then reverse to the right until reaching a point on the 3-SAT axis at a small ratio. Further action of DPLL leads to a rapid elimination of the remaining clauses and the trajectory ends up at the right lower corner S, where a solution is found.

Frieze and Suen [182] have shown that for the GUC heuristic, at ratios $\alpha_0 < \alpha_L \approx 3.003$ the number of backtrackings necessary to reach a solution is bounded from above by a power of $\log n$. Thus, the full search tree essentially reduces to a single branch, and is entirely described by the ODEs (1). The average size $\bar{Q}$ of the branch then scales linearly in n with a multiplicative factor $\gamma(\alpha_0) = \bar{Q}/n$ that can be computed analytically [97, 100]

The boundary α_L of this lower SAT region can be defined as the largest initial ratio α_0 such that the branch trajectory $p(t), \alpha(t)$ issued from α_0 never leaves the SAT phase in the course of DPLL resolution.

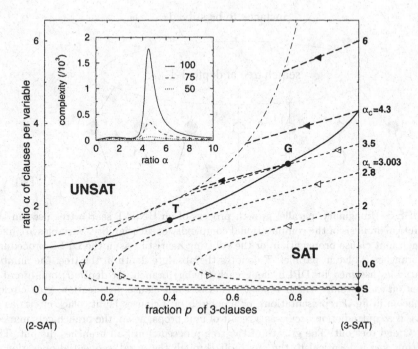

FIGURE 4   Phase diagram of 2+p-SAT and resolution trajectories under DPLL action. The bold solid line marking the threshold $\alpha_c(p)$ separates the SAT from UNSAT phase. Departure points for DPLL trajectories are located on the 3-SAT vertical axis. Arrows indicate the direction of "motion" along trajectories (dashed curves) parametrized by the fraction t of variables set by DPLL. For small ratios $\alpha < \alpha_L$ (≈ 3.003 when DPLL selects variables using the generalized unit clause heuristic), branch trajectories remain confined to the SAT phase and end in a solution **S** at coordinates $(1,0)$, found with a simple search process as in figure 1(a). For $\alpha > \alpha_c \approx 4.3$, proofs of unsatisfiability are given by complete search trees where all leaves contain contradictions, as in figure 1(b). The tree trajectories are represented by bold dashed lines (full arrows) ending near the halt (dot-dashed) line. For ratios $\alpha_L < \alpha < \alpha_c$, the branch trajectory intersects the threshold line at some point **G**. A contradiction almost surely arises and extensive backtracking up to **G** is needed, as in figure 1(c). Only with exponentially small probability does the trajectory (dashed curve) cross the "dangerous" region where contradictions are likely to occur, and then exit from this region to end up with a solution (lowest dashed trajectory). Inset: Resolution time of 3-SAT instances as a function of the ratio of clauses per variable α and for three different sizes. Data correspond to the median resolution time of 10,000 instances by DPLL; the mean time may be somewhat larger due to the presence of rare, exceptionally hard instances, cf. section 2.4. The computational complexity is linear for $\alpha < \alpha_L \approx 3.003$, exponential above.

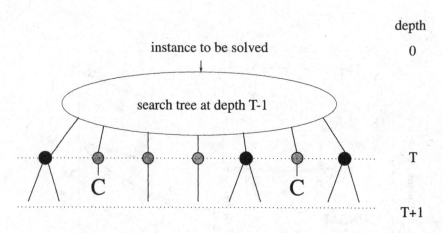

FIGURE 5 Imaginary, parallel growth process of an UNSAT search tree used in the theoretical analysis of the computational complexity of satisfiability. Variables are fixed through unit clause propagation, or the splitting heuristics as in the DPLL procedure, but branches evolve in parallel. T denotes the absolute depth in the tree: the number of variables assigned by DPLL along each (living) branch. At depth T, one literal is chosen on each branch, either among 1-clauses (unit clause propagation: grey circles, not shown in fig. 1 representation), or among 2- or 3-clauses (split: black circles as in fig. 1). If a contradiction occurs as a result of unit propagation, the branch gets marked with **C** and dies out. The growth of the tree proceeds until all branches die out. The resulting tree is identical to the one built through the usual, sequential operation of DPLL.

2.2.2 UNSAT Phase and Tree Trajectories.

For ratios above the threshold ($\alpha_0 > \alpha_c \approx 4.3$), instances almost never have a solution, but a considerable amount of backtracking is necessary before proving that clauses are incompatible. As shown in figure 1(b), a generic UNSAT tree includes many branches. The average number of nodes, $\bar{Q}$, or the average number of branches (leaves), $\bar{B} = \bar{Q}-1$, grows exponentially with n [95]. It is convenient to define its logarithm ω as $\bar{B} = 2^{n\omega}$. Contrary to the previous section, the sequence of points (p, α) characterizing the evolution of the 2+p-SAT instance solved by DPLL no longer constitutes a line, but rather a patch or a cloud of points with a finite extension in the phase diagram of figure 2.

We can compute analytically the logarithm ω of the size of these patches, as a function of α_0, extending the probabilistic analysis of DPLL to the UNSAT region. A priori, this would seem to be a very difficult task since the search tree of figure 1(b) is the output of a complex, sequential process: nodes and edges are added by DPLL through successive descents and backtrackings. We instead imagine a different construction, resulting in the same complete tree but mathematically analyzable: we grow the tree in parallel, layer by layer (fig. 5).

A new layer is added by assigning one more variable along each living branch, according to the DPLL heuristic. As a result, a branch may (1) split, (2) keep growing, or (3) result in a contradiction and die out. Cases 1, 2 and 3 are stochastic events, the probabilities of which depend on the characteristic parameters c_2, c_3 defining the 2+p-SAT instance carried by the branch, and on the relative depth (fraction of assigned variables) $t = T/n$ in the tree. We take into account the correlations between the parameters c_2, c_3 on each of the two branches issued from splitting (case 1), but neglect any further correlation between different branches at different levels in the tree [97, 100]. This Markovian approximation enables us to write an evolution equation for the logarithm $\omega(c_2, c_3, t)$ of the average number of branches with parameters c_2, c_3 as the depth t increases,

$$\frac{\partial \omega}{\partial t}(c_2, c_3, t) = H\left[c_2, c_3, \frac{\partial \omega}{\partial c_2}, \frac{\partial \omega}{\partial c_3}, t\right] \quad . \tag{3}$$

H incorporates the details of the splitting heuristic. In terms of the partial derivatives $y_2 = \partial \omega / \partial c_2$, $y_3 = \partial \omega / \partial c_3$, we find for the UC and GUC heuristics

$$H_{\text{UC}} = 1 + \frac{1}{\log 2}\left[\frac{3 c_3}{1-t}\left(e^{y_3}\frac{1+e^{-y_2}}{2} - 1\right) + \frac{c_2}{1-t}\left(\frac{3}{2}e^{-y_2} - 2\right)\right]$$

$$H_{\text{GUC}} = \log_2 \nu(y_2) + \frac{1}{\ln 2}\left[\frac{3 c_3}{1-t}\left(e^{y_3}\frac{1+e^{-y_2}}{2} - 1\right) + \frac{c_2}{1-t}\left(\nu(y_2) - 2\right)\right]$$

$$\text{where} \quad \nu(y_2) = \frac{1}{2} e^{y_2}\left(1 + \sqrt{1 + 4e^{-y_2}}\right) \quad . \tag{4}$$

Partial differential equation (3) is analogous to growth processes encountered in statistical physics [385]. (For a different perspective on surface growth and computational models, see also ch. 11.) The surface ω, growing with "time" t above the plane (c_2, c_3)—or equivalently from (2), above the plane (p, α), as shown in figure 6—describes the whole distribution of branches. The average number of branches at depth t in the tree equals $B(t) = \int dp\, d\alpha\, 2^{n\,\omega(p,\alpha,t)} \simeq 2^{n\,\omega^*(t)}$, where $\omega^*(t) = \max_{p,\alpha}$ is the maximum of $\omega(p, \alpha, t)$ over p, α, reached at $p^*(t), \alpha^*(t)$. In other words, the exponentially dominant contribution to $B(t)$ comes from branches carrying 2+p-SAT instances with parameters $p^*(t), \alpha^*(t)$, which define the tree trajectories on figure 4.

The hyperbolic line in figure 4 indicates the halt points, where contradictions prevent dominant branches from further growth. Each time DPLL assigns a variable through unit propagation, an average number $u(p, \alpha)$ of new 1-clauses is produced, resulting in a net addition of $u - 1$ 1-clauses. As long as $u < 1$, 1-clauses are quickly eliminated and do not accumulate. Conversely, if $u > 1$, 1-clauses tend to accumulate. Opposite 1-clauses x and $\bar{x}$ are likely to appear, leading to a contradiction [88, 182]. The halt line is defined by $u(p, \alpha) = 1$, and in the case of GUC, may be calculated explicitly as

$$\alpha = \left(\frac{3+\sqrt{5}}{2}\right) \log \left[\frac{1+\sqrt{5}}{2}\right] \frac{1}{1-p} \approx \frac{1.256}{1-p} \quad . \tag{5}$$

Along the tree trajectory in figure 4, $\omega^*(t)$ grows from 0 at the right vertical axis to some final positive value $\hat{\omega}$ on the halt line. This growth is seen in figure 6.

The value $\hat{\omega}$ is our theoretical prediction for the logarithm of the complexity (divided by n). Values of $\hat{\omega}$ obtained for $4.3 < \alpha_0 < 20$ by solving eq. (3) compare very well with numerical results [97, 100]. Although our calculation is not rigorous, it provides a very good quantitative estimate of the complexity. Furthermore, complexity is found to scale asymptotically as

$$\hat{\omega}(\alpha_0) \sim \frac{3+\sqrt{5}}{(6\log 2)\,\alpha_0} \left[\log\left(\frac{1+\sqrt{5}}{2}\right)\right]^2 \approx \frac{0.292}{\alpha_0} \quad (\alpha_0 \gg \alpha_c) . \tag{6}$$

This result exhibits the expected scaling [39]. It may indeed be exact: as α_0 increases, search trees become smaller and smaller, and correlations between branches become weaker and weaker.

2.2.3 Upper SAT Phase and Mixed Branch-Tree Trajectories.

The advantages of the trajectory approach proposed in this chapter are best seen in the upper SAT phase, namely for ratios α_0 ranging from α_L to α_c. This intermediate region juxtaposes branch and tree behaviors: see figure 1(c). The branch trajectory starts from the point $(p = 1, \alpha = \alpha_0)$ corresponding to the initial 3-SAT instance and hits the critical line $\alpha_c(p)$ at a point **G** with coordinates (p_G, α_G) after nt_G variables have been assigned by DPLL (fig. 4). The algorithm then enters the UNSAT phase and generates 2+p-SAT instances with no solution, requiring it to search through an entire dense subtree between **G** and the halt line (fig. 4). The size of this subtree is $2^{n(1-t_G)\hat{\omega}_G}$, where $\hat{\omega}_G$ corresponds to the complexity of the equivalent 2+p-SAT instance at **G** and can be predicted analytically from our theory for UNSAT instances. We expect that to a good approximation, the complexity of the full DPLL search tree is dominated by the complexity of the dense subtree below **G** in figure 1(c), and so $\hat{\omega} = \hat{\omega}_G(1 - t_G)$. We have verified this scenario experimentally for $\alpha_0 = 3.5$. The coordinates of the average highest backtracking node $(p_G \approx 0.78, \alpha_G \approx 3.02)$, coincide with the analytically computed intersection of the single branch trajectory and the critical line $\alpha_c(p)$ [97, 100]. As for complexity, experimental measures of ω from 3-SAT instances at $\alpha_0 = 3.5$, and of the analogous quantity ω_G from 2+0.78-SAT instances at $\alpha_G = 3.02$, obey the expected identity $\omega = \omega_G(1 - t_G)$ and are in very good agreement with theory [97, 100]. Therefore, the structure of search trees for 3-SAT reflects the existence of a critical line for 2+p-SAT instances.

Note that the upper SAT phase is characterized by large run-to-run complexity fluctuations, arising from fluctuations of the branch trajectory. We will

(a)

ω

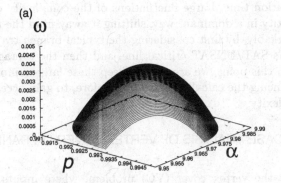

(b)

ω

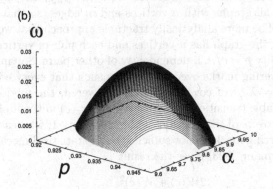

(c)

ω

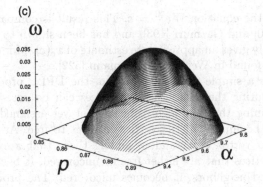

FIGURE 6   Snapshots of the surface $\omega(p, \alpha)$ for $\alpha_0 = 10$ at three different depths: $t = 0.01$ (a), $t = 0.05$ (b) and $t = 0.09$ (c). The height $\omega^*(t)$ of the top of the surface, with coordinates $p^*(t), \alpha^*(t)$, is the logarithm (divided by n) of the number of branches. The halt line is hit at $t_h \approx 0.094$.

see in section 2.4 how small complexity fluctuations can be exploited to shorten the average resolution time. Large fluctuations of the complexity contribute to the mean complexity in a dominant way, shifting it away from the median value of interest. Remarkably, by first considering the typical branch trajectory up to the crossing of the SAT/UNSAT critical line, and then the average size of the subtree built from this point, we are able to keep these large complexity fluctuations from influencing the calculation, and, therefore, to gain access directly to the median complexity.

2.3 AVERAGE-CASE ANALYSIS OF VERTEX COVER ON RANDOM GRAPHS

We now consider the vertex cover (VC) problem, where inputs are random graphs. One approach is to choose graphs from the $\mathcal{G}_{n,m}$ ensemble: uniformly at random among all graphs with n vertices and m edges, so that the mean degree is $c = 2m/n$. The more analytically tractable approach that we adopt here is the $\mathcal{G}_{n,p}$ ensemble: the graph has n vertices and each pair of vertices contains an edge with probability $p = c/n$, independently of other pairs. Solving VC requires distributing X covering marks over the vertices such that every edge is covered. As the density $x = X/n$ of covering marks is lowered, the model undergoes a coverable/uncoverable transition at a critical value $x_c(c)$ in the limit $n \to \infty$. For $x > x_c(c)$, vertex covers of size nx exist with probability 1, whereas for $x < x_c(c)$ the number of covering marks is not sufficient. The statistical mechanics analysis of Weigt and Hartmann [523] gives the result

$$x_c(c) = 1 - \frac{2W(c) + W(c)^2}{2c}, \qquad \text{for } c < e, \tag{7}$$

where $W(c)$ solves the equation $We^W = c$. This result is compatible with the bounds of Friez [180] and Gazmuri [193], and has been shown to be exact [37]. For $c > e$, eq. (7) only gives an approximate estimate of $x_c(c)$. More sophisticated calculations can be found in Weigt and Hartmann [522].

Let us consider a simple implementation of the DPLL procedure for the present problem. During the computation, vertices can be *covered, uncovered,* or simply *free,* meaning that the algorithm has not yet assigned any value to that vertex. In the beginning all the vertices are set to free. At each step the algorithm chooses a vertex i at random among those that are free. If i has any neighboring vertices that are either free or uncovered, it becomes covered. If i has only covered neighbors, it becomes uncovered. The process continues unless the number of covered vertices exceeds X. In that case, the algorithm backtracks and a previously assigned vertex is given the opposite assignment, unless this corresponds to making uncovered a vertex that has one or more uncovered neighbors. The algorithm halts if it finds a solution (in which case it declares the graph to be coverable), or after unsuccessfully exploring the entire search tree (in which case it declares the graph to be uncoverable).

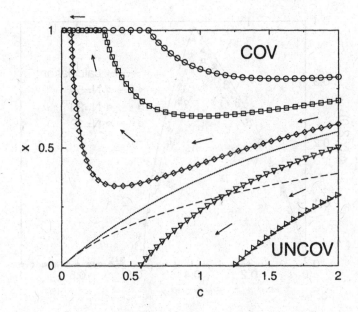

FIGURE 7 Phase diagram of VC. The low-x, high-c UNCOV phase is separated from the high-x, low-c COV phase by the dashed line $x_c(c)$, see eq. (7). The symbols (numerical results) and continuous lines (analytical predictions, see eq. (8)) refer to the simple search algorithm described in the text. The dotted line $x_L(c)$ separates the upper COV branch trajectories from the lower COV mixed trajectories.

Of course, one can improve on this algorithm by using smarter heuristics [521]. One remarkable example is the *leaf-removal algorithm* defined in Bauer and Golinelli [37]. Instead of picking a vertex at random, one chooses a degree-one vertex, declares it uncovered, and declares its neighbor covered. This is repeated on the subgraph of free nodes until no degree-one nodes are left. In the low-degree, coverable region $\{c < e, x > x_c(c)\}$, the procedure stops only when the graph is completely covered. As a consequence, this algorithm can solve VC in linear time with high probability in the entire region. No equally good heuristic exists for higher degree, $c > e$.

2.3.1 Branch Trajectories. Under the action of the algorithms above, the instance is progressively modified and the number of variables reduced. At each step, a vertex is selected and can be eliminated from consideration regardless of whether it is declared covered or uncovered. The analysis of the first algorithm is greatly simplified by the fact that, as long as backtracking has not begun, the new vertex is selected at random. This implies that the modified instance produced by the algorithm is still a random graph (see also ch. 8). Its evolution

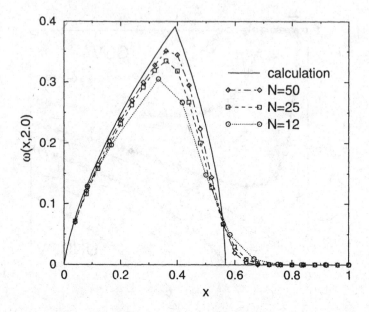

FIGURE 8   Number of operations required to solve (or to show that no solution exists to) the VC decision problem with the search algorithm described in the text. The logarithm of the number of nodes of the backtracking tree, divided by the size n, is plotted versus the density of covering marks. Here we consider random instances with mean degree $c = 2$. The phase transition is at $x_c(c = 2) \approx 0.3919$ and coincides with the peak in computational complexity.

can be described by a trajectory in the (c, x) space: starting from the parameters c_0, x_0, a straightforward calculation shows that after nt steps of the algorithm one ends up with a new instance of size $n(1 - t)$ and parameters [524]

$$c(t) = c_0(1 - t), \quad x(t) = \frac{x_0 - t}{1 - t} + \frac{e^{-c_0(1-t)} - e^{-c_0}}{c_0(1 - t)}. \tag{8}$$

Similar to the behavior we have seen with DPLL on random satisfiability, two types of trajectories under this algorithm start out as a branch: simple branches leading directly to a solution (cf. fig. 1(a)) and mixed cases eventually entering the uncoverable or UNCOV phase (cf. fig. 1(c)). This is shown in the phase diagram in figure 7. By solving eq. (8) for the values of x_0 and c_0 satisfying the limiting condition $x(t) = 1$ as $t \to 1$, one obtains the line separating the upper COV easy phase from the lower COV hard phase [524]

$$x_L(c) = 1 - \frac{1 - e^{-c}}{c}. \tag{9}$$

This is shown in figure 7 by the dotted line. Above the line, the algorithm solves the problem in linear time.

For more general heuristics the analysis becomes less straightforward, because a graph produced by an intermediate step of the algorithm does not necessarily belong to the standard random graph ensemble. It may be necessary to increase the number of parameters that describe the evolution of the instance. As an example, the leaf-removal algorithm mentioned in the previous section is conveniently described by three parameters, collectively characterizing the degree distribution of intermediate graphs [521].

2.3.2 Tree Trajectories. Below the critical line $x_c(c)$ (cf. eq. (7)), no solution exists to a typical random instance of VC. To prove this, our algorithm must explore a large backtracking tree, taking exponential time. The size of the backtracking tree can be computed along the lines of section 2.2.2. However, a good result can also be obtained from a simple "static" calculation [523].

As in figure 5, we imagine the evolution of the backtracking tree proceeding "in parallel." At the level l of the tree a set of l vertices has been visited. Call G_l the subgraph induced by these vertices. Since we put a covering mark on every vertex surrounded by uncovered vertices, each node on the backtracking tree represents a vertex cover for the associated subgraph G_l. Therefore, the number of backtracking nodes in the full tree is given by

$$Q = \sum_{l=1}^{n} N_{VC}(G_l; X),\qquad(10)$$

where $N_{VC}(G_l; X)$ is the number of VCs for G_l using at most X marks. A very crude estimate of the right-hand side of the equation above is

$$Q \le \sum_{l=1}^{n} \sum_{X'=0}^{\min(X,l)} \binom{l}{X'},\qquad(11)$$

where we bound the number of VC's of size X' on G_l by the number of ways of placing X' marks on l vertices. Weigt and Hartmann [524] provide a refined estimate based on the *annealed approximation* used in statistical mechanics. Figure 8 compares the results of this calculation with the numerics.

2.3.3 Mixed Trajectories. If the parameters characterizing an instance of VC lie in the region between $x_c(c)$ (cf. eq. (7)) and $x_L(c)$ (cf. eq. (9)) the problem can still be solved but our algorithm takes an exponential time to solve it. After a certain number of vertices have been visited and declared either *covered* or *uncovered*, the remaining subgraph G_{free} can no longer be covered with the leftover marks. Typically, this happens when the first descent trajectory (8) crosses the critical line (7).

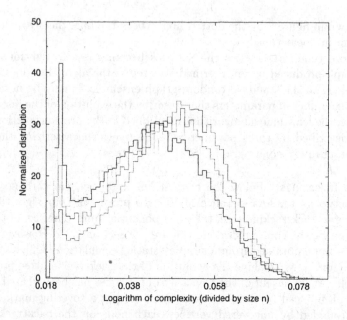

FIGURE 9 Probability distributions of the logarithm ω of the resolution complexity, based on 20,000 runs of DPLL on random 3-SAT instances with ratio $\alpha = 3.5$. Each distribution corresponds to one randomly drawn instance of size $n = 300$.

It takes some time for the algorithm to realize this fact. More precisely, it takes the time needed to prove that G_{free} is uncoverable. This time dominates the computational complexity in this region and can be calculated using methods similar to those sketched in the previous section. The result, once again, is reported in figure 8, clearly showing a computational peak at the phase boundary.

Finally, note that this mixed behavior is a consequence of the heuristic used in the DPLL algorithm, and is absent in the entire $c < e$ region when the leaf-removal procedure is adopted for the first descent.

2.4   DISTRIBUTION OF RESOLUTION TIMES

Up until now we have studied the typical resolution complexity. The study of the fluctuations of resolution times is interesting too, particularly in the upper SAT (lower COV) phase where solutions exist but are found at the price of a large computational effort. We may expect that there exist lucky but rare resolutions able to find a solution in a time much smaller than the typical one. Due to the stochastic character of DPLL, the complexity of the algorithm indeed fluctuates from run to run on the same instance. In figure 9 we show this run-to-run distribution of the logarithm ω of the resolution complexity for four instances

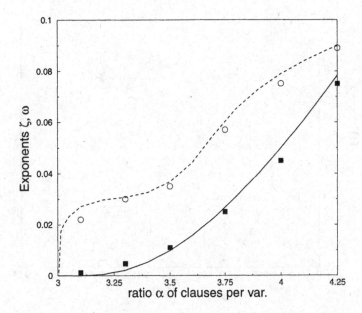

FIGURE 10   Resolution of random 3-SAT instances in the upper SAT phase: logarithm of complexity with DPLL (ω: circles show simulations, dotted line shows theory) and restarts (ζ: squares show simulations, solid line shows theory) as a function of ratio α.

of random 3-SAT with the same ratio $\alpha = 3.5$. The run-to-run distributions are qualitatively independent of the particular instances, and exhibit two peaks. The wide right one, located at $\omega \approx 0.035$, characterizes the majority of resolutions. It acquires more and more weight as n increases and corresponds to the typical behavior analyzed in section 2.2.3. The left peak characterizes much faster resolutions, taking place in linear time. The weight of this peak (fraction of runs with complexities falling within the peak) decreases exponentially fast with n, and can be estimated numerically as $W_{\mathrm{lin}} = 2^{-n\zeta}$ with $\zeta \approx 0.011$. Therefore, instances at $\alpha = 3.5$ are typically solved in exponential time while a tiny (exponentially small) fraction of runs only need linear time to find a solution.

A systematic stop-and-restart procedure may be introduced to take advantage of this fluctuation phenomenon and speed up resolution. If a solution is not found before n splits, DPLL is stopped and rerun after some random permutations of the variables and clauses. Since the expected number N_{rest} of restarts needed to find a solution is equal to the inverse probability $1/W_{\mathrm{lin}}$ of linear resolutions, the resulting complexity scales as $n\,W_{\mathrm{lin}}^{-1} \sim 2^{n\,\zeta}$.

To calculate ζ, Cocco and Monasson [98, 99] have analyzed the whole distribution of complexity for a given ratio α in the upper SAT phase, using methods

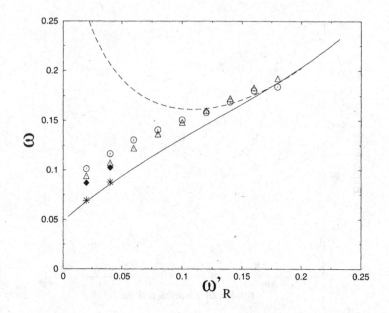

FIGURE 11 The computational complexity of the search algorithm for VC, with restarts after $\exp(n\omega'_R)$ backtracking steps. The complexity is defined as the logarithm of the total number of visited nodes, divided by the size n of the graph. Symbols refer to $n = 30$ (circles), 60 (triangles), and 120 (diamonds). The stars are the result of an $n \rightarrow \infty$ extrapolation. The continuous and dashed lines reproduce the theoretical prediction with and without taking into account fluctuations of the first descent trajectory.

similar to those for studying the growth of the search tree in the UNSAT phase, Linear resolutions are found to correspond to branch trajectories that cross the UNSAT phase without being hit by a contradiction, see figure 4. Results are reported in figure 10 and compare very well with the experimentally measured number $N_{\rm rest}$ of restarts necessary to find a solution. Throughout the upper SAT phase, the use of restarts offers an exponential gain with respect to the usual DPLL resolution (see fig. 10 for a comparison of ζ and ω). However, the DPLL algorithm with the stop-and-restart procedure is no longer a complete algorithm, and cannot prove the absence of solutions unless some sophisticated modifications are introduced [27].

A slightly more general restart strategy consists of stopping the backtracking procedure after a fixed number of nodes $Q_R = e^{n\omega'_R}$ have been visited. A new (and statistically independent) DPLL procedure is then started from the beginning. In this case one exploits lucky, but still exponentially numerous, stochastic runs. The tradeoff between the exponential gain of time and the exponential

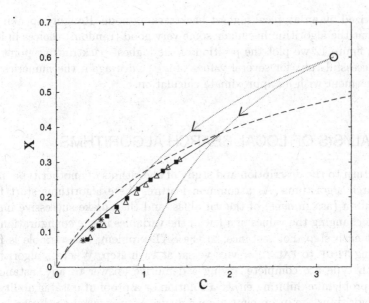

FIGURE 12   Restart experiments for VC with initial condition $c_0 = 3.2$, $x_0 = 0.6$ (empty circle). The long-dashed line is the critical line (7). The dotted line on the right is the typical trajectory. The dotted line on on the left is the rare trajectory, ending at the last (successful) restart of the algorithm for $\omega'_R = 0.1$. The symbols are numerical results for the (c, x) coordinates of the root of the backtrack tree generated by the algorithm since the last restart, for different values of ω'_R. Triangles, squares and stars denote $n = 30$, 60, 120, respectively. The solid line is an approximate analytical prediction for the same quantity.

number of restarts can be optimized by tuning the parameter ω'_R. This approach is analyzed in Montanari and Zecchina [408], taking VC as a working example. In figure 11 we show the computational complexity of such a strategy as a function of the restart parameter ω'_R. We compare the numerics with an approximate calculation [408]. The instances are random graphs with average degree $c = 3.2$ and $x = 0.6$ covering marks per vertex. The optimal choice of the parameter seems (in this case) to be $\omega'_R \approx 0$, corresponding to polynomial runs.

The analytical prediction reported in figure 11 requires, as for 3-SAT, an estimate of the execution-time fluctuations of the DPLL procedure (without restart). It turns out that one major source of fluctuations is, in the present case, the location in the (c, x) plane of the highest node in the backtracking tree. In a typical run this coincides with the intersection (c_G, x_G) between the first descent trajectory (8) and the critical line (7). However, once an upper bound ω'_R on the backtracking time is fixed, the problem is solved in those lucky runs characterized by an atypical highest backtracking node. Roughly speaking, this means that the algorithm has made some very good (random) choices in its first steps. In figure 12 we plot the position of the highest backtracking point in the (last) successful runs for several values of ω'_R. Once again the numerics are in good agreement with an approximate calculation.

3 ANALYSIS OF LOCAL SEARCH ALGORITHMS

We now turn to the description and study of algorithms of another type, namely local search algorithms. As a common feature, these algorithms start from a configuration (assignment) of the variables, and then make successive improvements by changing the values of a few of the variables in the configuration (local move) at each step. For instance, in the SAT problem, one variable is flipped from being TRUE to FALSE, or vice versa, at each step. Whereas algorithms of the DPLL type are complete, giving a definitive answer to any instance of a decision problem, exhibiting either a solution or a proof of unsatisfiability, local search algorithms are incomplete, giving a sure answer when a solution is found but unable to prove unsatisfiability. However, these algorithms can sometimes be turned into one-sided probabilistic algorithms, with an upper bound on the probability that after T steps of the algorithm an existing solution has not yet been found, decreasing to zero when $T \to \infty$ [411].

3.1 LANDSCAPE AND SEARCH DYNAMICS

Local search algorithms perform repeated changes to a configuration C of variables (values of the Boolean variables for SAT, vertex status—marked or unmarked—for VC) according to some criterion. This criterion is usually based on the comparison of the cost function F (number of unsatisfied clauses for SAT, number of uncovered edges for VC) evaluated at C and over its neighborhood. It is, therefore, clear that the shape of the multidimensional surface $C \to E(C)$, called the cost or energy function landscape, is of high importance. On intuitive grounds, if the landscape is relatively smooth with a unique minimum, local procedures such as gradient descent should be very efficient. Conversely, the presence of many local minima could hinder the search process (fig. 13). The fundamental underlying question is to what extent the performance of the dynamical process (ability to find the global minimum and time needed to reach it) can be understood in terms of an analysis of the cost function landscape alone.

This question was intensively studied and answered some years ago for a limited class of cost functions, called mean-field spin glass models [114]. Indeed, the characterization of landscapes is of huge importance in physical systems of this kind. The cost function is simply the physical energy, and local dynamics are usually low-temperature or zero-temperature Monte Carlo dynamics, essen-

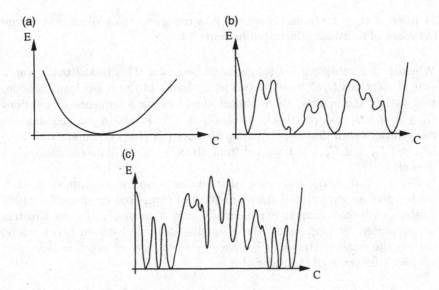

FIGURE 13 Landscapes corresponding to three different cost functions. Horizontal axis represents the space of configurations C, while vertical axis is the associated cost $E(C)$: (a) smooth cost function, with a single minimum easily reachable with local search procedures, e.g., gradient descent; (b) rough cost function with many local minima whose presence may damage the performances of local search algorithms. The various global minima are spread out homogeneously over the configuration space; (c) rough cost function with global minima clustered in some portions of the configuration space only.

tially equivalent to gradient descent.[3] Depending on the parameters of the input distribution, the minima of the cost functions may undergo structural changes, notably a phenomenon that in physics is called clustering.

Clustering has been shown rigorously to take place in the random 3-XORSAT problem [101, 112, 131, 170, 398, 445], and is likely to exist in many other random combinatorial problems such as 3-SAT [56, 395]. Instances of the 3-XORSAT problem with $m = \alpha n$ clauses and n variables almost surely have solutions as long as $\alpha < \alpha_c \approx 0.918$ [101, 131, 170, 398, 445]. The clustering phase transition

---

[3]The Monte Carlo algorithm we consider, e.g., in section 3.2 is a sequence of variable changes from an initial (random) configuration performed according to some simple rule allowing the stationary distribution of configurations to obey the Gibbs measure, $P(C) \propto \exp(-E(C)/\tau)$ where $\tau(\geq 0)$ is called temperature. The Metropolis scheme is one such rule: attempt to change the configuration from $C \to C'$; if $E(C') \leq E(C)$, accept the change; if $E(C') > E(C)$, accept the change with probability $p = \exp(-(E(C') - E(C))/\tau)$ and reject it with probability $1 - p$.

takes place at $\alpha_s \approx 0.818$ and is related to a change in the geometric structure of the space of solutions, illustrated in figure 13:

1. When $\alpha < \alpha_s$, the space of solutions is *connected*. This means that given a pair of solutions C, C', that is, two assignments of the n Boolean variables that satisfy the clauses, there almost surely exists a sequence of solutions $C_j, j = 0, 1, 2, \ldots, J$, with $C_0 \equiv C$, $C_J \equiv C'$, $J = O(n)$, connecting the two solutions such that the Hamming distance (number of different variables) between C_j and C_{j+1} is bounded from above by some finite constant when $n \to \infty$.
2. When $\alpha_s < \alpha < \alpha_c$, the space of solutions is no longer connected. It is made up of an exponential (in n) number of connected components, called clusters, each containing an exponentially large number of solutions. Clusters are separated by large voids: the Hamming distance between two clusters, namely the smallest Hamming distance between pairs of solutions belonging to these clusters, is of the order of n.

On intuitive grounds, a change in the statistical properties of the cost function landscape—such as in the structure of the solution space—could affect the search dynamics. This connection between static properties and dynamics has been established in numerous cases in the context of mean-field models of spin glasses [114], and subsequently also proposed in studies of local search algorithms in combinatorial optimization problems [56, 395, 494]. It is a crucial element in the algorithmic approach discussed in chapter 4. So far, there is no general explanation as to when and why features of dynamical phenomena that are *a priori* algorithm-dependent should be related to, or predictable from, statistical properties of the cost function landscape. In the following, we shall see some examples in which such a connection indeed exists (sec. 3.2) and others where its presence is far less obvious (sec. 3.3, 3.4).

3.2   ALGORITHMS FOR ERROR CORRECTING CODES

Coding theory is a rich source of computational problems (and algorithms) for which average-case analysis is deeply relevant [33, 481]. Let us focus, for the sake of concreteness, on the decoding problem. Codewords are sequences of symbols with built-in redundancy. If we consider the case of linear codes on a binary alphabet, this redundancy can be implemented as a set of linear constraints. In practice, a codeword is a vector $\vec{x} \in \{0, 1\}^n$ (with $n \gg 1$) satisfying the equation

$$\mathbb{H}\vec{x} = \vec{0} \quad (\text{mod } 2),\tag{12}$$

where $\mathbb{H}$ is an $m \times n$ binary matrix (*parity check matrix*). Each one of the m linear equations involved in eq. (12) is called a *parity check*. This set of equations can be represented graphically by a *Tanner graph*, as shown in figure 14. A Tanner

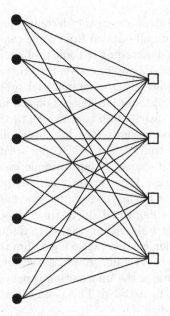

FIGURE 14   Tanner graph of a *regular* linear code. A left-hand node is associated with each variable, and a right-hand node with each parity check. A link is drawn between two nodes whenever the variable associated with the left-hand one enters in the parity check corresponding to the right-hand one.

graph is a bipartite graph highlighting the relations between the variables x_i and the constraints (parity checks) acting on them. The decoding problem consists of finding, among the solutions of eq. (12), the *closest* one $\vec{x}_\mathrm{d}$ to the output $\vec{x}_\mathrm{out}$ of some communication channel. This problem is, in general, NP-hard [49].

The precise meaning of *closest* depends upon the nature of the communication channel. Let us give two examples:

1. The binary symmetric channel (BSC). In this case the output of the communication channel $\vec{x}_\mathrm{out}$ is a codeword, that is, a solution of (12), in which a fraction p of the entries have been flipped. "Closest" is meant in the Hamming-distance sense. $\vec{x}_\mathrm{d}$ is the solution of eq. (12) minimizing the Hamming distance from $\vec{x}_\mathrm{out}$.
2. The binary erasure channel (BEC). The output $\vec{x}_\mathrm{out}$ is a codeword in which a fraction p of the entries have been erased. One needs to find a solution $\vec{x}_\mathrm{d}$ of eq. (12) that is compatible with the remaining entries. Such a problem has a "unique" solution for small enough erasure probability p.

There are two sources of randomness in the decoding problem: (1) the matrix $\mathbb{H}$ which defines the code is usually drawn from some random *ensemble*; (2) the message received is distributed according to some probabilistic model of the communication channel (in the two examples above, the bits to be flipped/erased are chosen randomly). Unlike many other combinatorial problems, there is, therefore, a "natural" probability distribution defined on the instances. Average-case analysis with respect to this distribution is of great practical relevance.

Recently, amazingly good performance has been obtained by using low-density parity check (LDPC) codes [93]. LDPC codes are defined by parity check matrices $\mathbb{H}$ that are large and sparse. As an example we can consider Gallager *regular* codes [188]. In this case $\mathbb{H}$ is chosen with flat probability distribution among the family of matrices having v ones per row and w ones per column. These are decoded using a suboptimal linear-time algorithm known as *belief propagation* or the *sum-product* algorithm [188, 431], discussed in greater length in chapter 4. Belief propagation is an iterative algorithm taking advantage of the locally tree-like structure of the Tanner graph, see figure 14, for LDPC codes. After T iterations it incorporates the information conveyed by the variables up to distance T from the one to be decoded. This can be done in a recursive fashion allowing for linear-time decoding.

Belief propagation decoding shows a striking threshold phenomenon as the noise level p crosses some critical (code-dependent) value p_d. While for $p < p_d$ the transmitted codeword is recovered with high probability, for $p > p_d$ decoding will almost always fail. The threshold noise p_d is, in general, smaller than the threshold p_c for optimal decoding (with unbounded computational resources).

Rigorous analysis in Richardson and Urbanke [446] allows a precise determination of the critical noise p_d under quite general circumstances. Nevertheless, some important theoretical questions remain. Can we find a smarter linear-time algorithm whose threshold is greater than p_d? Is there any "intrinsic," algorithm-independent, characterization of the threshold phenomenon taking place at p_d? As a first step towards answering these questions, Franz et al. [169] explore the dynamics of local optimization algorithms by using statistical mechanics techniques. The interesting point is that belief propagation is by no means a local search algorithm.

Let us focus on the BEC. In this case we can treat decoding as a combinatorial optimization problem within the space of bit sequences of length np (the number of erased bits, with the others being fixed by the received message). The cost function to be minimized is the *energy density*

$$\varepsilon(\vec{x}) = \frac{2}{n} d_H(\mathbb{H}\vec{x}, \vec{0}), \tag{13}$$

where we denote as $d_H(\vec{x}_1, \vec{x}_2)$ the Hamming distance between two vectors $\vec{x}_1$ and $\vec{x}_2$ and we introduce the normalizing factor for later convenience. Note that both arguments of d_H in eq. (13) are vectors in $\{0, 1\}^m$.

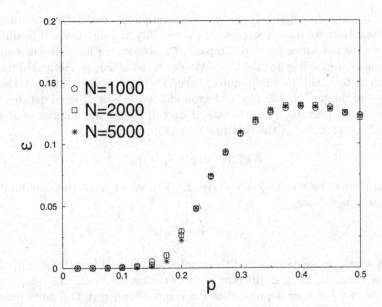

FIGURE 15 The $(6,3)$ Gallager code decoded by local search with 1-neighborhoods. At each time step, the algorithm looks for a bit (among the ones incorrectly received) such that flipping it decreases the cost function (13), which is the number of violated parity checks (multiplied by $2/n$). We plot the average cost after the algorithm halts, as a function of the erasure probability p.

We define the R-neighborhood of a given sequence $\vec{x}$ as the set of sequences $\vec{z}$ such that $d_H(\vec{x}, \vec{z}) \leq R$, and call R-stable states those bit sequences that are optima of the decoding problem within their R-neighborhood. One can easily devise local search algorithms [425] for the decoding problem that use the R-neighborhoods. The algorithm starts from a random sequence and, at each step, optimizes it within its R-neighborhood. This algorithm is clearly suboptimal and halts on R-stable states. Let us consider, for instance, a $(v = 6, w = 3)$ regular code and decode it by local search in 1-neighborhoods. Figure 15 shows the resulting energy density ε after the local search algorithm halts, as a function of the erasure probability p. We averaged over 100 different realizations of the noise and of the matrix $\mathbb{H}$. For the sake of comparison we note that the threshold for belief propagation decoding is $p_d \approx 0.429440$ [446], while the threshold for optimal decoding is $p_c \approx 0.488151$ [169]. It is evident that local search by 1-neighborhoods performs quite poorly.

A natural question is to what extent these performances can be improved by increasing R. It is, therefore, natural to study *metastable* states: states that are

R-stable for any $R = o(n)$.[4] There exists no completely satisfactory definition of such states. Here we merely suggest one possibility among others. The difficulty is that we do not know how to compare R-stable states for different values of n, making it impossible to use the asymptotic definition of metastability. Our approach is to count R-stable states, take the $n \to \infty$ limit and, at the end, the $R \to \infty$ limit [55]. On physical grounds, we expect R-stable states to be exponentially numerous. In particular, if we call $N_R(\varepsilon)$ the number of R-stable states taking a value ε of the cost function (13), we may write

$$N_R(\varepsilon) \sim \exp\{nS_R(\varepsilon)\}. \tag{14}$$

We then define the *physical complexity* $\Sigma(\varepsilon)$ (distinct from the computational complexity) as follows,

$$\Sigma(\varepsilon) \equiv \lim_{R\to\infty} S_R(\varepsilon). \tag{15}$$

Roughly speaking, we can say that the number of metastable states is $\exp\{n\Sigma(\varepsilon)\}$. Of course there are several different ways of taking the limits $R \to \infty$, $n \to \infty$, and we do not yet have a proof that these procedures give the same result for $\Sigma(\varepsilon)$. Nevertheless, it is quite clear that the presence of an exponential number of metastable states should dramatically affect the behavior of local search algorithms.

Methods from statistical mechanics [169] make it possible to determine the complexity $\Sigma(\varepsilon)$ [404]. In "difficult" cases (such as for error-correcting codes), the actual computation may involve an approximation, that is, the use of a variational Ansatz. Nevertheless, the outcome is usually quite accurate. In figure 16 we consider a $(6,3)$ regular code on the binary erasure channel. We report the resulting complexity for three different values of the erasure probability p. The general picture is as follows. Below p_d there is no metastable state, except the one corresponding to the correct codeword. Between p_d and p_c there is an exponential number of metastable states ($\Sigma(\varepsilon)$ is strictly positive) when the energy density belongs to an interval $\varepsilon_{GS} < \varepsilon < \varepsilon_D$. Above p_c, $\varepsilon_{GS} = 0$. The maximum of $\Sigma(\varepsilon)$ is always at ε_D.

Since complexity is a property of infinitely large neighborhoods, this picture suggests that any local algorithm will run into difficulties above p_d. As confirmation, Franz et al. [169] have performed numerical computations using simulated annealing for the decoding algorithm, for large codes ($n = 10^4$ bits). At each value of p, the simulation starts with a fixed fraction $(1 - p)$ of bits set to one (this part is kept fixed all along the run). The remaining pn spins are the dynamical variables updated during annealing in order to try to satisfy all the parity checks. The energy of the system measures the number of unsatisfied parity checks.

---

[4]We use the standard notation $f_n = o(n)$ if $\lim_{n\to\infty} f_n/n = 0$.

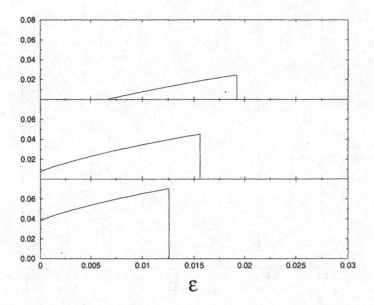

FIGURE 16 The complexity $\Sigma(\varepsilon)$ of a $(6,3)$ code on the BEC, for (top to bottom) $p = 0.45$ (below p_c), $p = 0.5$, and $p = 0.55$ (above p_c). Recall that $\Sigma(\varepsilon)$ is positive only above $p_d \approx 0.429440$.

The cooling schedule is chosen in the following way: Monte Carlo sweeps take place[5] at each of 1000 equidistant temperature values between $\tau = 1$ and $\tau = 0$. The highest temperature is such that the system equilibrates very rapidly. The simulation described here uses 1000 Monte Carlo sweeps per temperature value.

Notice that, for any fixed cooling schedule, the computational complexity of the simulated annealing method is linear in n. We expect it to be affected by metastable states of energy ε_D, which are present for $p > p_d$: the energy relaxation should be strongly reduced around ε_D and eventually blocked completely. Results are plotted in figure 17 together with the theoretical prediction for ε_D. The good agreement confirms our picture. The algorithm gets stuck in metastable states, which in the great majority of cases have energy density ε_D.

Both "belief propagation" and local search algorithms fail to decode correctly between p_d and p_c. This leads naturally to the conjecture that no linear-time algorithm can decode in this regime of noise. The (typical case) computational complexity changes from being linear below p_d to superlinear above p_d. In the

---

[5] Each Monte Carlo sweep consists of n proposed bit flips. Each proposed bit flip is accepted or rejected according to the Metropolis scheme.

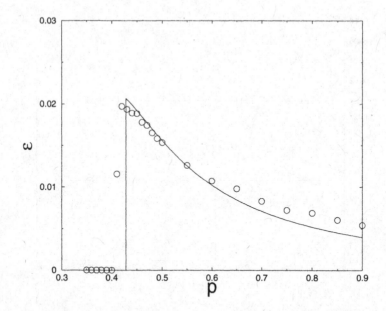

FIGURE 17   The $(6,3)$ LDPC code on the BSC decoded by simulated annealing. The circles give the number of violated checks in the resulting sequence. The continuous line is the analytical result for the typical energy density of metastable states (ε_D in fig. 16).

case of the binary erasure channel, it remains polynomial up to p_c, since optimal decoding can be realized with linear algebra methods. However, it is plausible that for a general channel it becomes non-polynomial.

Recently, statistical physics and coding theory have inspired an important development in the field of local search algorithms: the "survey propagation" algorithm [395, 397] discussed in chapter 4. This is a message-passing algorithm like belief propagation. Unlike belief propagation, however, it is designed to deal with situations in which metastable states proliferate exponentially. The new algorithm is very efficient on random 3-SAT and graph coloring, where clusters of solutions are an example of metastable states.

It is, therefore, natural to ask whether the new algorithm implies any improvement in the original decoding problem. The answer is no. Survey propagation is constructed to treat in an average fashion the exponentially numerous metastable states with positive complexity $\Sigma(\varepsilon) > 0$. However, in the interesting regime $p_d < p < p_c$, the solution of the decoding problem ($\varepsilon = 0$) is separated by a gap from such states, as seen at the top of figure 16. Moreover, it is statistically unrelated to them.

3.3   GRADIENT DESCENT AND XORSAT

The local procedure we now consider is gradient descent (GD). In the language of satisfiability, GD is defined as follows.

1. Start from an initial randomly chosen configuration of the variables. Let E be the number of unsatisfied clauses.
2. If $E = 0$ then stop (a solution is found). Otherwise, pick one variable at random, say x_i, and compute the number E' of unsatisfied clauses when this variable is negated. If $E' \leq E$, accept this change, i.e., replace x_i with $\bar{x}_i$ and E with E'. If $E' > E$, reject the change. Repeat step 2.

The study of the performance of GD in finding the minima of cost functions related to statistical physics models has recently motivated various studies [119, 221, 386, 482, 493]. Numerics indicate that GD is typically able to solve random 3-SAT instances with ratios $\alpha < 3.9$ [395, 494], close to the onset of clustering [56, 395, 428]. We will now show that this is not the case for 3-XORSAT.

Recall that XORSAT differs from SAT in that literals (variables or their negations) within a clause are connected by the XOR logical operator. Let us apply GD to an instance of XORSAT. The instance has a graph representation illustrated in figure 18. Vertices are in one-to-one correspondence with variables. A clause is fully described by a plaquette joining three variables and a Boolean label equal to the number of negated variables it contains, modulo 2 (not shown in fig. 18). Once a configuration of the variables is chosen, each plaquette may be labelled by its status, S or U, denoting whether the associated clause is satisfied or unsatisfied. A fundamental property of XORSAT is that each time a variable is changed, that is, its value is negated, the clauses it belongs to change status as well.

This property facilitates the analysis of certain properties of GD. Consider the hypergraph made up of 15 vertices and 7 plaquettes in figure 19, and suppose the central plaquette is violated (U) while all other plaquettes are satisfied (S). The number of unsatisfied clauses is $E = 1$. Now run GD on this special instance of XORSAT. Two cases arise, symbolized in figure 19, depending on whether or not the variable to be flipped belongs to the central plaquette. It is easy to check that in both cases, $E' = 2$ and the change is rejected by GD. We will refer to the hypergraph of figure 19 as an *island*. When the status of the central plaquette is U and the peripheral plaquettes are S, the island is called blocked. Even though the instance of the XORSAT problem encoded by a blocked island is in fact satisfiable (by negating simultaneously the variable at a vertex V of the central plaquette and a variable in each of the two peripheral plaquettes joining the central plaquette at V), GD will never be able to find the solution and will be blocked forever at the $E = 1$ local minimum.

We show in this section that this situation is typical for random instances of XORSAT. More precisely, while almost all instances of XORSAT with a ratio of

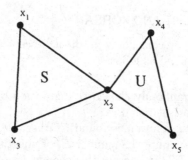

FIGURE 18 Graphical representation of an XORSAT instance with two clauses involving variables x_1, x_2, x_3 and x_2, x_4, x_5. Each clause or equation is represented by a plaquette whose vertices are the variables included in it. When the variables are assigned values, the clauses can be either satisfied (S) or unsatisfied (U).

clauses per variable below $\alpha \approx 0.918$ have a lot of solutions, GD is almost never able to find one. Even worse, with high probability when $n \to \infty$, the number of violated clauses reached by GD is bounded from below by $\Psi(\alpha) n$ where

$$\Psi(\alpha) = \frac{729}{1024} \alpha^7 e^{-45\alpha} \quad . \tag{16}$$

In other words, the number of clauses remaining unsatisfied at the end of a typical GD run is of the order of n. Our analysis, inspired from Häggström [221], is based on the fact that, with high probability, a random instance of XORSAT contains a large number of blocked islands of the type of figure 19.

To make the proof easier, we shall study the following fixed-clause probability ensemble. Instead of requiring the number of clauses to be equal to $m(= \alpha n)$, we allow any triplet τ of three vertices (among n) to carry a plaquette with probability $\mu = \alpha n / \binom{n}{3} = 6\alpha/n^2 + O(1/n^3)$. Notice that this probability ensures that, on the average, the number of plaquettes equals αn. Let us now draw a hypergraph with this distribution. For each triplet τ of vertices, we define $I_\tau = 1$ if τ is the center of a island, 0 otherwise. We shall calculate the average value of the total number of islands $I = \sum_\tau I_\tau$ in the large n limit, and show that I is highly concentrated at this average value.

The expectation value of I_τ is equal to

$$\mathbf{E}[I_\tau] = \frac{(n-3) \times (n-4) \times \ldots \times (n-13) \times (n-14)}{8 \times 8 \times 8} \times \mu^A (1-\mu)^B , \tag{17}$$

where $A = 7$ is the number of plaquettes in the island, and

$$B = \binom{n}{3} - \binom{n-15}{3} - 7 \quad , \tag{18}$$

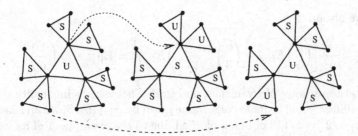

FIGURE 19 A blocked island (left) is an instance of 7 clauses (1 central, 6 peripheral) with variables such that the central plaquette is unsatisfied and all peripheral plaquettes are satisfied. Inversion of any variable increases the number of unsatisfied clauses by 1, be it attached to the central (middle) or to a peripheral (right) plaquette.

is the number of triplets not carrying a plaquette but having at least one vertex among the 15 vertices in the island. The explanation for eq. (17) is straightforward. Since the central triplet τ occupies three vertices, there are $\binom{n-3}{2}$ ways to pick vertices for the first peripheral plaquette of the island, and then $\binom{n-5}{2}$ ways to pick vertices for the other peripheral plaquette having a common vertex with the first one. Since the order in which these two plaquettes are built does not matter, an additional factor $1/2$ prevents double counting. The remaining four peripheral plaquettes have multiplicities calculable in the same way (with correspondingly fewer available vertices). The terms in μ and $1 - \mu$ represent the probability that such a 7-plaquette configuration is drawn on the 15 vertices of the island, and is disconnected from the remaining $n - 15$ vertices. The expectation value of the number $i = I/n$ of islands per vertex then reads

$$\lim_{n\to\infty} \mathbf{E}[i] = \lim_{n\to\infty} \frac{1}{n}\binom{n}{3}\mathbf{E}[I_\tau] = \frac{729}{8}\alpha^7 e^{-45\alpha} . \tag{19}$$

To show that i is concentrated around this average value, let us calculate the second moment of the number of islands, $\mathbf{E}[I^2] = \sum_{\tau,\sigma} \mathbf{E}[I_\tau I_\sigma]$. Clearly, $\mathbf{E}[I_\tau I_\sigma]$ depends only on the number $\ell = 0, 1, 2, 3$ of vertices common to triplets τ and σ. It is obvious that no two triplets of vertices can both be centers of islands when they have $\ell = 1$ or $\ell = 2$ common vertices. If $\ell = 3$, $\tau = \sigma$ and $E_{\ell=3} \equiv \mathbf{E}[I_\tau^2] = \mathbf{E}[I_\tau]$ has been calculated above. For $\ell = 0$, a similar calculation gives

$$E_{\ell=0} = \frac{(n-6)(n-7)...(n-29)}{2^{18}} \mu^{14}(1-\mu)^{B'} \tag{20}$$

$$B' = \binom{n}{3} - \binom{n-30}{3} - 14 .$$

Finally, we obtain

$$\mathbf{E}[i^2] = \frac{1}{n^2}\left[\binom{n}{3}E_{\ell=3} + \binom{n}{3}\binom{n-3}{3}E_{\ell=0}\right] = \mathbf{E}[i]^2 + O\left(\frac{1}{n}\right) \quad . \tag{21}$$

Therefore, the variance of i vanishes, and from Chebyshev's inequality, i is, with high probability, equal to its average value given by eq. (19). Since an island has a probability $1/2^7 = 1/128$ of being blocked due to the assignment of its variables, the number of blocked islands per vertex in a random XORSAT instance with ratio α is almost surely equal to $\Psi(\alpha)$ given by eq. (16). Furthermore, each blocked island has one unsatisfied clause, so this is also a lower bound on the number of violated clauses per variable. In practice, of course, $\Psi(\alpha)$ is very small: it is bounded from above by 1.5×10^{-9} over the range of interest, $0 < \alpha < 0.918$. Therefore, one could need billions of variables before entering the true asymptotic regime of GD where solutions cannot be reached.

The proof can easily be generalized to versions of gradient descent where one looks ahead more than one step. To extend the notion of blocked islands to the case where GD is allowed to invert R variables at a time (rather than only 1), it is sufficient to have $R + 1$ peripheral plaquettes (rather than only 2) attached to each vertex of the central plaquette. The calculation of the lower bound $\Psi(\alpha, R)$ on the number of violated clauses per variable reached by GD is straightforward and not reproduced here. Qualitatively, the consequence is the same: GD, even with R simultaneous flips allowing the algorithm to overcome local barriers, almost surely remains trapped at an extensive ($O(n)$) number of violated clauses for any finite R. The lower bound $\Psi(\alpha, R)n$ tends to zero only if R is of the order of $\log n$.

Interestingly, the statistical physics calculation of physical complexity Σ (see sec. 3.2) predicts that there are no metastable states for $\alpha < 0.818$ [170, 445], even though GD is almost surely trapped by the presence of blocked islands for any $\alpha > 0$. This apparent discrepancy comes from the fact that GD is sensitive to the presence of configurations blocked for finite R, whereas the physical complexity only reflects states that are metastable in the limit $R \to \infty$ [55]. It is worth noting that where GD is unable to reach solutions, Monte Carlo, with a low and eventually decreasing temperature, might. A study of this algorithm and of the dependence of its performance upon the annealing scheme would be a welcome development.

3.4   THE WALKSAT PROCEDURE

The Pure Random WalkSAT (PRWSAT) algorithm for solving k-SAT is defined by the following rules [424].

1. Choose a random configuration of the Boolean variables.
2. If all clauses are satisfied, output "satisfiable" and terminate.

3. If not, choose randomly one of the unsatisfied clauses and one of the k variables in this clause. Flip (invert) the chosen variable. The selected clause is now satisfied, but the flip operation may have violated other clauses that were previously satisfied.
4. Repeat at step 2, until a predefined limit on the number of flips has been reached. Then output "don't know" and terminate.

If the algorithm outputs "satisfiable," there is an associated solution. If the algorithm outputs "don't know," no certainty on the status of the formula is reached. This procedure was first introduced for $k = 2$ [424], where it was shown that with high probability it solves any satisfiable 2-SAT instance in a number of steps (flips) of the order of n^2. Recently, Schöning [458] has proven the following very interesting result for 3-SAT [458]. Define a trial as a run of PRWSAT consisting of a random initial configuration followed by $3n$ steps of the procedure. If none of T successive trials on a given instance has successfully provided a solution, then the probability that this instance is satisfiable is lower than $\exp(-T(3/4)^n)$. In other words, after $T \gg (4/3)^n$ trials of PRWSAT, most of the configuration space has been probed, and if there were a solution, it would likely have been found. Although this local search algorithm is not complete, the uncertainty on its output can be made as small as desired and it can be used to prove unsatisfiability (in a probabilistic sense).

This bound holds for *any* instance. Restriction to specific input distributions leads to stronger results: instances of random 3-SAT with clause-to-variable ratio $\alpha < 1.63$ are in fact, with high probability, solved by PRWSAT in polynomial time [14].

3.4.1 Behavior of the Algorithm.

In this section, we briefly sketch the behavior of PRWSAT, as seen from numerical experiments [430] and the analysis of [36, 472]. A dynamical threshold α_d (≈ 2.7 for 3-SAT) is found, separating two regimes:

1. For $\alpha < \alpha_d$, the algorithm finds a solution very quickly, with the number of flips growing linearly with the number of variables n. Figure 20(a) shows the fraction φ_0 of unsatisfied clauses as a function of relative time t (number of flips divided by the number of clauses $m = \alpha n$) for one instance with $n = 500$ variables and ratio $\alpha = 2$. The plot displays a rapid decrease from the initial value (in the large n limit, $\varphi_0(t = 0) = 1/8$ independent of α) down to zero on a time scale $t_{\mathrm{res}} = O(1)$. Fluctuations decrease as n grows. t_{res} is an increasing function of α. This *relaxation* regime corresponds to the study above [14]: as expected, $\alpha_d > 1.63$.
2. For instances in the range $\alpha_d < \alpha < \alpha_c$, the initial relaxation phase taking place on a time scale $t = O(1)$ is not sufficient to reach a solution (fig. 20(b)). The fraction φ_0 of unsatisfied clauses then fluctuates around some plateau value for a very long time. On the plateau, the system is trapped in a *metastable* state. The lifetime of this metastable state, or trapping time,

is so huge that it is meaningful to define a quasi-equilibrium probability distribution $p_n(\varphi_0)$ for the fraction φ_0 of unsatisfied clauses (second inset of fig. 20(b)). The distribution of φ_0 is peaked around an average value (mean height of the plateau), and the left and right tails decrease exponentially fast in n: $p_n(\varphi_0) \sim \exp(n\bar\zeta(\varphi_0))$ with $\bar\zeta \leq 0$. Eventually a large negative fluctuation will bring the system to a solution $\varphi_0 = 0$. Assuming that these fluctuations are independent random events occuring with probability $p_n(0)$ on an $O(1)$ interval of time, the resolution time is a stochastic variable with exponential distribution. Its average is, to leading exponential order, the inverse of the probability of resolution on the $O(1)$ time scale: $t_{\text{res}} \sim \exp(n\zeta)$ with $\zeta = -\bar\zeta(0)$. The time scale for escape from the metastable state is therefore exponentially large in n, as confirmed by numerical simulations for different sizes. Note that the probabilistic result mentioned above for successive trials of PRWSAT [458] can be interpreted as a lower bound $\bar\zeta(0) > \log(3/4)$, bounding the probability by $p_n(0) > (3/4)^n$ for any instance.

The plateau energy, or the fraction of unsatisfied clauses reached by PRWSAT on the linear time scale, is plotted in figure 21. The *dynamic* critical value α_d, above which the plateau energy is positive (PRWSAT stops finding a solution in linear time), is strictly smaller than the *static* ratio α_c where formulas go from being satisfiable with high probability to unsatisfiable with high probability. In the intermediate range $\alpha_d < \alpha < \alpha_c$, instances are almost surely satisfiable but PRWSAT needs an exponentially large time to prove this. Interestingly, α_d and α_c coincide for 2-SAT, in agreement with the result above [424] that with high probability PRWSAT solves any satisfiable 2-SAT instance in polynomial time. Finally, note that the dynamical transition does not appear to be related to the onset of clustering, which takes place at $\alpha_s \approx 3.9$.

3.4.2 Results for the Linear Phase $\alpha < \alpha_d$.

When PRWSAT finds a solution easily, the number of steps it requires is of the order of n, or equivalently, m. Let us call $t_{\text{res}}(\alpha, k)$ the average of this number divided by the number of clauses m. By definition of the dynamic threshold, t_{res} diverges when $\alpha \to \alpha_d^-$. Assuming that $t_{\text{res}}(\alpha, k)$ can be expressed as a series of powers of α, we obtain the expansion [472]

$$t_{\text{res}}(\alpha, k) = \frac{1}{2^k} + \frac{k(k+1)}{k-1} \frac{1}{2^{2k+1}} \alpha$$
$$+ \frac{4k^6 + k^5 + 6k^3 - 10k^2 + 2k}{3(k-1)(2k-1)(k^2-2)} \frac{1}{2^{3k+1}} \alpha^2 + O(\alpha^3) \ . \qquad (22)$$

around $\alpha = 0$. Only a finite number of terms in this expansion have been computed, so we do not control its radius of convergence. However, as shown in figure 22, numerical experiments provide convincing evidence in favor of its validity.

The calculation leading to eq. (22) is based on two facts. First, for $\alpha < 1/(k(k-1))$ the instance under consideration splits into independent subinstances

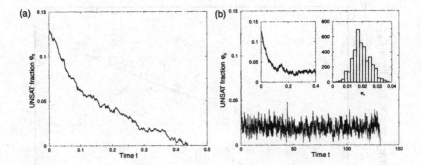

FIGURE 20   Fraction φ_0 of unsatisfied clauses as a function of time t (number of flips over number of clauses m) during the action of PRWSAT on two randomly drawn $n = 500$ instances of 3-SAT with ratios $\alpha = 2$ (a) and $\alpha = 3$ (b). Note the difference of time scales between the two figures. Left inset of figure (b): enlargement of the initial relaxation of φ_0, taking place on the $O(1)$ time scale as in (a). Right inset of figure (b): histogram $p_{500}(\varphi_0)$ of the fluctuations of φ_0 over the plateau $1 \le t \le 130$.

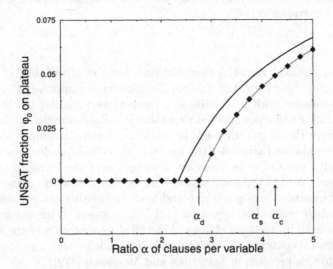

FIGURE 21   Fraction φ_0 of unsatisfied clauses on the metastable plateau of PRWSAT for 3-SAT, as a function of the ratio α of clauses per variable. Diamonds show an infinite-size extrapolation from numerical simulations at sizes ranging from $n = 1,000$ to $n = 10,000$, with 1,000 instances at each size. The dotted line serves as a guide to the eye. The ratio at which φ_0 begins being positive, $\alpha_d \approx 2.7$, is smaller than the threshold $\alpha_s \approx 3.9$ at which solutions gather into distinct clusters, and smaller than the threshold $\alpha_c \approx 4.3$ above which instances almost surely have no solution. The full line is the prediction of the Markovian approximation of section 3.4.3.

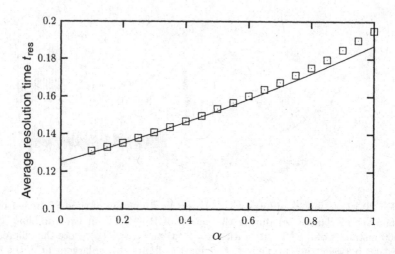

FIGURE 22   Average resolution time $t_{res}(\alpha,3)$ for PRWSAT on 3-SAT. Symbols: numerical simulations, averaged over $1,000$ runs for $n = 10,000$. Solid line: prediction from the cluster expansion (22).

(involving no common variable) that contain a number of variables of the order of $\log n$ at most. Moreover, the number of "connected components" containing j clauses, computed with probabilistic arguments very similar to those of section 3.3, contribute to a power series expansion in α only at order α^j. Second, the number of steps the algorithm needs to solve the instance is simply equal to the sum of the numbers of steps needed for each of the independent subinstances. This additivity remains true when one averages over the initial configuration and the choices made by the algorithm. One is then left with enumerating the different subinstances of a given size and with calculating the average number of steps for their resolution. Equation (22) is the output of the enumeration of subinstances with up to three clauses. A detailed presentation of the method is given in a general context in Semerjian and Cugliandolo [471], and applied more specifically to this problem in Semerjian and Monasson [472].

3.4.3   Results for the Exponential Phase $\alpha > \alpha_d$.   The small α expansion above does not allow us to investigate the $\alpha > \alpha_d$ regime. We turn now to an approximate method better adapted to this situation.

Let us denote by C an assignment of the Boolean variables. PRWSAT defines a Markov process on the space of the configurations C, a discrete set of cardinality 2^n. It is impossible to follow the probabilities of all these configurations as a function of the number of steps T of the algorithm. Instead, one looks for a simpler description of the state of the system during the evolution of the algorithm. The simplest, and crucial, quantity to follow is the number of clauses violated by the current assignment of the Boolean variables, $m_0(C)$. As soon as this value vanishes, the algorithm has found a solution and stops.

A crude approximation consists of assuming that, at each time step T, all configurations with a given number of unsatisfied clauses are equiprobable. This, along with the fact that the Hamming distance between two configurations visited at step T and $T + K$ of the algorithm is at most K, allows us to derive a Markovian evolution equation for the probability that m_0 clauses are unsatisfied after T steps. The results obtained from the approximation are surprisingly good. Using methods similar to the ones in section 2.2, we find [36, 472]:

1. the average fraction of unsatisfied clauses, $\varphi_0(t)$, after $T = tm$ steps of the algorithm. For ratios $\alpha > \alpha_d(k) = (2^k - 1)/k$, φ_0 remains positive at large times, meaning that a large formula typically will not be solved by PRWSAT, and that the fraction of unsatisfied clauses on the plateau is $\varphi_0(t \to \infty)$. The predicted value for $k = 3$, $\alpha_d = 7/3$, is in good though not perfect agreement with the estimates from numerical simulations, around 2.7. The plateau height, $2^{-k}(1 - \alpha_d(k)/\alpha)$, is compared to numerics in figure 21.
2. the probability $p_n(\varphi_0) \sim \exp(n\bar{\zeta}(\varphi_0))$ that the fraction of unsatisfied clauses is φ_0. It has been argued above that the distribution of resolution times in the $\alpha > \alpha_d$ phase is expected to be, at leading order, an exponential distribution with average $e^{n\zeta}$ where $\zeta = -\bar{\zeta}(0)$. Predictions for $\bar{\zeta}(0)$ are plotted and compared to experimental values of ζ in figure 23. Despite the roughness of our Markovian approximation, theoretical predictions are in qualitative agreement with numerical experiments.

A similar study of the behavior of PRWSAT has also been performed on XORSAT problems [36, 472], with qualitatively similar conclusions: there exists a dynamic threshold α_d for the algorithm, smaller than both the satisfiability and clustering thresholds (known exactly in this case [101, 131, 398]). For low values of α, the resolution time is linear in the size of the formula; between α_d and α_c resolution occurs on exponentially large time scales, due to fluctuations around a plateau value for the number of unsatisfied clauses. In the XORSAT case, the agreement between numerical experiments and this approximate study (which predicts $\alpha_d = 1/k$) is quantitatively better and seems to improve with increasing k.

4   CONCLUSION AND PERSPECTIVES

In this chapter, we have aimed to give an overview of the studies that physicists have devoted to the analysis of algorithms. This presentation is certainly not exhaustive, and further methods and results are discussed in the next three chapters. A few other examples outside of the scope of this volume include binary

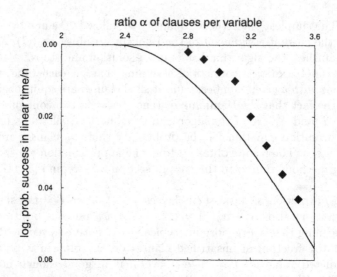

FIGURE 23 Large deviations for the action of PRWSAT on 3-SAT. The logarithm $\bar{\zeta}$ of the probability of successful resolution within $O(n)$ time steps, divided by n, plotted as a function of the ratio α of clauses per variable. Prediction for $\bar{\zeta}$ has been obtained within the approximations of section 3.4.3. Diamonds correspond to (minus) the logarithm ζ of the average resolution times obtained from numerical simulations at sizes ranging from $n = 500$ to $n = 4,000$, divided by n and extrapolated to $n \to \infty$. Number of samples ranges from 2,000 to 10,000, depending on the values of α and n. Error bars are of the order of the size of the diamond symbol. Lower bound [458] is $\zeta \geq \log(3/4) \approx -0.288$.

search trees [374], learning in neural networks [146] and extremal optimization [58, 60].

The objection may be made that algorithms are well-defined mathematical objects and, as such, can properly be analyzed with rigorous techniques only. While this is clearly a desirable goal, the state of available probabilistic and combinatorial tools compared with the sophisticated nature of computer science algorithms makes it unrealistic at present. We hope the reader is now convinced that ideas and techniques from statistical physics can be of help in acquiring a quantitative intuition or even in formulating conjectures on the average performance of search algorithms. A wealth of concepts familiar to physicists, such as phase transitions and diagrams, dynamical renormalization flow, out-of-equilibrium growth phenomena, metastability and perturbative approaches have proven useful in understanding the behavior of algorithms. It is a safe bet that this list will get longer in the near future, and that increasingly powerful methods derived from modern theoretical physics will find their place in the field.

Numerous open questions remain. Variants of DPLL with complex splitting heuristics or random backtracking [27], or applied to combinatorial problems with internal symmetries [142], are worth further study. On the subject of local search algorithms, it would be very interesting to study refined versions of the Pure WalkSAT procedure that alternate random and greedy steps [259, 384, 468], in order to understand the observed existence and properties of optimal strategies (a simple case of this is considered by Weigt [521]). One of the main related challenges is understanding to what extent performance is related to intrinsic features of the combinatorial problem, rather than to details of the search algorithm [353]: as we have seen, the structures of the cost function landscape can induce trapping or slowing down of search algorithms [428]. Finally, the input distributions of instances we have focused on here are far from being realistic. Real instances have structure that strongly influence the performance of algorithms. Adapting present methods of analysis to more realistic distributions—or, better yet, obtaining results that hold for all instances—would be of great value to this evolving field.

ACKNOWLEDGMENTS

This work was partly funded by the ACI Jeunes Chercheurs "Algorithmes d'optimisation et systèmes désordonnés quantiques" from the French Ministry of Research.

CHAPTER 4

Constraint Satisfaction by Survey Propagation

Alfredo Braunstein
Marc Mézard
Martin Weigt
Riccardo Zecchina

1 INTRODUCTION

Methods and analyses from statistical physics are of use not only in studying the performance of algorithms, but also in developing efficient algorithms. Here, we consider survey propagation (SP), a new approach for solving typical instances of random constraint satisfaction problems. SP has proven successful in solving random k-satisfiability (k-SAT) and random graph q-coloring (q-COL) in the "hard SAT" region of parameter space [79, 395, 397, 412], relatively close to the SAT/UNSAT phase transition discussed in the previous chapter. In this chapter we discuss the SP equations, and suggest a theoretical framework for the method [429] that applies to a wide class of discrete constraint satisfaction problems. We propose a way of deriving the equations that sheds light on the capabilities of the algorithm, and illustrates the differences with other well-known iterative probabilistic methods.

Our approach takes into account the clustered structure of the solution space described in chapter 3, and involves adding an additional "joker" value that

Computational Complexity and Statistical Physics, edited by
Allon G. Percus, Gabriel Istrate, and Cristopher Moore, Oxford University Press.

variables can be assigned. Within clusters, a variable can be *frozen* to some value, meaning that the variable always takes the same value for all solutions (satisfying assignments) within the cluster. Alternatively, it can be *unfrozen*, meaning that it fluctuates from solution to solution within the cluster. As we will discuss, the SP equations manage to describe the fluctuations by assigning joker values to unfrozen variables. The overall algorithmic strategy is iterative and decomposable in two elementary steps. The first step is to evaluate the marginal probabilities of frozen variables using the SP *message-passing* procedure. The second step, or *decimation* step, is to use this information to fix the values of some variables and simplify the problem. The notion of message passing will be illustrated throughout the chapter by comparing it with a simpler procedure known as belief propagation (mentioned in ch. 3 in the context of error correcting codes) in which no assumptions are made about the structure of the solution space.

The chapter is organized as follows. In section 2 we provide the general formalism, defining constraint satisfaction problems as well as the key concepts of factor graphs and cavities, using the concrete examples of satisfiability and graph coloring. In section 3 we introduce the notions of *warnings* and *local fields*, whose histograms lead to the belief propagation equations. Finally, in Section 4 we discuss the role of clusters and derive the SP equations. The equations are given explicitly for both 3-SAT and 3-COL, and the decimation procedure is discussed.

2　GENERALITIES

2.1　CONSTRAINT SATISFACTION PROBLEMS

Consider a *constraint satisfaction problem* (CSP) defined on a set of n discrete variables, x_i for $i \in I = \{1, \ldots, n\}$. We use the vector notation $\vec{x} = (x_i)_{i \in I}$ to denote this *configuration* or set of variables. Each x_i can take on q possible values, so $\vec{x} \in X = \{1, \ldots, q\}^n$. Note that it is straightforward to generalize this to the case where the number of possible values depends on i.

The variables are subject to a set of m constraints, C_a for $a \in A = \{1, \ldots, m\}$. The index sets I and A are disjoint, so that their elements uniquely determine a single variable or constraint. Assume each constraint C_a can involve only a subset of variables $(x_i)_{i \in I(a)}$, where $I(a) \subset I$. Equivalently, each variable x_i is only involved in the constraints $(C_a)_{a \in A(i)}$ where $A(i) \subset A$. The constraint C_a is defined as a mapping $C_a : \{1, \ldots, q\}^{|I(a)|} \to \{0, 1\}$, where the value $C_a = 0$ corresponds to a satisfied constraint, and $C_a = 1$ to an unsatisfied constraint.

We define the *cost function*

$$C[\vec{x}] = \sum_{a \in A} C_a[(x_i)_{i \in I(a)}] , \tag{1}$$

counting the number of unsatisfied constraints. Our goal is to satisfy all constraints simultaneously, that is, to find a solution configuration $\vec{s} \in X$ with $C[\vec{s}] = 0$. We thus introduce the subset $S_C \subset X$ of solutions to our CSP instance as

$$S_C = \{\vec{s} \mid \vec{s} \in X, \ C[\vec{s}] = 0\} . \tag{2}$$

The algorithm aims at finding one solution $\vec{s} \in S_C$. We concentrate *a priori* on instances that possess a non-empty solution set S_C.

2.2 FACTOR GRAPH

The factor graph [351] representation for a CSP is as follows:

Definition 2.1. *For any instance of the CSP problem, its **factor graph** is a bipartite undirected graph $G = (V, E)$. The vertex set V contains two types of nodes:*

- *variable nodes $i \in I$ and*
- *function nodes $a \in A$.*

Edges can only connect one node type with the other. The edge (i, a) belongs to the edge set E if and only if the constraint C_a involves the variable x_i, that is, if $a \in A(i)$ or equivalently $i \in I(a)$. More formally, we define the vertex set $V = A \cup I$ and the edge set $E = \{(i, a) \mid i \in I, a \in A(i)\} = \{(a, i) \mid a \in A, i \in I(a)\}$.

In the figures in this chapter, we represent variable nodes by circles and function nodes by squares. This notation will help to distinguish between the different meanings of the two node types.

2.3 CAVITIES

Given a CSP and its factor graph, we will use the cavity graphs obtained by removing a variable:

Definition 2.2. *Given a factor graph G and one variable node $i \in I$, the **cavity graph** $G^{(i)}$ is obtained by deleting from G all function nodes $a \in A(i)$ adjacent to i, as well as all edges incident to these function nodes.*

The cavity graph $G^{(i)}$ defines a new CSP, with cost function

$$C^{(i)} = C - \sum_{a \in A(i)} C_a = \sum_{b \notin A(i)} C_b . \tag{3}$$

Note that in this new problem the variable x_i is isolated, and can take any value without violating a constraint. The solution set $S^{(i)}$ for the cavity problem $G^{(i)}$ is larger than the original solution set S_C, since constraints have been removed.

2.4 TWO EXAMPLES: SATISFIABILITY AND COLORING

Although in principle the survey propagation algorithm applies to arbitrary CSP, we present two specific examples: satisfiability and coloring.

In the satisfiability problem a constraint C_a is a clause, violated by only one assignment of the variables $(x_i)_{i \in I(a)}$. In random 3-SAT each clause involves three variables $(|I(a)| = 3)$, the indices of which are chosen randomly with a uniform distribution in I. This is shown in figure 1. For a given a and $I(a)$, there are eight different types of constraints C_a, corresponding to the combinations of possible negations of literals in one clause. In random 3-SAT the clauses are chosen uniformly at random from among these eight types.

In the q-coloring problem we are given an undirected graph. The problem is to color the vertices, using q colors, so that two vertices connected by an edge have different colors. One constraint is, therefore, associated with each edge of the original graph, and the factor graph is a decoration of the original graph (fig. 2) where function nodes are added on each original edge. There is only one type of function node. In the random q-COL problem, the original graph is a random graph from the $\mathcal{G}_{n,p}$ ensemble with mean degree pn.

We are particularly interested in algorithmic behavior for large n. Note that both k-SAT and q-COL are problems where $|A(i)|$ has a limiting Poisson distribution with finite mean when $n \to \infty$, so $|A(i)|$ is typically much smaller than n. Moreover, the structure of the factor graph is locally tree-like. This will guide us in the definition of the algorithm below, and appears to be an important ingredient in the algorithm's success.

3   BELIEF PROPAGATION

3.1   WARNINGS AND FIELDS

Given a CSP and a configuration $\vec{x} \in X$, we define [79, 395] the following three quantities associated with $\vec{x}$:

Definition 3.1. *For a given edge (a, i) of the factor graph, with $a \in A$ and $i \in I(a)$, the* **warning** *is the q-dimensional vector $\vec{u}_{a \to i}(\vec{x}) \in \{0, 1\}^q$ with components:*

$$u^p_{a \to i}(\vec{x}) = C_a \left[(x_j)_{j \in I(a) \setminus i} \mid x_i \leftarrow p \right] , \quad p = 1, ..., q .$$

This notation means that C_a is calculated with all variables of the configuration $\vec{x}$ that are neighbors of constraint a except for x_i, which is assigned the value p. Thus, $\vec{u}_{a \to i}(\vec{x})$ may be interpreted as a "message" from constraint a to variable i, warning it not to take on any value p for which $u^p_{a \to i}(\vec{x}) = 1$, or else the constraint will be violated. Note that since the warning depends explicitly only on $(x_j)_{j \in I(a) \setminus i}$, we do not need to know the value of x_i for computing $\vec{u}_{a \to i}(\vec{x})$.

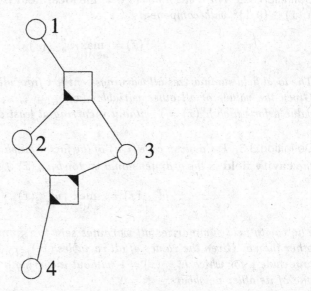

FIGURE 1 3-SAT: the factor graph corresponding to the simple formula: $(x_1 \vee \overline{x}_2 \vee x_3) \wedge (x_2 \vee \overline{x}_3 \vee \overline{x}_4)$. Variable nodes are represented as circles, clauses (function nodes) as squares. A triangle-shaped mark indicates that the corresponding literal is negated.

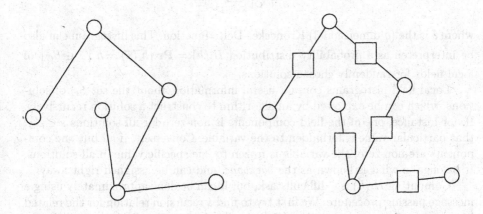

FIGURE 2 Graph coloring: the original graph (left) and its factor graph (right).

Definition 3.2. *For a given node $i \in I$, the* **local field** *is the q-dimensional vector $\vec{h}_i(\vec{x}) \in \{0,1\}^q$ with components:*

$$h_i^p(\vec{x}) = \max_{a \in A(i)} u_{a \to i}^p(\vec{x}) \ .$$

The local field summarizes all warnings sent to i from all neighboring constraints. Given the values of all other variables $(x_j)_{j \in I(a)\backslash i}$, x_i cannot be assigned any value p for which $h_i^p(\vec{x}) = 1$ without incurring at least one constraint violation.

Definition 3.3. *For a given edge (i,a) of the factor graph, with $i \in I$ and $a \in A(i)$, the* **cavity field** *is the q-dimensional vector $\vec{h}_{i \to a}(\vec{x}) \in \{0,1\}^q$ with components:*

$$h_{i \to a}^p(\vec{x}) = \max_{b \in A(i)\backslash a} u_{b \to i}^p(\vec{x}) \ .$$

The cavity field summarizes all warnings sent to i from neighboring constraints other than a. Given the values of all variables $(x_j)_{j \in I(a)\backslash i}$, x_i cannot be assigned any value p for which $h_{i \to a}^p(\vec{x}) = 1$ without incurring a constraint violation with one of its other neighbors.

3.2 HISTOGRAMS

The elementary messages above are defined for an arbitrary configuration $\vec{x}$. We are ultimately interested in knowing, for each variable i, the *histogram of local fields* for the configurations that are solutions to the CSP:

$$H_i(\vec{h}) = \frac{1}{|S_C|} \sum_{\vec{s} \in S_C} \delta_{\vec{h}, \vec{h}_i(\vec{s})} \ , \tag{4}$$

where δ is the (q-dimensional) Kronecker-Delta function. This histogram can also be interpreted as a probability distribution $H_i(\vec{h}) = \mathbf{Pr}\left[\vec{h}_i(\vec{s}) = \vec{h} \mid \vec{s} \in S_C\right]$ of local fields for randomly chosen solutions.

Local field histograms contain useful information about the set S_C of solutions, which can be exploited by an algorithm to construct a solution recursively. If, for instance, one of the field components is non-zero for all solutions $\vec{s} \in S_C$, that particular value is forbidden to the variable. Conversely, if all but one components are non-zero, the variable is frozen to one specific value in all solutions. It belongs to what is known as the *backbone*, and can be assigned right away.

Computing $H_i(\vec{h})$ is a difficult task, but it can be done approximately using a message passing procedure. We first try to find a recursion relation for the related histograms of the warnings $\vec{u}_{a \to i}(\vec{s})$ over all solutions $\vec{s} \in S_C$ [79]. Considering figure 3 as an example, note that the histogram of $\vec{u}_{a \to i}(\vec{s})$ depends on the "joint" histogram of all the warnings $\vec{u}_{b \to j}(\vec{s})$ sent to all variables $j \in \{j_1, j_2, j_3\}$ "above" function node a. We call these the *incoming warnings*. The obvious problem

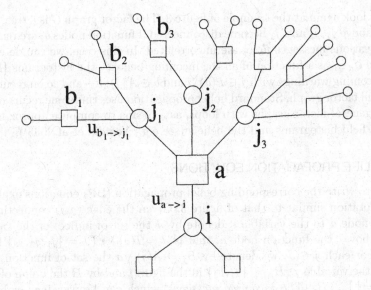

FIGURE 3 Iteration for $\vec{u}$ warnings.

is that their joint distribution is not known. If the $\vec{u}_{b \to j}(\vec{s})$ were independent variables, we would be able to factorize the joint histogram into the product of all individual histograms of warnings $\vec{u}_{b \to j}(\vec{s})$, and then obtain a recursion. But, in general, there is no reason for them to be independent. Moreover, they cannot even be approximately independent, as the variables "above" variable nodes j—the small unnamed ones in the figure—are connected to each other by very short paths, via at most three function nodes. Those variables in turn define the $\vec{u}_{b \to j}(\vec{s})$ messages.

This is where the cavity graph becomes useful. For each edge (b, j) of the factor graph, we define the *belief* $U_{b \to j}(\vec{u})$ as the histogram of the warnings $\vec{u}_{b \to j}$ over the configurations $s \in S^{(j)}$ that are solutions of the problem on the cavity graph $G^{(j)}$:

$$U_{b \to j}(\vec{u}) = \frac{1}{|S^{(j)}|} \sum_{\vec{s} \in S^{(j)}} \delta_{\vec{u}, \vec{u}_{b \to j}(\vec{s})}$$

$$= \mathbf{Pr}\left[\vec{u}_{b \to j}(\vec{s}) = \vec{u} \mid \vec{s} \in S^{(j)}\right]. \qquad (5)$$

The second line in eq. (5) refers again to the probabilistic interpretation: $U_{b \to j}(\vec{u})$ describes the probability of having a warning $\vec{u}$ for a randomly chosen solution of $G^{(j)}$. Note that even though the function node b is itself absent from the cavity graph, the warning $\vec{u}_{b \to j}$ is still well defined, with respect to the full factor graph.

Now look again at the example of figure 3. The factor graph G is a tree, so the vertices above j_1, j_2 and j_3 become disconnected if function nodes b_i are removed, and the various messages $\vec{u}_{b \to j}$ are uncorrelated. In this case, we can determine the belief $U_{a \to i}$ as a function of all the incoming beliefs—the histograms $\{U_{b \to j}\}$ of the incoming warnings with $j \in I(a) \setminus i$ and $b \in A(j) \setminus a$—and so on recursively for the full factor graph. Standard belief propagation uses this same recursion also in more general factor graphs with loops, as a means to compute approximately the local field histograms and the beliefs (see e.g., Yedidia et al. [533]).

3.3 BELIEF PROPAGATION EQUATIONS

In order to write the corresponding belief propagation (BP) equations explicitly, we use notation similar to that of figure 3. Given the edge (a, i) connecting the function node a to the variable i, denote by J the set of indices of the variable nodes "above" the function node a, that is $J = I(a) \setminus i$ ($J = \{j_1, j_2, j_3\}$ in the figure). For each $j \in J$, we denote by $B_j = A(j) \setminus a$ the set of function nodes "above" the variable j ($B_{j_1} = \{b_1, b_2\}$ in the figure) and by B the union of these sets, $B = \bigcup_{j \in J} B_j$. The *incoming messages*, which can be warnings or beliefs, are all the messages propagated on the edges $b \to j$, where $j \in J$, and for each such j, $b \in B_j$.

Let us first consider a set of incoming warnings $\{\vec{u}_{b \to j}\}$. This warning set may or may not lead self-consistently to a configuration $(s_j)_{j \in J}$ satisfying all constraints $(C_b)_{b \in B}$. One can easily carry out an enumerative procedure to evaluate all configurations $(s_j)_{j \in J}$ compatible with the warning set. First compute the cavity fields (Definition 3.3) component-wise: $h^p_{j \to a} = \max_{b \in B_j} (u^p_{b \to j})$. For each $j \in J$, the allowed values of s_j are those where $h^{s_j}_{j \to a} = 0$. We denote by $T(\{\vec{h}_{j \to a}\}) \subset \{1, ..., q\}^{|J|}$ the set of allowed configurations for the s_j variables:

$$T(\{\vec{h}_{j \to a}\}) = \left\{ (s_j)_{j \in J} \mid \forall j \in J : h^{s_j}_{j \to a} = 0 \right\}. \tag{6}$$

For each (s_j) in $T(\{\vec{h}_{j \to a}\})$, one can then determine the outgoing warning $\vec{u}_{a \to i}$ using Definition 3.1.

This procedure can be embedded into the probabilistic description of solutions on the cavity graph. Assuming that incoming warnings are "independent," we follow the steps above, first calculating from the incoming beliefs the histogram of cavity fields. This is the probability of having a cavity field $\vec{h}_{j \to a} = \vec{h}$ for a randomly chosen solution of the cavity graph $G^{(j)}$, or equivalently, the fraction of such solutions sending warnings to j that produce a cavity field $\vec{h}$:

$$H_{j \to a}(\vec{h}) = \sum_{\{\vec{u}_{b \to j}\}_{b \in B_j}} \delta_{\vec{h}, \vec{h}_{j \to a}} \prod_{b \in B_j} U_{b \to j}(\vec{u}_{b \to j}), \tag{7}$$

where the sum is over sets of warnings $\{\vec{u}_{b \to j}\}_{b \in B_j}$ with all possible warning values $\vec{u}_{b \to j} \in \{0, 1\}^q$. The new distribution of warnings $\vec{u}_{a \to i}$ is then given by an average over cavity fields,

$$U_{a \to i}(\vec{u}) = \mathcal{Z}^{-1} \sum_{\{\vec{h}_{j \to a}\}_{j \in J}} \left[\sum_{\vec{s} \in T(\{\vec{h}_{j \to a}\})} \delta_{\vec{u}, \vec{u}_{a \to i}(\vec{s})} \right] \prod_{j \in J} H_{j \to a}(\vec{h}_{j \to a}) . \quad (8)$$

The pre-factor $\mathcal{Z}^{-1}$ is a normalization constant. Note that each cavity field configuration $\{\vec{h}_{j \to a}\}$ contributes $|T(\{\vec{h}_{j \to a}\})|$ terms. As a result, contradictory messages never contribute to eq. (8).

The BP eqs. (7) and (8) are equivalent to the so-called sum-product (or belief network, or Bayesian network) equations [188, 431]. One can try to solve them by iteration, starting from randomly chosen beliefs and then updating $U_{a \to i}$ sequentially on randomly chosen (a, i) edges. In some cases the process converges to a unique solution, independently of the updating scheme. When the belief propagation equations converge, one can use the resulting beliefs to estimate the histogram of local fields, using:

$$H_j(\vec{h}) \simeq \sum_{\{\vec{u}_{b \to j}\}_{b \in A(j)}} \delta_{\vec{h}, \vec{h}_{j \to a}} \prod_{b \in A(j)} U_{b \to j}(\vec{u}_{b \to j}) , \quad (9)$$

and this histogram can be used for decimation.

3.4   AN EXAMPLE OF BELIEF PROPAGATION: 3-COL

For the sake of clarity, let us work out BP on a simple example of the 3-COL problem ($q = 3$), for which the part of the factor graph is shown in figure 4. Since function nodes are connected to two variable nodes only (constraints represent edges in the original graph), there is only one variable node j above function node a. For a given configuration of incoming warnings $\{\vec{u}_{b \to j}\}$, we can make a table of allowed values s_j, and for each of them compute the outgoing warning $\vec{u}_{a \to i}(s_j)$. The only possible warnings are $(1, 0, 0)$, $(0, 1, 0)$, $(0, 0, 1)$, since a function node can only forbid one color: the value of the other variable connected to the function node.

- Suppose that $\vec{u}_{b_1 \to j} = (1, 0, 0)$, $\vec{u}_{b_2 \to j} = (0, 1, 0)$, and $\vec{u}_{b_3 \to j} = (0, 0, 1)$. Then $h_{j \to a} = (1, 1, 1)$ and we find a contradictory message. No satisfiable configuration exists for s_j. According to the procedure given above, this configuration does not contribute to $U_{a \to i}$.
- Suppose that $\vec{u}_{b_1 \to j} = \vec{u}_{b_2 \to j} = (1, 0, 0)$, and $\vec{u}_{b_3 \to j} = (0, 1, 0)$. Then $h_{j \to a} = (1, 1, 0)$, and the only possible coloring assignment for j is $s_j = 3$. For this configuration, we have only one possible outgoing warning: $\vec{u}_{a \to i} = (0, 0, 1)$.
- Suppose that $\vec{u}_{b_1 \to j} = \vec{u}_{b_2 \to j} = \vec{u}_{b_3 \to j} = (1, 0, 0)$. Then $h_{j \to a} = (1, 0, 0)$, and there are two possible colors for s_j, namely the values 2 and 3. For the first one we have $u_{a \to i} = (0, 1, 0)$, and for the second one $u_{a \to i} = (0, 0, 1)$. Both contribute with equal weight to $U_{a \to i}$.

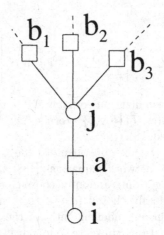

FIGURE 4 An example of the coloring problem. This part of the factor graph is the one necessary to compute the messages (warning and belief) passed from the function node a to the variable node i.

- All other configurations are simple color permutations of the three cases mentioned above, and are handled analogously.

From eqs. (7) and (8), we can easily deduce the equation giving the probability distribution $U_{a \to i}$ in terms of all distributions $\{U_{b_l \to j}; l = 1, 2, 3\}$. Parametrizing $U_{a \to i}$ according to the three possible messages as

$$U_{a \to i}(\vec{u}) = \eta^1_{a \to i} \delta_{\vec{u},(1,0,0)} + \eta^2_{a \to i} \delta_{\vec{u},(0,1,0)} + \eta^3_{a \to i} \delta_{\vec{u},(0,0,1)} , \qquad (10)$$

we find

$$\eta^p_{a \to i} = \frac{\prod_{l=1}^{3}(1 - \eta^p_{b_l \to j})}{\sum_{r=1}^{3} \prod_{l=1}^{3}(1 - \eta^r_{b_l \to j})} . \qquad (11)$$

This expression can be understood easily: $\eta^p_{a \to i}$ equals the probability that color p is forbidden for node i, which means that node j has already taken this color, $s_j = p$. Now, node j can take color p if and only if it is not forbidden by any incoming warning: the numerator in eq. (11) simply calculates the probability that none of the incoming messages forbids color p, and the denominator guarantees normalization. Note that configurations in which all variables b_l take the same color r are counted twice, namely in the expressions for both values of $p \neq r$. According to the discussion above, this is correct because we have two new configurations for s_j, and two corresponding messages $\vec{u}_{a \to i}$ can be sent.

Finally, note that due to the symmetry among colors, a trivial solution to the BP equations is $\eta^p_{a \to i} = 1/q$ for all edges $(a, i) \in E$ and all colors p. However, in a recursive coloring algorithm some variable nodes would be assigned a color at the outset. This would explicitly break the symmetry.

4 SURVEY PROPAGATION

4.1 CLUSTERING

Unfortunately, the belief propagation dynamics are known not to converge for the random version of many combinatorial problems (including again 3-SAT and q-COL) in the region of the parameters near the SAT/UNSAT threshold. Recently, as discussed in earlier chapters, it has become possible using tools from statistical physics to gain an understanding of what happens in the solution space around the threshold [392, 395, 397]. Well below the threshold, where the number m/n of constraints per variable is relatively small, a generic problem has exponentially many solutions, which tend to form one giant cluster: for any two solutions, it is possible to find a connecting path via other solutions that requires short steps only (each pair of consecutive assignments in the path is close together in Hamming distance). Close to the critical threshold, however, the solution space breaks up into many smaller clusters. Solutions in separate clusters are generally far apart. In addition, the cost function $C[\vec{x}]$ has exponentially many local minima, separated from each other by large cost "barriers." These local cost minima are exponentially more numerous than the solution clusters. As seen explicitly in the example of error correcting codes in chapter 3, their metastability causes them to act as traps for local search algorithms.

According to the statistical physics analysis, which considers the infinite size limit $n \to \infty$, there exist exponentially many widely separated clusters of solutions. Within a given cluster of solutions, we may identify two types of variables: those that are frozen in one single assignment for all configurations belonging to the cluster, and those—unfrozen—that fluctuate from solution to solution inside the cluster. Note also that the variables that are frozen within one solution cluster may change their value when we go to another cluster, where they may even be unfrozen. While in general the distinction above can only provide an approximate description of clusters, it appears from numerical experiments that in many hard random CSPs, such as k-SAT or q-COL, this type of approximation is already rather accurate.

4.2 THE JOKER ASSIGNMENT

Survey propagation (SP) turns out [79, 427] to be able to deal with this clustering phenomenon for large (finite) sizes n. Although the original derivation uses subtle statistical physics ideas, one can also develop it more directly in algorithmic terms. The key intuition is that we no longer work with individual solutions $\vec{s} \in S_C$, but rather with entire clusters of solutions. The variables that are frozen within a cluster retain one single value $s_j \in \{1, ..., q\}$ in our description. Other variables may take several values within the cluster. For handling these, we introduce an additional joker value denoted by "$\star$" so that within each cluster, $s_j \in \{1, ..., q, \star\}$. We can then generalize the constraint to this enlarged space and work out the corresponding belief propagation equations.

An even finer description, useful for general CSPs, would use multiple jokers to describe the set of allowed values for the variable, so that $s_j \in \mathcal{P}$ where $\mathcal{P}$ is the ensemble built from all subsets of $\{1, ..., q\}$. Within each cluster one could then assign exactly one of these generalized values to each variable. However, we will not develop this "derivation" in further detail, since in any event it does not give any rigorous construction. Rather, we will directly write the SP equations themselves, in terms of the original variables $\vec{x} \in \{1, ..., q\}^n$, and then analyze them.

4.3 GENERALIZED MESSAGES

We first need to define the generalizations of the warnings, local fields, and cavity fields used in survey propagation. In order to simplify the presentation, we shall often omit the "generalized" qualifier, and use the same notation for generalized warning as we used for warnings in the BP section. The reader should bear in mind that in the context of SP, all these messages are taken to be "generalized" messages.

For a given CSP, we define the warning:

Definition 4.1. *For a given edge (a, i) of the factor graph, with $a \in A$ and $i \in I(a)$, let S be a set of possible values for the variables $(x_j)_{j \in J}$ "above" a. ($J = I(a) \setminus i$.) The* **warning** *is the q-dimensional vector $\vec{u}_{a \to i}(\vec{x}) \in \{0, 1\}^q$ with components:*

$$u_{a \to i}^p(S) = \min_{(x_j) \in S} C_a\left[(x_j)_{j \in J}\,\middle|\, x_i \leftarrow p\right] , \quad p = 1, ..., q .$$

This generalized warning is also known in the literature as *cavity bias* [395]. Note that the set of possible warnings is enlarged in SP: for the example of 3-COL, the *null message* $(0, 0, 0)$ is added to $(0, 0, 1)$, $(0, 1, 0)$ and $(1, 0, 0)$. As in section 3.4, the non-null messages are sent if the node "above" a function node is assigned a fixed color in the solution cluster. Correspondingly, the null message is sent if this vertex is not fixed to a single color, that is, if it is has the joker value.

Based on these warnings, we define local and cavity fields according to definitions 3.2 and 3.3, with the single configuration argument $\vec{x}$ again replaced by a set S of configurations. Using the J and B_j notation from section 3.3,

$$h_i^p(S) = \max_{a \in A(i)} u_{a \to i}^p(S) \text{ and}$$
$$h_{j \to a}^p(S) = \max_{b \in B_j} u_{b \to j}^p(S) . \tag{12}$$

4.4 HISTOGRAMS

Histograms of warnings and fields are now defined over clusters rather than over individual solutions. Letting S_C^α represent solution cluster α, and n_{cl} the total number of clusters, the histogram of local fields is given by

$$H_i(\vec{h}) = \frac{1}{n_{cl}} \sum_{\alpha=1}^{n_{cl}} \delta_{\vec{h}, \vec{h}_i(S_C^\alpha)} \ . \tag{13}$$

The histogram of the generalized warning on an edge (b, j) is called the *survey*, denoted by $Q_{b \to j}(\vec{u})$. It is defined in terms of the clusters of solutions for the cavity graph $G^{(j)}$. Calling $S_C^{\alpha,(j)}$ the corresponding solution cluster, and $n_{cl}^{(j)}$ the corresponding number of clusters, one defines:

$$Q_{b \to j}(\vec{u}) = \frac{1}{n_{cl}^{(j)}} \sum_{\alpha=1}^{n_{cl}^{(j)}} \delta_{\vec{u}, \vec{u}_{b \to j}(S_C^{\alpha,(j)})} \ . \tag{14}$$

4.5 SURVEY PROPAGATION EQUATIONS

Based on these definitions, one can easily infer the generalized recurrence equations for the (approximate) probabilities $Q_{a \to i}(\vec{u})$ that implement the solutions in this enlarged configuration space. These SP equations lead to a small, yet fundamental modification of the BP equations. The basic assumption is again that incoming warnings are independent. In this case, however, contradictory messages have to be explicitly forbidden. Keeping figure 3 in mind, we use the incoming set of surveys $\{Q_{b \to j}\}$ with $b \in B_j$ and $j \in J$ to calculate the cavity field distributions exactly as in eq. (7):

$$H_{j \to a}(\vec{h}) = \sum_{\{\vec{u}_{b \to j}\}_{b \in B_j}} \delta_{\vec{h}, \vec{h}_{j \to a}} \prod_{b \in B_j} Q_{b \to j}(\vec{u}_{b \to j}) \ . \tag{15}$$

Recall that these fields lead to contradictions if and only if $\vec{h}_{j \to a} = (1, 1, \dots, 1)$ for at least one j. Therefore, we introduce the ensemble of all *non-contradictory* cavity field configurations,

$$\mathcal{M}_{a \to i} = \left\{ \{\vec{h}_{j \to a}\}_{j \in J} \mid \forall j \in J : \ \vec{h}_{j \to a} \in \{0, 1\}^q, \ \vec{h}_{j \to a} \neq (1, \dots, 1) \right\} \ . \tag{16}$$

Then, for an element of $\mathcal{M}_{a \to i}$—one specific set of $\{\vec{h}_{j \to a}\}_{j \in J}$—we again define

$$T(\{\vec{h}_{j \to a}\}) = \left\{ (s_j)_{j \in J} \mid \forall j \in J : \ h_{j \to a}^{s_j} = 0 \right\} \ , \tag{17}$$

the set of allowed configurations for the variable nodes above function node a. Now the difference with respect to BP arises: since all elements of $T(\{\vec{h}_{j \to a}\})$

give rise to a single outgoing warning, they all belong to the same cluster. The new warning is thus computed on the set of allowed configurations, and is given by $\vec{u}_{a \to i}(T(\{\vec{h}_{j \to a}\}))$. Its distribution follows:

$$Q_{a \to i}(\vec{u}) = \tilde{\mathcal{Z}}^{-1} \sum_{\{\vec{h}_{j \to a}\} \in \mathcal{M}_{a \to i}} \delta_{\vec{u}, \vec{u}_{a \to i}(T(\{\vec{h}_{j \to a}\}))} \prod_{j \in J} H_{j \to a}(\vec{h}_{j \to a}) . \qquad (18)$$

Equations (15) and (18) are the SP equations. Note that eq. (18) produces a dramatic change in the iteration of the probabilities compared with the BP eq. (8): every allowed cavity field configuration contributes only one term to the sum. Note also that contradictory messages have to be excluded "explicitly" by summing only over $\mathcal{M}_{a \to i}$. In BP, for each configuration of input messages one takes the full collection of possible outputs, thereby introducing a bifurcation mechanism that can easily become unstable. In SP, on the contrary, the presence of multiple outputs is collapsed into a null message (which in the example of graph coloring does not even exist in the belief propagation formalism). A variable receiving a message with at least two zero components will be "unfrozen" in the corresponding cluster.

The eqs. (15)–(18) provide a closed set of equations for the surveys. Practically, this recurrence defines a map

$$\Lambda : \left\{ Q_{a \to i}^{\mathrm{old}} \right\}_{a \in A(i)}^{i \in I} \mapsto \left\{ Q_{a \to i}^{\mathrm{new}} \right\}_{a \in A(i)}^{i \in I} \qquad (19)$$

and we look for a fixed point of this map, obtained numerically by starting with some (random) initial $\left\{ Q_{a \to i}^{0} \right\}$ and applying Λ iteratively:

$$\left\{ Q_{a \to i}^{SP} \right\} = \lim_{N \to \infty} \overbrace{\Lambda \circ \cdots \circ \Lambda}^{N \text{ times}} \left\{ Q_{a \to i}^{0} \right\} . \qquad (20)$$

Such a fixed point will be called a *self-consistent* set of surveys.

4.6   AN EXAMPLE OF SURVEY PROPAGATION: 3-COL

For the 3-COL example, because of the additional null message, the warning distribution now reads [78]

$$Q_{a \to i}(\vec{u}) = \eta_{a \to i}^{\star} \delta_{\vec{u},(0,0,0)} + \eta_{a \to i}^{1} \delta_{\vec{u},(1,0,0)} + \eta_{a \to i}^{2} \delta_{\vec{u},(0,1,0)} + \eta_{a \to i}^{3} \delta_{\vec{u},(0,0,1)} , \quad (21)$$

and the SP equations corresponding to figure 4 are given by

$$\eta_{a \to i}^{p} = \frac{\prod_{l=1}^{3}(1 - \eta_{b_l \to j}^{p}) - \sum_{r \neq p} \prod_{l=1}^{3}(\eta_{b_l \to j}^{\star} + \eta_{b_l \to j}^{r}) + \prod_{l=1}^{3} \eta_{b_l \to j}^{\star}}{\sum_{r=1}^{3} \prod_{l=1}^{3}(1 - \eta_{b_l \to j}^{r}) - \sum_{r=1}^{3} \prod_{l=1}^{3}(\eta_{b_l \to j}^{\star} + \eta_{b_l \to j}^{r}) + \prod_{l=1}^{3} \eta_{b_l \to j}^{\star}} , \qquad (22)$$

for $p \in \{1, 2, 3\}$. Then $\eta^\star_{a \to 1}$ can be computed by normalization:

$$\eta^\star_{a \to i} = 1 - \left(\eta^1_{a \to i} + \eta^2_{a \to i} + \eta^3_{a \to i} \right). \tag{23}$$

The interpretation of this equation is again straightforward. We explain it for color 1: now $\eta^1_{a \to i}$ is given by the probability that s_j is forced to take value 1, that is, by the probability that the cavity field equals $\vec{h}_{j \to a} = (0, 1, 1)$, conditioned on non-contradictory cavity fields. The numerator calculates the unconditioned probability. The first term includes all cases where $h^1_{j \to a} = 0$: $(0,0,0), (0,0,1), (0,1,0), (0,1,1)$. The second term then excludes those cases where $h^1_{j \to a} = h^r_{j \to a} = 0$, summed over $r \neq 1$: $(0,0,0), (0,0,1)$ for $r = 2$; $(0,0,0), (0,1,0)$ for $r = 3$. Finally, the third term includes $(0,0,0)$ again since it was double-counted in the second term. The denominator then provides for conditioning on non-contradictory fields, by giving the probability that $\vec{h}_{j \to a} \neq (1, 1, 1)$. The counting of possible cases follows a similar inclusion-exclusion principle as for the numerator.

Note that as with belief propagation, the symmetry among colors leads to a trivial solution: $\eta^\star_{a \to i} = 1$ for all edges (a, i) of the factor graph, that is, only null messages are sent. Clearly, this is not the correct solution in the clustered regime, and the color symmetry is not valid at the level of solution clusters. In fact, it is the appearance of a nontrivial solution for the $\eta^p_{a \to i}$ that marks the onset of clustering.

4.7 AN EXAMPLE OF SURVEY PROPAGATION: K-SAT

In the case of SAT, $q = 2$: possible $\vec{u}$ warnings are $(0,0), (1,0), (0,1)$, and $(1,1)$. As any clause can be satisfied by any given variable (choosing the variable's value according to whether or not the corresponding literal is negated), the $(1,1)$ message will never appear. Moreover, for a given edge (a, i), the sign of the literal at i will completely determine whether $(1,0)$ or $(0,1)$ can appear on $\vec{u}_{a \to i}$. So we can parametrize distributions $Q_{a \to i}$ with only one real number $\eta_{a \to i}$, namely the probability of the nontrivial $\vec{u}_{a \to i}$ message, that is, a message other than $(0,0)$. The probability of $(0,0)$ is then $1 - \eta_{a \to i}$. The corresponding equations have been written and implemented in Braunstein et al. [79] and at the Survey Propagation web site [536]. In the case of 3-SAT, they read

$$\eta_{a \to i} = \prod_{j \in J} \left[\frac{\Pi^u_{j \to a}}{\Pi^u_{j \to a} + \Pi^s_{j \to a} + \Pi^0_{j \to a}} \right], \tag{24}$$

where

$$\Pi^u_{j \to a} = \left[1 - \prod_{b \in A^u_a(j)} (1 - \eta_{b \to j}) \right] \prod_{b \in A^s_a(j)} (1 - \eta_{b \to j}),$$

$$\Pi_{j \to a}^s = \left[1 - \prod_{b \in A_a^s(j)} (1 - \eta_{b \to j}) \right] \prod_{b \in A_a^u(j)} (1 - \eta_{b \to j}) \; ,$$

$$\Pi_{j \to a}^0 = \prod_{b \in B_j} (1 - \eta_{b \to j}) \; . \tag{25}$$

$A_a^u(j), A_a^s(j)$ are the two sets into which $A(j)$ decomposes $(A(j) = A_a^u(j) \cup A_a^s(j))$ where the indices s and u refer to the neighbors b for which the literals (b, j) and (a, j) agree and disagree, respectively. This separation corresponds to the distinction of which neighbors cause the clause a to be satisfied or unsatisfied by variable j.

For example, the product $\prod_{b \in A_a^s(j)} (1 - \eta_{b \to j})$ gives the probability that no nontrivial message arrives at j from the function nodes $b \in A_a^s(j)$ (empty products are set to 1 by definition).

4.8 DECIMATION

Once convergence is reached in eq. (20) (we stop when $\max_{i \in I, a \in A(i)}$ $|Q_{a \to i}^{old} - Q_{a \to i}^{new}|$ becomes small enough), we can use the information computed so far to find a solution to the original problem [79, 395]. We can easily compute the (approximate) local field distributions $\{H_i\}_{i \in I}$ introduced in eq. (13) by considering all neighboring function nodes, and forbidding contradictory messages. Recall that in the cavity graph we delete the constraints containing variable i, whereas in H_i we have to restrict the sum to messages that can be extended to solutions of the complete problem. In the example of 3-COL, $H_i(\vec{h})$ is given by

$$H_i(\vec{h}) = \mathcal{Z}'^{-1} \sum_{\{\vec{u}_{a \to i}\}_{a \in A(i)}} \left(1 - \delta_{\vec{h}, (1,1,1)} \right) \delta_{\vec{h}, \vec{h}_i} \prod_{a \in A(i)} Q_{a \to i}(\vec{u}_{a \to i}) \; , \tag{26}$$

with $\vec{h}_i$ determined according to eq. (12).

Given the vector $\vec{h}_0$ with a 0 entry at component p and 1 at the other two components, the value $H_i(\vec{h}_0)$ gives the probability for a variable i to be frozen to a certain value p. A simple decimation procedure can then be implemented. Select the variable that is frozen with the highest probability, and fix it to its most frozen value. Then simplify the problem: certain constraints may already be satisfied independently of the values of other participating variables, and can be deleted from the problem instance. Other constraints might immediately fix single variables to one value (unit clause resolution). Reconverge the warning distributions on the smaller subproblem.

The decimation algorithm can lead to three types of behaviors:

1. The algorithm can solve the problem fixing all, or almost all variables (some variables may not need to be fixed, even if the problem is already solved).

2. The surveys converge at some stage to the trivial solution concentrated on null messages, $Q_{a \to i}(u) = \delta_{h,(0,0,0)}$ for all $(a,i) \in E$. In this case SP has nothing more to offer. Luckily, the resulting subproblems are generally under-constrained and then easy to solve by other means. Note that, for q-COL, the trivial solution always exists. In numerical experiments, we found that in the case of the existence of another solution, the latter was the correct one. Therefore, even if a trivial solution is found once, it is reasonable to restart the iteration of the SP equations. Only if no nontrivial solution can be found after several restarts does the subproblem need to be passed to a different solver.

3. The SP algorithm never converges, even if the initial problem was satisfiable.

On large random instances of 3-SAT [79, 395, 397, 429] and q-COL [78] in the hard SAT region, though not too close to the satisfiability threshold, numerical experiments show that the algorithm behaves as in case 2. The subproblems generated turn out to be very simple to solve by other conventional heuristics, such as WalkSAT [470] or unmodified belief propagation.

Case 3 generally occurs very close to the SAT/UNSAT transition. It is not yet clear whether this outcome appears due to the existence of finite loops in the original problem (which make the SP equations only approximate), due to the simple decimation heuristic that always fixes the most frozen variable, or due to problems that go beyond the validity of the SP equation itself.

5 WHAT'S NEXT

Among all the possible directions of research that may follow from the algorithm we have presented, we would like to highlight two in particular. The first is to formalize rigorously the notions suggested in section 4, establishing precise definitions for the clusters, and a corresponding derivation of the SP equations. The second, of great computational relevance, is to generalize SP. SP has been presented here in its purest form, but can be adapted to deal with correlations between warnings that arise from local problem structures such as small loops in the factor graph. Similar extensions have been considered for BP [533]. A further possible generalization would include diverse structures of the solution space. Notions of *replica symmetry breaking*, discussed in chapter 1, argue for considering clusters of solution clusters or even a hierarchical construction of clusters. Developing this might be a further step towards more fully applying theory and analysis from statistical physics to algorithmic methods.

ACKNOWLEDGMENTS

It is a pleasure to thank R. Mulet, A. Pagnani, and F. Ricci-Tersenghi for numerous discussions. M. Mézard and M. Weigt acknowledge the hospitality of the ICTP Trieste, where a portion of this work was done. The work has been supported in part through the EC "STIPCO" network, grant No. HPRN-CT-2002-00319.

CHAPTER 5

The Easiest Hard Problem:
Number Partitioning

Stephan Mertens

1 INTRODUCTION

The number partitioning problem (NPP) is defined easily: Given a list $a_1, a_2, \ldots,$ a_n of positive integers, find a partition, that is, a subset $\mathcal{A} \subset \{1, \ldots, n\}$, minimizing the discrepancy

$$E(\mathcal{A}) = \left| \sum_{i \in \mathcal{A}} a_i - \sum_{i \notin \mathcal{A}} a_i \right|. \tag{1}$$

A *perfect partition* is a partition with $E = 0$ for $\sum a_j$ even, or $E = 1$ for $\sum a_j$ odd.

Number partitioning is of considerable importance, both practically and theoretically. Its practical applications range from multiprocessor scheduling and the minimization of VLSI circuit size and delay [102, 504], to public key cryptography [387], to choosing up sides in a ball game [237]. Number partitioning is also one of Garey and Johnson's six basic NP-hard problems that lie at the heart of the theory of NP-completeness [191, 388], and is in fact the only one of these

Computational Complexity and Statistical Physics, edited by
Allon G. Percus, Gabriel Istrate, and Cristopher Moore, Oxford University Press. **125**

problems that actually deals with numbers. Hence, it is often chosen as a base for NP-completeness proofs of other problems involving numbers, such as bin packing, multiprocessor scheduling [38], quadratic programming, and knapsack problems.

The computational complexity of the NPP depends on the type of input numbers $\{a_1, a_2, \ldots, a_n\}$. Consider the case where the values of a_j are positive integers bounded by a constant A. Then the discrepancy E can take on at most nA different values, so the size of the search space is $O(nA)$ instead of $O(2^n)$ and it is straightforward to devise an algorithm that explores this reduced space in time polynomial in nA [191]. Of course, such an algorithm does not prove P = NP: a concise encoding of an instance requires $O(n \log_2 A)$ bits, and A is not bounded by any power of $\log_2 A$. This feature of the NPP is called *pseudo-polynomiality*. The NP-hardness of the NPP becomes apparent when input numbers are of a size exponentially large in n or, after division by the maximal input number, of exponentially high precision.

To study typical properties of the NPP, the input numbers are often taken to be independent, identically distributed random variables. Under this probabilistic assumption, the minimal discrepancy E_0 is a stochastic quantity. For real-valued input numbers (infinite precision, see above), Karmarkar et al. [298] proved that the *median* value of E_0 is $O(\sqrt{n}2^{-n})$. Lueker [370] showed that the same scaling holds for the *mean* value of E_0. From numerical simulations [157] it is known that the standard deviation of E_0 is of the same order of magnitude as the mean: E_0 is *non-self-averaging*.

Another surprising feature of the NPP is the poor quality of heuristic algorithms [281, 448]. The differencing method, discussed below, is the best polynomial time heuristic known to date, and for real-valued a_j yields minimum discrepancies $O(n^{-\alpha \log n})$ with some positive constant α [532]. This is far above the true optimum, yet it is the best that one can get for large systems! The poor quality of polynomial time heuristics is a very peculiar feature that distinguishes the NPP from many other hard optimization problems such as the Euclidean traveling salesman problem [444], for which satisfactory approximation algorithms do exist.

The NP-hardness of the NPP tells us that for numbers a_j bounded by $A = 2^{\kappa n}$, the worst-case complexity of any exact algorithm is almost certainly exponential in n for all $\kappa > 0$. Numerical simulations show that the typical complexity on instances of the random ensemble is exponential only for $\kappa > \kappa_c > 0$. For $\kappa < \kappa_c$ it is polynomial. The critical value κ_c marks a transition point, where the random ensemble somehow changes its character. Below κ_c, typical instances seem to have a special property that can be exploited by an exhaustive algorithm. This abrupt change of an averaged quantity, as a parameter of a statistical ensemble is varied, is called a *phase transition* by analogy with the transitions observed in thermodynamic systems. Phase transitions in the average complexity have been observed in many NP-hard problems such as satisfiability [236, 319], or Hamiltonian circuit [91], and are discussed throughout this volume.

Their study forms the base of an emerging interdisciplinary field of research that encompasses the efforts of computer scientists, mathematicians and physicists [133].

The NPP illustrates the interdisciplinary character of the field. Fu [185], a physicist, first mapped partitioning to an infinite-range, antiferromagnetic spin glass, concluding (incorrectly) that this model did not have a phase transition. Gent and Walsh [194], computer scientists, demonstrated the existence of the phase transition using numerical simulations. They introduced the control parameter κ and estimated the transition point close to $\kappa_c = 0.96$. Mertens [389], a physicist, reconsidered Fu's spin glass analogy and derived a phase transition at $\kappa_c = 1 - (\log_2 n/2n) + O(1/n)$. Then Borgs, Chayes and Pittel [71], mathematicians, took over and established the phase transition and its characterization rigorously. The mathematical proofs for the phase transitions are another exceptional feature of the NPP. For other NP-hard problems such as satisfiability, much less is known from rigorous techniques and the sharpest results have been obtained by the powerful but non-rigorous techniques from statistical mechanics [395], as seen in the previous two chapters.

It is this combination of algorithmic hardness and analytical tractability that earns the NPP the description of *easiest hard problem*, a phrase coined by Brian Hayes [237]. In this chapter, we exploit the easiness of the NPP to provide an understanding of some of its remarkable properties.

2   ALGORITHMS AND COMPLEXITY

In view of the NP-hardness of the NPP, it is wise to abandon the idea of an exact solution and to ask instead for an approximate but fast heuristic algorithm. An obvious approach is to place the largest number in one of the two subsets, then continue to place the largest among the remaining numbers in the subset with the smaller total sum so far, until all numbers are assigned. The idea behind this *greedy heuristic* is to keep the discrepancy small with every decision. In the worst case, the two subsets could be perfectly balanced just before the last number is assigned: since numbers are assigned in decreasing order, this leads to the discrepancy scaling as $O(n^{-1})$ for real-valued a_j. That, of course, is extremely bad compared to the optimum discrepancy of $O(\sqrt{n}\, 2^{-n})$. The time complexity of the greedy algorithm is given by the time complexity to sort n numbers, or $O(n \log n)$. Applied to the set $\{a_j\} = \{8, 7, 6, 5, 4\}$, the greedy heuristic misses the perfect solution and yields a partition $\{8, 5, 4\}\{7, 6\}$ with discrepancy 4.

The differencing method of Karmarkar and Karp [297], also called the KK heuristic, is another polynomial time approximation algorithm. The key idea of this algorithm is to reduce the size of the numbers. This is achieved by replacing the two largest numbers with the absolute value of their difference. This differencing operation is equivalent to committing the numbers to different subsets without actually fixing which subset each will go into. With each differencing

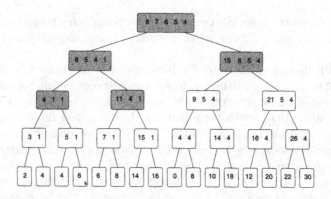

FIGURE 1 Search tree of the complete differencing algorithm. Left branch means "replace two largest numbers with their difference," right branch means "replace them with their sum." With appropriate pruning rules only the shaded nodes have to be visited to find the optimum solution.

operation the number of numbers decreases by one, and the final number is the discrepancy. Applied to $\{8, 7, 6, 5, 4\}$, the differencing method yields a discrepancy of 2 that results from the partition $\{8, 6\}$ $\{7, 5, 4\}$. Note that reconstructing the partition requires some additional bookkeeping that we did not mention in our brief description of the algorithm. Again the heuristic misses the perfect solution, but at least the outcome is better than the greedy result. Yakir [532] has proven that the differencing method applied to random real-valued $a_j \in [0, 1]$ produces mean discrepancies $n^{-\alpha \log n}$ with a constant $\alpha = 0.72$. Again this is much better than the greedy result, yet it is still far from the optimum. The time complexity of the differencing method is dominated by the complexity of selecting the two largest numbers. This is done most efficiently by sorting the initial list and keeping the order throughout all iterations, leaving us with a time complexity $O(n \log n)$.

Either one of these heuristics can be used as a base for an exact algorithm, analogous to the search tree methods analyzed in chapter 3. At each iteration, the greedy algorithm places a number in the subset with the smaller total sum so far. The only alternative is to place the number in the other subset. Exploring both alternatives means searching a binary tree that contains all 2^n possible partitions. In the KK heuristic, the corresponding alternative is to replace the two largest numbers by their sum rather than by their difference, equivalent to committing them to the same subet. Korf [341] calls the algorithms that explore both alternatives *complete greedy* and *complete differencing* algorithms. Figure 1 shows the search tree of the complete differencing method for our example $\{8, 7, 6, 5, 4\}$.

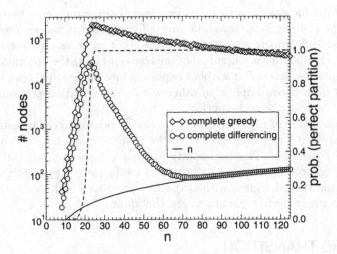

FIGURE 2 Number of nodes visited by the complete greedy and the complete differencing algorithms. Instances are sets (of cardinality n) of random 20-bit integers, each data point representing an average over 10^4 instances. The dashed line indicates the empirical probability that a given instance has a perfect solution.

Both complete algorithms have exponential time complexity in the worst case, but it is possible to prune parts of the search tree using simple rules. For the complete differencing method these rules are:

1. If fewer than 5 numbers are left, take the left branch (apply the differencing operation).
2. If the largest number in the set is larger than or equal to the sum of all the other numbers, stop branching: the best solution in this subtree is to place the largest number in one set, and all the other numbers in the other set.
3. If a perfect partition has been found, stop the process.

The first rule needs some thought, but it can in fact be proven that the KK heuristic always yields the optimum for $n \leq 4$. Similar pruning rules can be added to the complete greedy method. Figure 1 shows an example in which the rules chop off large parts of the search tree.

The question is how pruning affects the search in general and for large instances. Figure 2 shows the number of nodes visited by the complete greedy and the complete differencing algorithms while solving large instances of random 20-bit integers. For small values of n, the number of nodes grow exponentially with n, that is, the pruning shows only little effect on the performance. For systems beyond $n = 23$ the situation changes drastically: the number of nodes not only stops increasing with n, it decreases. Larger problems become easier to solve! The pruning gets more and more effective as n increases, especially for the complete differencing algorithm. For $n > 80$, it explores only n nodes of the search tree, that is, the very first leaf of the tree represents the optimum solution, and the algorithm "knows" it without exploring any further. This can only mean that rule 3 from above applies, in other words, the partition generated by the differencing heuristic must be perfect.

The appearance of perfect partitions is closely related to the transition in the average complexity, as can be seen from the probability that a random instance has a perfect partition. This probability jumps precisely at the point where the algorithmic complexity changes its behavior, see figure 2. Apparently, there is a computationally hard regime without perfect partitions and a computationally easy regime where perfect partitions are abundant.

3   PHASE TRANSITION

As we have seen in the preceding section, the average complexity of algorithms for the random NPP depends on the presence of perfect partitions. The probability of perfect solutions is a property of the ensemble of instances, and can be studied independently of algorithms. That is what we do in this section.

A partition $\mathcal{A}$ can be encoded by binary variables $s_j = \pm 1$: $s_j = +1$ if $j \in \mathcal{A}$, $s_j = -1$ otherwise. The cost function then reads $E = |D(s)|$ where

$$D = \sum_{j=1}^{n} a_j s_j \tag{2}$$

is the signed discrepancy. An alternative cost function is $H = D^2$ or

$$H = -\sum_{i,j} J_{ij} s_i s_j \qquad \text{with } J_{ij} = -a_i a_j . \tag{3}$$

H is the Hamiltonian of an infinite-range, antiferromagnetic spin glass, which has been studied by physicists [157, 185, 389] within the canonical framework of statistical mechanics. Here we follow another, very simple approach that has been used recently to analyze the multiprocessor scheduling problem [38].

The signed discrepancy D can be interpreted as the distance from the origin of a one-dimensional walk with steps to the left ($s_j = -1$) and to the right ($s_j = +1$), and with random stepsizes (a_j). The average number of walks that end at D reads

$$\Omega(D) = \sum_{\{s_j\}} \left\langle \delta \left(D - \sum_{j=1}^{n} a_j s_j \right) \right\rangle \tag{4}$$

where angular brackets denote averaging over the random numbers a. By the central limit theorem, for a fixed walk $\{s_j\}$ and large n, the sum $\sum_{j=1}^{n} a_j s_j$ is

Gaussian with mean

$$\langle D \rangle = \langle a \rangle \sum_j s_j \tag{5}$$

and variance

$$\langle D^2 \rangle - \langle D \rangle^2 = n(\langle a^2 \rangle - \langle a \rangle^2). \tag{6}$$

The sum over $\{s_j\}$ is basically an average over all trajectories of our random walk. For large n this average is dominated by trajectories with $\sum s_j = 0$, leading to $\langle D \rangle = 0$. Hence the probability density for ending the walk at distance D reads

$$p(D) = \frac{1}{\sqrt{2\pi n \langle a^2 \rangle}} \exp\left(-\frac{D^2}{2n \langle a^2 \rangle}\right). \tag{7}$$

Note that our walk involves only a sublattice of $\mathbb{Z}$ with lattice spacing 2: movements are confined to either the even or odd numbers, depending on whether $\sum a_j$ is even or odd. Hence the average number of walks ending at distance D, when D is of the same parity as $\sum a_j$, is given by

$$\Omega(D) = 2^n 2p(D) = \frac{2^{n+1}}{\sqrt{2\pi n \langle a^2 \rangle}} \exp\left(-\frac{D^2}{2n \langle a^2 \rangle}\right). \tag{8}$$

For the location of the phase transition we can concentrate on perfect partitions, that is, assume $D = 0$. If the a's are uniformly distributed κn-bit integers (for large n, without loss of generality $\sum a_j$ can be taken to be even),

$$\langle a^2 \rangle = \frac{1}{3} 2^{2\kappa n} \left(1 - O(2^{-\kappa n})\right) \tag{9}$$

and so

$$\log_2 \Omega(0) = n(\kappa_c - \kappa) \tag{10}$$

with

$$\kappa_c = 1 - \frac{\log_2 n}{2n} - \frac{1}{2n} \log_2 \left(\frac{\pi}{6}\right). \tag{11}$$

This is our phase transition: according to eq. (10) we have an exponential number of perfect partitions for $\kappa < \kappa_c$, and no perfect partition for $\kappa > \kappa_c$. Our derivation is a bit sloppy, of course, but the result agrees with the rigorous theory of Borgs et al. [71].

From eq. (10), we expect the entropy $S = \log_2 \Omega(0)$ of perfect partitions for fixed but large n to be a linear function of κ. In fact this can already be observed for rather small problem sizes in figure 3. Linear extrapolation of the simulation data for $\log_2 \Omega(0)$ gives numerical values for the transition points $\kappa_c(n)$. Again the numerical data for small systems agree very well with the predictions of the asymptotic theory (fig. 4). The strong finite size corrections of order $\log n/n$ lead to the curvature of $\kappa_c(n)$ and they are responsible for the incorrect value $\kappa_c = 0.96$ that Gent and Walsh extrapolated from their simulations [194].

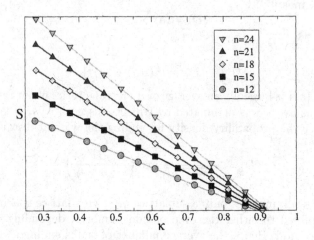

FIGURE 3 Entropy $S = \log_2 \Omega(0)$ of perfect partitions vs. κ. Theory (eq. (10)) compared to numerical enumerations (symbols).

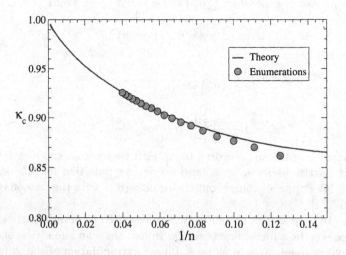

FIGURE 4 Numerical data for the transition points $\kappa_c(n)$ have been obtained by linear extrapolation of the data for $S = \log_2 \Omega(0)$ from figure 3. The solid line is eq. (11).

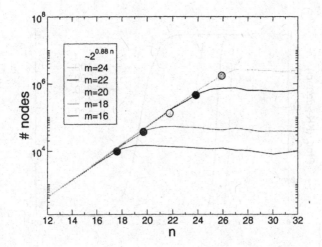

FIGURE 5 Partitioning m-bit numbers with the complete greedy algorithm: number of search nodes visited vs. n. The curves are averages over 10^4 random samples, and the symbols mark the values n_c given by eq. (12). The fitted curve $2^{0.88n}$ shows that pruning has almost no effect for $n < n_c$.

The phase transition at κ_c is a property of the instances. In contrast to the analysis of chapter 3, it is by no means clear how this transition affects the dynamical behavior of search algorithms. Note that even for $\kappa < \kappa_c$, the fraction of perfect partitions is exponentially small, and finding one of these is non-trivial.

In numerical experiments like the one shown in figure 2, the number $m = \kappa n$ of bits is usually fixed and n is varied. Then κ_c translates into a critical value $n_c = m/\kappa_c$ or

$$\frac{m}{n_c} = 1 - \frac{\log_2 n_c}{2n_c} - \frac{1}{2n_c} \log_2 \left(\frac{\pi}{6} \right). \tag{12}$$

For $m = 20$ this gives $n_c = 21.8$, in good agreement with the location of the hardest instances in figure 2. Figure 5 shows that the average time complexity of the complete greedy algorithm changes its dependence on n precisely at the values n_c given by eq. (12). It is well justified to classify the two regimes $\kappa < \kappa_c$ and $\kappa > \kappa_c$ as *easy* and *hard*.

4 EASY PHASE

The hallmark of the easy phase is the exponential number of perfect partitions, but the easy phase is not homogeneous: the number of perfect partitions increases with decreasing κ. This phenomenon might yield an interesting structure with

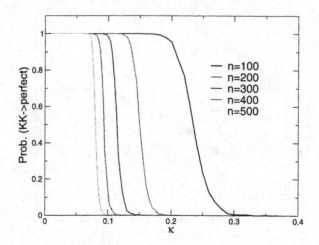

FIGURE 6   Probability of the Karmarkar-Karp differencing heuristic yielding a perfect partition.

regard to algorithms: the performance of an algorithm improves as one moves away from the phase boundary towards smaller values of κ. In fact, figure 2 indicates that complete differencing finds a perfect partition with its very first descent in the search tree if κ is small enough (n is large enough). Does this mean that the situation is reminiscent of satisfiability (see ch. 3) and the $\kappa < \kappa_c$ region disintegrates into two phases, one in which complete differencing hits a perfect solution on the first try and another one in which it needs to backtrack?

To test this hypothesis, we investigate the Karmarkar-Karp (KK) heuristic solution for the NPP. Recall that this solution is the first one generated by the complete differencing algorithm. Let D_{kk} be the discrepancy of the KK solution. Our hypothesis would then be: there is a value $0 \leq \kappa_{kk} \leq \kappa_c$ such that

$$\lim_{n \to \infty} \mathbf{Pr}(D_{kk} \leq 1) = \begin{cases} 1, & \kappa < \kappa_{kk}; \\ 0, & \kappa > \kappa_{kk}. \end{cases} \tag{13}$$

Figure 6 shows the result of a simulation of the KK algorithm. While there is a sharp transition at a value κ_{kk}, the value depends on n and seems to go to 0 as $n \to \infty$.

A simple argument explains why this happens. We know from the work of Yakir [532] that given real-valued input numbers $a_j \in [0, 1]$, the KK algorithm generates partitions with mean discrepancy $n^{-\alpha \log n}$ for some constant $\alpha > 0$. So if the numbers are integers with $m = \kappa n$ bits, we would expect that on average

$$D_{kk} = 2^{\kappa n} n^{-\alpha \log n}. \tag{14}$$

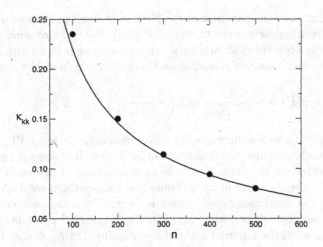

FIGURE 7   Threshold value below which Karmarkar-Karp differencing yields perfect solutions. Solid line denotes κ_{kk} from eq. (15), symbols show results of numerical simulations.

Therefore, $D_{kk} \leq 1$ as long as $\kappa \leq \kappa_{kk}(n)$ with

$$\kappa_{kk}(n) = \alpha \frac{(\log n)^2}{n \log 2}. \tag{15}$$

Figure 7 shows $\kappa_{kk}(n)$ compared with the results from simulations, where we have measured κ_{kk} as the value where the probability of generating a perfect partition is $1/2$. For α, we take the value 0.72 reported by Yakir for the average discrepancy of the KK solution.

Note that a similar argument suggests that even the greedy heuristic eventually yields perfect partitions for sufficiently small values of κ. At the value $m = 20$ used in figure 2, we expect the greedy heuristic to generate perfect partitions for $n > 839000$.

5   HARD PHASE

Figure 2 shows that in the easy phase, complete differencing outperforms complete greedy, and in view of the exponentially small fraction of perfect partitions, both algorithms outperform exhaustive search through all partitions. Figure 2 also indicates that complete greedy and complete differencing perform similarly to each other in the hard phase. In fact, in the hard phase neither is superior to blind random search, as we will see in this section.

A first hint as to the hardness of the NPP in its hard phase was provided by the *random cost approximation* to the NPP [391]. Here, the original problem is replaced by the problem of locating the minimum number in an unsorted list of 2^{n-1} "independent" random, positive numbers E drawn from the distribution

$$p(E) = \frac{2}{\sqrt{2\pi n \langle a^2 \rangle}} \exp\left(-\frac{E^2}{2n \langle a^2 \rangle}\right) \qquad (E \geq 0). \qquad (16)$$

This is exactly the probability density of discrepancies in the NPP, as seen in eq. (7), although of course those discrepancies in the NPP are not independent random variables. On the other hand, the approximation of independence allows us to calculate the statistics of the optimal and near-optimal solutions.

Consider the continuous case, where $\kappa \to \infty$. Then the cost values E are real, positive numbers drawn from eq. (16). There are 2^{n-1} possible cost values, corresponding to all the different ways of partitioning. Let E_k denote the $k+1$th lowest of these cost values, so that E_0 is the minimum (optimal) cost, followed by E_1 (lowest near-optimal) and so on. The probability density ρ_0 of E_0 can easily be calculated:

$$\rho_0(E_0) = 2^{n-1} p(E_0) \left(1 - \int_0^{E_0} p(E') dE'\right)^{2^{n-1}-1}. \qquad (17)$$

To get a finite right-hand side in the large n limit, E_0 must be small. Hence we may approximate

$$\rho_0(E_0) \simeq 2^{n-1} p(0) \left(1 - E_0 p(0)\right)^{2^{n-1}-1}$$
$$\simeq 2^{n-1} p(0) e^{-2^{n-1} p(0) E_0}.$$

This means that the rescaled minimum,

$$\varepsilon_0 = 2^{n-1} p(0) E_0 \qquad (18)$$

is an exponential random variable,

$$\rho_0(\varepsilon) = e^{-\varepsilon} \qquad (\varepsilon > 0). \qquad (19)$$

Along similar lines, one can show [187] that the density ρ_k of the $k+1$th lowest (kth near-optimal) rescaled number is

$$\rho_k(\varepsilon) = \frac{\varepsilon^k}{k!} e^{-\varepsilon} \qquad k = 1, 2, 3, \ldots . \qquad (20)$$

Figures 8 and 9 compare eqs. (19) and (20) with the probability density of the rescaled optimal and near-optimal discrepancies for the NPP in the $\kappa \to \infty$ limit of real-valued input numbers. The agreement is amazing, even for small values of n. In fact, eqs. (19) and (20) have been established as the asymptotic

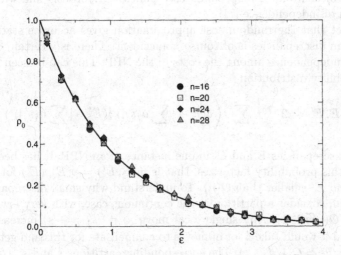

FIGURE 8 Probability density of the rescaled optimum discrepancy in the hard phase. Symbols: numerical simulations. Solid line: prediction by the random cost approximation.

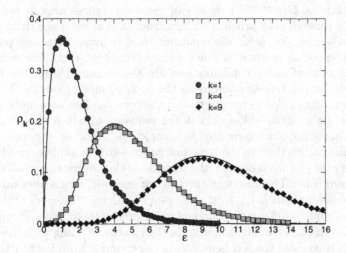

FIGURE 9 Probability densities of the kth best partition in the hard phase. Symbols: numerical simulations for $n = 24$. Solid lines: predictions by the random cost approximation.

probability measure for the optimum discrepancies—rigorously and without the assumption of independence [71].

The fact that the random cost approximation gives accurate statistics for the optimum discrepancies is of course no accident. There is a certain degree of statistical independence among the costs in the NPP. This can be seen from the joint probability distribution

$$p(E, E') = 2^{-2n} \sum_{\{s_j, s_j'\}} \left\langle \delta(E - |\sum_j a_j s_j|)\, \delta(E' - |\sum_j a_j s_j'|) \right\rangle \qquad (21)$$

of finding discrepancies E and E' in one instance of an NPP. It has been shown [390] that this probability factorizes, that is, $p(E, E') = p(E)p(E')$ for discrepancies E and E' smaller than $O(n)$. To understand why small discrepancies are uncorrelated, consider a partition in the continuous case, with very low discrepancy $E = O(\sqrt{n}\,2^{-n})$. Any single local move $s_j \mapsto s_j' = -s_j$ increases E by $O(n^{-1})$, and it would take a lot of moves to compensate for this and get another discrepancy $E' = O(\sqrt{n}\,2^{-n})$. The corresponding partitions s and s' would then have vanishingly small overlap, which leads to the factorization of $p(E, E')$.

The random cost problem is an algorithmic nightmare. No smart heuristic can be quicker than exhaustive search. This is the reason why there are no good heuristics in the hard phase of the NPP, and why complete algorithms cannot really take advantage of pruning rules. But there are differences in the quality of heuristic solutions: recall the result from greedy, $O(n^{-1})$, and from the KK heuristic, $O(n^{-\alpha \log n})$. How can these differences arise if the NPP is essentially a random cost problem? The answer is that both algorithms exploit correlations among the *large* discrepancies to stay away from bad partitions, and the differencing method is much more efficient at this. The correlations between large discrepancy configurations are also responsible for the fact that the complete barrier tree characterizing the energy landscape of the NPP looks different from the complete barrier tree of the pure random cost problem [483].

Complete algorithms differ only in the sequence in which they explore the partitions. In the sequence generated by complete differencing, the true optimum might appear earlier than in the sequence generated by complete greedy. But if the random cost picture is correct, the location of the optimum is random in any prescribed sequence. This has been checked, for example, for another smart algorithm proposed by Korf [341]. Korf suggested reordering the leaves of the search tree of the complete differencing method according to the number of *right turns* (violations of the differencing heuristic) in their paths, starting with those leaves that deviate least from the KK heuristic. In our example from figure 1 the leaves would be visited in the sequence $(2, 4, 4, 6, 0, 6, 8, 14, 8, 10, 12, 16, 18, 20, 22, 30)$, and in fact the perfect solution would appear earlier than in the order shown in figure 1. Numerical simulation, however, revealed that in the hard phase the position of the optimum in the sequence generated by this method is completely random—as predicted by the random cost problem [390].

· Apparently, there is no way to overcome the random cost nature of the NPP in the hard phase. When the NPP is hard, it's very hard.

6 CONCLUSIONS

We have seen that random NPP has a phase transition in average complexity, and that this phase transition goes hand in hand with a transition in probability of perfect solutions. The control parameter κ of both transitions is the ratio m of the number of bits in the input variables to the number n of variables, and $\kappa_c = 1 - \log_2(n)/2n + O(n^{-1})$ is the critical value that separates the hard $(\kappa > \kappa_c)$ from the easy $(\kappa < \kappa_c)$ phase. Much more can be said about the phase transition, notably concerning the width of the transition window and the probability of perfect solutions inside that window. Another proven fact is the uniqueness of the solution in the hard phase. For all this (and much more), the reader is referred to the paper of Borgs, Chayes, and Pittel [71]. Their work answers most of the open questions on random NPP that are not related to algorithms. The major open problem is putting the random cost approximation on rigorous grounds and clarifying its relevance for algorithms. From a practical point of view it would be very nice to have a polynomial time algorithm that yields better results than the differencing method. After all, there is much room between $O(n^{-\alpha \log n})$ and $O(\sqrt{n}\, 2^{-n})$.

The NPP as shown here can be generalized and modified in various directions. An obvious generalization is to partition the numbers into $q \geq 2$ subsets. This is called the multiprocessor scheduling problem, and in physics parlance this corresponds to a Potts spin glass or to a walk with random stepsizes in $q - 1$ dimensions. The latter approach has been used to analyze an "easy-hard" phase transition in multiprocessor scheduling [38].

Another variant is the constrained NPP where the cardinality of the subsets is fixed. This is necessary for problems such as choosing up sides in a ball game [237], where both teams need to have the same number of players. The cardinality difference of the subsets is a control parameter that triggers another phase transition in computational complexity, giving rise to a two-dimensional phase diagram [72].

ACKNOWLEDGMENTS

Discussions with Heiko Bauke are gratefully acknowledged. Part of the numerical simulations have been performed on *Tina* [500] a 156-CPU Beowulf cluster built in-house at Otto-von-Guericke-Universität, Magdeburg.

CHAPTER 6

Ground States, Energy Landscape, and Low-Temperature Dynamics of $\pm J$ Spin Glasses

Sigismund Kobe
Jarek Krawczyk

1 INTRODUCTION

The previous three chapters have focused on the analysis of computational problems using methods from statistical physics. This chapter largely takes the reverse approach. We turn to a problem from the physics literature, the spin glass, and use the branch-and-bound method from combinatorial optimization to analyze its energy landscape. The spin glass model is a prototype that combines questions of computational complexity from the mathematical point of view and of glassy behavior from the physical one. In general, the problem of finding the ground state, or minimal energy configuration, of such model systems belongs to the class of NP-hard tasks.

The spin glass is defined using the language of the Ising model, the fundamental description of magnetism at the level of statistical mechanics. The Ising model contains a set of n spins, or binary variables s_i, each of which can take on the value up $(s_i = 1)$ or $down$ $(s_i = -1)$. Finding the ground state means finding the spin variable values minimizing the Ising Hamiltonian energy (cost)

Computational Complexity and Statistical Physics, edited by
Allon G. Percus, Gabriel Istrate, and Cristopher Moore, Oxford University Press.

function, written in general as

$$E = - \sum_{i<j}^{n} J_{ij}\, s_i\, s_j \tag{1}$$

for given interaction strengths J_{ij}. This is a problem of nonlinear discrete optimization. When J_{ij} is positive, interactions are called *ferromagnetic*. In this case, there is a trivial solution: all spins are aligned, meaning they have identical signs. When J_{ij} is negative, interactions are called *antiferromagnetic*. Physically, the spins are often taken to lie on a lattice. For a square or cubic lattice with negative J_{ij} for neighboring pairs of spins and $J_{ij} = 0$ otherwise, the ground state is clearly the configuration where adjacent spins have opposite signs.

If all nonzero interaction strengths J_{ij} are equal, the system is said to be *ordered*. For ordered systems with antiferromagnetic interactions between nearest neighbors, but where neighbors of a given spin are also neighbors of each other, *frustration* prevents certain interactions from being "satisfied." An example is the triangular lattice: to quote the early work of Wannier, "antiferromagnetism does not fit into the triangular pattern" [517]. While the solution to the optimization problem is straightforward, one third of all interactions lead to conflicts that increase the ground-state energy. The structural sensitivity of antiferromagnetic order has been discussed by Sato and Kikuchi [453] for the face-centered cubic lattice. Other ordered systems have been considered by Liebmann [361].

The problem becomes more complex when *disorder* arises, and interaction strengths are not equal. Often, such systems can only be solved by numerical methods. The time complexity of an algorithm is defined by the growth of the solution time as a function of input size [230]. For many disordered spin models, it can be shown that finding ground states is NP-hard [31, 214], and so the time complexity likely grows faster than any polynomial. In order to address this, Kobe and Handrich [335] introduced a "misfit" parameter characterizing the degree of frustration, and used it to find exact ground states in a two-dimensional system of $n = 23$ hard disks (an amorphous Ising model) with distance-dependent antiferromagnetic interactions. Further exact results for two-dimensional ($n = 40$) and three-dimensional systems ($n = 30$) were obtained by Kobe [334] and Kobe and Hartwig [336] using the branch-and-bound method of combinatorial optimization [137, 354, 363].

Another concept for studying systems with disorder and competing interactions was introduced by Toulouse [502]. He analyzed the frustration effect in a two-dimensional lattice model with a random distribution of ferromagnetic and antiferromagnetic nearest-neighbor interactions J_{ij} of equal strength, known as the Edwards-Anderson $\pm J$ model. The system may be described by plaquettes representing elementary lattice regions, such as a unit cell on a square lattice. The quantity $\Phi = \prod_c J_{ij}$, taken over the contour c forming the perimeter of the plaquette, measures frustration: $\Phi = -1$ if the plaquette is frustrated, $\Phi = 1$ if it is not. The exact ground state is then associated directly with a matching [139] of frustrated plaquettes that minimizes the sum of lattice distances between matched pairs. The multiplicity of ground states, or degeneracy, comes from the total number of ways to create such a minimal matching. This approach only works for two-dimensional systems, but it is an efficient one, since minimal matching can be solved to optimality in polynomial time. In the years following Toulouse's work, the matching method of optimization was used widely [32, 52].

This chapter is organized as follows. In section 2, we introduce the branch-and-bound algorithm as a prototype for a numerical procedure of nonlinear discrete optimization. Then, in section 3, we describe the Edwards-Anderson $\pm J$ spin glass model and give an overview of numerical results for the ground-state energy and entropy. In section 4 the low-energy landscape of finite three-dimensional $\pm J$ spin glasses (consisting of clusters and valleys) is analyzed and visualized. The correlation with the real-space picture shows the existence of rigid spin domains in the ground state. We discuss dynamical consequences in section 5, focusing on the transition from one ground-state cluster to another by way of a saddle cluster. It can be shown that internal structure contributes to the slowing of relaxation processes. Finally, we point out the progress and challenges of complexity theory for a better microscopic understanding of glassy behavior.

2   BRANCH-AND-BOUND

The ground state of the Ising model with n spins $s_i = \pm 1$ is the spin configuration with energy

$$E_0 = \min_{s_i = \pm 1} \left(-\sum_{i<j}^{n} J_{ij}\, s_i\, s_j \right). \tag{2}$$

For interactions J_{ij} of arbitrary sign and magnitude, finding the exact ground state is an NP-hard problem. Since the number of states increases with 2^n, only for very small n can eq. (2) be solved by complete enumeration.

Complete algorithms for combinatorial optimization problems aim to reduce the numerical effort while still giving an exact solution. The general principle can be demonstrated for the branch-and-bound algorithm. The strategy of branch-and-bound is to exclude as many states with high energy values as possible, in an early stage of calculation [336]. Let us consider a small cluster with $n = 8$ spins and J_{ij} values of differing strengths. To simplify matters and without loss of generality, we take the case where there are only antiferromagnetic interactions, representing an amorphous antiferromagnetic cluster with dilution. The upper triangle of the interaction matrix $\mathbf{J} = (J_{ij})$ is given by

$$\mathbf{J} = \begin{pmatrix} 0 & -5 & -2 & -5 & -6 & -1 & 0 & 0 \\ & 0 & -10 & -4 & 0 & -2 & -1 & 0 \\ & & 0 & 0 & 0 & -3 & 0 & -1 \\ & & & 0 & -3 & -5 & -7 & -4 \\ & & & & 0 & -4 & -5 & -8 \\ & & & & & 0 & 0 & -1 \\ & & & & & & 0 & 0 \\ & & & & & & & 0 \end{pmatrix}. \tag{3}$$

In figure 1, a tree is constructed by successively fixing spin values. At the branching depth $l = 1$, spin number 1 is set to the positive direction $(+)$. At depth $l = 2$ the spin number 2 is fixed, and so on. At each branching node a configuration $(s_1, ..., s_l)$ and an energy value E_l is shown. For $l = 1$ the starting energy $E_1 = E_{id}$ is chosen, where $E_{id} = -\sum_{i<j} |J_{ij}|$ is a lower bound on the ground-state energy E_0 in eq. (2), representing the situation where all interactions are satisfied and no conflict is present. The other values E_l for $1 < l \leq n$ can be obtained by the following rule:

$$E_l = E_{l-1} + 2 \sum_{k(\|l)}^{l-1} |J_{kl}|. \tag{4}$$

In the example of eq. (3), where all interactions are antiferromagnetic, $k(\|l)$ denotes those k for which spin k has already been fixed in the same direction as the spin l. More generally, when both positive and negative J_{ij} values are present, the sum contains those contributions that arise due to conflicts of spin l with all spins fixed earlier. In figure 1 the values of the summation term in eq. (4) are given at the branching lines. From eq. (4) it follows that

$$E_l \geq E_{l-1}. \tag{5}$$

It is easy to recognize that all configurations of the system (modulo a global spin flip) and their associated energies can be found at the end of the fully branched tree, at $l = n$. The goal of the branch-and-bound strategy is to prune some branches. In order to do this, a heuristic is used to generate an approximate solution, that is, the greedyindexbranch-and-bound algorithm procedure of steepest descent shown in figure 1 where at each step the new contribution to the sum in eq. (4) is minimized. In our example, the energy of the resulting configuration is -47. This value is used as E_{bound}, and signals that branching can stop at any node where $E_l > E_{bound}$. From eq. (5) it is certain that all branches pruned in this way can lead only to states with $E_n \geq E_{bound}$, and so none of them can yield a solution to eq. (2). Therefore, in place of a complete enumeration of all states, the pruned tree in figure 1 can be used to search for

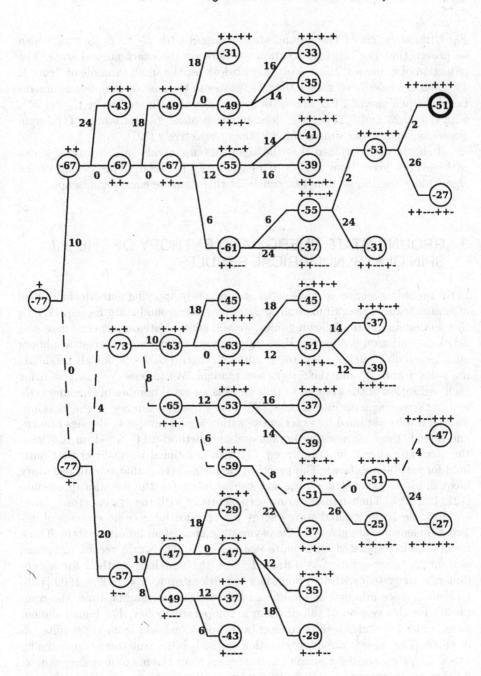

FIGURE 1   Branch-and-bound tree for a cluster with $n = 8$ spins given by the interaction matrix **J** in eq. (3); $E_{id} = -77$, $E_{bound} = -47$ obtained by steepest descent (dashed line). The exact ground state with the energy $E_0 = -51$ is marked in bold.

E_0. Ultimately, either the ground state is found with $E_0 < E_{bound}$, or it can be proven that the heuristic solution was already the exact ground state. The reduction of numerical effort is already obvious for the small example of figure 1: 49 nodes are calculated rather than 128 states in the case of complete enumeration. The increase of CPU time with system size is estimated to be $t_{calc} = 2^{\alpha n}$, with $\alpha = 0.23$ and 0.27 for the determination of all ground states of $\pm J$ spin glasses on square and simple cubic lattices respectively [327].

It should be mentioned that the algorithm also yields "all" low-lying states with energies lower than E_{bound}, if $E_{bound} > E_0$ is chosen. This variant of the algorithm is used in section 4 to construct the complete energy landscape.

3   GROUND-STATE ENERGY AND ENTROPY OF THE $\pm J$ SPIN GLASS: NUMERICAL RESULTS

In the preceding section we have given an example of applying numerical methods of nonlinear discrete optimization to determine the ground state E_0 (eq. (2)). In this section and in the following ones, we will concentrate on a special case, the Edwards-Anderson $\pm J$ model. Here, interactions are between nearest neighbors on a hypercubic lattice, they are of equal strength ($|J_{ij}| = J$ for all neighboring spins i and j), and their signs are random. We impose $\sum_{i<j}^{n} J_{ij} = 0$ for each realization of the system, so that there is an equal number of ferromagnetic and antiferromagnetic interactions. We first present a survey of the best numerical results obtained by exact optimization algorithms [484]. Besides branch-and-bound, these include the branch-and-cut method [214] based on rewriting the quadratic energy function in eq. (2) with additional inequalities that must hold for feasible solutions. The practical challenge here is that not all necessary inequalities are known *a priori*, and can arise during the iteration procedure [121, 122, 230]. Their number grows exponentially with the system size.

In table 1, the ground-state energy per spin for hypercubic systems of different dimensions are given, in the asymptotic limit of an infinite system. These results are extrapolated from finite-size numerics. The world record in system size for an exact solution is obtained using the matching method for a two-dimensional system with free boundary conditions up to $n = 1800 \times 1800$ [422]. Of course, since minimal matching can be solved in polynomial time, the complexity for this version of the problem is comparatively low. For higher dimensions, table 1 includes results coming both from exact and from approximation methods. The accuracy of approximation methods is in many cases supported by exact values obtained for smaller system sizes than the maximum shown here. As they are incomplete methods, it is generally impossible to supply any further evidence for their exactness [230]. However, the inclusion of such methods with a "high level of reliability" [262] provides the possibility of considering systems of larger size than would be otherwise available, and thus to extrapolate more convincingly to infinite lattices. Much less is known about the exact ground-state energy for other than hypercubic lattices.

TABLE 1   Ground-state energy per spin e_0 and entropy per spin s_0 of the hypercubic $\pm J$ spin glass in d dimensions. Results for infinite systems are extrapolated from system sizes up to $n = L_{max}^d$. Parenthetical numbers denote error bar in final digit(s).

d	method	L_{max}	e_0	s_0	Ref.
2	matching*	1800	$-1.40193(2)$		Palmer and Adler [422]
2	branch-and-cut	50	$-1.4015(8)$		De Simone et al. [122]
2	branch-and-bound	8	$-1.40(6)$	0.077(21)	Klotz [327]
2	genetic cluster appr.	40	$-1.4015(3)$		Hartmann [232]
2	genetic cluster appr.	40		0.078(5)	Hartmann [228]
2	transfer matrix$^\times$	11	$-1.4024(12)$	0.0701(5)	Cheung and McMillan [92]
2	expansion-fall-invasion-spring	10	-1.40169		Vogel et al. [513]
2	genetic	20	$-1.401(1)$		Gropengiesser [211]
2	flat histogram sampling	32	$-1.4007(85)$	0.0709(6)	Zhan et al. [537]
3	branch-and-bound	4	$-1.778(14)$	0.054(16)	Klotz [327]
3	extremal optimization	12	$-1.7865(3)$		Boettcher and Percus [61]
3	genetic	10	$-1.787(3)$		Gropengiesser [211]
3	genetic cluster appr.	8		0.051(3)	Hartmann [228]
3	genetic cluster appr.	14	$-1.7876(3)$		Hartmann and Rieger [230]
3	multicanonical sampling	12		0.04412(46)	Berg et al. [47]
4	genetic cluster appr.	7	$-2.095(1)$		Hartmann and Rieger [230]
4	genetic cluster appr.	6		0.027(5)	Hartmann [228]
4	extremal optimization	7	$-2.093(1)$		Boettcher and Percus [61]
5	extremal optimization$^+$	4	-2.3511		Boettcher [57]

* free boundary conditions
$^\times$ rectangular lattice ($L \times W$) with $L_{max} = 11$ (periodic boundary conditions) and $W_{max} = 10^4 \cdots 10^5$ (free boundary conditions)
$^+$ without extrapolation

A shortcoming of presenting the ground-state energy per spin is that the value is not comparable across different dimensions, lattice types, etc. For that reason, a universal measure of frustration has been introduced by the *misfit* parameter

$$\mu_0 = \frac{1}{2}\left(1 + \frac{E_0}{\sum_{i<j}|J_{ij}|}\right),\tag{6}$$

TABLE 2 Misfit parameter μ_0 of the $\pm J$ spin glass in d dimensions. Estimate for infinite system, extrapolated from numerics.

lattice	d	μ_0	E_0 from
honeycomb	2	0.09	Lebrecht and Vogel [356]
square	2	0.150	Table 1
triangular	2	0.22	Vogel et al. [511]
simple cubic	3	0.202	Table 1
hypercubic	4	0.24	Boettcher and Percus [61]
hypercubic	5	0.26	Boettcher [57]

representing the mean fraction of unsatisfied bonds in the ground state [337]. For the $\pm J$ spin glass, μ_0 values from numerical simulations are compiled in table 2. They may be compared with $\mu_0 = 1/3$ for the antiferromagnetic triangular or face-centered cubic lattice, and $\mu_0 = 1/2$ for fully frustrated hypercubic and face-centered cubic lattices in the limiting case of infinite dimensions [16, 120]. Moreover, it can be seen that the $\pm J$ spin glass is less frustrated on the honeycomb lattice, and more frustrated on the triangular lattice, than on the square one.

4 ENERGY LANDSCAPE

An advantage of the branch-and-bound algorithm is that it is very easy to implement a variant allowing the calculation of all near-optimal solutions. For these purposes, a certain $E_{\text{bound}} > E_0$ has to be chosen and fixed during the calculation. All states of the system with energy $E_i < E_{\text{bound}}$ can then be found. (Note that here, the subscript i denotes an excited state of the system, that is, with higher energy than the ground state, rather than an intermediate level of branch-and-bound as in section 2.) Through subsequent analysis of these states with respect to their neighborhood structure, the complete low-energy landscape in the high-dimensional configuration space can be obtained. The situation in this space is analagous to that of "fog in the mountains" in a real landscape: all areas below the upper limit of the fog are covered.

Let us first investigate the low-energy landscape of a three-dimensional system of size $n = 4 \times 4 \times 4$, with periodic boundary conditions. All $N = 1635796$ configurations up to the third excitation (fourth-lowest energy state) were calculated using branch-and-bound [231]. The configurations were then studied with regard to their one-spin neighborhood. Two configurations that differ in the orientation of only one spin are considered neighbors. Consequently, each of the N configurations can have at most n neighbors belonging to the set of N. The

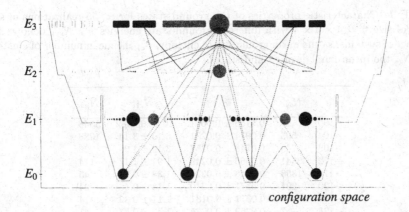

configuration space

FIGURE 2   Schematic picture of the exact low-energy landscape up to the third excitation for one system of size $n = 4 \times 4 \times 4$. Clusters are marked by circles of sizes proportional to the number of configurations in the cluster: the two ground-state clusters on the left, for instance, consist of 12 and 18 configurations. (Note that the scale is different for different energy levels, so the largest clusters in the first, second, and third excitations contain 819, 82,960, and 1,503,690 configurations, respectively.) Lines denote single spin-flip connections. All clusters connected to the same neighborhood structure are pooled in a box.

low-energy landscape is formed by all states of energy E_k, with $k \le 3$. Due to the discreteness of the coupling constants J_{ij}, the energy values are degenerate. E_0 is the ground-state energy and $E_k = E_0 + 4k$ are the excitation energies.

An energy landscape is thus formed, consisting of clusters, valleys and saddles [328, 329, 330]. A set of configurations is called a *cluster* if a *chain* connecting them exists. The chain is built up by neighboring configurations with the same energy. The landscape is symmetric, due to eq. (2). Two clusters of different energies are "connected" whenever at least one configuration of the first cluster is a neighbor of one configuration of the second cluster. A schematic picture of this low-energy landscape is illustrated in figure 2. Finally, *valleys* can be associated with ground-state clusters. A valley consists of clusters that have connections to one single ground-state cluster. Different valleys are connected by *saddle* clusters, which mediate the transition over energy barriers.

Note that there is a broad distribution of realizations of the $\pm J$ systems. The ground-state energy of 8555 systems of the size $n = 4 \times 4 \times 4$ varies between $E_0 = -100$ and -128. The respective values for the mean ground-state entropy $\overline{s}_0$, the number of clusters $\overline{N}_{cl}$, and the number of ground states $\overline{N}_{gs}$, are given in table 3.

In table 4, corresponding values characterizing the structure of the first excitations of the same set of realizations are given. Here, the following average

TABLE 3   Characteristic properties of the ground states for 8,555 realizations of systems of size $n = 4 \times 4 \times 4$ with different ground-state energies E_0. N_{sys} denotes the number of systems, $\bar{s}_0$ the mean ground-state entropy, $\overline{N}_{cl}$ the mean number of clusters, and $\overline{N}_{gs}$ the mean number of ground states.

E_0	N_{sys}	$\bar{s}_0$	$\overline{N}_{cl}$	$\overline{N}_{gs}$
−100	5	0.1153 ± 0.0091	10.20 ± 2.82	3848
−104	505	0.0974 ± 0.0231	6.19 ± 3.14	1088
−108	2769	0.0748 ± 0.0257	3.19 ± 1.99	326
−112	3541	0.0566 ± 0.0249	1.91 ± 1.17	114
−116	1358	0.0448 ± 0.0221	1.38 ± 0.74	45
−120	291	0.0371 ± 0.0210	1.18 ± 0.46	24
−124	52	0.0311 ± 0.0181	1.11 ± 0.32	14
−128	7	0.0259 ± 0.0235	1.33 ± 0.57	41
	8555	0.0623 ± 0.0285	2.47 ± 1.98	228

values are specified: $\overline{N}_1$ is the mean number of states in the first excitation: of these, $\overline{N}_s$ belong to saddle clusters and $\overline{N}_m$ are metastable states without direct connections to one of the ground states. $\overline{N}_{cl1}$ is the mean number of clusters: of these, $\overline{N}_{cls}$ are saddle clusters and $\overline{N}_{clm}$ are metastable clusters. It can be seen that systems with higher ground-state energies (i.e., higher frustration) also possess more complex energy landscapes with larger entropies and many clusters.

The relation between the energy landscape in configuration space and the spin structure in real space is demonstrated in figure 3. Here an example with $n = 6 \times 6 \times 6$ spins is shown. The ground states can be grouped into four clusters, similar to the situation in figure 2. Two clusters contain 5632 states and two clusters contain 1280 states. The degeneracy within the clusters is caused by the existence of *free spins* that feel no internal field and can thus be flipped without energy input. Let us first consider the two clusters that remain when one ignores the *mirror states* arising from a global spin flip. All spins in real space that are free in either of these clusters are marked by empty circles. The remaining spins are divided into two groups, marked by full circles and shaded triangles. In each of these groups the relative orientation of any given spin is fixed with respect to all others in the group. Due to this internal rigidity, the two groups are called *spin domains* [230]. When one includes the mirror states, there are four different orientations of the two spin domains, resulting in the four ground-state clusters in configuration space, see also Hed et al. [238]. Many of the free spins are situated physically between the spin domains. Thus, the low-energy excitations in figure 2 can be understood as a successive softening of the spin domains starting from the boundary region of free spins between them. Consequently, a transition over

TABLE 4 Characteristic properties of the first excitations for 8,555 realizations of systems of size $n = 4 \times 4 \times 4$ with different ground-state energies E_0. $\overline{N}_1$ denotes the mean number of first excited states, $\overline{N}_{cl1}$ the mean number of clusters, $\overline{N}_s$ the mean number of saddle states, $\overline{N}_{cls}$ the mean number of saddle clusters, $\overline{N}_m$ the mean number of metastable states, and $\overline{N}_{clm}$ the mean number of metastable clusters.

E_0	$\overline{N}_1$	$\overline{N}_{cl1}$	$\overline{N}_s$	$\overline{N}_{cls}$	$\overline{N}_m$	$\overline{N}_{clm}$
-100	384825	61.00 ± 8.51	191598	0.70 ± 0.45	351	7.20 ± 3.56
-104	102879	47.64 ± 15.76	50016	0.98 ± 0.68	543	6.31 ± 3.58
-108	25469	33.48 ± 14.37	11079	0.99 ± 0.90	375	4.59 ± 2.73
-112	6653	23.02 ± 10.81	2199	0.54 ± 0.77	151	2.57 ± 1.98
-116	1895	17.01 ± 7.76	375	0.30 ± 0.62	42	1.25 ± 1.28
-120	775	14.18 ± 5.07	81	0.16 ± 0.41	14	0.59 ± 0.94
-124	395	12.81 ± 4.11	22	0.15 ± 0.44	2	0.14 ± 0.36
-128	322	13.42 ± 4.75	13	0.14 ± 0.38	0.43	0.14 ± 0.37
	17634	26.5 ± 14.4	7326	0.68 ± 0.83	225	3.14 ± 2.73

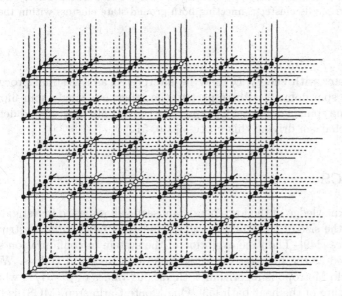

FIGURE 3 Two spin domains of a $\pm J$ spin glass with $n = 6 \times 6 \times 6$, marked by full circles and shaded triangles. All spins that are free in either of the ground-state clusters are marked by empty circles.

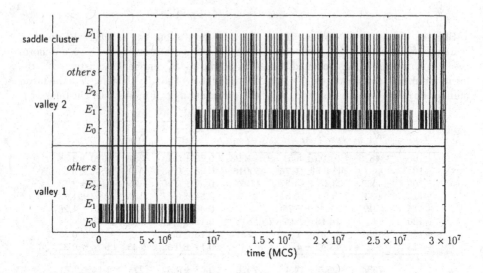

FIGURE 4   An individual Monte Carlo run through the landscape vs. time, at inverse temperature $\beta = 2.5$ for one system of size $n = 4 \times 4 \times 4$ (fig. 2). The process starts from an arbitrary state within the ground-state cluster on the left in figure 2. The vertical axis shows different energies belonging to valleys 1 and 2, respectively, and the energy E_1 of the saddle cluster connecting both ground-state clusters within the first excitation.

the saddle cluster with energy E_1 may be interpreted as a gradual process of reversal of one spin domain with respect to the other, one single spin flip at a time. By flipping spins, additional free spins are continually created and deleted: that is the mechanism driving this process [230, 512].

5   DYNAMICS

The complete knowledge of the low-energy landscape allows us to investigate the influence that the size of clusters and valleys and their neighborhood structure has on dynamics [349]. The time evolution of the system in configuration space can be described as the progressive exploration of clusters and valleys. We use the Monte Carlo Metropolis algorithm with various values of $\beta = 1/\tau$, where τ is the temperature of the heat bath [53]. One Monte Carlo step (MCS) is taken as the time unit. An individual run through the landscape is shown in figure 4. We start from an arbitrary state in the leftmost ground-state cluster of figure 2.

At first, the system walks in the valley, sometimes touching the saddle cluster in the first excitation. After an escape time t_{esc} of the order of 10^7 MCS, the system leaves the first valley and goes through the saddle cluster to the second

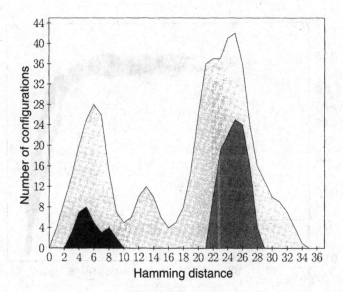

FIGURE 5 The transition profile of the saddle cluster with energy E_1 in figure 2 illustrated by the number of configurations vs. Hamming distance from a reference state (see text). The shaded area marks all configuration in the saddle cluster. States having connections with valley 1 (dark) and 2 (middle) are shown in black and grey respectively.

one. This transition is governed by the internal structure of the saddle cluster, shown as its transition profile in figure 5. First, all pairs of configurations are checked to find the largest Hamming distance h_d (the number of spin values differing between the two configurations). Then, using one of these states as the reference state, the h_d values of all configurations in the saddle cluster with respect to the reference state are calculated. Two sets of states are marked, one consisting of states connected by a single spin flip with the first valley and the other with the second valley. These sets denote the input and the output areas for a transition from one valley to the other. Considering a transition as a walk between these sets, it is clearly slowed down by the small numbers of states in between.

Quantitatively, the random walk can be described by the spin correlation function

$$q(t) = \frac{1}{n} \left\langle \sum_{i=1}^{n} s_i^G(0) s_i(t) \right\rangle, \tag{7}$$

where $s_i^G(0)$ is the ith spin of the starting configuration chosen arbitrarily from the ground states of valley 1 or 2. The brackets denote the average of 100 runs starting from the same state (fig. 6).

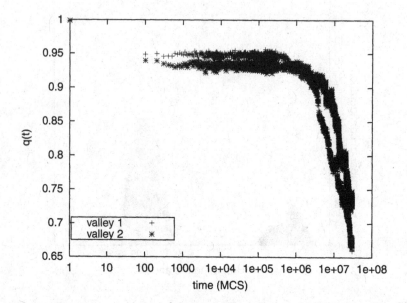

FIGURE 6 The spin correlation function vs. time for the system of size $n = 4 \times 4 \times 4$ (fig. 2). The starting configuration is selected from the set of ground states of valley 1 and 2. The Monte Carlo process is run at inverse temperature $\beta = 2.5$.

The spin correlation function $q(t)$ vs. time is characterized by a plateau with the value q_{pl} followed by a temperature-dependent decay. It should be noted that such a plateau is typical for supercooled liquids, where the dynamical process is called α-relaxation. To examine the correlation between the structure of the landscape and the dynamics, we compare q_{pl} with the size of the valley, keeping in mind that the spin correlation within the valley can be calculated using the mean Hamming distance $\overline{h}_d$ of all pairs of states by

$$q_{pl}^{(Ham)} = 1 - 2\overline{h}_d/n. \tag{8}$$

We find an agreement between q_{pl} and $q_{pl}^{(Ham)}$ (table 5), where the average in eq. (8) approximated by the average over all states in the corresponding ground-state clusters.

The plateau thus reflects the dynamics within the valley. The subsequent decay of $q(t)$ shows the escape from the valley. The escape time t_{esc} depends on the temperature and can be fitted by $t_{esc} \sim exp(\beta \, \Delta E_{eff})$. We found $\Delta E_{eff} = 4.24 \pm 0.08$ for valley number 1 and $\Delta E_{eff} = 4.46 \pm 0.09$ for valley number 2. The effective energy barrier is larger than the real one, which is $\Delta E = E_1 - E_0 = 4$ in our example. Moreover, ΔE_{eff} is larger for valley 2 than for 1. This reflects the fact that the system can leave the saddle cluster more easily in the direction of 2, as there are more exit connections (see fig. 5).

6 SUMMARY

Due to the physical complexity of the spin glass problem, advanced methods of combinatorial optimization are required. In recent years, powerful numerical algorithms have become available, enabling us to study model systems of small and moderate sizes from the microscopic point of view. For example, it is possible to determine the internal structure of an energy landscape in a high-dimensional configuration space. Understanding the slow dynamics of glassy systems is a current challenge of solid state physics. Spin glasses are good candidates for modeling glassy behavior.

In this chapter, we have discussed the $\pm J$ spin glass model, and shown the correlation between the microscopic structure of the energy landscape and the dynamical behavior. The characteristic shape of the correlation function may be attributed to the restricted connectivity of clusters and valleys in the energy landscape and to their internal profiles. Finding better algorithms for NP-hard problems remains an ongoing challenge. Our hope is that with the development of improved algorithms, the restriction to small system sizes can be eased, and the ground-state behavior of $\pm J$ spin glasses can be analyzed with improved confidence [534].

ACKNOWLEDGMENTS

The authors wish to thank A. Heuer, S. Boettcher, and A. K. Hartmann for valuable discussions. Thanks to A. K. Hartmann also for permission to use his data concerning the ground state of a three-dimensional system with $n = 6 \times 6 \times 6$. This work has been supported by Graduiertenkolleg "Struktur- und Korrelationseffekte in Festkörpern."

TABLE 5 The values of q_{pl} obtained from simulations (fig. 6) and calculation (eq. (8))

	Figure 6	Equation (8)
q_{pl} (1)	0.947 ± 0.004	0.936
q_{pl} (2)	0.932 ± 0.004	0.924
Δq_{pl}	0.015 ± 0.004	0.012

Part 3: Identifying the Threshold

CHAPTER 7

The Satisfiability Threshold Conjecture:
Techniques Behind Upper Bound
Improvements

Lefteris M. Kirousis
Yannis C. Stamatiou
Michele Zito

1 INTRODUCTION

One of the most challenging problems in probability and complexity theory is
to establish and determine the *satisfiability threshold,* or phase transition, for
random k-SAT instances: Boolean formulas consisting of clauses with exactly k
literals. As the previous part of the volume has explored, empirical observations
suggest that there exists a critical ratio of the number of clauses to the number of
variables, such that almost all randomly generated formulas with a higher ratio
are unsatisfiable while almost all randomly generated formulas with a lower ratio
are satisfiable. The statement that such a crossover point really exists is called
the *satisfiability threshold conjecture.* Experiments hint at such a direction, but
as far as theoretical work is concerned, progress has been difficult. In an important advance, Friedgut [177] showed that the phase transition is a sharp one,
though without proving that it takes place at a "fixed" ratio for large formulas.
Otherwise, rigorous proofs have focused on providing successively better upper
and lower bounds for the value of the (conjectured) threshold. In this chapter,

Computational Complexity and Statistical Physics, edited by
Allon G. Percus, Gabriel Istrate, and Cristopher Moore, Oxford University Press.

our goal is to review the series of improvements of upper bounds for 3-SAT and the techniques leading to these. We give only a passing reference to the improvements of the lower bounds as they rely on significantly different techniques, one of which is discussed in the next chapter.

Let ϕ be a random k-SAT formula constructed by selecting, uniformly and with replacement, m clauses from the set of all possible clauses with k literals (no variable repetitions allowed within a clause) over n variables. It has been experimentally observed that as the numbers n, m of variables and clauses tend to infinity while the ratio or *clause density* m/n is fixed to a constant α, the property of satisfiability exhibits a phase transition. For the case of 3-SAT, when α is greater than a number that has been experimentally determined to be approximately 4.27, then almost all random 3-SAT formulas are unsatisfiable; that is, the fraction of unsatisfiable formulas tends to 1. The opposite is true when $\alpha < 4.27$. Analogous phenomena have been observed for k-SAT with $k > 3$, and the experimentally determined threshold point increases with k. The experiments that led to these conclusions were initiated by the work of Cheeseman et al. [91]. For detailed numerical results see Crawford and Auton [110] and Mitchell et al. [400]. For $k = 2$, it has been rigorously established, independently by Chvátal and Reed [94], Goerdt [201, 202], and Fernandez de la Vega [156], that a transition from almost certain satisfiability to almost certain unsatisfiability takes place at a clause-to-variable ratio equal to 1.

For $k \geq 3$, finding the exact value of the threshold point where this transition occurs—or even proving that such a threshold exists—is still an open problem. The following is known. Friedgut [177] has shown that for k-SAT the transition is sharp, so that in the large n limit, the probability of satisfiability changes from arbitrarily close to 1 to arbitrarily close to 0, as the density α moves along arbitrarily short intervals. However, it is not known whether these intervals converge to a fixed point. Also, Istrate et al. [273] have shown that the transition is *first order*: as α moves along these intervals of asymptotically zero length, the value of a certain combinatorial parameter of the random formula jumps from zero to a nonzero multiple of n. Such parameters are called *order parameters* in statistical physics. The specific one used in 3-SAT is the size of the formula's *spine*, defined as the set of all literals l for which a subformula $\psi \subseteq \phi$ can be found, so that l is FALSE in every truth assignment satisfying ψ. Furthermore, recent theoretical work in statistical physics [395] has supplied additional and almost conclusive evidence—though not a formal proof in the mathematical sense—for the existence of the threshold point. Some of this has been discussed in chapter 4.

Apart from the results above, much effort has been put into rigorously establishing upper and lower bounds for the region where the k-SAT transition occurs. These efforts have resulted in interesting and novel probabilistic techniques. In this chapter we will mainly concentrate on presenting the upper-bound results and the techniques that lead to them (see also the review by Dubois [129]).

2   GENERATING RANDOM 3-SAT FORMULAS

Let Ω denote the set of all $2^3\binom{n}{3}$ possible 3-SAT clauses. A random 3-SAT formula ϕ on $m = \alpha n$ clauses can be formed using one of the following frequently employed probability models:

1. Model $\mathcal{G}_{m,m}$: select the m clauses of ϕ by drawing them uniformly at random, independently of one another and with replacement, from Ω;
2. Model $\mathcal{G}_m$: as above, but with no replacement;
3. Model $\mathcal{G}_p$: place each clause of Ω in ϕ independently of the others and with probability p; and
4. Model $\mathcal{G}_{3,\alpha n}$: fill each of the $3\alpha n$ possible literal positions (αn clauses each having 3 literals) with literals chosen uniformly at random, independently and with replacement, from the set of $2n$ possible literals over the n variables. Note that this model allows the formation of clauses containing variable repetitions.

All of these models are variations on the *fixed clause length* model introduced by Franco and Paull [167]. That model was an adaptation of the classical model for random graphs introduced by Erdős and Rényi in a series of seminal papers published starting in 1959 [147, 148] (see the book of Bollobás [62] for the historical development of the field of random graphs).

The fixed clause length model is in sharp contrast to the *variable clause length* model introduced by Goldberg et al. [204] in order to study the average time complexity of satisfiability algorithms. In the variable clause length model, each of a fixed number of clauses is formed by placing every possible literal in the clause with some probability, and independently of the others. This model has the disadvantage of inducing, on the set of all Boolean formulas with given n, a probability distribution that favors easy instances. The fixed clause length model does not have this feature, since it allows the manipulation of the instance hardness by means of the clause density parameter (clause-to-variable ratio) α.

Each of these models has its own distinct advantages and disadvantages. The model $\mathcal{G}_{m,m}$ usually leads to tighter results than $\mathcal{G}_p$. On the other hand, the latter has the important property of independence for events involving "non-intersecting" sets of clauses, events that may be dependent in $\mathcal{G}_{m,m}$. Finally, as we will see later, $\mathcal{G}_{3,\alpha n}$ enables one to study as well as manipulate individual literal appearances in a formula. This fact leads to a finer description of the formula than the detail that the other models can achieve. As we discuss in section 6, this may lead to better upper bound values, as one usually applies the techniques we will examine on a more limited and well-defined set of formulas. However, it can be shown that if a threshold exists in any one of the models above, it exists in all of them and its value is equal in all of them, even though the bounds obtained by a given method may differ from model to model.

In the sections where we examine the rigorous techniques that have been used in order to bound the satisfiability threshold from above, we will see examples of the advantages and disadvantages mentioned and how they are exploited or circumvented, respectively. Unless stated otherwise, we will assume throughout this chapter that we work with the model $\mathcal{G}_{m,m}$.

3   THE SUCCESSIVE THRESHOLD APPROXIMATIONS

For the purposes of this chapter, we will accept the satisfiability threshold conjecture, and denote the k-SAT transition point in the large n limit by α_k. The basic mathematical tool employed for bounding α_k from above is a probabilistic technique known as the *first moment method*. This method makes use of *Markov's inequality*: let X be a nonnegative integer random variable and let $\mathbf{E}[X]$ be the expectation of X, then $\mathbf{Pr}[X \geq 1] \leq \mathbf{E}[X]$. In our case Markov's inequality is applied on a sequence of random variables $X = X_n, n = 0, 1, \ldots$, that depend on certain *control parameters*. If one finds a condition on the control parameters that forces $\mathbf{E}[X]$ to approach zero as n approaches infinity, then the probability of X being nonzero also vanishes in the large n limit as long as that condition holds. Despite its simplicity, the first moment method is a powerful tool that quickly provides us with a condition (though most often not the tightest possible) for proving that asymptotically a random variable is almost certainly zero,

The connection of the first moment method with the satisfiability threshold conjecture was observed by a number of researchers, including Franco and Paull [167], Simon et al. [475] and Chvátal and Szemerédi [95]. Let ϕ be a random 3-SAT formula on n variables generated according to $\mathcal{G}_{m,m}$ and let $\mathcal{A}_n(\phi)$—or simply $\mathcal{A}_n$ if ϕ is implied by the context—be the random set consisting of the truth assignments that satisfy ϕ. The probability that a truth assignment satisfies a single clause is 7/8, so given 2^n possible truth assignments, $\mathbf{E}[\|\mathcal{A}_n\|] = 2^n (7/8)^m$. Since $\mathbf{Pr}[\phi \text{ is satisfiable}] = \mathbf{Pr}[|\mathcal{A}_n| \geq 1]$, from Markov's inequality it follows that

$$\mathbf{Pr}[\phi \text{ is satisfiable}] \leq 2^n \left(\frac{7}{8}\right)^{\alpha n}. \tag{1}$$

If by α_M we denote the exact solution of the equation $2(7/8)^\alpha = 1$ (so that $\alpha_M = \log 2 / \log(8/7) \approx 5.19$), then we observe that under the condition $\alpha > \alpha_M$ the right-hand side of eq. (1) tends to zero. This establishes the value α_M as an upper bound for the critical value α_3.

It is perhaps instructive at this point to provide the Markov inequality computations for model $\mathcal{G}_p$ as an example of the difference in accuracy that can be obtained using various random models. In $\mathcal{G}_p$, the probability that a truth assignment satisfies a random formula is the probability that none of the $\binom{n}{3}$ clauses violated by the assignment are part of the formula, or $(1 - p)^{\binom{n}{3}}$. Let us set $p = (6\alpha)/(8n^2)s$, so that for large n the mean number of clauses in ϕ is αn. Note that for such a choice of selection probability, it holds that if the event "ϕ is satisfiable" has a vanishingly small probability in the $\mathcal{G}_p$ model, the probability of this event is also small in $\mathcal{G}_m$ and $\mathcal{G}_{m,m}$ for $m = \alpha n$, as well as in $\mathcal{G}_{3,\alpha n}$. By Markov's inequality in $\mathcal{G}_p$ we have

$$\mathbf{Pr}[\phi \text{ is satisfiable}] \leq \mathbf{E}[|\mathcal{A}_n|] = 2^n (1 - p(n))^{\binom{n}{3}} = 2^n \left(1 - \frac{6\alpha}{8n^2}\right)^{\binom{n}{3}}, \quad (2)$$

so asymptotically, $\mathbf{Pr}[\phi \text{ is satisfiable}] \leq 2^n e^{-\alpha n/8}$. This leads to the inequality $\alpha_3 < 8 \log 2 \approx 5.545$, a weaker one than for $\mathcal{G}_{m,m}$. Equations (1) and (2) provide a simple demonstration of a frequently occurring tradeoff among the various probabilistic models: accuracy of results vs. ease of handling complicated situations, such as the computation of the probability of conjunctions of events.

The first observation that the inequality $\alpha_3 < 5.19$ is not the best one possible came from Broder, Frieze, and Upfal [81], who pointed out that the condition $\alpha > \alpha_M - 10^{-7}$ is sufficient to guarantee that $\mathbf{Pr}[\phi \text{ is satisfiable}]$ tends to zero. El Maftouhi and Fernandez de la Vega [145] obtained a further improvement, by showing that the condition can be relaxed to $\alpha > 5.08$. Then Kamath et al. [292] obtained the improved condition $\alpha > 4.758$ using a numerical computation while also giving an analytical proof of the condition $\alpha > 4.87$. Using a refinement of Markov's inequality based on the definition of a restricted class of satisfying truth assignments, Kirousis, Kranakis, and Krizanc [323] proved an upper bound value $\alpha > 4.667$. Using the same class of satisfying truth assignments, after more accurate but lengthier computations, Dubois and Boufkhad [130] independently obtained the upper bound 4.642. Also, Kirousis et al. [324] give the bound 4.602 by what they call "the method of local maxima." Later, Janson, Stamatiou, and Vamvakari [278] lowered this value to 4.596 through two different approaches: by viewing a formula as a physical spin system and taking advantage of techniques from statistical physics to compute an asymptotic expression for its energy, and by obtaining an improved upper bound to the Rogers-Szegő polynomials. In Zito's doctoral thesis [538] the upper bound was further improved to about 4.58 while Kaporis et al. [293] obtained the value 4.571 using a new upper bound for the q-binomial coefficients obtained in Kirousis et al. [325]. Finally, Dubois, Boufkhad, and Mandler [132, 134] gave an upper bound of 4.506 using an approach involving formulas with a "typical" number of appearances of signed occurrences of their variables.

For general k, Franco and Paull [167] used the first moment method and derived an upper bound for the value of the satisfiability threshold of k-SAT equal to $2^k \log 2$, while the same derivation was also observed by Simon et al. [475] and Chvátal and Szemerédi [95]. Kirousis, Kranakis, Krizanc and Stamatiou [324] and, independently, Dubois and Boufkhad [130] gave techniques that improved this general upper bound without, however, improving the leading term that in both approaches is equal to $2^k \log 2$.

On the lower bound side, Chao and Franco [88, 89] were the first to analyze the asymptotic behavior of algorithms that apply a heuristic in order to iteratively assign a truth value to all the variables of a formula. If the heuristic is sure to succeed at a given value of α, this clearly provides a lower bound on the threshold. One of the algorithms they analyzed applied the *unit clause* heuristic defined in chapter 3. Using a technique relying on differential equations in order to model the workings of their algorithm, they showed that the algorithm succeeds with positive probability (but *not* necessarily with high probability) for clause-to-variable ratio less than 2.9. Following this, the first lower bound for 3-SAT was established by Franco [166], who analyzed an algorithm that satisfies only literals whose complements do not appear in the formula (pure literals). He showed that for $\alpha < 1$, the algorithm succeeds almost certainly—meaning with probability approaching one in the large n limit—in finding a satisfying truth assignment to all the variables. Broder, Frieze and Upfal [81] then showed that the pure literal heuristic actually succeeds almost certainly in satisfying a formula if the ratio is smaller than 1.63. Frieze and Suen [182] improved the lower bound to 3.003 by analyzing the *generalized unit clause* heuristic (GUC) with limited backtracking and showing that it succeeds almost certainly for ratios lower than 3.003, as discussed in chapter 3. Finally, using the differential equations method developed by Wormald [529] for approximating the evolution of discrete random processes, Achlioptas [2] and Achlioptas and Sorkin [5] reached the values 3.143 and 3.26, respectively. They developed a framework for a special class of algorithms called *myopic*, and showed that no algorithm in this class can succeed almost certainly in satisfying formulas with clause-to-variable ratios larger than 3.26. Recently, Kaporis, Kirousis, and Lalas [294, 295] analyzed a simple greedy heuristic using the methodology discussed in chapter 8, where the literal that is selected to be satisfied at each step is the one with the maximum number of occurrences in the formula. They obtained the lower bound of 3.42. This was the first time that a heuristic making use of information related to the number of appearances of literals in a random formula (*degree sequence*) has been analyzed. With a little more complicated greedy heuristics that at each step satisfy a literal with a large degree but whose negation has a small degree, a lower bound of more than 3.52 can be attained. This is currently the best value.

The best currently known *general* lower bound for k-SAT, for any fixed value of k, is given by a recent result by Achlioptas and Moore [3] who showed that $\alpha_k \geq 2^k \log 2/2 - c$, for some constant $c > 0$ independent of k. This result essentially bridged the asymptotic gap between the $2^k \log 2$ general upper bound and the $1.817(2^k/k)$ previously best general lower bound obtained by Frieze and Suen [182]. Moreover, Frieze and Wormald [183] showed that α_k is asymptotic to $2^k \log 2$ if k is a function of n and $k - \log_2 n \to \infty$. Both results are the first successful efforts (to the best of our knowledge) in applying the *second moment method* in order to prove a lower bound to the satisfiability threshold, something that previously was feasible only through the probabilistic analysis of satisfiability algorithms relying on specific heuristics for random formulas, as discussed above. Finally, using a technique known in physics as the *replica method*, Monasson and Zecchina predicted [405] that the asymptotic (in k) expression for the threshold is equal to $2^k \log 2$, although their approach was not a rigorous one.

4 UPPER BOUND APPROACHES BASED ON THE HARMONIC MEAN

The first moment method is simple to apply, but does not lead to the best possible upper bounds for k-SAT. For values of the clause-to-variable ratio smaller than α_M as defined in the previous section, the expected number of satisfying truth assignments of a random formula tends to infinity, even though the empirical evidence suggests that most such formulas have no satisfying truth assignment at all. This is due to the fact that there exist very rare formulas that are satisfiable and have a large number of satisfying assignments. El Maftouhi and Fernandez de la Vega [145] and, independently, Kamath et al. [292], studied this situation in detail. They resorted to the harmonic mean formula, first introduced (or formalized) by Aldous [13] to address the problem.

Aldous's result. Let $(B_i : i \in I)$ be a finite family of events in a probability space. For a permutation π of I, call (B_i) *invariant under* π if

$$\mathbf{Pr}[B_{i_1} \cap B_{i_2} \ldots \cap B_{i_r}] = \mathbf{Pr}[B_{\pi(i_1)} \cap B_{\pi(i_2)} \ldots \cap B_{\pi(i_r)}]$$

for all $\alpha \geq 1$ and $i_1, \ldots, i_r \in I$. Call the family (B_i) *transitive invariant* if for each $i_1, i_2 \in I$ there exists π such that $\pi(i_1) = i_2$ and (B_i) is invariant under π. In particular, transitive invariance implies that $\mathbf{Pr}[B_i] = p$ is actually independent of i.

Let N be the random variable counting the number of B_i's that occur. Then, if $(B_i : i \in I)$ is a transitive invariant family of events (with $p = \mathbf{Pr}[B_i]$ independent of i),

$$\mathbf{Pr}[\textstyle\bigcup_{i \in I} B_i] = p \cdot |I| \cdot \mathbf{E}[N^{-1}|B_j]$$

for any $j \in I$. The method gives a new expression for $\mathbf{Pr}[\phi$ is satisfiable], if one interprets B_i as the event "assignment A_i satisfies ϕ." (Note that $|\mathcal{A}_n|$, the number of truth assignments satisfying ϕ, is denoted by $|Mod(\mathcal{F})|$ in El Maftouhi and Fernandez de la Vega [145] and $\#F$ in Kamath et al. [292].) Let T_i be the set of formulas satisfied by the ith truth assignment when these assignments are placed in reverse lexicographic order, so that T_1 consists of those formulas satisfied by all variables set to TRUE. In that case, letting $j = 1$ without loss of generality, the following is a restatement of Aldous's result in the context of 3-SAT formulas:

$$\mathbf{Pr}[\phi \text{ is satisfiable}] = \mathbf{E}[|\mathcal{A}_n|] \times \textstyle\sum_{\psi \in T_1} \frac{1}{|\mathcal{A}_n(\psi)| \cdot |T_1|} \;.$$

Notice that an expression equivalent to the equation above is the following (this is the one proven explicitly in El Maftouhi and Fernandez de la Vega [145, eq. (1)]):

$$\mathbf{E}_{\phi \in \mathrm{SAT}}[\|\mathcal{A}_n\|] = \frac{|T_1|}{\sum_{\psi \in T_1} \frac{1}{|\mathcal{A}_n(\psi)|}}$$

where $\mathbf{E}_{\phi \in \mathrm{SAT}}[\|\mathcal{A}_n\|]$ is the expectation of $|\mathcal{A}_n|$ with respect to all satisfiable formulas on n variables and m clauses. El Maftouhi and Fernandez de la Vega [145] prove that it is possible to define a class of formulas $T_1^* \subseteq T_1$ of size at least $(1 - 2^{-\delta n})|T_1|$, where δ is a constant, such that each formula in T_1^* has at least $2^{\delta n}$ satisfying truth assignments. As we will see in subsection 4.1, this implies $\mathbf{E}_{\phi \in \mathrm{SAT}}[\|\mathcal{A}_n\|] \geq 2^{\delta n - 1}$. Therefore, the probability that a random 3-SAT formula is satisfiable is at most

$$2^n \left(\frac{7}{8}\right)^{\alpha n} 2^{1-\delta n}.$$

The authors set $\alpha = 5.08$, and using a simple random experiment they find a class of formulas T_1^* satisfying the conditions above when $\delta = 0.02137$. The satisfiability probability goes to zero asymptotically for these values, establishing the improved bound $\alpha_3 < 5.08$. The different quality of the bounds derived in El Maftouhi and Fernandez de la Vega [145] and Kamath et al. [292] is due not only to the use of coarse upper bounds rather than exact asymptotics in El Maftouhi and Fernandez de la Vega [145] for estimating the proportion of "interesting" formulas with a particular structure—it can in fact be proven that the difference between the two is vanishingly small—but also to the different experiment used to count this proportion. In the following sections we report, briefly, the results in the two papers. The careful reader will be able to pick up the similarities and the differences in the two approaches.

4.1   ACCOUNTING FOR RARE FORMULAS WITH MANY SATISFYING TRUTH ASSIGNMENTS: DISPENSABLE VARIABLES

El Maftouhi and Fernandez de la Vega [145] define the subset T_1^* of T_1 such that $|T_1^*| \geq (1 - 2^{-\delta n})|T_1|$ and all formulas in T_1^* have at least $2^{\delta n}$ satisfying assignments. Notice that this can be rewritten as $\mathbf{Pr}[|\mathcal{A}_n| \geq 2^{\delta n} \mid \phi \in T_1] \geq 1 - 2^{-\delta n}$. Since $|\mathcal{A}_n| \geq 1$ for any $\phi \in T_1$, one can write:

$$\sum_{\psi \in T_1} \frac{1}{|\mathcal{A}_n(\psi)|} = \sum_{\psi \in T_1^*} \frac{1}{|\mathcal{A}_n(\psi)|} + \sum_{\psi \in T_1 \setminus T_1^*} \frac{1}{|\mathcal{A}_n(\psi)|}$$

$$\leq \frac{|T_1^*|}{2^{\delta n}} + (|T_1| - |T_1^*|) \leq \frac{|T_1|}{2^{\delta n}} + \frac{|T_1|}{2^{\delta n}}.$$

Therefore $\mathbf{E}_{\phi \in \mathrm{SAT}}[\|\mathcal{A}_n\|] \geq \frac{|T_1|}{2|T_1|/2^{\delta n}} = 2^{\delta n - 1}$.

In order to describe how T_1^* is defined, let $\mathcal{C}_i = \mathcal{C}_i(\psi)$ be the set of clauses in ψ containing exactly i positive literals. We first estimate $|\mathcal{C}_i|$ under the assumption that $\psi \in T_1$. Notice that no formula in T_1 can contain a clause with only negated variables, therefore, $|\mathcal{C}_0| = 0$. Furthermore, for formulas in T_1 with n variables and αn clauses, it is fairly easy to compute the asymptotic distribution of the formulas with $|\mathcal{C}_i| = m_i$ for each $i \in \{1, 2, 3\}$ (where $\alpha n = m_1 + m_2 + m_3$):

$$\mathbf{Pr}[m_1, m_2, m_3] = \frac{\binom{\alpha n}{m_1, m_2, m_3} \left[n\binom{n}{2}\right]^{m_1 + m_2} \binom{n}{3}^{m_3}}{\left[\binom{2n}{3} - \binom{n}{3}\right]^{\alpha n}}.$$

Using Stirling's approximation for the various factorials involved and setting $\gamma_i = m_i/n$, it is easy to prove that $\mathbf{Pr}[m_1, m_2, m_3]^{1/n}$ is asymptotic to $(6\alpha/7)^\alpha / (2\gamma_1)^{\gamma_1} (2\gamma_2)^{\gamma_2} (6\gamma_3)^{\gamma_3}$, assuming all m_i's tend to infinity. Considered as a function of γ_1, γ_2 and γ_3, this expression reaches its maximum (equal to one) for $\gamma_1 = \gamma_2 = \frac{3\alpha}{7}$ and $\gamma_3 = \frac{\alpha}{7}$. Now let $T_1^* \subseteq T_1$ be the set of all those formulas in T_1 with $\gamma_1 \leq 2.37$, $\gamma_2 \leq 2.37$ and $\gamma_3 \leq 0.87$ (recall that $\alpha = 5.08$ for all formulas in T_1). It may be shown from the asymptotic probability expression [145] that these inequalities hold with probability greater than $1 - 2^{-0.02137n}$, implying that $|T_1^*| > (1 - 2^{-0.02137n})|T_1|$.

To prove that 5.08 is an upper bound to the satisfiability threshold, following the reasoning given earlier, it remains to demonstrate that the formulas in T_1^* have, with sufficiently high probability, at least $2^{0.02137n}$ satisfying truth assignments. To this end, the authors introduce the notion of *dispensable variables*. Given a formula ϕ, a truth assignment A that satisfies ϕ and a set D consisting of certain variables taking the values dictated by A, we call D a set of *dispensable* variables if its elements can be set in any arbitrary way and still result in the truth assignment satisfying ϕ. Let $D(\phi)$ be the set of dispensable variables in ϕ with respect to the assignment that sets all variables to TRUE. Clearly $|\mathcal{A}_n(\phi)| \geq 2^{|D(\phi)|}$, so it is then sufficient to show that for all $\phi \in T_1^*$, $|D(\phi)| \geq 0.02137n$ with high probability. The authors do this by analyzing the size of the set of dispensable variables returned by the following "greedy" algorithm:

1. Take all clauses in C_1, and call I_1 the set of all positive literals in these clauses. These are known as *isolated* literals. Let $n_1 = |I_1|$.
2. Take all clauses in C_2 whose two positive literals are both absent from I_1, and for each such clause select at random one of its two positive literals. Call I_2 the set of all such literals. Set $J_2 = I_1 \cup I_2$. Let $n_2 = |I_2|$, so that $|J_2| = n_1 + n_2$.
3. Take all clauses in C_3 whose three positive literals are all absent from J_2, and for each such clause select at random one literal. Call I_3 the set of all such literals. Set $J_3 = J_2 \cup I_3$. Let $n_3 = |I_3|$, so that $|J_3| = n_1 + n_2 + n_3$.

One may readily verify that all variables *not* represented in J_3 form a set of dispensable variables, so $|J_3|$ needs to be bounded from above. For the range of values of γ_i that defines T_1^*, an estimate on $|J_3|$ is obtained by finding upper bounds on: n_1; n_2 conditioned on n_1; and n_3 conditioned on n_2 and n_1.

In order to estimate n_1, the authors resort to the *occupancy problem*. In this problem, one throws μn balls (μ is a constant) uniformly at random into n boxes and asks for the distribution of the random variable Y that counts the number of *non-empty* boxes. Then for any $\epsilon > 0$, $r = r(\epsilon) = (1 + \epsilon)(1 - e^{-\frac{\mu}{1+\epsilon}})$ and $s = s(\epsilon) = 1 - r(\epsilon)$, the following is established:

$$\frac{1}{n} \log \mathbf{Pr}[Y \geq \lfloor r(\epsilon)n \rfloor] \leq (1 - o(1)) \log \frac{(s+\epsilon)^{s+\epsilon}(1+\epsilon)^{\mu-1-\epsilon}}{s^s}.$$

As n_1 can be viewed as the number of non-empty boxes that result from the random placement of $\gamma_1 n$ balls into n boxes, we have that $Y = n_1$ and $\mu = \gamma_1$. Setting $\epsilon = 0.062$ and exponentiating both sides of the inequality above, we obtain for $\gamma_1 \leq 2.37$ that

$$\mathbf{Pr}[n_1 \leq 0.94800n] \geq 1 - e^{-0.01513n}. \tag{3}$$

Now define m_2' as the number of clauses in $\mathcal{C}_2$ (clauses with two positive literals) identified by the greedy algorithm as having both of their positive literals absent from I_1. This is binomially distributed, with number of trials $\gamma_2 n$ and success probability $(1 - n_1/n)(1 - (n_1 - 1)/n)$, where success means "absent from I_1." Conditioning on $n_1 \leq 0.94800n$, we can use the Chernoff bound on the upper tail of the binomial distribution, $\mathbf{Pr}[B(m, p) \geq \beta mp] \leq (e^{\beta-1}/\beta^\beta)^{mp}$, setting $\beta = 3.84$ and $mp = 0.006408n$ to obtain for $\gamma_2 \leq 2.37$ that $\mathbf{Pr}[m_2' \leq 0.02461n | n_1 \leq 0.94800n] \geq 1 - e^{-0.01490n}$. Since $n_2 \leq m_2'$,

$$\mathbf{Pr}[n_2 \leq 0.02461n | n_1 \leq 0.94800n] \geq 1 - e^{-0.01490n}. \tag{4}$$

Similarly, define m_3' as the number of clauses in $\mathcal{C}_3$ identified by the greedy algorithm as having all of their literals absent from J_2. Again bounding the tail of the relevant binomial distribution, we obtain for $\gamma_3 \leq 0.87$ that $\mathbf{Pr}[m_3' \leq 0.00356n | n_1 + n_2 \leq 0.97261n] \geq 1 - e^{-0.0153n}$. Since $n_3 \leq m_3'$,

$$\mathbf{Pr}[n_3 \leq 0.00356n | n_1 + n_2 \leq 0.97261n] \geq 1 - e^{-0.0153n}. \tag{5}$$

Finally, multiplying together (3), (4) and (5) we may verify that for sufficiently large n, $\mathbf{Pr}[n_1 + n_2 + n_3 \leq 0.97617n] \geq 1 - e^{-0.01481n} = 1 - 2^{-0.02137n}$. Thus, with probability at least $1 - 2^{-0.02137n}$, $|D(\phi)| \geq 0.02383n > 0.02137n$ for $\phi \in T_1^*$.

4.2 SHARPER ESTIMATE OF OCCUPANCY PROBABILITIES: INDEPENDENT VARIABLES

Kamath et al. [292] performed a similar investigation of the structure of the typical $\phi \in T_1$. A variable x is said to *cover* a clause C if x occurs unnegated in C—that is, as a positive literal. For instance, in the formula below (which does not belong to T_1), represented by the sequence of sets of literals forming individual clauses in it,

$\phi(x_1, x_2, x_3, x_4, x_5) =$

C_3 $\{x_1, x_2, x_3\}, \{x_2, x_3, x_4\}, \{x_3, x_4, x_5\},$

C_2 $\{\overline{x}_2, x_3, x_4\}, \{x_1, x_4, \overline{x}_5\}, \{x_1, \overline{x}_2, x_5\}, \{x_1, \overline{x}_2, x_4\}, \{x_1, \overline{x}_3, x_5\}, \{x_3, x_4, \overline{x}_5\},$
$\{x_2, x_4, \overline{x}_5\}, \{x_2, \overline{x}_3, x_4\}, \{\overline{x}_3, x_4, x_5\}, \{x_1, x_3, \overline{x}_4\},$

C_1 $\{x_2, \overline{x}_3, \overline{x}_5\}, \{\overline{x}_1, x_4, \overline{x}_5\}, \{\overline{x}_1, \overline{x}_3, x_5\}, \{\overline{x}_1, \overline{x}_2, x_5\}, \{\overline{x}_1, x_3, \overline{x}_4\}, \{\overline{x}_3, x_4, \overline{x}_5\},$
$\{\overline{x}_2, x_4, \overline{x}_5\}, \{\overline{x}_1, x_4, \overline{x}_5\}, \{x_1, \overline{x}_3, \overline{x}_5\},$

C_0 $\{\overline{x}_1, \overline{x}_2, \overline{x}_3\}, \{\overline{x}_1, \overline{x}_4, \overline{x}_5\}, \{\overline{x}_2, \overline{x}_3, \overline{x}_4\}, \{\overline{x}_1, \overline{x}_2, \overline{x}_4\}, \{\overline{x}_1, \overline{x}_3, \overline{x}_5\}$

the variable x_1 covers the clauses:

$$\{x_1, x_2, x_3\}, \{x_1, x_4, \overline{x}_5\}, \{x_1, \overline{x}_2, x_5\}, \{x_1, \overline{x}_2, x_4\}, \{x_1, \overline{x}_3, x_5\}, \{x_1, x_3, \overline{x}_4\},$$
$$\{x_1, \overline{x}_3, \overline{x}_5\}.$$

A set of variables V covers a set of clauses if every one of these clauses is covered by at least one variable in V. Such a variable set is called a *cover*. Obviously, a random formula $\phi \in T_1$ has a trivial cover, namely the set consisting of all the n variables. However, it is possible that there exists a smaller cover than the trivial one. For instance, Figure 1 shows a formula in T_1 with the sets of clauses in C_1, C_2, C_3, the set X containing all variables, a set I_1 of variables covering C_1, a second set of variables (from the set R of remaining variables) needed to cover the uncovered portions of C_2 and C_3, and the remaining *independent set I*. The set $X \setminus I$ in the figure is an example of a cover for all the clauses of the formula that is smaller than the trivial one. Therefore, setting the variables in $X \setminus I$ to TRUE is sufficient to satisfy the formula. Since all the variables in the independent set I can be set arbitrarily, if ϕ has a cover of size s then $|\mathcal{A}_n(\phi)| \geq 2^{n-s}$.

To estimate $\mathbf{E}_{\phi \in \mathrm{SAT}}[|\mathcal{A}_n|] = |T_1| / \sum_{\psi \in T_1} \frac{1}{|\mathcal{A}_n(\psi)|}$, we partition T_1 into "slices" containing formulas with minimal cover of size s, and use:

$$\sum_{\psi \in T_1} \frac{1}{|\mathcal{A}_n(\psi)| \cdot |T_1|} = \sum_{s=1}^{n} \sum_{\psi \in T_1 : |\mathrm{cover}(\psi)| = s} \frac{1}{|\mathcal{A}_n(\psi)| \cdot |T_1|}$$

$$\leq \sum_{s=1}^{n} \sum_{\psi \in T_1 : |\mathrm{cover}(\psi)| = s} \frac{\mathbf{Pr}[|\mathrm{cover}(\psi)| = s]}{|\mathcal{A}_n(\psi)|}$$

$$\leq \sum_{s=1}^{n} \sum_{\psi \in T_1 : |\mathrm{cover}(\psi)| = s} 2^{s-n} \mathbf{Pr}[|\mathrm{cover}(\psi)| = s].$$

The problem thus reduces to one of estimating, as accurately as possible, the probability that an arbitrary formula in T_1 has minimal cover size s. As in subsection 4.1, this is done using asymptotic expressions for binomial tails and occupancy probabilities.

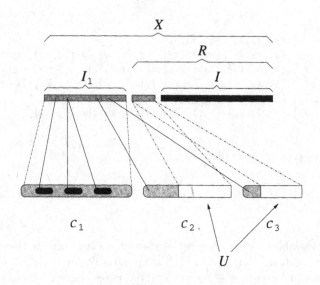

FIGURE 1 A set X of variables and the clauses in C_1, C_2, C_3 that it covers. Broken lines denote covered regions; solid lines represent some of the specific clauses covered by variables in I_1.

1. First fix the size m_1 of C_1, the set of clauses containing a single unnegated variable. The probability $\mathbf{Pr}[u]$ that this number is within u times its mean can be shown to be close to 1 using bounds on binomial tails.

2. Then determine the set I_1 of isolated variables ($X \setminus R$ in fig. 1). Conditioning on m_1 being within u of its mean, the probability $\mathbf{Pr}[v|u]$ that the size n_1 of I_1 is within v times its mean is estimated using occupancy asymptotics (again we are throwing clauses "into" variables: the empty bins correspond to the variables in $X \setminus I_1$).

3. Next, compute the number of clauses in $C_2 \cup C_3$ that are *not* covered by I_1, conditioned on n_1 and m_1. The *set* of these clauses is denoted by U in figure 1. The probability that this number is within w times its mean, $\mathbf{Pr}[w|u,v]$, is again a binomial tail.

4. Finally, bound the size of the variable set needed to cover U.

The improvement in Kamath et al. [292] comes from estimating the size of U, and from adding to the cover only those variables needed to cover U rather than the whole set $I_2 \cup I_3$ (as done in the other paper, in the second and third selection step).

5 SPECIAL CLASSES OF SATISFYING TRUTH ASSIGNMENTS

The next improvements resulted from a different kind of exploitation of rare formulas with many satisfying truth assignments.

Since the main disadvantage of Markov's inequality can be attributed to rare formulas having a large number of satisfying truth assignments, a plausible approach for improvement is to use in the inequality not the expected cardinality of the set of satisfying truth assignments of a random formula, but the expected cardinality of a smaller set. Of course one needs to prove that the expectation of the new random set still provides an upper bound on the probability that ϕ is satisfiable.

This idea was introduced by Kirousis, Kranakis, and Krizanc [323] ("single flips") and independently by Dubois and Boufkhad [130]. In this section we describe these approaches and several others derived from them, and we report the resulting improvements on the estimate of α_3. With regard to the techniques described in sections 5.1 and 5.2 in particular, we should point out in advance the following important difference between them. The technique described in section 5.1 approximates α_3 by computing an upper bound on the expected cardinality of a special class of satisfying truth assignments, employing a simple correlation inequality that bounds from above the probability that some dependent events hold simultaneously. On the other hand, the technique described in section 5.2 results in a slightly better approximation of α_3 by computing *exactly* the expected cardinality of the same class of satisfying truth assignments. The former method, however, is much simpler to apply and easily generalizes to k-SAT random formulas for any $k > 3$ while the latter is complicated and cannot be readily applied to k-SAT in general.

The following formula

$$\phi(x_1, x_2, x_3, x_4) = \{x_1, \overline{x}_2, x_4\}, \{\overline{x}_1, \overline{x}_2, \overline{x}_4\}, \{x_1, \overline{x}_3, \overline{x}_4\}, \{\overline{x}_1, x_2, \overline{x}_3\}$$

whose satisfying assignments are

	x_1	x_2	x_3	x_4
A_1	FALSE	FALSE	FALSE	FALSE
A_2	FALSE	FALSE	FALSE	TRUE
A_3	FALSE	FALSE	TRUE	FALSE
A_4	FALSE	TRUE	FALSE	TRUE
A_5	TRUE	FALSE	FALSE	FALSE
A_6	TRUE	FALSE	FALSE	TRUE
A_7	TRUE	TRUE	FALSE	FALSE
A_8	TRUE	TRUE	TRUE	FALSE

will be used as an example in the next subsection, to convey a better understanding of the various results.

5.1   SINGLE FLIPS

The strategy described here was introduced in Kirousis et al. [323]. In what follows it may be convenient to identify classes of truth assignments on n variables with sets of lexicographically ordered sequences over a two-letter alphabet (say the numbers 0 and 1 with $0 < 1$).

Given a random formula ϕ, the set $\mathcal{A}_n^1$ is defined as the class of truth assignments A such that the following two conditions hold: (1) A satisfies ϕ, and (2) any assignment obtained from A by changing exactly one FALSE value to TRUE does not satisfy ϕ. Such a change is called a *single flip* and will be denoted by sf. The truth assignment that results from the flip will be denoted by A^{sf}. The class $\mathcal{A}_n^1$ contains the elements of $\mathcal{A}_n$ that are *local maxima* with respect to single flips. In other words, a truth assignment belongs to $\mathcal{A}_n^1$ if it satisfies ϕ and if no other possible satisfying truth assignment can be obtained from it by changing a single FALSE value to TRUE—by performing all possible single flips in isolation.

In our example formula, the first truth assignment A_1 does not belong to $\mathcal{A}_n^1$: if we change the value assigned to x_1 the resulting truth assignment is still in $\mathcal{A}_n$. However, the fourth truth assignment A_4 does belong to $\mathcal{A}_n^1$: changing the value assigned to x_1 produces the assignment $A' \notin \mathcal{A}_n$ where all variables except x_3 are set to TRUE, and changing the value of x_3 similarly leads to the ϕ not being satisfied. Since all possible transformations changing a FALSE value result in truth assignments that do not satisfy ϕ, the assignment A_4 is in $\mathcal{A}_n^1$. It is easy to verify that the set $\mathcal{A}_n^1$ for ϕ is formed by the assignments A_3, A_4, A_6, and $A_8.c$

Since $\mathcal{A}_n^1 \subseteq \mathcal{A}_n$, $\mathbf{E}[|\mathcal{A}_n^1|] \leq \mathbf{E}[|\mathcal{A}_n|]$. Thus, to relax Markov's inequality we need only establish that $\mathbf{Pr}[\phi \text{ is satisfiable}] \leq \mathbf{E}[|\mathcal{A}_n^1|]$. This can easily be seen as follows. Let I_ϕ be the random indicator for the property "ϕ is satisfiable." Clearly $I_\phi \leq |\mathcal{A}_n^1|$. If we now write

$$\mathbf{Pr}[\phi \text{ is satisfiable}] = \sum_\phi I_\phi \mathbf{Pr}[\phi]$$

then the desired inequality follows immediately. To exploit this technique one then needs to prove a bound on $\mathbf{E}[|\mathcal{A}_n^1|]$, asymptotically smaller than $2^n (7/8)^{\alpha n}$.

Using a correlation inequality to compute the probability that a single flip results in an assignment not satisfying ϕ, it can be proven that in the random formula model $\mathcal{G}_{m,m}$, the expected size of class $\mathcal{A}_n^1$ is at most $(7/8)^{\alpha n}(2 - e^{-3\alpha/7} + o(1))^n$. Therefore, the unique positive solution of the equation $(7/8)^\alpha (2 - e^{-3\alpha/7}) = 1$ gives an upper bound for the satisfiability threshold critical value α_3. This solution is approximately 4.667.

If instead one uses the $\mathcal{G}_p$ ensemble, one avoids having to compute probabilities of conjunctions of *dependent* events. Applying Markov's inequality then leads to the solution of the equation $e^{-\alpha/8}(2 - e^{-3\alpha/7}) = 1$. This expression, however, gives an upper bound equal to 5.07—worse than the bound given for $\mathcal{G}_{m,m}$.

5.2   THE SET OF NEGATIVELY PRIME SOLUTIONS (NPS)

Independently from Kirousis et al., Dubois and Boufkhad introduced a class of satisfying truth assignments that they called *negatively prime solutions* (NPS) [130]. This class turns out to coincide with the class $\mathcal{A}_n^1$ described in subsection 5.1.

Dubois and Boufkhad proved the following exact expression for the expected cardinality of NPS for k-SAT:

$$\mathbf{E}[|\text{NPS}|] = \sum_{i=0}^{n} \sum_{j=i}^{m} 2^{-km} 2^i \binom{n}{i} \binom{m}{j} S_2(j,i) i! \left(\frac{k}{n}\right)^j (2^k - 1 - k)^{m-j} \qquad (6)$$

where $S_2(j,i)$ are the *Stirling numbers of the second kind* that count the number of ways of partitioning a set of j elements into i *non-empty* subsets. By way of a series of asymptotic manipulations, the authors then arrived at a closed-form upper bound for (6), showing that it converges to 0 for values of the clause-to-variable ratio greater than 4.642.

5.3   RESTRICTING FURTHER THE CLASS OF SATISFYING TRUTH ASSIGNMENTS: DOUBLE FLIPS

Kirousis et al. [324] define as a *double flip* the change of exactly two variables x_i and x_j, with $i < j$, where x_i is changed from FALSE to TRUE and x_j from TRUE to FALSE. Notice that the restriction $i < j$ implies that a double flip always leads to a lexicographically "greater" assignment. Let A^{df} denote the truth assignment that results from A after the application of the double flip df. Let $\mathcal{A}_n^{2\sharp}$ be the set of truth assignments A that have the following three properties: (1) A satisfies ϕ, (2) for all possible single flips sf of A, A^{sf} does not satisfy ϕ, and (3) for all possible double flips df of A, A^{df} does not satisfy ϕ.

It is proven in [324] that the following inequality holds:

$\mathbf{Pr}[\phi \text{ is satisfiable}]$

$$\leq \mathbf{E}[|\mathcal{A}_n^{2\sharp}|] = (7/8)^{\alpha n} \sum_{A \in S} \mathbf{Pr}[A \in \mathcal{A}_n^1 \mid A \in \mathcal{A}_n] \mathbf{Pr}[A \in \mathcal{A}_n^{2\sharp} \mid A \in \mathcal{A}_n^1], \qquad (7)$$

where S is the set of all 2^n possible truth assignments on the n variables. As before, to get an upper bound on α_3 it suffices to find the smallest possible value for the clause-to-variable ratio for which the right-hand side of this inequality tends to 0. In what follows, $sf(A)$ denotes the total number of possible single flips of A (which is simply the number of variables assigned the value FALSE in A) and $df(A)$ denotes the total number of possible double flips.

It can be proven that $\mathbf{Pr}[A \in \mathcal{A}_n^1 \mid A \in \mathcal{A}_n]$ may be bounded from above by an expression of the form $P^{sf(A)}$, where P depends only on the clause-to-variable ratio α (this is in fact the expression used to derive the improved upper bound in subsection 5.1). The hard part is computing the second probability, involving the realization of the double flip events conditional upon the realization of the single flip events. As it turns out, the computation of this probability in the model $\mathcal{G}_{m,m}$ involves dependencies among events of a very complicated nature. In $\mathcal{G}_p$, on the other hand, there at least are no dependencies ensuing from the fundamental requirement of $\mathcal{G}_{m,m}$ that the size of the formula is fixed. The remaining dependencies are those arising from the fact that some of the double flip events involve double flips sharing a particular FALSE variable. The computation of an upper bound to this probability was made possible by the use of a version of Suen's correlation inequality [492] proven by Janson [277]. The bound has the form $Q^{df(A)}$ with Q dependent on n and α. The reader may consult [324] for the derivation of this bound. Inequality (7) may then be rewritten as follows:

$$\mathbf{Pr}[\phi \text{ is satisfiable}] \leq 3m^{1/2}(7/8)^{\alpha n} \sum_{A \in S} P^{sf(A)} Q^{df(A)}, \qquad (8)$$

with the polynomial factor $3m^{1/2}$ arising due to the change from $\mathcal{G}_{m,m}$ to $\mathcal{G}_p$ (see Bollobás [62]). To complete the derivation of the improved bound, the authors noted the following combinatorial identity, which can be proven by induction on n:

$$\sum_{A \in S} P^{sf(A)} Q^{df(A)} = \sum_{i=0}^{n} \begin{bmatrix} n \\ i \end{bmatrix}_Q P^i, \qquad (9)$$

where $\begin{bmatrix} n \\ i \end{bmatrix}_q = \frac{(q^n-1)(q^n-q)\cdots(q^n-q^{i-1})}{(q^i-1)(q^i-q)\cdots(q^i-q^{i-1})}$ are the *q-binomial* or *Gaussian* coefficients [192] for $0 \leq i \leq n$ and $q \neq 1$. The right-hand expression in eq. (9) is also known as the *Rogers-Szegő polynomial* $F_{n,Q}(P)$, and leads to the inequality

$$\sum_{A \in S} P^{sf(A)} Q^{df(A)} \leq \prod_{i=0}^{n-1}(1 + PQ^{i/2}), \qquad 0 \leq P^2 \leq Q \leq 1. \qquad (10)$$

Equation (8) thus becomes

$$\mathbf{Pr}[\phi \text{ is satisfiable}] \leq 3m^{1/2}(7/8)^{\alpha n} \prod_{i=0}^{n-1}(1 + PQ^{i/2}). \qquad (11)$$

The product on the right-hand side can be estimated by making use of *hypergeometric series* (see also Gasper and Rahman [192]) and an inequality derived in Kirousis [322], ultimately leading to the bound $\alpha_3 < 4.602$.

5.4 OCCUPANCY BOUNDS AND Q-BINOMIAL COEFFICIENTS

As we have just seen, a key step in the improvement of the upper bound to 4.602 is the derivation of an upper bound to the sum in eq. (8) through its connection with the q-binomial coefficients. This bound can be improved further: two approaches have been given by Janson, Stamatiou, and Vamvakari [278]. Both result in the same value, namely $\alpha_3 < 4.596$. However, these approaches are interesting in their own right. The first approach links the problem of determining upper bounds to the satisfiability threshold with the study of *Ising spin systems* in statistical mechanics, while the second approach links the problem with the branch of mathematics dealing with q-hypergeometric series and their generating functions.

More specifically, in the first approach the sum in eq. (8) is written as

$$\sum_{\varepsilon_1,\ldots,\varepsilon_n \in \{0,1\}} \exp\left(a \sum_{i=1}^{n} \varepsilon_i + \frac{b}{n} \sum_{1 \le i < j \le n} \varepsilon_i(1 - \varepsilon_j) \right), \qquad (12)$$

with the outer sum ranging over all the 2^n sequences $\varepsilon_1,\ldots,\varepsilon_n$ of 0's and 1's, each of them coding a truth assignment A with 0 and 1 representing TRUE and FALSE respectively. This sum is indeed equal to the sum of eq. (8) when $a = \log P$ and $b = n \log Q$.

The expression in eq. (12) enables the application of an optimization technique common in statistical physics, resulting in an asymptotic expression for the sum. This particular form of the sum is precisely the *partition function* $Z = \sum_{\varepsilon_1,\ldots,\varepsilon_n} \exp(-\beta H)$ for a system with n spin sites, each having a spin value $\varepsilon_i \in \{0,1\}$ and with an energy function equal to $H = -a \sum_{i=1}^{n} \varepsilon_i - \frac{b}{n} \sum_{1 \le i < j \le n} \varepsilon_i(1 - \varepsilon_j)$, in units where the inverse temperature $\beta = 1$. The first term in H corresponds to an external field acting on all the spins of the system, the second to an interaction acting between arbitrary pairs of spin sites with the left site having spin 1 and the right site having spin 0. The energy function can easily be rewritten into a more conventional form: $H = \sum_{i=1}^{n}(-a - b + b\frac{i}{n})\varepsilon_i + \frac{b}{n}\sum_{i<j}\varepsilon_i\varepsilon_j$, or, substituting $\varepsilon_i = (1 + s_i)/2$ to have more traditional (and symmetric) spins with values ± 1,

$$H = -\frac{a}{2}n - \frac{b}{8}(n-1) + \sum_{i=1}^{n}\left(-\frac{a}{2} + b\frac{i - (n+1)/2}{2n}\right)s_i + \frac{b}{4n}\sum_{i<j}s_is_j.$$

The value H may be interpreted in statistical physics as the energy function for a mean-field Ising model with an inhomogeneous (linear) external field. Ultimately, this leads to an asymptotic expression for the partition function, and an estimate for the sum in eq. (8), resulting in $\alpha_3 < 4.596$.

In the second approach, a sharp upper bound is derived for the sum in eq. (8). Recall that it is equal to the Rogers-Szegő polynomial $F_{n,Q}(P)$. Then, using the *Eulerian* generating function and a technique described in Lemma 8.1

of Odlyzko [417], the following upper bound is obtained (see Janson et al. [278]) for any t, $0 < t < \min(1, 1/P)$:

$$F_{n,\dot{Q}}(P) \leq \frac{t^{-n}}{(1-t)(1-tP)} \exp\left[-\frac{1}{\log Q}\left(\text{Li}_2(tP) + \text{Li}_2(t) + \text{Li}_2(Q^n) - \text{Li}_2(Q)\right)\right]$$

where $\text{Li}_2(y) = \text{dilog}(1-y) = \text{Polylog}(2, y) = \sum_{i \geq 1} \frac{y^i}{i^2}$ is the *dilogarithm* function. By finding the value of t that optimizes this upper bound and plugging it into eq. (8), we obtain precisely the same upper bound as in the first approach, $\alpha_3 < 4.596$.

5.5 BALLS AND BINS

The calculations described in the previous sections are useful, but limited. The idea of single flips, although leading to a good improvement of the upper bound, only takes into account a very limited range of locality around a given satisfying assignment. The results described in subsection 5.3 exploit wider locality ranges, but because of the complexity of the resulting numerical expressions, the authors were forced to use weak bounds on $\mathbf{Pr}[A \in \mathcal{A}_n^1 \mid A \in \mathcal{A}_n]$ and the overall $\mathbf{E}[|\mathcal{A}_n^{2\sharp}|]$. Finally, the two approaches in subsection 5.4 reached the limits of what can be exploited from the upper bound shown in eq. (8). In order to obtain further improvements, one must step back from the derivation of eq. (8) and attempt to realize improvements on the probabilities involved.

Kaporis et al. [293] have achieved an improved bound of 4.571 using sharp estimates for certain probabilities related to the classical occupancy problem that we have seen in subsection 4.1. For a given satisfying assignment A, the probability that no single flip satisfies ϕ is best computed (up to polynomial factors) by noticing the following "structural" condition imposed on ϕ by the event in question: for each variable x set to FALSE in A, the formula must contain a *critical* clause $\{\overline{x}, \ell_1, \ell_2\}$ with $A(\ell_1) = A(\ell_2) = \text{FALSE}$.

If a satisfying assignment A sets j variables to FALSE, no single flip satisfies ϕ when: (1) some $l \geq j$ clauses out of $m = \alpha n$ are critical (the remaining ones being consistent with A^{sf}), and (2) these l clauses can be seen as a sequence of balls that are dropped into j distinct bins (corresponding to different single flips) in a way that leaves no bin completely empty.

Asymptotic estimates on the occupancy probability that the l critical clauses indeed cover all possible j single flips [292], as well as a change of models from $\mathcal{G}_{m,m}$ to $\mathcal{G}_m$ in order to be able to formulate our problem in the balls and bins framework, lead to a sharper bound of $\mathbf{Pr}[A \in \mathcal{A}_n^1 \mid A \in \mathcal{A}_n]$. Note that Zito [538] has performed a similar analysis using coupon collector probabilities instead, deriving a bound of about 4.58. The analysis in Kaporis et al. [293] improves on the previous results for another reason as well: the overall bound on $\mathbf{E}[|\mathcal{A}_n^{2\sharp}|]$ is tightened by means of a more direct estimate of the q-binomial coefficient involved. Using simple generating function inequalities (and elementary calculus) it is possible to bound the term $\begin{bmatrix} n \\ i \end{bmatrix}_Q$ directly and avoid the use of Rogers-Szegő polynomials.

Finally, to obtain their results, the authors had to establish a relationship between the probabilities of the event, $A \in \mathcal{A}_n^{2\sharp} \mid A \in \mathcal{A}_n^1$, in the models $\mathcal{G}_{m,m}$ and $\mathcal{G}_p$. Using results described in Bollobás [62, ch. II], it is easy to prove the desired relationship for *unconditional* events when the average length of a random formula constructed in the model $\mathcal{G}_p$ equals m. However, the conditioning here may bias the expected length of the formula to higher values. The authors have shown how to adjust p appropriately so as to obtain the bound above.

6   TYPICAL FORMULAS

In the last section, all the techniques have worked by placing restrictions on the *assignments* (*semantics*, in some sense) satisfying a formula and for which the expectation, which is required by the first moment method, is computed. As mentioned above, the application of this technique to the kinds of assignment restrictions described in subsections 5.1, 5.2, and 5.3 results provably in no further upper bound improvement.

Dubois, Boufkhad, and Mandler [132, 134] consider random formulas with the special characteristic that the numbers of appearances of their literals fall within certain ranges that are "typical" for randomly generated formulas. In this way, they are able to disallow the rare formulas that seem to prevent Markov's inequality from giving an upper bound close to the experimentally determined value. By computing the expected number of negative prime solutions for these formulas only, making use of the model $\mathcal{G}_{3,an}$, they achieve an upper bound improvement. In contrast to the semantic methods that rely on restricting the set of truth assignments taking part in the application of the first moment method, this approach can be characterized as *syntactic*: it focuses on restricting the *form* or *syntax* of the set of formulas participating in the first moment method calculations. However, the approach also limits the possible truth assignments using the restricted sets defined in Sections 5.1 and 5.2. Without going into detail, Dubois, Boufkhad and Mandler give an expression for the expected number of negative prime solutions for these formulas. In so doing, they obtain $\alpha_3 < 4.506$, the best upper bound to date for the location of the random 3-SAT threshold.

ACKNOWLEDGMENTS

We would like to thank the editors as well as the anonymous referee for their invaluable contribution to the improvement of the presentation in the chapter. This work has been supported by the University of Patras Research Committee (Project C. Carathéodory no. 20445) and by the EU within the 6th Framework Programme under contract 001907 (DELIS).

CHAPTER 8

Proving Conditional Randomness using the Principle of Deferred Decisions

Alexis C. Kaporis
Lefteris M. Kirousis
Yannis C. Stamatiou

1 INTRODUCTION

In order to prove that a certain property holds asymptotically for a restricted class of objects such as formulas or graphs, one may apply a heuristic on a random element of the class, and then prove by probabilistic analysis that the heuristic succeeds with high probability. This method has been used to establish lower bounds on thresholds for desirable properties such as satisfiability and colorability: lower bounds for the 3-SAT threshold were discussed briefly in the previous chapter. The probabilistic analysis depends on analyzing the mean trajectory of the heuristic—as we have seen in chapter 3—and in parallel, showing that in the asymptotic limit the trajectory's properties are strongly concentrated about their mean. However, the mean trajectory analysis requires that certain random characteristics of the heuristic's starting sample are retained throughout the trajectory.

We propose a methodology in this chapter to determine the conditional that should be imposed on a random object, such as a conjunctive normal form (CNF)

Computational Complexity and Statistical Physics, edited by
Allon G. Percus, Gabriel Istrate, and Cristopher Moore, Oxford University Press.

formula or a graph, so that conditional randomness is retained when we run a given algorithm. The methodology is based on the principle of deferred decisions. The essential idea is to consider information about the object as being stored in "small pieces," in separate registers. The contents of the registers pertaining to the conditional are exposed, while the rest remain unexposed. Having separate registers for different types of information prevents exposing information unnecessarily. We use this methodology to prove various randomness invariance results, one of which answers a question posed by Molloy [402].

2   PRINCIPLE OF DEFERRED DECISIONS

Let $G \in \mathcal{G}_{n,m}$ be a graph chosen uniformly at random, conditional on its number of vertices n and number of edges m. All G with n vertices and m edges are thus equiprobable. Intuitively, if we delete from G a vertex v chosen uniformly at random and also delete all edges incident on v, the new graph should be random conditional on the new number of vertices, $n - 1$, and the new number of edges m', where m' is a random variable. In other words, given m', the new graph is equiprobable among all graphs with $n - 1$ vertices and m' edges. Note that here and in what follows, "random" will mean "uniformly random," that is, equiprobable, on conditionals that will be either explicit or clear from the context.

Knuth [332, Lecture 3] has introduced a method, known as the *principle of deferred decisions*, by which randomness claims such as the one above can be verified. In the specific example of vertex deletion from a $\mathcal{G}_{n,m}$ graph, it works as follows. Consider $n+m$ cards facing down, or more precisely, $n+m$ registers with unexposed content. The first n of them correspond to the vertices of the graph and the remaining m to its edges. The register of a vertex v contains pointers to the registers of the edges incident on v. The register of an edge e contains pointers to the registers of the two endpoints of e. That the registers are unexposed means that the pointers can be specified randomly. To delete a random vertex, do the following: point randomly to a vertex register; expose its contents; expose all edge registers pointed to by this vertex register; delete the exposed vertex register and the exposed edge registers; nullify pointers in other vertex registers that point to deleted edge registers (without exposing these vertex registers). The registers that have not been deleted remain unexposed and, therefore, they can be filled in randomly. The only conditional, that is, the only exposed information about the graph, is the new number of vertex registers and the new number of edge registers.

The principle of deferred decisions states that conditional randomness is retained as long as no new information about the current contents of unexposed registers can be determined, at any given update step, from information exposed up until that step. The method can be applied in more complicated situations. Consider a random graph conditional on (i) the number of vertices, (ii) the number of edges, and (iii) for each $i = 0, \ldots, n - 1$, the number of vertices of degree i (the degree sequence). We claim that upon deleting a random vertex of degree i (for any i) and its i incident edges, the new graph is random conditional on the same type of information. Indeed, it suffices to augment the argument of the previous paragraph with the additional assumption that for each vertex v there is an *exposed* degree register containing an integer equal to its degree. This degree register needs to be exposed so that the algorithm may choose, at random, a vertex of a given degree. After a deletion step, the contents of the remaining vertices are updated. After the update, no information about the new values of the unexposed registers can be determined from what still is, or previously was, exposed. Therefore, the new graph is random given the number of its vertices, the number of its edges, and its degree sequence.

Notice that keeping a register unexposed is not in itself sufficient to guarantee that its contents stay random. Randomness is destroyed if one could even *implicitly* infer additional information about the current contents of an unexposed register from the combined knowledge of the current and previous contents of exposed registers. Therefore, in all cases, a proof is necessary that no new information about the current values of unexposed registers can be implicitly revealed. On the other hand, it is permissible for a given update step to implicitly reveal information about previous contents—subsequently overwritten—of an unexposed register. This does not destroy randomness, in that it is the *updated* structure that must be proven random. Since revealing past secret information causes no harm as long as no current secret information is revealed, it is convenient to imagine an omniscient "intermediary": an agent independent of the deleting algorithm who updates all necessary registers in total confidence (see, in this respect, the "card model" in Achlioptas [1]). Randomness is retained even if the actions (updates) of the intermediary combined with all exposed information implicitly yield some information about past values of unexposed registers, as long as no information about their current contents is revealed. Of course, this construct of "intermediary" is not a formal notion, but simply a convenient way to describe the updating mechanism.

Notice also that one should not assume that *all* previously unexposed information that is going to be overwritten is necessarily exposed at an update. Doing so might make it possible to infer additional implicit information about the updated contents of unexposed registers. In general, only part of the information to be overwritten needs to be known in order to carry out the update, and thus is implicitly revealed. The construct of the omniscient intermediary operating in secrecy frees us from having to make explicit exactly what secret information (to be overwritten) is implicitly revealed at an update. We simply need to make sure that no updated secret information is implicitly revealed after the update.

We illustrate these points by a further example. Consider a random graph conditional on (i) the number of vertices, (ii) the number of edges, (iii) the number of vertices of degree 1, and (iv) the number of vertices of degree 0 (isolated vertices). We claim that upon deleting a random vertex of degree 1 and its incident edge, the new graph is random conditional on the same type of information. This randomness claim is an immediate consequence of a more general theorem proven in Pittel et al. [436] (see also Broder et al. [81]), where the degrees of the vertices to be deleted are allowed to take values up to an arbitrary fixed integer k, assuming that the degree sequence of the graph is given up to k (we have seen in the previous example that this is true if we allow the degrees to range up to $n - 1$). The proof in Pittel et al. [436] depends upon counting all possibilities. However, the result can also be proven using the principle of deferred decisions. Assume that for each vertex v there is an *exposed* degree register that contains a three-valued parameter, indicating whether the degree of that vertex is 0, 1, or ≥ 2. In contrast to the case where the whole degree sequence was known, updating these registers after a deletion step presupposes knowledge of *unexposed* information. For instance, to update the degree register of a vertex that had degree at least 2 before the deletion, and which lost an incoming edge because of the deletion, we need to know whether its degree was previously exactly 2 or strictly more. However, it is easy to see that no information about the *updated* value of the unexposed registers is revealed by the combined knowledge of what currently is and previously was exposed: if an updated degree register ends up with the value ≥ 2, beyond this information we still have no knowledge of its actual degree. Therefore, randomness is retained. The omniscient intermediary secretly carries out the updating, using unexposed information. Even though the intermediary might reveal implicit information about the past values of registers, an observer cannot obtain any knowledge about the current contents of any unexposed register from what is and was unexposed.

On the other hand, the fact that additional current information is implicitly revealed is sometimes hard to notice. The subtlety of implicit disclosure can be illustrated by the following example. Let a *B&W graph* be a graph whose *edges* are either black or white. Call a vertex *all-white* if all the edges incident on it are white. Let the w-degree of a vertex v be the number of all-white vertices that v is connected with (see figs. 1 through 3). Notice that a black edge incident on v does not count towards the w-degree of v, while a white edge incident on v may or may not count towards the w-degree of v. Suppose we are given a random B&W graph G conditional on the number of vertices, and for each vertex v, the w-degree of v as well as the number of black edges and the number of white edges incident on v. All other characteristics of G are assumed to be random. Formally, given a fixed integer n and a fixed array of integers $d_{w,i,j}$ where $w, i, j = 0, \ldots, n - 1$, then G is chosen with equal probability among all B&W graphs such that $d_{w,i,j}$ is the number of vertices in the graph with w-degree w, i incident white edges and j incident black edges. We assume that the values of the array are such that there is at least one such graph. Suppose now that we delete from G a vertex v, chosen at random among all vertices with a specified w-degree (say 0). Suppose we also delete all edges, black and white, incident on v. Is the new graph random conditional on the same type of information?

Prima facie, one may think that the answer to this question is yes. Indeed, suppose that the exposed registers give for each vertex its w-degree, as well as the number of black edges and the number of white edges incident on it. All other information about the graph is assumed to be unexposed, that iss, random. After the deletion of a vertex v as previously described, and the subsequent deletion of all edges incident on v, all registers are updated. We may be tempted to conclude that the same type of information about the graph is known before and after the deletion, leading to an affirmative answer to the question. Unfortunately, this argument is erroneous. To see why, observe what happens if, after the deletion of v, the exposed w-degree of another vertex u increases. Using the combined knowledge of the current and previous contents of exposed registers, we can infer that in the new graph there exists at least one vertex v' that has just become all-white (as the result of the deletion of a black edge joining v with v'). Additionally, we learn that u is connected with at least one of these newly-all-white vertices. However, this last type of information is not supplied by the currently exposed registers, which give only the w-degree of u and the number of black and white edges incident on it. They do not specify a subset of the all-white vertices connected with u. The fact that we have implicit access to that information means that randomness cannot be retained in the new graph.

We now show a specific case of this. Consider the list of degree parameters (w-degree, number of incident white edges and number of incident black edges) given in figure 1(a) for each vertex of a random B&W graph. Then, by an easy case analysis we may verify that the only graphs having these degree parameters are the two depicted in figure 1(b) and (c). These two graphs are equiprobable, and any information about them other than what is in the upper table is assumed to be stored in unexposed registers. Suppose now that we delete the vertex v_5 from the random graph. Then the resulting graph, depending on which the original one was, will have the degree parameters given either in figure 2(a) or in figure 3(a). Suppose the resulting graph has the degree parameters of figure 2(a), so that the original graph was the one in figure 1(b)—examining this case will be sufficient for the purposes of demonstration. Again, by an easy case analysis we can verify that the only graphs having these degree parameters are the two depicted in figure 2(b) and 2(c). (If the original graph was the one in fig. 1(c), then the only possible graph having the degree parameters of fig. 3(a) is the one depicted in fig. 3(b)—we do not examine that case here.)

If deleting vertex v_5 did not destroy randomness, then both graphs in figure 2(b) and 2(c) should be equiprobable. However, from the *combined* knowledge of the tables in figure 1(a) and figure 2(a), we can easily infer that the graph in figure 2(c) is impossible. This is so because combining the information in the last columns of the tables in figure 1(a) and 2(a) we find that the newly all-white vertex is v_6 (it is the only vertex that previously had, but no longer has, an incident black edge). Also, from the combined information in the third and fourth rows of the second columns of these tables we see that both v_3 and v_4 are adjacent to v_6, as their w-degree has increased. Continuing with an easy case analysis,

vertices	w-degree	# of white incident edges	# of black incident edges
v_1	0	2	0
v_2	1	1	1
v_3	1	2	2
v_4	0	1	1
v_5	0	0	1
v_6	0	2	1

(a)

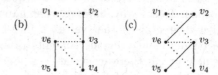

FIGURE 1 Original B&W graph: (a) exposed register values; (b) and (c) the two possible graphs corresponding to these values. Solid lines represent black edges and dashed lines represent white edges.

we conclude that the only graph that has the degree parameters of figure 2(a) and was obtained from a graph that has the degree parameters of figure 1(a) by deleting v_5 is the graph in figure 2(b). In other words, the combined knowledge of the two tables—the one before the deletion and the one after—reveals additional information that cannot be obtained exclusively from the current table, after the deletion. This proves that randomness is not retained. It is instructive to note that if no information were given about the w-degree of the vertices and we dealt only with information about the ordinary degrees (even if they were categorized by the number of incident white edges and the number of incident black edges) then randomness would be retained. That is true because combined knowledge of the two consecutive tables would not then be enough for us to infer additional unexposed information about the resulting graph.

The execution of an algorithmic step on the graph, such as the deletion of a vertex and the edges incident on it, can thus implicitly but subtly expose additional information about the current values of unexposed registers. In section 4, we describe more fully the methodology that is helpful in checking whether any implicit exposure of additional information has taken place as the result of the application of an algorithmic step. As we have seen here, the basic idea is to store information about the random structure in registers, in sufficiently "small pieces." The payoff of doing so is that implicit disclosure of information can be detected easily. Again, we do not require that updates be performed only on the basis of exposed information: unexposed information can be made available to the omniscient "intermediary" doing the updating. But there must be no way for us to infer this information.

vertices	w-degree	# of white incident edges	# of black incident edges
v_1	0	2	0
v_2	1	1	1
v_3	2	2	2
v_4	1	1	1
—	-	-	-
v_6	0	2	0

(a)

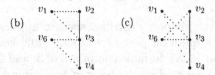

FIGURE 2   B&W graph from figure 1(b) with vertex v_5 deleted: (a) exposed register values; (b) and (c) the two possible graphs corresponding to these values.

vertices	w-degree	# of white incident edges	# of black incident edges
v_1	0	2	0
v_2	1	1	1
v_3	1	2	1
v_4	0	1	1
—	-	-	-
v_6	0	2	1

(a)

FIGURE 3   B&W graph from figure 1(c) with vertex v_5 deleted: (a) exposed register values; (b) the only possible graph corresponding to these values.

One might say that a safer way to prove conditional randomness claims is by rigorous counting arguments, rather than through the principle of deferred decisions. In complicated situations, however, counting arguments are practically impossible. As we will see from specific applications, our methodology makes it easy to specify what the *a priori* exposed information should be in order to retain randomness throughout the execution of an algorithm, given the type of operations that the algorithm allows. Such considerations have attracted much attention lately, in view of the increased interest in the probabilistic analysis of heuristics on random Boolean formulas and graphs. This has been discussed in chapter 3 (see also Molloy [403] for an overview of satisfiability and colorability thresholds). The probabilistic analysis involves analyzing the mean path of the heuristic [529], while showing that randomness is retained throughout the course of the heuristic. It is in situations like this where our methodology is particularly useful. This approach can ultimately be used to obtain lower bounds on threshold locations: indeed, the best lower bound to date on the satisfiability threshold [294, 295], mentioned in the previous chapter, has been proven using the principle of deferred decisions.

The rest of the chapter describes specific applications of this nature. We answer, notably, a question posed by Molloy [402] concerning a Davis-Putnam heuristic acting on a CNF formula comprised of 3- and 2-clauses, when the literals to be satisfied are selected on the basis of how often they appear in each of the two types of clauses. Using the principle of deferred decisions, we show what characteristics must be conditional in order to retain randomness throughout the procedure (theorem 4.2 in section 4), and conjecture that this is the minimal set of conditionals needed.

3   TERMINOLOGY AND NOTATION

Our results can be applied in various contexts related to random graphs or formulas. However, for concreteness, we first present them in the context of random formulas comprised only of 3- and 2-clauses. We introduce below the related terminology and notation.

Let V be a set of variables of cardinality n. Let L be the set of literals of V, that is, elements of V and their negations. A k-clause is a disjunction of exactly k literals from L. Let ϕ be a Boolean formula in conjunctive normal form (CNF), comprised of 3- and 2-clauses. Let m be the total number of clauses of the formula. Let C_3 and C_2 denote the collections of 3-clauses and 2-clauses of ϕ, respectively, and let c_3, c_2, and l be the respective cardinalities of the sets C_3, C_2, and L. Clearly $c_3 + c_2 = m$, and $l = 2n$. (Note that the notation used here is slightly different from that of chapter 3: there, C_3 and C_2 were the numbers of 3- and 2-clauses, and c_3 and c_2 were the respective *densities*. Note also that C_3 and C_2 are distinct from C_3 and C_2 from the previous chapter, where they denoted the collections of clauses containing exactly 3 and 2 *positive* literals, respectively.)

For $i = 0, 1, \ldots, 3c_3 + 2c_2$, let D_i be the set of literals in L that have exactly i occurrences in ϕ. The elements of D_i are said to have *degree* i. Literals whose negation is in D_0 are called *pure*. Notice that according to our terminology, a literal in L whose variable does not appear at all in the formula is pure.

Let D_1^3 and D_1^2 be the sets of literals that have exactly one occurrence in ϕ, in a 3-clause and 2-clause, respectively. D_1 is then the disjoint union of D_1^3

and D_1^2. Let also $D_{1\times1}^2$ be the subset of D_1^2 comprised of literals that appear in a 2-clause whose second literal also belongs to D_1^2.

Let d_i, d_1^3, d_1^2, and $d_{1\times1}^2$ be the respective cardinalities of D_i, D_1^3, D_1^2, and $D_{1\times1}^2$. Obviously, $d_1 = d_1^3 + d_1^2$.

Consider the collection of formulas comprised of 3- and 2-clauses that have given, fixed values for the parameters l, c_3, c_2, d_0, d_1^3, d_1^2, and $d_{1\times1}^2$. Make this collection into a probability space by assigning to each one of its elements the same probability (we assume that the values of the parameters are such that this space is not empty). An element of this space is called a random $\{3,2\}$-CNF formula conditional on the values of l, c_3, c_2, d_0, d_1^3, d_1^2, and $d_{1\times1}^2$. One could define random graphs similarly, conditional, for instance, on the number of edges and vertices, as we did in the previous section. Such formulas and graphs are called *conditionally random objects*.

We will consider algorithms on random $\{3,2\}$-CNF formulas that only apply steps of the following three types (one step may comprise several constituent substeps):

- *Set a pure literal.* Select at random a pure literal, set it to TRUE and delete all clauses where it appears.
- *Set a degree-one literal from a 3-clause.* Select at random a literal in D_1^3, set it to FALSE, delete it from the 3-clause where it appears and delete all clauses where its negation appears.
- *Set a degree-one literal from a 2-clause.* Select at random a literal in D_1^2, set it to FALSE, delete it from the 2-clause where it appears and delete all clauses where its negation appears. This can create a 1-clause. As long as there are 1-clauses, choose one at random, set its literal to TRUE, delete all clauses where it appears and delete its negation from any clause in which it appears. Ignore (delete) any empty and thus trivially unsatisfiable clause that may occur during this step. This last provision is simply a technicality introduced to study the randomness of the formula independently of its satisfiability. Of course, when such a step is used as a subroutine of an algorithm for satisfiability, the occurrence of an empty clause is an indication to stop immediately and report unsatisfiability.

4   RESULTS

Theorem 4.1. *Let ϕ be a random $\{3,2\}$-CNF formula conditional on the values of the parameters l, c_3, c_2, d_0, d_1^3, d_1^2, and $d_{1\times1}^2$. If any algorithmic step like the ones described above is applied to ϕ, then the formula obtained is a random $\{3,2\}$-CNF formula conditional on the new values of the parameters l, c_3, c_2, d_0, d_1^3, d_1^2, and $d_{1\times1}^2$.*

Proof Notice that no algorithmic step differentiates between degree-one literals appearing in 2-clauses on the basis of the degree of the other literal in the 2-clause. Still, according to the statement of the theorem, randomness is preserved if it is conditional not only on d_1^2 but also on $d_{1 \times 1}^2$. The reason for this will become clear later in this proof.

We first introduce some general notions, in more formal terms than before. An object such as a formula or a graph can be modeled by a data structure. Let us think of a data structure as a collection of registers containing information about the object. For example, a data structure modeling a graph includes a register for each vertex, with pointers to the registers of the edges incident on the vertex. It also includes a register for each edge, with pointers to the registers of the vertices on which the edge is incident. A data structure modeling a formula includes a register for each literal, with pointers to the registers of the literal appearing in the clause. It also includes a register for each clause (more information about the registers of a formula is given below).

Registers are partitioned into groups. The elements of each group contain various types of information for the same part of the modeled object. For example, for each vertex of a graph, we may have several registers in one group: one with pointers to the edges incident on the vertex, another with the degree of this vertex, etc. For the present purposes, we refer to the registers belonging to the same group as sub-registers of the group. We also imagine, for each group, a head register with pointers to its sub-registers. When a sub-register of a group contains a pointer to another group, it is assumed to point to the head register of that other group. Intuitively, the reason for storing different types of information in separate sub-registers is to avoid exposing all information about a part of the modeled object when it is necessary to expose only a "small piece" of it.

A *data structure with unexposed information* is a data structure whose (sub-)registers are partitioned into two categories, called *unexposed* and *exposed* registers. The partitioning is done according to rules given in the definition of the structure. These rules are based on the type of contents of the registers. The head registers of the groups are always exposed. Intuitively, one may think of such a structure as modeling an object whose characteristics stored in the unexposed registers are random, conditional on the information stored in the exposed registers. The same group may contain both exposed and unexposed sub-registers. For example, although the specific edges where a vertex appears may not be exposed, its degree may be exposed.

In general, given a conditionally random object, we associate with it a data structure as above. An algorithmic step that deletes an element of the object (such as the deletion of a vertex or the assignment of a variable) corresponds to the deletion of the group of registers associated with the deleted element of the object. After the deletion, all registers are updated.

Definition 1. *An algorithmic step is called randomness preserving if, after the corresponding deletions and updates of registers, no information about the contents of unexposed registers can be inferred from what currently is and previously was exposed, beyond what can be inferred from what is currently exposed. In other words, no additional information is implicitly revealed by knowing both past and current exposed information.*

To prove a randomness claim such as the theorem under consideration, it suffices to find a data structure with unexposed information that models the conditionally random object in the claim, and then to show (i) that the algorithmic steps are randomness preserving and (ii) that the information in the conditional is exactly the information that can be extracted from the exposed registers of the structure.

We describe below a structure S, with unexposed information, that models a random $\{3, 2\}$-CNF formula conditional on the parameters l, c_3, c_2, d_0, d_1^3, d_1^2, and $d_{1\times 1}^2$.

- For each literal t in L, the structure S contains a group of sub-registers collectively called literal sub-registers. These contain information about the degree of the literal, its occurrences in the formula and its negation. The information that is assumed exposed is (i) the degree and (ii) the position in the formula of literals with a single occurrence that happens to be in a 2-clause. All other information is unexposed. More formally, one of these sub-registers contains two bits of information indicating whether t belongs to D_0 (t does not appear in the formula), D_1^3 (t has degree 1 and appears in a 3-clause), D_1^2 (t has degree 1 and appears in a 2-clause) or none of these (t has degree at least 2). This sub-register is exposed. Also, we assume that there are sub-registers containing pointers to the positions of all occurrences of t in the formula (to the heads of all clause sub-registers where t appears; see below). These sub-registers are exposed if t is in D_1^2 and unexposed otherwise. The reason for exposing the position in the formula of literals in D_1^2 will become apparent later. Finally, we assume that there is an unexposed sub-register pointing to the head of the literal sub-register of the negation of t. It is important to notice that because the pointer to the negation of a literal is unexposed, each literal is paired with its logical negation randomly.
- For each clause in the formula, the structure S contains a group of sub-registers collectively called clause sub-registers. These contain information about the type of the clause (3-clause or 2-clause) and pointers to the heads of literal sub-registers corresponding to the literals that appear in the clause. The information about the type of the clause is exposed, while the pointers to the literal registers are unexposed.

It is straightforward to verify that after the application of any of the algorithmic steps, no information about an unexposed register can be deduced from what is and previously was exposed. Under these circumstances, the randomness of the structure S is preserved under an algorithmic step. The need for having the positions of literals in D_1^2 exposed can be seen in the event that under an update step, exactly one 3-clause shrinks to a 2-clause and exactly one literal moves from D_1^3 to D_1^2. In that case, the information about the type of each clause and the degree of each literal is sufficient to allow us to infer the position of this literal.

Now the theorem follows because the information that can be extracted from S consists only of the values of the following parameters: l (the number of groups of literal sub-registers), c_2 (the number of groups of clause sub-registers for 2-clauses), c_3 (the number of groups of clause sub-registers for 3-clauses), d_0, d_1^3, d_1^2, and $d_{1\times1}^2$. The value of $d_{1\times1}^2$ can be obtained from S because the positions in the formula of literals in D_1^2 are exposed. All other information that can be extracted from S can be expressed in terms of the values of the parameters l, c_3, c_2, d_0, d_1^3, d_1^2, and $d_{1\times1}^2$, only. (One can immediately see, for instance, that the number of 2-clauses where both positions are filled with literals of degree at least 2 or the number of 2-clauses where one position contains a literal of degree at least two and the other a literal of degree exactly one can be expressed in terms of the values of the parameters l, c_3, c_2, d_0, d_1^3, d_1^2, and $d_{1\times1}^2$). This completes the proof of Theorem 4.1.

We now come to the generalization of the previous result to arbitrary degrees, where algorithms making use of the overall number of occurrences of literals in 3-clauses and 2-clauses, separately, are allowed. To preserve randomness in this case, a conditional given by a number of integer parameters—as in the previous theorem—is not enough. We have to assume that the positions of all literals appearing in 2-clauses are known, regardless of their degree: this information is revealed when a 3-clause shrinks to a 2-clause and the exposed degree information of literals is updated. However, no information about negations of literals or identification of literals need be revealed, nor does information on the positions of literals appearing in 3-clauses. In other words, we have to assume that the *pattern* in which literals are paired in 2-clauses is conditional, though the pattern need not reveal the pairing of literals of opposite logical sign. This is still a severe restriction on the randomness of the formula. Below, we formalize the notion of pattern.

Fix an even integer $2n$ representing the number of literals of a formula, and an integer c_3 representing the number of 3-clauses in a formula. A *pattern for 2-clauses and degree sets that is transparent with respect to negations* (pattern, in short) is a set of unordered pairs $\underline{C}_2$ of integers from $\{1, \ldots, 2n\}$, representing the collection of 2-clauses of the formula, together with a collection of sets $D_i^3 \subseteq \{1, \ldots, 2n\}, i = 0, \ldots, c_3$, such that $\sum_i i|D_i^3| = 3c_3$, representing the collection of sets of literals whose number of occurrences in 3-clauses is i.

Now fix a pattern P as described above. A random formula ϕ conditional on P is constructed as follows: randomly choose c_3 unordered triplets from $1, \ldots, 2n$

so that all integers in each D_i^3 appear in exactly i such triplets; denote this set by $\underline{C}_3$; randomly select a one-to-one and onto mapping neg : $\{1, \ldots, n\} \rightarrow \{n+1, \ldots, 2n\}$ representing the negations; in the tuples of $\underline{C}_3$ and of $\underline{C}_2$, replace each $k = 1, \ldots, n$ with variable x_k and each neg(k), $k = 1, \ldots, n$, with its negation $\overline{x_k}$, and denote by C_3 and C_2, respectively, the sets of clauses thus obtained; let the formula ϕ be the one that has as 3-clauses and as 2-clauses the sets C_3 and C_2, respectively. Notice that since the negation function "neg" was random, a literal and its negation may appear in the same clause. If we wish to avoid this, "neg" may instead be a random one-to-one and onto mapping made conditional on the fact that for no $i = 1, \ldots, n$ can both i and neg(i) appear in the same tuple of either $\underline{C}_3$ or $\underline{C}_2$. Based on the method of proof of the previous theorem, one can obtain the following result that answers an open question posed by Molloy [402].

Theorem 4.2. *Let ϕ be a random $\{3,2\}$-CNF formula conditional on a given pattern P, as described above. For arbitrary i and j, choose at random a literal t with i occurrences in 3-clauses and j occurrences in 2-clauses. Assign to t the value* TRUE *and perform the necessary deletions and shrinking of clauses accompanied by repeated setting to* TRUE *of literals in 1-clauses, as long as 1-clauses exist. The new formula is then random, conditional on its new pattern P'.*

Proof Again, we introduce a structure $\mathcal{S}$ that contains groups of sub-registers corresponding to literals and to clauses. This time, the exposed degree sub-registers of a literal t contain two integers: one giving the number of occurrences of t in 3-clauses and the other giving the number of occurrences of t in 2-clauses. Furthermore, the group of literal sub-registers of t contains information on which 3-clauses and which 2-clauses include t. The information regarding 3-clauses is unexposed. The information regarding 2-clauses, however, must be exposed because after an algorithmic step, it can be inferred from the knowledge of the previous and current values of the registers giving the type of each clause (3-clause or 2-clause) and the degrees of the literals. One may readily confirm that nothing can then be inferred about the unexposed registers after the application of an algorithmic step. It is also immediately apparent that the information that can be extracted from such a structure $\mathcal{S}$ is given by the pattern P.

Note that if the algorithm does not make use of the number of occurrences of literals separately in 3-clauses and 2-clauses, but only needs the total number of occurrences of a literal in the formula, then the conditional does not have to include the pairing of literals in 2-clauses. It is sufficient in this case for the conditional to contain the total degree sequence, the number of 3-clauses, and the number of 2-clauses.

Finally, as a further application, let us see what information must be placed in the conditional for an algorithm deleting vertices of a specified w-degree from a random B&W graph, as discussed in section 2.

Given a B&W-graph G, let $W \subseteq G$ be the subgraph comprised of the vertices of G, with vertices marked according to whether or not they are all-white (in the sense of G), and all white edges with at least one endpoint incident on an all-white vertex. Call W the subgraph of w-degree *witnesses*. Without giving details, one can again define a notion of random B&W graphs conditional on the number of vertices, the total number of edges and the precise subgraph of w-degree witnesses. Note that to construct the rest of the graph from this information, one can arbitrarily place edges between vertices that are not all-white and then arbitrarily color them black or white, taking care that at least one black edge is incident on each vertex that is not all-white.

Then the following theorem holds. We omit its easy proof, as the notion of B&W graphs was introduced only for illustrative purposes.

Theorem 4.3. *If we delete a random vertex of a specified arbitrary w-degree from a B&W graph that is random conditional on the number of vertices, the total number of edges and the subgraph of w-degree witnesses, then the new graph is random conditional on the new number of vertices, the new total number of edges and the new subgraph of w-degree witnesses.*

An analogous result holds if the deleted vertex has specified numbers of white and black edges incident on it (the conditional in the latter case must be augmented to contain the sequence d_{ij} giving the number of vertices with i white and j black edges incident on them).

We conclude this chapter by the following

Informal Conjecture. The conditionals of theorems 4.1, 4.2, and 4.3 contain the least information possible. With weaker conditionals, randomness would not be retained.

ACKNOWLEDGMENTS

This research has been supported by the University of Patras, Research Committee (Project C. Carathéodory no. 2445). We would like to thank an anonymous referee and the editors for their comments that led to substantial improvements. The second author thanks D. Achlioptas and M. Molloy for several discussions about probabilistic arguments, and acknowledges partial support by the EU within the 6th Framework Programme under contract 001907 (DELIS).

CHAPTER 9

The Phase Transition in the Random HornSAT Problem

Demetrios D. Demopoulos
Moshe Y. Vardi

1 INTRODUCTION

This chapter presents a study of the satisfiability of random Horn formulas and a search for a phase transition. In the past decade, phase transitions or *sharp thresholds*, have been studied intensively in combinatorial problems. Although the idea of thresholds in a combinatorial context was introduced as early as 1960 [147], in recent years it has been a major subject of research in the communities of theoretical computer science, artificial intelligence, and statistical physics. As is apparent throughout this volume, phase transitions have been observed in numerous combinatorial problems, both for the probability that an instance of a problem has a solution and for the computational cost of solving an instance. In a few cases (2-SAT, 3-XORSAT, 1-in-k SAT) the existence and location of these phase transitions have also been formally proven [7, 94, 101, 131, 156, 202].

The problem at the center of this research is that of *3-satisfiability* (3-SAT). An instance of 3-SAT consists of a conjunction of clauses, where each clause is a disjunction of three literals. The goal is to find a truth assignment that satisfies

Computational Complexity and Statistical Physics, edited by Allon G. Percus, Gabriel Istrate, and Cristopher Moore, Oxford University Press.

all clauses. The *density* of a 3-SAT instance is the ratio of the number of clauses to the number of Boolean variables. We call the number of variables the *size* of the instance. Experimental studies [110, 395, 397, 466, 469] have shown that there is a shift in the probability of satisfiability of random 3-SAT instances, from 1 to 0, located at around density 4.27 (this is also called the *crossover point*). So far, in spite of much progress in obtaining rigorous bounds on the threshold location, highlighted in the previous chapters, there is no mathematical proof of a phase transition taking place at that density [1, 132, 177]. Experimental studies also show a peak of the computational complexity around the crossover point. In Kirkpatrick and Selman [319], finite-size scaling techniques were used to suggest a phase transition at the crossover point. Later, in Coafra et al. [96], experiments showed that a phase transition of the running time from polynomial in the instance size to exponential is solver-dependent, and for several different solvers this transition occurs at a density lower than the crossover point. This phenomenon has been further discussed in chapter 3. A restriction on all the experimental studies is imposed by the inherent difficulty of the problem, especially around the crossover point. We can only study instances of limited size (usually up to a few hundred) before the problems get too hard to be solved in reasonable time using available computational resources.

A problem similar to random 3-SAT is that of the satisfiability of random Horn formulas, also called random HornSAT. A Horn formula in conjunctive normal form (CNF) is a conjunction of Horn clauses; each Horn clause is a disjunction of literals of which *at most one* can be positive. Unlike 3-SAT, HornSAT is a tractable problem. The complexity of the HornSAT is linear in the size of the formula [128]. The linear complexity of HornSAT allows us to study experimentally the satisfiability of the problem for much bigger input sizes than those used in similar research on other problems like 3-SAT or 3-Colorability [96, 110, 253, 469].

An additional motivation for studying random HornSAT comes from the fact that Horn formulas are related to several other areas of computer science and mathematics [375]. In particular, Horn formulas are connected to automata theory, as the transition relation, the starting state, and the set of final states of an automaton can be described using Horn clauses. For example, if we consider automata on binary trees (see definition below), then Horn clauses of length three can be used to describe its transition relation, while Horn clauses of length one can describe the starting state and the set of the final states of the automaton (we elaborate on that later). Then, the question about the emptiness of the language of the automaton can be translated to a question about the satisfiability of the formula. There is also a close relation between knowledge-based systems and Horn formulas, though we do not consider that relation in this chapter. Finally, there is a correspondence between Horn formulas and hypergraphs that we use to show how results on random hypergraphs relate to our research on random Horn formulas.

The probability of satisfiability of random Horn formulas generated according to a variable clause length model has been studied by Istrate [271], who showed that random Horn formulas have a *coarse* rather than a sharp satisfiability threshold, meaning that the problem does not have a phase transition. The variable clause length distribution model used by Istrate is ideally suited to studying Horn formulas in connection with knowledge-based systems [375].

Motivated by the connection between the *automata emptiness* problem and Horn satisfiability, we study the satisfiability of two types of random Horn formulas in conjunctive normal form (CNF) that are generated according to a variation of the *fixed* clause length distribution model mentioned in chapter 7. We consider the 1-3-HornSAT, where formulas consist of clauses of length one and three only, and 1-2-HornSAT, where formulas consist of clauses of length one and two only. We are looking to identify regions in the problems' space where instances are almost surely satisfiable or almost surely unsatisfiable. We are also interested in finding if the problems exhibit a sharp threshold.

The random 1-2-HornSAT problem is related to the random 1-3-HornSAT problem in the same way that random 2-SAT is related to random 3-SAT. That is, as some algorithm searches for a satisfying truth assignment for a random 1-3-Horn formula by assigning truth values to the variables, a random 1-2-Horn formula is created as a subformula of the original formula. This is a result of 3-clauses being shortened to 2-clauses by a subtitution of truth values. The relation between random 2-SAT and random 3-SAT has been exploited by Achlioptas [1] to improve on the lower bound for the threshold of random 3-SAT. In this work, Achlioptas uses differential equations to analyze the execution of a broad family of SAT algorithms. In general, one can try to analyze phase transitions using differential equations (cf. Istrate [272]). The 1-2-HornSAT problem can also be analyzed with the help of random graphs [62]. We show how results on random digraph connectivity, presented by Karp [300], can be used to model the satisfiability of random 1-2-Horn formulas. These results can be used to show that there is no phase transition for 1-2-HornSAT and are matched by our experimental data.

Our experimental investigation of 1-3-HornSAT shows that there are regions where a random 1-3-Horn formula is almost surely satisfiable and regions where it is almost surely unsatisfiable. Analysis of the satisfiability percentile window and finite-size scaling methods [485] suggest that there is a sharp threshold line between these two regions. Just as 1-2-HornSAT can be analyzed using random digraphs, 1-3-HornSAT can be analyzed using random hypergraphs. We show that some recent results on random hypergraphs [116] fit our experimental data well. Unlike the data analysis, however, the hypergraph-based model suggests that the transition from the satisfiable to unsatisfiable regions is a steep function rather than a step function. It is, therefore, not clear if the problem exhibits a phase transition, in spite of our having made use of experimental data for instances of large size.

Our results here also relate to those of Kolaitis and Raffill [339], who carried out a search for a phase transition in another NP-complete problem, that of AC-matching. The similarity between their work and ours is that the experimental data provide evidence that both problems have a slowly emerging phase transition. The difference is that in our case, because of the linear complexity of Horn satisfiability, we are able to test instances of Horn satisfiability of much larger size than the instances of AC-matching in Kolaitis and Raffill [339], or for that matter of most NP-complete problems such as 3-SAT and 3-COL.

2 PRELIMINARIES AND FINITE AUTOMATA

Before discussing our main results on thresholds in HornSAT, let us review some definitions related to combinatorial phase transitions, and show explicitly the relationship between HornSAT and finite automata. Let X be a finite set and $|X| = n$. Let A be a random subset of X constructed by a random procedure according to the probability space $\Omega(n, m)$ with measure:

$$\Pr_{\Omega(n,m)}(A) = \begin{cases} 1/\binom{n}{m^*} & \text{if } |A| = m^*; \\ 0 & \text{otherwise}, \end{cases}$$

where m is an integer and

$$m^* = \begin{cases} 0 & \text{if } m < 0; \\ m & \text{if } 0 \le m \le n; \\ n & \text{if } m > n. \end{cases}$$

The random procedure consists of selecting m^* elements of X without replacement. A (set) property Q of X is a subset of 2^X, the power set of X consisting of all subsets of X. Q is increasing if $A \in Q$ and $A \subseteq B \subseteq X$ implies $B \in Q$. Q is non-trivial if $\varnothing \notin Q$ and $X \in Q$. A property sequence Q consists of a sequence of sets $\{X_n : n \ge 1\}$ such that $|X_n| < |X_{n+1}|$ and a family $\{Q_n : n \ge 1\}$ where each Q_n is a property of X_n. Q is increasing if Q_n is increasing for every $n \ge 1$, and Q is non-trivial if Q_n is non-trivial for every $n \ge 1$.

Let Q_n be an increasing non-trivial property sequence, and $\theta : \mathbb{N} \to \mathbb{R}^+$ a strictly positive function. We say that θ is a threshold for Q if for every $f : \mathbb{N} \to \mathbb{N}$:

1. If $\lim_{n\to\infty} f(n)/\theta(n) = 0$ then $\lim_{n\to\infty} \Pr_{\Omega(n,f(n))}(Q_n) = 0$
2. If $\lim_{n\to\infty} f(n)/\theta(n) = \infty$ then $\lim_{n\to\infty} \Pr_{\Omega(n,f(n))}(Q_n) = 1$.

θ is a sharp threshold Q if for every $f : \mathbb{N} \to \mathbb{N}^+$:

1. If $\sup_{n\to\infty} f(n)/\theta(n) < 1$ then $\lim_{n\to\infty} \Pr_{\Omega(n,f(n))}(Q_n) = 0$
2. If $\inf_{n\to\infty} f(n)/\theta(n) > 1$ then $\lim_{n\to\infty} \Pr_{\Omega(n,f(n))}(Q_n) = 1$.

We say that Q exhibits a phase transition if it has a sharp threshold. Our interest is in satisfiability of Horn formulas. Thus, in our framework X_n is the set of Horn clauses over a set with n Boolean variables. A set of Horn clauses is a Horn formula.

Our main motivation for studying the satisfiability of Horn formulas is that, unlike 3-SAT, this problem is tractable. Therefore, we will have numerical data for instances of much larger size to help us answer questions similar to those previously asked about 3-SAT.

Apart from that, it is also of interest to us that Horn formulas can be used to describe finite automata. A finite automaton A is a 5-tuple $A = (S, \Sigma, \delta, s, F)$, where S is a finite set of states, Σ is an alphabet, δ is a transition relation, s is a starting state, and $F \subseteq S$ is the set of final (accepting) states.

In a word automaton, δ is a function from $S \times \Sigma$ to 2^S. In a binary-tree automaton δ is a function from $S \times \Sigma$ to $2^{S \times S}$. Intuitively, for word automata δ provides a set of successor states, while for binary-tree automata δ provides a set of successor state pairs. A run of an automaton on a word $a = a_1 a_2 \cdots a_n$ is a sequence of states $s_0 s_1 \cdots s_n$ such that $s_0 = s$ and $(s_{i-1}, a_i, s_i) \in \delta$. A run is successful if $s_n \in F$: in this case we say that A accepts the word a. A run of an automaton on a binary tree t labeled with letters from Σ is a binary tree r labeled with states from S such that $\text{root}(r) = s$ and for a node i of t, $(r(i), t(i), r(\text{left-child-of-}i), r(\text{right-child-of-}i)) \in \delta$. Thus, each pair in $\delta(r(i), t(i))$ is a possible labeling of the children of i. A run is successful if for all leaves l of r, $r(l) \in F$: in this case we say that A accepts the tree t. The language $L(A)$ of a word automaton A is the set of all words a for which there is a successful run of A on a. Likewise, the language $L(A)$ of a tree automaton A is the set of all trees t for which there is a successful run of A on t. An important question in automata theory that is also of great practical importance in the field of formal verification [510] is, given an automaton A, is $L(A)$ non-empty? We can show how the problem of non-emptiness of automata languages translates to Horn satisfiability.

Consider first a word automaton $A = (S, \Sigma, \delta, s_0, F)$. Construct a Horn formula ϕ_A over the set S of variables as follows:

- create a clause $(\overline{s_0})$
- for each $s_i \in F$ create a clause (s_i)
- for each element (s_i, a, s_j) of δ create a clause $(\overline{s_j}, s_i)$,

where $(s_i, \ldots, s_k)$ represents the clause $s_i \vee \cdots \vee s_k$ and $\overline{s_j}$ is the negation of s_j.

Theorem 2.1. *Let A be a word automaton and ϕ_A the Horn formula constructed as described above. Then $L(A)$ is non-empty if and only if ϕ_A is unsatisfiable.*

Proof ($\Rightarrow$) Assume that $L(A)$ is non-empty, i.e., there is a path $\pi = s_{i_0} s_{i_1} \cdots s_{i_m}$ in A such that $s_{i_0} = s_0$ and $s_{i_m} = s_k$ where s_k is a final state. Since s_k is a final state, (s_k) is a clause in ϕ_A. Also $(\overline{s_k}, s_{i_{m-1}})$ is a clause in ϕ_A. For ϕ_A to be satisfiable s_k must be TRUE, and consequently $s_{i_{m-1}}$ must be TRUE. By induction on the length of the path π we can show that for ϕ_A to be satisfiable s_0 must be TRUE, which is a contradiction.

($\Leftarrow$) Assume that ϕ_A is unsatisfiable. It then must have positive-unit resolution refutation [239], i.e., a proof by contradiction where in each step one of the resolvents must be a positive literal and the last resolution step is with the clause $(\overline{s_0})$. Let (s_i) be the first positive literal resolvent in the proof. By construction, s_i is a final state of A. By induction on the length of the refutation, we can construct a path in A from s_0 to s_i, Therefore, $L(A)$ is non-empty.

Similarly to the word automata case, we can show how to construct a Horn formula from a binary-tree automaton. Let $A = (S, \Sigma, \delta, s_0, F)$ be a binary-tree automaton. Then we can construct a Horn formula ϕ_A using the construction above with the only difference that since δ in this case is a function from $S \times \{\alpha\}$ to $S \times S$, for each element (s_i, α, s_j, s_k) of δ we create a clause $(\overline{s_j}, \overline{s_k}, s_i)$. It is not difficult to see that also in this case we have:

Theorem 2.2. *Let A be a binary-tree automaton and ϕ_A the Horn formula constructed as described above. Then $L(A)$ is non-empty if and only if ϕ_A is unsatisfiable.*

Motivated by the connection between tree automata and Horn formulas described in theorem 2.2, we study the satisfiability of two types of random Horn formulas. More precisely, let $H^{1,2}_{n,d_1,d_2}$ denote a random formula in CNF over a set of variables $X = \{x_1, \ldots, x_n\}$, containing:

- a single negative literal chosen uniformly among the n possible negative literals;
- $d_1 n$ positive literals that are chosen uniformly, independently and without replacement among all $n - 1$ possible positive literals (the negation of the single negative literal already chosen is not allowed); and
- $d_2 n$ clauses of length two that contain one positive and one negative literal chosen uniformly, independently and without replacement, among all $n(n-1)$ possible clauses of that type.

We call the number of variables n the *size* of the instance.

Let also $H^{1,3}_{n,d_1,d_3}$ denote a random formula in CNF over the set of variables $X = \{x_1, \ldots, x_n\}$, containing:

- a single negative literal chosen uniformly among the n possible negative literals;
- $d_1 n$ positive literals that are chosen uniformly, independently and without replacement among all $n - 1$ possible positive literals (the negation of the single negative literal already chosen is not allowed); and
- $d_3 n$ clauses of length three that contain one positive and two negative literals chosen uniformly, independently and with replacement among all $n(n - 1)(n - 2)/2$ possible clauses of that type.

The sampling spaces $H^{1,3}$ and $H^{1,2}$ are slightly different: we sample with replacement in the first, and without replacement in the second. Here we explain why. Assume that we sample dn clauses out of N uniformly at random with replacement. Let us consider the (asymptotic) expected number of distinct clauses we get. Each one of the N clauses will be chosen with probability $1 - (1 - 1/N)^{dn}$. The expected number of distinct chosen clauses is $N(1 - (1 - 1/N)^{dn})$. Notice that $N(1 - (1 - 1/N)^{dn}) \simeq dn - O((dn)^2/N)$. In the case of a random $H^{1,3}_{n,d_1,d_3}$ formula $N = n(n - 1)(n - 2)/2$ and clearly the expected number of distinct clauses we sample is asymptotically equivalent to dn; thus we sample with replacement for experimental ease. In the case of a random $H^{1,2}_{n,d_1,d_2}$ formula, we sample without replacement to ensure that we do not have many repetitions among the chosen clauses.

3   1-2-HORNSAT

In this section we present our results on the probability of satisfiability of random 1-2-Horn formulas. We first present an experimental investigation of the satisfiability on the $d_1 \times d_2$ quadrant. We then discuss the relation between random 1-2-Horn formulas and random digraphs and show that our data agree with analytical results on graph reachability presented in Karp [300].

To study the probability of satisfiability of $H^{1,2}_{n,d_1,d_2}$ random formulas in the $d_1 \times d_2$ quadrant, we have generated and solved 1200 random instances of size 20000 per data point. Figure 1 shows the average satisfiability probability versus the two input parameters d_1 and d_2 (a) and the corresponding contour plot (b).

The satisfiability plot in figure 1 suggests that the problem does not have a phase transition. This can also be observed if we fix the value of one of the input parameters. In figure 2 we show the satisfiability plot for random 1-2-HornSAT for various instance sizes ranging from 500 to 32000, and for fixed $d_1 = 0.1$. We now explain why random 1-2-HornSAT does not have a phase transition, based on known results on random digraphs.

There are two most frequently used models of random digraphs. The first one, $\mathcal{G}_{n,m}$ consists of all digraphs on n vertices having m edges; all digraphs have equal probability. The second model, $\mathcal{G}_{n,p}$ with $0 < p < 1$, consists of all digraphs on n vertices in which the edges are chosen independently with probability p.

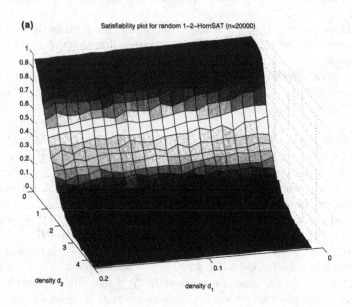

(a)

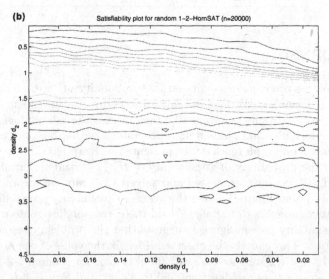

(b)

FIGURE 1   Satisfiability probability of a random 1-2-Horn formula of size 20,000 (a) and the corresponding contour plot (b). The contour plot contains 25 lines that separate consecutive percentage intervals $[0\% - 4\%), [4\% - 8\%), \ldots, [96\% - 100\%]$.

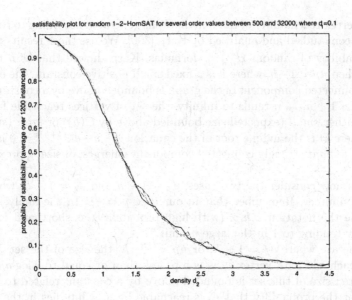

satisfiability plot for random 1–2–HornSAT for several order values between 500 and 32000, where q=0.1

FIGURE 2   Satisfiability probability of random 1-2-Horn formulas when $d_1 = 0.1$

It is known that in most investigations the two models are interchangeable, provided certain conditions are met. In what follows, we will take advantage of this equivalence in order to show how our experimental results relate to analytical results on random digraphs [300].

We will first show that there is a relation between the satisfiability of a random $H^{1,2}_{n,d_1,d_2}$ formula and the vertex reachability of a random digraph $\mathcal{G}_{n,m=d_2n}$. Let $\phi \in H^{1,2}_{n,d_1,d_2}$, $(\overline{x_0})$ be the unique single negative literal in ϕ, and F be the set of all variables that appear as single positive literals in ϕ. Obviously $|F| = d_1n$. Construct a graph G_ϕ such that for every variable x_i in ϕ there is a corresponding node v_i in G_ϕ and for each clause $(\overline{x_i}, x_j)$ of ϕ there is a directed edge in G_ϕ from v_i to v_j. G_ϕ is a random digraph from the $\mathcal{G}_{n,m=d_2n}$ model.

It is not difficult to see that ϕ is unsatisfiable if and only if the node v_0 in G_ϕ is reachable from a node v_i such that $x_i \in F$. In other words, the probability of unsatisfiability of a random $H^{1,2}_{n,d_1,d_2}$ formula ϕ is equal to the probability that a vertex of the random digraph $\mathcal{G}_{n,m=d_2n}$ is reachable from a set of vertices of size d_1n. (A vertex is reachable from a set of vertices if it is reachable by at least one of the vertices of the set.)

As mentioned above, the $\mathcal{G}_{n,m}$ and $\mathcal{G}_{n,p}$ models can be used interchangeably, when $m \simeq \binom{n}{2}p$ [62]. Therefore, the relation we have established between satisfiability of a random $H^{1,2}_{n,d_1,d_2}$ formula ϕ and the vertex reachability of a random digraph $\mathcal{G}_{n,m=d_2n}$ also holds between ϕ and a random digraph $\mathcal{G}_{n,p=d_2/n}$.

The vertex reachability of random digraphs generated according to the model $\mathcal{G}_{n,p}$ has been studied and analyzed by Karp [300]. We use those results to study the satisfiability of random $H_{n,d_1,d_2}^{1,2}$ formulas. Karp showed that as n tends to infinity, when $np < 1 - h$, where h is a fixed small positive constant, the expected size of a connected component of the graph is bounded above by a constant $C(h)$. When $np > 1 + h$, as n tends to infinity, the set of vertices reachable from one vertex is either *small* (expected size bounded above by $C(h)$) or *large* (size close to Θn, where Θ is the unique root of the equation $1 - x - e^{-(1+h)x} = 0$ in $[0, 1]$). Moreover, a *giant* strongly connected component emerges, of size approximately $\Theta^2 n$.

Let us now consider the two cases, $d_2 = 1 - h$ and $d_2 = 1 + h$, where h is a positive number. Remember that in our case $p = \frac{d_2}{n}$. In the analysis below we will use the notation w.h.p. (with high probability) as shorthand for "with probability tending to 1 in the large n limit."

In the case where $d_2 = 1 - h$, or $np < 1 - h$, the size of the set $X(v_i)$ of vertices reachable by a vertex v_i is w.h.p. less than or equal to $3 \log n h^{-2}$, and the expected size of this set is bounded above by a constant related to h. Thus we get that the probability that v_0 is reachable by v_i w.h.p. lies in the interval $[0, 3 \log n / n(1 - d_2)^2]$, and its expected value is bounded above by a constant. The expected probability that v_0 is reachable by a set of $d_1 n$ vertices should increase with d_1. The plots in figures 1 and 2 show that when $d_2 < 1$, the probability of satisfiability of ϕ (1 minus the probability that v_0 is reachable by a set of $d_1 n$ vertices in G_ϕ), decreases as we increase d_2 and/or d_1.

When $d_2 = 1 + h$, or $np > 1 + h$, we know that the set $X(v_i)$ of vertices reachable by a vertex v_i is w.h.p. either in the interval $[0, 3 \log n / (1 - d_2)^2]$ or around Θn. We also know that the probability that $X(v_i)$ is small tends to $1 - \Theta$. Therefore, w.h.p. at least one of the $d_1 n$ vertices will have a large reachable set. That is, the probability that v_0 is reachable by a set of $d_1 n$ vertices is bounded below from Θ. Notice that Θ increases with d_2. Again, the plots in figures 1 and 2 show that when $d_2 > 1$, the probability of satisfiability of ϕ decreases as d_2 increases. So the experimental observations are in agreement with the expectations based on the digraph reachability analysis.

Going back to digraphs' reachability, Karp's results show that for each vertex the set of its reachable vertices is very small up to the point where $np = 1$. We can observe the same behavior in 1-2-HornSAT if we change our distribution model by setting $d_1 = c/n$ for some constant c. By doing so, we are adjusting our model to fit the reachability analysis done by Karp that is based on a single starting vertex in the digraph. The result of this modification is that d_1 is no longer a factor on the probability of satisfiability of ϕ, which now depends solely on d_2. See figure 3, where we show the satisfiability plot in that case, and contrast with the picture that emerges when d_1 is a constant (shown in fig. 2). While before the satisfiability probability was steadily decreasing as we increased d_2, now the satisfiability probability is practically 1 until d_2 becomes larger than one. In both

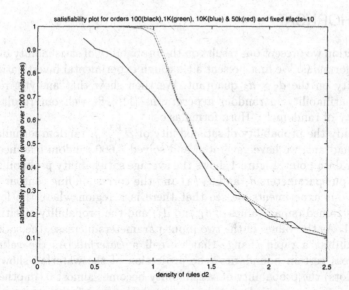

satisfiability plot for orders 100(black),1K(green), 10K(blue) & 50k(red) and fixed #facts=10

FIGURE 3 Satisfiability probability of random 1-2-Horn formulas when $d_1 = 10/n$ for sizes 100 (lower curve), 1,000, 10,000, and 50,000 (upper curve).

cases, however, the reachability analysis and the experimental data show that the satisfiability of random 1-2-Horn formulas is a problem that lacks a phase transition.

Remark 1. *The probability of satisfiability of 1-2-Horn can in fact be calculated exactly. Using the combinatorics of labeled trees, one can calculate exactly the probability $P(k)$ that a given vertex v has an out-tree of size k, not including itself, in a random digraph with mean out-degree d_2. This is*

$$P(k) = \frac{e^{-(k+1)d_2} d_2^k}{k!}(k+1)^{k-1}.$$

The probability of satisfiability is then

$$\mathbf{Pr}[\text{SAT}] = \sum_{k=0}^{\infty} P(k)(1-d_1)^k.$$

Numerical computation indicates a close fit with our experimental results.

4   1-3-HORNSAT

In this section we present our results on the probability of satisfiability of random 1-3-Horn formulas. We first present a thorough experimental investigation of the satisfiability on the $d_1 \times d_3$ quadrant. We then show that analytic results on vertex identifiability in random hypergraphs [116] fit well our results on the satisfiablity of random 1-3-Horn formulas.c

To study the probability of satisfiability of $H^{1,3}_{n,d_1,d_3}$ random formulas in the $d_1 \times d_3$ quadrant, we have generated and solved 3,600 random instances of size 20,000 per data point. Figure 4 shows the average satisfiability probability versus the two input parameters d_1 and d_3 (a) and the corresponding contour plot (b).

From our experiments we see that there is a region where the formula is underconstrained (small values of d_1 and d_3) and the probability of satisfiability is almost 1. As the values of the two input parameters increase, the satisfiability terrain exhibits a rapid change that we call a *waterfall*. As the values of d_1 and d_3 cross certain boundaries (the projection of the waterfall shown in the contour plots) the probability of satisfiability becomes almost 0. In other words, the transition appears to be similar to those observed in other combinatorial problems such as 3-SAT and 3-COL.

There is a significant difference though, between these previously studied transitions and the one we observe in 1-3-HornSAT. In cases such as 3-SAT or 3-COL there are two input parameters describing a random instance; the size and the constrainedness of the instance. The constrainedness is defined as the ratio of clauses to variables for satisfiability, and edges to vertices for graph coloring. In random 1-3-HornSAT, there are three parameters: the size of the instance and the two densities, namely d_1 and d_3. By taking a cut along the three-dimensional surface shown in figure 4(a), we can study the problem as if it had only two input parameters.

We have taken two straight-line cuts of the surface. For the first cut, we fix d_1 to be 0.1, we let d_3 take values in the range $[1, 5.5]$ with step 0.1, and we choose instance sizes 500, 1,000, 2,500, 5,000, 10,000, 20,000, and 40,000. See figure 5(a), where we plot the probability of satisfiability along this cut. This plot reveals a quick change on the probability of satisfiability as the input parameter d_3 passes through a critical value, around 3. One technique that has been used to support experimental evidence of a phase transition is finite-size scaling. This is a technique coming from statistical mechanics that has been used in studying the phase transitions of several NP-complete problems, such as k-SAT and AC-matching [319, 339]. The technique uses data from finite-size instances to extrapolate to infinite-size instances. The transformation is based on a rescaling according to a power law of the form $d' = d - d_c/d_c n^r$, where d is the density, d' is the rescaled parameter, d_c is the critical value, n is the instance size and r is a scaling exponent. As a result, a function $f(d, n)$ is transformed to a function $f(d')$. We apply finite-size scaling to our data to observe the sharpness of the transition, following the procedure presented by Kolaitis et al. [339]. Our

(a)

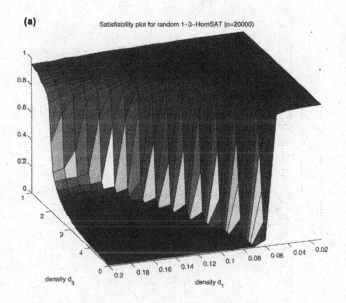

(b)

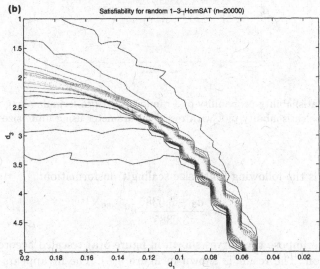

FIGURE 4   Satisfiability probability of a random 1-3-Horn formula of size 20,000 (a) and the corresponding contour plot (b). The contour plot contains 25 lines that separate consecutive percentage intervals $[0\% - 4\%), [4\% - 8\%), \ldots, [96\% - 100\%]$.

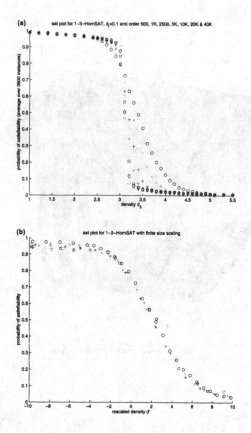

FIGURE 5 Satisfiability probability of a random 1-3-Horn formula along the $d_1 = 0.1$ cut (a) and the satisfiability plot with rescaled parameter using finite-size scaling (b).

analysis yields the following finite-size scaling transformation:

$$d' = \frac{d_3 - 3.0385}{3.0385} n^{0.4859}.$$

We then superimpose the curves shown in figure 5(a) rescaled according to this transformation. The result is shown in figure 5(b). The fit appears to be very good around zero, where curves collapse to a single universal curve, although as we move away it gets weaker. In the plot, the universal curve seems to be monotonic with limits $\lim_{d' \to -\infty} f(d') = 1$ and $\lim_{d' \to \infty} f(d') = 0$. This evidence would seem to suggest a phase transition near $d_3 = 3$ for $d_1 = 0.1$.

We repeat the same experiment and analysis with the second cut, a straight line cut along the diagonal of the $d_1 \times d_3$ quadrant. In this case our formal parameter is an integer i. An instance with input parameter value i corresponds to an instance with densities $d_1 = i/200$ and $d_3 = i/10 + 1$. Here, by making d_1 and d_3 dependent, we effectively reduce the number of input parameters of the problem from three, (d_1, d_3, n), to two, (i, n). We let i take values in the range $[1, 40]$ in increments of 1, and use instance sizes 500, 1,000, 2,500, 5,000, 10,000, 20,000, and 40,000. In figure 6(a) we plot the probability of satisfiability along this cut. This plot, as the one for the previous cut, reveals a quick change on the probability of satisfiability as the input parameter i passes through a critical value (around 19). We again use finite-size scaling on these data, looking for further support of a phase transition. For this cut, the analysis yields the following transformation:

$$i' = \frac{i - 19.1901}{19.1901} n^{0.2889}.$$

In figure 6(b) we superimpose the curves shown in the same figure (a) using the transformation above. As with the previous cut, the fit seems quite good, especially around zero, and the universal curve seems to have limits 1 and 0 in the infinities.

In an attempt to find further evidence of a phase transition, we perform the following experiment for the cut used to produce the data in figure 5 ($d_1 = 0.1$). For several instance sizes between 500 and 200,000 and for density d_3 taking values in the range $[2.7, 3.8]$ in increments of 0.02, we generate and solve 1,200 instances. We record for each different instance size the values of density d_3 for which the average probability of satisfiability is 0.1, 0.2, 0.8, and 0.9, respectively. (We actually used linear regression on the two closest points to compute the density for each satisfiability percentage.) The idea behind this experiment is that if the problem has a sharp threshold, then as the size of the instances increases the window between the 10th and 90th probability percentiles, as well as that between the 20th and the 80th probability percentiles, should shrink and become zero at the large n limit. In figure 7 we plot these windows. Indeed, they do get smaller as the instance size increases.

Similar analysis has been performed in the past for k-SAT. The *width* of the satisfiability phase transition, namely the amount by which the number of clauses of a random instance needs to be increased so that the probability of satisfiability drops from $1 - \epsilon$ to ϵ, is thought to grow as $\Theta(n^{1-\frac{1}{\nu}})$, with the exponent ν for $2 \leq k \leq 6$ estimated in Kirkpatrick and Selman [319], Kirkpatrick et al. [321], and Monasson et al. [406, 407]. Notice that the window that we estimate is equal to the normalized width (divided by the instance size). It was also conjectured that as k gets large, ν tends to 1. However, Wilson has proven [527] that for all $k \geq 3$, $\nu \geq 2$, so the transition width is at least $\Theta(n^{1/2})$. Our experiments suggest that the window of the satisfiability transition for 1-3-HornSAT shrinks as fast as $n^{-1/2}$, thus the transition width grows as $n^{1/2}$. We believe that the analysis in Wilson [527] can be applied in the case of 1-3-HornSAT, and can complement our experimental findings.

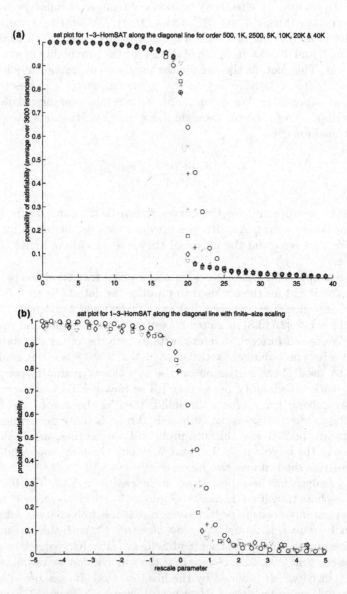

FIGURE 6   Satisfiability probability of a random 1-3-Horn formula along the diagonal cut (a) and the satisfiability plot with rescaled parameter using finite-size scaling (b).

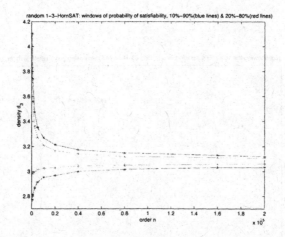

FIGURE 7   Windows of satisfiability probability of random 1-3-Horn formulas along the $d_1 = 0.1$ cut. The outer two curves show the 10%–90% probability window, and the inner two curves show the 20%–80% probability window.

Although figure 7 shows that these windows indeed shrink as the instance size increases, it is not at all clear whether in the limit they would go to zero. A further curve-fitting analysis is more revealing. In figure 8 we plot the size of the 10%–90% probability of satisfiability window (a) and the 20%–80% probability of satisfiability window (b) as a function of the instance size. Using MATLAB to do curve fitting on our data, we find that both windows decrease almost as fast as $1/\sqrt{n}$. The correlation coefficient r^2 is almost 0.999, giving high confidence for the validity of the fit. This analysis suggests that, indeed, the two windows should be zero at the limit, evidence supporting the existence of a phase transition for 1-3-HornSAT.

In the rest of this section we will discuss the connection between random Horn formulas and random hypergraphs. We will see that recent results on random hypergraphs provide a good fit for our experimental data on random 1-3-HornSAT presented so far. On the other hand, these results suggest that the transition is steep, but not the step function needed for a sharp threshold.

There is a one-to-one correspondence between random Horn formulas and random directed hypergraphs. Let ϕ be a $H_{n,d_1,d_3}^{1,3}$ random formula. We can represent ϕ with the following hypergraph G_ϕ:

- represent each variable x_i in ϕ with a node v_i in G_ϕ;
- represent each unit clause $\{x_k\}$ as a hyperedge in G_ϕ over v_k (hyperedges over vertices are also called *patches* [116] or *loops* [135]); and
- represent each clause $\{x_j, \overline{x_k}, \overline{x_l}\}$ as a directed hyperedge in G_ϕ over the set $\{v_j, v_k, v_l\}$.

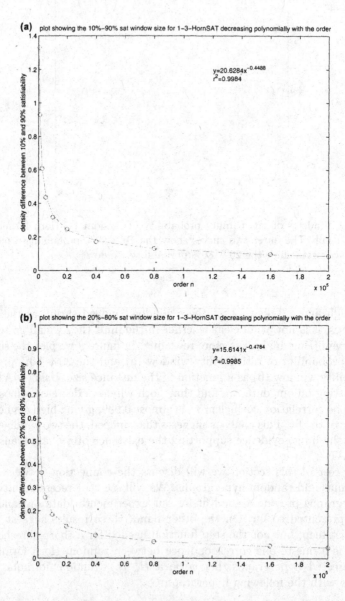

FIGURE 8 Plot of the 10%–90% satisfiability probability window (a) and of the 20%–80% satisfiability probability window (b) as a function of the intance size n.

Note that we omit the single negative literal appearing in ϕ.

In a recent development, Darling and Norris [116] proved certain results on vertex identifiability in random undirected hypergraphs. A vertex v of a hypergraph is *identifiable in one step* if there is a hyperedge over v. A vertex v is *identifiable in n steps* if there is a hyperedge over a set S, such that $v \in S$ and all other elements of S are identifiable in fewer than n steps. Finally, a vertex v is *identifiable* if it is identifiable in n steps for some positive n. We now establish the equivalence between the satisfiability of ϕ and the *identifiability* of vertex v_k of G_ϕ, where $\{\overline{x}_k\}$ is the unique single negative literal clause of ϕ.

First, we introduce a simple algorithm for deciding whether a Horn formula is satisfiable or not, presented by Dowling and Gallier [128] (see also Beeri and Bernstein [41]). The algorithm runs in time $O(n^2)$ where n is the number of variables in the formula. Dowling and Gallier actually describe in their work how to improve this algorithm to run in linear time, though for our purposes and for the sake of simplicity we use the simple quadratic algorithm.

Algorithm A.

```
begin
        let φ = {c₁,...,cₘ}
        consistent:=TRUE; change:=TRUE;
        set each variable xᵢ to be FALSE;
        for each variable xᵢ such that {xᵢ} is a clause in φ
            set xᵢ to TRUE
        endfor;
        while (change and consistent) do
            change:=FALSE;
            for each clause cⱼ in φ do
                if (cⱼ is of the form (x̄₁,...,x̄_q)
                    and all x₁,...,x_q are set to TRUE) then
                        consistent:=FALSE;
                else
                    if cⱼ is of the form {x₁,x̄₂,...,x̄_q}
                        and all x₂,...,x_q are set to TRUE
                        and x₁ is set to FALSE
                            then set x₁ to TRUE; change:=TRUE; φ := φ − cⱼ
                    endif
                endif
            endfor
        endwhile
end
```

If Algorithm A terminates with consistent:=TRUE, then a satisfying truth assignment has been found. Otherwise, the formula ϕ is unsatisfiable.

Given a formula ϕ, its corresponding directed hypergraph G_ϕ, and a variable x_i, we prove the following relation between the truth value that Algorithm A assigns to x_i and the identifiability of vertex v_i of G_ϕ:

Lemma 1. *Algorithm A running on ϕ assigns the value TRUE to x_i if and only if the vertex v_i of G_ϕ is identifiable.*

Proof It is easy to show the equivalence by induction on the number of steps required to identify v_k (equivalently the number of iterations of the **while** loop of Algorithm A needed to set the value of x_k to TRUE).

Base Case: If v_k is identifiable in one step, then $\{x_k\}$ is a clause in ϕ and Algorithm A immediately assigns the value TRUE to it, and vice versa.

Inductive Hypothesis: A vertex is identifiable in $n-1$ steps if and only if the corresponding variable is set to TRUE by Algorithm A in no more than $n-1$ iterations of the **while** loop.

Inductive Step: A vertex v_j that is identifiable in n steps corresponds to a variable that appears in a clause of the form $\{v_j, \overline{v_{i_1}}, \ldots, \overline{v_{i_q}}\}$, and since all of $x_{i_1}, \ldots, x_{i_q}$ are already set to TRUE, A will set x_j to TRUE in the nth iteration of the **while** loop. Conversely, if x_j is set to TRUE in the nth iteraton of the **while** loop of Algorithm A, then we derive that it appears in a clause of the form $\{x_j, \overline{x_{i_1}}, \ldots, \overline{x_{i_q}}\}$, where all of $x_{i_1}, \ldots, x_{i_q}$ are already set to TRUE. But this implies that all $v_{i_1}, \ldots, v_{i_q}$ are identifiable in $n-1$ steps; therefore v_j is identifiable in n steps.

As an immediate result of this lemma we obtain:

Corollary 4.1. *Let ϕ be a $H_{n,d_1,d_3}^{1,3}$ random formula and $\{\overline{x_k}\}$ be the unique single negative literal clause of ϕ. Let G_ϕ be the directed hypergraph corresponding to ϕ. The formula ϕ is satisfiable if and only if the vertex v_k of G_ϕ is not identifiable.*

Darling and Norris [116] studied the vertex identifiability in random undirected hypergraphs. Although Horn formulas correspond to directed hypergraphs, we have decided to use the results of Darling and Norris in an effort to approximate the satisfiability of Horn formulas. The authors use the notion of a *Poisson random hypergraph*. A Poisson random hypergraph on a set V of n vertices with non-negative parameters $\{\beta_k\}_{k=0}^\infty$ is a random hypergraph Λ, where the numbers $\Lambda(A)$ of hyperedges of Λ over sets $A \subseteq V$ of vertices are independent random variables, depending only on $|A|$, such that $\Lambda(A)$ has distribution $\text{Poisson}(n\beta_k/\binom{n}{k})$ where $|A| = k$. Thus, the number of hyperedges of size k is $\text{Poisson}(n\beta_k)$, distributed uniformly at random among all vertex sets of size k. (Recall that the distribution function of $\text{Poisson}(\lambda)$ is $f(x) = \exp(-\lambda)\lambda^x/x!$. The expectation of $\text{Poisson}(\lambda)$ is λ.) Note that this model allows for more than one edge over a set $A \subseteq V$; for our purposes we only care whether $\Lambda(A) = 0$ or not.

One of the key results they proved is the following:

Theorem 4.1 (Darling and Norris [116]). *Let $\beta = (\beta_j : j \in \mathbb{Z})$ be a sequence of non-negative parameters. Let $\beta(t) = \Sigma_{j\geq0}\beta_j t^j$ and $\beta'(t)$ the derivative of $\beta(t)$. Let $z^* = \inf\{t \in [0,1) : \beta'(t) + \log(1-t) < 0\}$; if the infimum is not well-defined then let $z^* = 1$. Denote by ζ the number of zeros of $\beta'(t) + \log(1-t)$ in $[0, z^*)$.*

Assume that $z^* < 1$ and $\zeta = 0$. For $n \in \mathbb{N}$, let V^n be a set of n vertices and let G^n be a Poisson(β) hypergraph on V^n. Then, as $n \to \infty$ the number V^{n*} of identifiable vertices satisfies the following limit w.h.p.: $V^{n*}/n \to z^*$.

If we ignore the direction of the hyperedges then the random hypergraph G_ϕ representing an $H^{1,3}_{n,d_1,d_3}$ random formula corresponds to a Poisson(β) hypergraph G^n. To see that, notice that the hyperedges in G_ϕ are distributed uniformly at random among all possible 1- and 3-sets of vertices, just as in a Poisson random hypergraph with only two non-zero parameters, β_1 and β_3. To find the values of these parameters, we set equal the probabilities that a hyperedge exists in the two hypergraphs G_ϕ and G^n. In G_ϕ, the probability that a variable x_i is selected as a positive unit literal is d_1. In G^n, the probability that there are zero hyperedges on x_i is e^{β_1}. From this we get $\beta_1 = -\log(1 - d_1)$. In G_ϕ, the probability that a 3-clause is selected (ignoring directions) is $nd_3/\binom{n}{3}$. In G^n, the probability that there are zero edges on the three variables in that clause is $e^{-n\beta_3/\binom{n}{3}} \simeq 1 - n\beta_3/\binom{n}{3}$ (as $n \to \infty$). From this we get $\beta_3 = d_3$.

Note that ignoring the direction of the hyperedges is equivalent to adding to the formula, for each clause $(x \vee \overline{y} \vee \overline{z})$, two more clauses $(\overline{x} \vee y \vee \overline{z})$ and $\overline{x}\vee\overline{y}\vee z$. Therefore, we expect that the probability of satisfiability we get from the hypergraph model should be lower than the actual probability as it is measured by our experiments. This is indeed the case, as will be apparent in figure 10.

We used MATLAB to compute z^* for the hypergraph G^n on the quadrant $d_1 \times d_3$ (the Darling-Norris Theorem does not provide us with an explicit result for z^*). From corollary 1, we get that the probability of satisfiability of ϕ is 1 minus the probability that v_k is identifiable in G^n, which, by theorem 4.1, is $1 - z^*$. In figure 9(a) we plot the satisfiability probability of ϕ against the input parameters d_1 and d_3. A contour plot is given in figure 9(b).

Comparing the results derived by this model (fig. 9) and the results obtained by our experiments (fig. 4), we see that the results from the hypergraph analysis provide a very good fit of the experimental data. This is also clear in figure 10 where we plot the 50 percent satisfiability line according to the model above (the rough curve) and according to our experimental data (smoother curve).

Finally, we used our model to estimate the probability of satisfiability along the same two cuts that we presented earlier (the $d_1 = 0.1$ and the diagonal cut). See figure 11 for the probability estimation along the two cuts according to the hypergraph-based model, and compare with our experimental findings shown in figure 5(a) and figure 6(a). For both cuts, the estimated probability has a steep drop that happens at the exact same point that the respective drop is observed in the experimental data. In table 1 we give the raw data that correspond to the

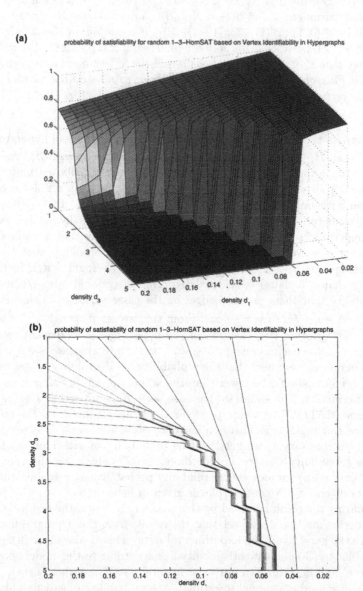

FIGURE 9 Satisfiability probability of a random 1-3-Horn formula according to the vertex-identifiability model (a) and the corresponding contour plot (b).

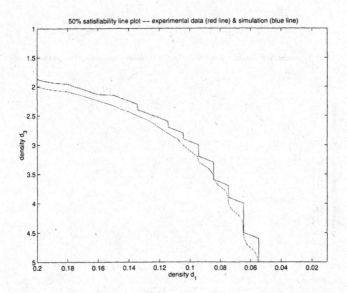

FIGURE 10 50% satisfiability line, according to the model derived through hyper-graphs (rough line) and according to our experimental data (smoother line).

plots in figure 11. Notice that, despite the very steep transition, the estimated curve is not a step function as we would expect from our data and the limiting curve under finite-size scaling analysis (figs. 5(b) and 6(b)). Should this be an accurate model for the 1-3-HornSAT, the probability of satisfiability is not a step function at the limit, so the threshold function is not in fact a constant function.

5   CONCLUSIONS

We have set out to investigate the existence of a phase transition for the satisfiability of the random 1-3-HornSAT problem. This is a problem that is similar to 3-SAT, but its polynomial complexity allows us to collect data for much higher instance sizes.

We first showed, through our experimental findings and an analysis based on known results from digraphs' reachability, that the 1-2-HornSAT is a problem lacking a phase transition.

On the other hand, our experiments provide evidence that the 1-3-HornSAT has a phase transition. By thoroughly sampling the $d_1 \times d_3$ quadrant, solving a large number of random instances of large size, we document a waterfall-like probability of satisfiability surface. In addition, by taking cuts of this surface, we are able to observe a quick transition from a satisfiable to an unsatisfiable

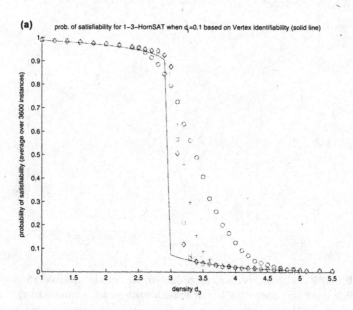

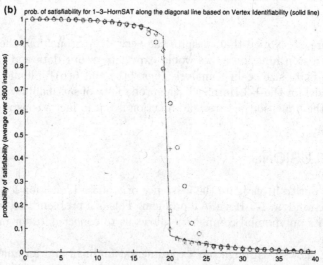

FIGURE 11   Satisfiability probability of a random 1-3-Horn formula according to the vertex-identifiability model, along the $d_1 = 0.1$ cut (a) and the diagonal cut (b). The solid line corresponds to the model; experimental data points are shown for comparison.

TABLE 1   Data for the satisfiability probability of a random 1-3-Horn formula according to the vertex-identifiability model, along the $d_1 = 0.1$ and the diagonal cut.

$d_1 = 0.1$ cut		diagonal cut	
d_3	sat. prob.	input parameter i	sat. prob.
1	0.98775	1	0.99997
1.1	0.98619	2	0.99988
1.2	0.98455	3	0.9997
1.3	0.98282	4	0.99941
1.4	0.98098	5	0.99899
1.5	0.97903	6	0.99841
1.6	0.97694	7	0.99764
1.7	0.9747	8	0.99664
1.8	0.9723	9	0.99537
1.9	0.96969	10	0.99376
2	0.96685	11	0.99175
2.1	0.96372	12	0.98924
2.2	0.96026	13	0.98611
2.3	0.95637	14	0.98217
2.4	0.95194	15	0.97717
2.5	0.94679	16	0.97069
2.6	0.94062	17	0.96202
2.7	0.9329	18	0.94968
2.8	0.92244	19	0.9294
2.9	0.90522	20	0.072832
3	0.072832	21	0.063411
3.1	0.063588	22	0.055476
3.2	0.055745	23	0.048727
3.3	0.049039	24	0.042943
3.4	0.043267	25	0.038
3.5	0.038272	26	0.0335
3.6	0.033928	27	0.029856
3.7	0.030137	28	0.026559
3.8	0.026815	29	0.023665
3.9	0.023896	30	0.021117
4	0.021324	31	0.018868
4.1	0.019052	32	0.016878
4.2	0.017041	33	0.015114
4.3	0.015257	34	0.013547
4.4	0.013672	35	0.012153
4.5	0.012262	36	0.01091
4.6	0.011006	37	0.0098016
4.7	0.0098849	38	0.0088112
4.8	0.0088836	39	0.0079255
4.9	0.0079881	40	0.0071324

region. Finite-size scaling applied along these cuts suggests that there is a phase transition, and analysis of the transition window provides further evidence of this.

We then used recent results on random hypergraphs to generate a model for our experimental data. By comparing the waterfall-like probability surface against the estimated probability according to this model, we see that the hypergraph-based model fits our experimental data well. This suggests that further analysis based on hypergraphs could provide a rigorous analysis of the conjectured phase transition for the 1-3-HornSAT. Such a development would be very significant since very few phase transitions have been proven analytically (2-SAT, 3-XORSAT, 1-in-k SAT) [7, 94, 101, 131, 156, 202]. Interestingly, in spite of how well this model fits our data, when calculating the estimated probability along the two cuts we see that in the limit of large instance sizes, the probability of satisfiability is a very steep function, but does not have a discontinuity. This last result conflicts with our experimental findings and demonstrates the difficulty of using numerics to show a phase transition, even for tractable problems such as 1-3-HornSAT.

ACKNOWLEDGMENTS

We thank one of the anonymous referees for pointing out the exact calculation of the 1-2-HornSAT satisfiability probability, given in Remark 1.

Part 4: Extensions and Applications

CHAPTER 10

Phase Transitions for Quantum Search Algorithms

Tad Hogg

1 INTRODUCTION

Phase transitions have long been studied empirically in various combinatorial searches and theoretically in simplified models [91, 264, 301, 490]. The analogy with statistical physics [397], explored throughout this volume, shows how the many local choices made during search relate to global properties such as the resulting search cost. These studies have led to a better understanding of typical search behaviors [514] and improved search methods [195, 247, 261, 432, 433].

Among the current research questions in this field are the range of algorithms exhibiting the transition behavior and the algorithm-independent problem properties associated with the difficult instances concentrated near the transition. Towards this end, the present chapter examines quantum computer [123, 126, 158, 486] algorithms for nondeterministic polynomial (NP) combinatorial search problems [191].

As with many conventional methods, they exhibit the easy-hard-easy pattern of computational cost as the degree of constraint in the problems varies. We describe how properties of the search space affect the algorithms and identify an additional structural property, the *energy gap*, motivated by one quantum algorithm but applicable to a variety of techniques, both quantum and classical. Thus, the study of quantum search algorithms not only extends the range of algorithms exhibiting phase transitions, but also helps identify underlying structural properties.

Specifically, the next two sections describe a class of hard search problems and the form of quantum search algorithms proposed to date. The remainder of the chapter presents algorithm behaviors, relevant problem structure, and an approximate asymptotic analysis of their cost scaling. The final section discusses various open issues in designing and evaluating quantum algorithms, and relating their behavior to problem structure.

2   RANDOM SATISFIABILITY PROBLEMS

The k-satisfiability (k-SAT) problem, as discussed earlier in this volume, consists of n Boolean variables and m clauses. A clause is a logical **OR** of k variables, each of which may be negated. A solution is an assignment, that is, a value for each variable, TRUE or FALSE, satisfying all the clauses. An assignment is said to conflict with any clause it does not satisfy. Thus, a possible 2-SAT problem instance with 3 variables and 2 clauses might be (x_1 **OR** $\overline{x_2}$) **AND** (x_2 **OR** x_3), which has 4 solutions: for example, x_1 = FALSE, x_2 = FALSE and x_3 = TRUE is one of them. When $k \geq 3$, k-SAT is NP-complete [191], and so it is among the most difficult NP problems.

Evaluating a search algorithm's average cost requires defining a problem ensemble, meaning a class of problem instances and probabilities for their selection.

The random k-SAT ensemble with given n and m consists of instances whose m clauses are selected uniformly at random. Specifically, for each clause, a set of k variables is selected randomly from among the $\binom{n}{k}$ possibilities. Then each selected variable is negated with probability $1/2$ to produce the clause. Each of the m clauses is, therefore, selected, with replacement, uniformly from among the $N_{\text{clauses}} = \binom{n}{k}2^k$ possible clauses. This ensemble (called $\mathcal{G}_{m,m}$ in ch. 7) has a high concentration of hard instances when the *clause-to-variable ratio* $\alpha \equiv m/n$ is near a critical value where the fraction of solvable instances exhibits a phase transition [91, 254, 319], dropping abruptly from near 1 to near 0. For random 3-SAT this transition is at $\alpha \approx 4.27$.

The quantum algorithms discussed here are incomplete methods: failure to find a solution does not guarantee no solution exists. Thus, for empirical evaluation, we restrict attention to instances with at least one solution (determined via exhaustive classical search of the randomly generated instances). This restriction gives the random solvable k-SAT ensemble.

3   QUANTUM SEARCH METHODS

The quantum algorithms considered in this chapter consist of a series of trials, each operating on vectors of size 2^n, whose components consist of a complex number, or *amplitude*, for each assignment or *search state*. These vectors are often described as *superpositions* of all search states. After each trial, observing or measuring the superposition randomly produces a single assignment, with probabilities equal to the squared magnitudes of the final amplitudes. This result is then tested with a conventional computer, a rapid operation for NP problems. Trials repeat until a solution is found.

A trial starts with equal amplitudes, so that the initial vector has components $\psi_s^{(0)} = 2^{-n/2}$, for s ranging over all 2^n assignments. The trial consists of a prespecified number of steps j, unlike classical algorithms which can halt as soon as they find a solution. For step $h = 0, \ldots, j$ we define the *step fraction* $f = h/j$ as the fraction of steps completed.

A single step performs a matrix multiplication on the superposition, giving new values for the amplitudes. Quantum algorithms generally perform this operation in two parts, corresponding to multiplying by two matrices. First, the phases of the amplitudes are adjusted based on properties of the problem instance to be solved. Typically, this adjustment to the amplitude ψ_s associated with search state s depends on the *state cost* $c(s)$. In the case of k-SAT, $c(s)$ is the number of the m clauses conflicting with s. The phase adjustment has the form $e^{-i\rho(f,c(s))}$ where the *cost phase function* ρ is a real-valued function of the step fraction and the state cost.

The second part of a step mixes amplitudes among different states, corresponding to multiplication by a unitary matrix with nonzero off-diagonal terms. Usually, the mixing matrix for step h is taken to have the form $U^{(h)} = WT^{(h)}W$ with W and T defined as follows. W is the Walsh-transform, a $2^n \times 2^n$ matrix with elements $W_{rs} = 2^{-n/2}(-1)^{|r \wedge s|}$ where $|r \wedge s|$ is the number of 1's the two assignments have in common when viewed as bit-vectors ($0 \leq r, s \leq 2^{n-1}$). For instance, when $n = 1$, $W = \frac{1}{\sqrt{2}} \begin{pmatrix} 1 & 1 \\ 1 & -1 \end{pmatrix}$. The matrix $T^{(h)}$ is diagonal with $T_{ss}^{(h)} = e^{-i\tau(f,|s|)}$, where $|s|$ denotes the number of 1-bits in bit-vector s and the *mixing phase function* τ is another real-valued function. With these definitions, $U_{rs}^{(h)}$ depends only on the Hamming distance $d(r, s)$ between the states [250], that is, the number of variables they assign different values. Thus, the mixing matrix has the form $U_{rs}^{(h)} = u_{d(r,s)}^{(h)}$ with the u_d values determined by the choice of τ.

Combining these operations, a single step is[1]

$$\psi_r^{(h)} = \sum_s u_{d(r,s)}^{(h)} e^{-i\rho(f,c(s))} \psi_s^{(h-1)} . \tag{1}$$

Although the vectors have exponentially many components, quantum computers perform these operations efficiently [76, 215, 255].

Observing the final superposition gives an assignment having c conflicts with probability

$$P_{\text{conf}}^{(j)}(c) = \sum_{s|c(s)=c} |\psi_s^{(j)}|^2$$

with the sum over all assignments with c conflicts. In particular, $P_{\text{soln}}(j) = P_{\text{conf}}^{(j)}(0)$ is the probability to find a solution in a single trial. For good performance, the choices for ρ and τ should ensure a large value of $P_{\text{soln}}(j)$ after only a modest number of steps j.

Optimization versions of the search considered in this chapter amount to finding states with the minimum cost. This use of "cost" associated with individual states should not be confused with the *search cost*, that is, the number of elementary computation steps required to find a solution. For the probabilistic algorithms considered here, we focus on the expected value of the search cost and usually consider its median value over an ensemble of problems rather than its value for any single instance. This corresponds to the notion of average complexity in chapter 3.

As a reminder concerning notation, to compare function growth rates [208], $F = O(G)$ indicates F grows no faster than G as a function of n when $n \to \infty$. Conversely, $F = \Omega(G)$ means F grows at least as fast as G, and $F = \Theta(G)$ means both functions grow at the same rate.

The remainder of this section describes choices for ρ and τ giving unstructured search and then techniques exploiting problem structure.

3.1   UNSTRUCTURED SEARCH

In thec notation introduced above, Grover's unstructured search [215] has phase functions

$$\rho(f,c) = \begin{cases} \pi & \text{if } c = 0 \\ 0 & \text{otherwise} \end{cases}$$

$$\tau(f,b) = \begin{cases} \pi & \text{if } b = 0 \\ 0 & \text{otherwise} \end{cases}$$

---

[1]To provide a more direct connection with the Hamiltonian formulation of this algorithm, in section 3.4, the values of ρ and τ used here are $-\pi$ times the values introduced previously in the literature [250].

With these choices, which are the same for all steps (i.e., independent of f), the phase adjustment simply multiplies amplitudes for solutions by -1, leaving the others unchanged, and the mixing is a diffusion matrix: $u_d = -\delta_{d0} + 2^{1-n}$ where δ_{ab} is one if $a = b$ and zero otherwise.

The probability of finding a solution after j steps is [76]

$$P_{\text{soln}}(j) = \sin((2j+1)\theta)^2 \tag{2}$$

where $\theta \equiv \sin^{-1}\sqrt{S/2^n}$ and S is the number of solutions. For hard, solvable random k-SAT, θ is exponentially small. Thus the solution probability $P_{\text{soln}} \approx 1$ when the number of steps is $j \approx \pi/(4\theta) \approx \frac{\pi}{4}\sqrt{2^n/S}$, that is, after exponentially many steps for hard problems.

The corresponding unstructured classical algorithm, generate-and-test, requires on average $\frac{1}{2}2^n/S$ state tests to find a solution. The quantum method thus achieves a square-root speedup, the best possible improvement for unstructured search [76].

In practice, the number of solutions S and hence the best choice for the number of steps j are not known a priori. Moreover, since the solution probability $P_{\text{soln}}(j)$ oscillates with the number of steps j, picking j too large not only increases the search cost for each trial but can also result in a smaller value of P_{soln} and hence require more trials. One approach to this difficulty selects j differently for each trial as follows [76]: Starting with $J = 1$,

- perform a single trial with j selected uniformly at random between 0 and $J-1$
- if a solution is found, stop. Otherwise, set $J = \min(2^{n/2}, 6J/5)$ and repeat.

To evaluate the expected search cost, from eq. (2) the probability of obtaining a solution is [76]

$$p_{\text{random}}(J) = \frac{1}{J}\sum_{j=0}^{J-1} P_{\text{soln}}(j) = \frac{1}{2} - \frac{\sin(4J\theta)}{4J\sin(2\theta)} \tag{3}$$

which approaches $1/2$ as J increases. The trial with a given J takes $(J-1)/2$ steps, on average. With probability $1 - p_{\text{random}}(J)$ the trial is not successful. Thus the expected search cost for all trials starting with J is

$$\text{cost}(J) = \frac{J-1}{2} + (1 - p_{\text{random}}(J))\, \text{cost}(\min(2^{n/2}, 6J/5)). \tag{4}$$

When $J \geq 2^{n/2}$, further iterations have $J = 2^{n/2}$ so eq. (4) gives

$$\text{cost}(2^{n/2}) = \frac{2^{n/2}-1}{2\,p_{\text{random}}(2^{n/2})}.$$

This condition and eq. (4) enable us to compute the full expected search cost, $\text{cost}(1)$, recursively. This technique, allowing a different number of steps j for each trial, increases the expected search cost by at most a factor of 4 [76] compared to having prior knowledge of S.

3.2   SINGLE-STEP SEARCH

Unstructured search ignores all properties of search states except whether they are solutions. Fortunately, many problems allow efficient evaluation of additional useful properties. An extreme example is a problem with one solution and an efficient method giving the distance of any state to that solution. We then take this distance value to be the cost associated with that state.

Such problems are quite easy: classical methods can solve them with only a linear number of state evaluations. For instance, pick a random state, compute its distance to the solution, and then evaluate the distance for each of its n neighboring states (assignments that differ from the original by changing a single variable's value). Selecting the value for each variable giving the smaller distance then directly constructs a solution.

For a corresponding quantum search [249], take cost phase $\rho(f, c) = \frac{\pi}{2}c$ and mixing phase $\tau(f, b) = \frac{\pi}{2}b$ and let σ be the solution. The mixing matrix value is then $u_d = (e^{-i\pi/4}/\sqrt{2})^n i^d$. Since we take $c(s) = d(\sigma, s)$ and the initial state has equal amplitudes, a single step gives

$$\psi_r^{(1)} = 2^{-n} e^{-in\pi/4} \sum_s i^{d(r,s)}(-i)^{d(\sigma,s)} . \tag{5}$$

For $r = \sigma$, all terms in the sum are 1, that is, all contributions to the amplitude associated with the solution add in phase, giving $\psi_\sigma^{(1)} = e^{-in\pi/4}$ with absolute value 1. The amplitudes for the remaining states are zero. Thus, this quantum algorithm finds a solution, with probability 1, in just a single step.

This algorithm can work well even with some error in estimating the distances. As an extreme example, if the estimated solution distance has an error of any multiple of four, the quantum algorithm's behavior is unchanged. By contrast, such errors would change conventional algorithms based on comparing the distance values for neighboring states.

This scenario is not applicable to hard search problems, which lack efficient methods to determine distance to solution from most states. Nevertheless the single-step method illustrates how quantum computers exploit problem structure, in this case a strong correlation between easily computed measures (e.g., number of conflicts) and the distance to desired states. As described below, this observation, combined with the typical properties of problem structure, gives qualitative insight into why quantum algorithms show the phase transition behavior.

3.3   USING PROBLEM STRUCTURE

The previous two subsections described algorithms for two extremes: first the case in which a solution can be recognized when it is found, but no other information is available, and second the case of perfect information in which it is easy to determine the distance to the solution from any state. Typical NP search problems are between these extremes. Readily computed information about search states gives some information on the location of solutions, but is not always accurate. Using such information in the quantum algorithm of eq. (1) is conceptually straightforward. For a problem ensemble, such as random k-SAT, pick the phase functions $\rho(f,c)$ and $\tau(f,b)$ and number of steps j to minimize the search cost for typical instances.

We thus have another example of a common situation with heuristics: tuning algorithm parameters with respect to a class of problems. Generally, heuristics are too complicated to permit a useful analytical relation between the parameter values and algorithm search cost. Instead, numerical optimization can find good parameter values for a sample of problem instances, in the hope such values will also work well on other instances from the same problem ensemble.

When optimizing algorithm parameters for a sample of instances on a quantum machine, each trial requires only polynomial time, provided we pick the number of steps j to grow only polynomially with n. On the other hand, at least for most parameter choices, the solution probability P_{soln} is exponentially small, thus requiring exponentially many trials to estimate P_{soln} on the sample instances because each trial gives only a single state. Hence a direct attempt to find parameter values minimizing the median search cost would require exponentially many trials on a quantum computer. One way to address this difficulty is to identify how good parameter choices scale with n and then extrapolate values based on optimization with smaller n. Another approach uses the shift in amplitudes towards low-cost states, shown later in section 5: instead of maximizing P_{soln}, we could minimize the expected cost of the state produced by a trial, that is, $\langle c \rangle = \sum_c c P_{\text{conf}}^{(j)}(c)$, a quantity easily estimated with a modest number of trials.

Currently, however, we must simulate the quantum algorithm on conventional machines, so each trial requires exponential search cost and memory but has the benefit of giving P_{soln} directly from evaluating a single trial.

Another approach to finding good phase functions, discussed in section 6.2, uses an approximate analytical theory of the algorithm performance. The theory allows rapid, though approximate, performance evaluation for large problem sizes. Numerical optimization then finds phases giving high performance according to this approximation.

Algorithms using problem structure usually take the phase functions to have the form:

$$\rho(f,c) = \rho(f)c\,\Delta \tag{6}$$
$$\tau(f,b) = \tau(f)b\,\Delta$$

with Δ a parameter used to characterize how these functions scale with the number of steps j. We also call the single-parameter functions $\rho(f)$ and $\tau(f)$ the cost and mixing phase functions. The mixing matrix becomes [250]:

$$u_d^{(h)} = \left(e^{-i\tau\Delta/2}\cos\left(\frac{\tau\Delta}{2}\right)\right)^n \left(i\tan\left(\frac{\tau\Delta}{2}\right)\right)^d \tag{7}$$

which depends on the step fraction f through $\tau(f)$.

Completing the algorithm requires explicit forms for the phase functions, $\rho(f)$ and $\tau(f)$, and values for Δ and the number of steps j. Ideally, these quantities would minimize the expected search cost for the particular problem instance. For hard problems, such optimal choices are not known *a priori*. We therefore focus instead on functional forms giving good performance on average for random k-SAT, so depending only on the ensemble parameters n, k and m. While the values could vary from one trial to the next, by analogy with the procedure described in sec. 3.1 for unstructured search when the number of solutions is not known, for simplicity we use the same values for each trial. The expected cost of finding a solution is then $j/P_{\text{soln}}(j)$, the number of steps per trial multiplied by the expected number of times trials must be repeated to give a solution.

3.4   HAMILTONIAN FORMULATION

An alternate formulation of the algorithm steps involves the Hamiltonians producing the unitary operators used with eq. (1). For the phases given by eq. (6), in matrix form the step is

$$e^{-i\tau(f)H_0\Delta}e^{-i\rho(f)H_c\Delta}\psi,$$

(8)

with H_0 and H_c defined as follows. The mixing Hamiltonian has $(H_0)_{r,s}$ equal to $n/2$ when $r = s$, $-1/2$ when states r and s differ by exactly one bit, and 0 otherwise. The problem cost Hamiltonian H_c is diagonal with values equal to the state costs: $(H_c)_{r,r} = c(r)$.

The algorithm's initial state, with all amplitudes the same, is the ground state of H_0, with eigenvalue 0. Since H_c encodes the costs of the search states, its ground state corresponds to having nonzero amplitudes only in solutions (or, if there are no solutions, in states with the minimum number of conflicts).

When Δ is small, eq. (8) gives [503] $\psi^{(h)} \sim \exp(-iH(f)\Delta)\psi^{(h-1)}$ where $H(f) \equiv \tau(f)H_0 + \rho(f)H_c$. Defining the state vector $\psi(f) \equiv \psi^{(h)}$ and $T = j\Delta$, eq. (1) becomes

$$\frac{d\psi(f)}{df} = -iTH(f)\psi(f).$$

(9)

Thus, for small Δ, the algorithm steps closely approximate the continuous evolution of this Schrödinger equation with the time-dependent Hamiltonian $H(f)$ for $0 \leq f \leq 1$.

A significant application of this correspondence is the adiabatic limit [151]: for T sufficiently large, $\psi(f)$ remains close to the ground state of $H(f)$ if it starts in the ground state of $H(0)$. Since the state with uniform amplitudes is the ground state of H_0, the initial condition is achieved if $H(0) \propto H_0$, i.e., $\rho(0) = 0$. If we also have $\tau(1) = 0$, then $H(1) = H_c$ so the final state $\psi(1)$ will be close to the ground state of H_c, namely the solution (or a linear combination of solutions in case of multiple solutions). Thus, for a fixed problem size n, taking $T \to \infty$

and $\Delta \to 0$ leads to the solution probability approaching one, $P_{soln} \to 1$. An important open question is how many steps are sufficient to achieve large values of P_{soln}: algorithms of this form cannot efficiently solve worst-case instances of SAT [508], but it remains to be seen how effective they are on average.

By comparison, the heuristic method using eq. (6) has $\Delta = 1/j$ so $T = 1$. Hence, the adiabatic limit does not apply and, in general, the solution probability P_{soln} is exponentially small in n. However, with suitable phase functions $\rho(f)$ and $\tau(f)$ the expected number of steps to find a solution is significantly lower than that of the adiabatic limit for random 3-SAT (see sec. 5.1), at least for small n. The approximation of section 6.2 suggests this favorable scaling continues for larger problems.

A third possibility is phase adjustments whose size is independent of the number of steps, with Δ held constant instead of approaching zero as j increases. We can take the constant to be $\Delta = 1$, since any other value amounts to rescaling ρ and τ. In this case eq. (1) does not closely approximate the continuous evolution of eq. (9). Nevertheless, when $\rho(0) = 0 = \tau(1)$, a discrete version of the adiabatic theorem applies: the state vector starts in an eigenstate of the initial mixing operator, and is then multiplied by a series of slowly changing unitary matrices. When the changes are sufficiently small, that is, with a large number of steps j, the state vector remains close to an eigenstate of the matrices. In particular, the final state will be close to an eigenstate of the final operator, corresponding to states with a particular cost. Unlike the continuous adiabatic method, this final eigenstate need not correspond to solutions [246]. Ensuring the final eigenstate does correspond to solutions requires that the phase functions, and hence Δ, not exceed a threshold value that depends on the problem instance. Above this threshold, the changing eigenvectors take the initial ground state to an eigenvector of H_c other than its ground state. Thus, applying the discrete adiabatic limit requires identifying a suitable threshold value for the problem ensemble and so requires some parameter tuning but, since any values below the threshold will give $P_{soln} \to 1$ as j increases, identifying suitable values need not be as accurate as for the heuristic method. On the other hand, exceeding this threshold slightly can sometimes be beneficial by giving high solution probabilities for intermediate numbers of steps j, even though $P_{soln} \to 0$ as $j \to \infty$ [246].

Table 1 summarizes the various approaches to incorporating problem structure in quantum algorithms. For good performance, it is not necessary that the solution probability P_{soln} be very close to one: somewhat smaller values give lower expected costs j/P_{soln}, an observation that applies to a variety of quantum [76, 151, 383] and classical methods [368].

TABLE 1   Summary of quantum search algorithms using problem structure. The single-step and heuristic methods require finding appropriate choices for the phase functions to give good performance. Here Δ characterizes the scaling of the phase functions with number of steps, and $T = j\Delta$ characterizes the total phase changes applied over the course of a trial.

algorithm	parameters	phase functions
single-step	$T = 1, \quad \Delta = 1$	with suitable ρ, τ
heuristic	$T = 1, \quad \Delta \to 0$	with suitable ρ, τ
adiabatic: continuous	$T \to \infty, \Delta \to 0$	$\rho(0) = 0 = \tau(1)$
adiabatic: discrete	$T \to \infty, \Delta = 1$	$\rho(0) = 0 = \tau(1),$
		values for other f not too large

4   MAXIMALLY CONSTRAINED 1-SAT

For a simple illustration of quantum search behavior, consider 1-SAT problems with a single solution. In this case, the number of conflicts $c(s)$ in state s equals its distance to the solution. Thus, from eq. (1), the amplitudes for step h have the form $\psi_s \propto (Z_h)^{c(s)}$ with Z_h a complex number. Initially, all amplitudes are the same, so $Z_0 = 1$. Including the overall normalization, the solution probability corresponding to Z is

$$P_{\text{soln}} = \frac{1}{\sum_{c=0}^n \binom{n}{c} |Z|^{2c}} = (1 + |Z|^2)^{-n} \tag{10}$$

so $|Z| \ll 1/\sqrt{n}$ gives $P_{\text{soln}} \to 1$. How Z changes in one step is determined by eq (1), giving:

$$Z_{h+1} = \frac{-ie^{-i\rho\Delta} Z_h + v}{-i + e^{-i\rho\Delta} Z_h v} \tag{11}$$

with $v \equiv \tan(\tau\Delta/2)$, and the phase functions ρ and τ can depend on $f = h/j$.

If $\rho\Delta = \tau\Delta = \pi/2$ then $Z_1 = 0$, so all amplitude is in the solution after a single step, providing an example of the discussion of section 3.2. While this problem is simple enough to solve in a single step, it is also instructive to consider its behavior with other phase choices. The remainder of this section examines the limit $\Delta \to 0$ as the number of steps increases. In this case, eq. (9) gives

$$\frac{dZ}{df} = -iT\left(\rho Z - \frac{\tau}{2}(1 - Z^2)\right) \tag{12}$$

with $Z(0) = 1$.

We first consider $\Delta = 1/j$ so $T = 1$. For suitable choices of the phase functions, eq. (12) gives $Z(1) = 0$. One such choice is $\rho = \tau = \pi/\sqrt{2}$, independent of f, in which case

$$Z(f) = -1 + \frac{4 - i\sqrt{2}\sin(\pi f)}{3 - \cos(\pi f)}. \tag{13}$$

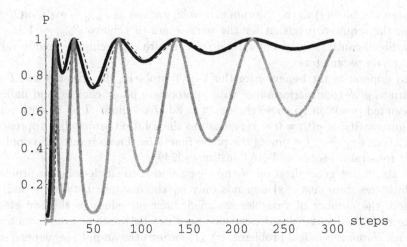

FIGURE 1 Solution probability, $P_{\text{soln}}(j)$, vs. number of steps j used in the trial, for a maximally constrained 1-SAT problem with $n = 100$ using $\Delta = 1/\sqrt{j}$, $\rho = \gamma f$, $\tau = \gamma(1 - f)$ with $\gamma = 0.828$ selected to give $P_{\text{soln}}(10) = 1$. Solid: exact (from eq. (11)), dashed: continuous approximation (eq. (12)). For comparison, the gray curve is for $n = 1000$.

The exact discrete map, eq. (11), for these parameters, gives $Z_j \sim \Theta(1/j)$ so $P_{\text{soln}} \sim \exp(-O(1)n/j^2)$. Hence, when the number of steps is $j \gg \sqrt{n}$, the solution probability approaches one, giving considerably lower search cost than the $\Theta(2^{n/2})$ value for unstructured search.

Second, consider the limit $T \to \infty$ using $1/j \ll \Delta \ll 1$. The adiabatic theorem applies if $\rho(0) = 0 = \tau(1)$. A simple choice is linear variation: $\rho = f$, $\tau = 1 - f$. In this limit eq. (12) gives $Z(f)$ close to the ground state of $H(f)$, which is proportional to $\Lambda(f)^c$ with

$$\Lambda(f) = \frac{\sqrt{1 - 2f + 2f^2} - f}{1 - f} \tag{14}$$

and $\Lambda(1) = 0$. Evaluating eq. (11) with $\Delta = 1/\sqrt{j}$ shows $Z(1)$ rapidly approaches the value from eq. (12) and this solution, in turn, approaches 0 as $1/T$. Thus the solution probability scales as $P_{\text{soln}} \sim \exp(-\Theta(1)n/T^2)$.

Figure 1 gives an example of this limit, showing $P_{\text{soln}} \to 1$ as the number of steps j increases. Furthermore, the probability oscillates, reaching values very close to 1 for relatively few steps, $T = \Theta(1)$. Exploiting these oscillations for rapid search requires identifying appropriate parameter values and ensuring that any implementation errors in these values are sufficiently small. If the parameter values vary by $O(\epsilon)$ from the ideal values giving $Z(1) = 0$, the value of Z at the final step will be $O(\epsilon)$ so the solution probability scales as $P_{\text{soln}} \sim \exp(-nO(\epsilon^2))$. Hence, the required precision for the parameters to achieve $P_{\text{soln}} \sim 1$ is $\epsilon \ll 1/\sqrt{n}$. Significantly, these techniques do not require exponentially precise values of the phase parameters.

To summarize the behavior for this 1-SAT problem, the one-step and $T = 1$ algorithms give good performance with appropriate phase choices, and indicate the required precision on those choices. The adiabatic limit, $T \to \infty$ with phase functions satisfying $\rho(0) = 0 = \tau(1)$, ensures the solution probability approaches one without any need for tuning the phase functions. These results also apply to highly constrained solvable k-SAT instances [249].

A significant generalization of this discussion is to single-solution problems in which the state cost $c(s)$ depends only on the distance between s and the solution: the number of variables assigned different values in the two states. Unlike the 1-SAT case, this dependence need not be linear or even monotonic. For such *Hamming-weight* problems, eq. (1) ensures the amplitudes depend only on the costs. This simplification allows studying the performance of quantum algorithms with a variety of cost structures [508], though classical algorithms can efficiently solve such problems by using the cost symmetry.

5 RANDOM K-SAT

On average, for k-SAT, the solution probability P_{soln} decreases exponentially with n for most phase function choices. Section 4 showed particular parameter choices leading to much better performance for 1-SAT with a single solution. As described in this section, the same options apply to hard random k-SAT problems, but, not surprisingly, do not perform as well.

5.1 SEARCH COST SCALING

For trials consisting of a single step or, more generally, a constant number of steps independent of n, the expected value of the solution probability P_{soln} always decreases exponentially when $m \propto n$ [251]: no choices are as good as those for the 1-SAT example of section 4. Nevertheless, selecting the best parameters for each value of the clause-to-variable ratio $\alpha = m/n$ exhibits the easy-hard-easy pattern as a function of α [251].

Better performance requires the number of steps in a trial, j, to increase with problem size. The approximate analysis of section 6.2 suggests choices for ρ and τ that appear to work well with $j \gg \sqrt{n}$. One example, with $\alpha = 4.25$ (close to the critical threshold), $j = n$ and $\Delta = 1/j$ is the phase functions [250]

$$\rho(f) = \pi(4.86376 - 4.18118(1 - f)) \tag{15}$$
$$\tau(f) = \pi(1.2 + 3.1(1 - f)).$$

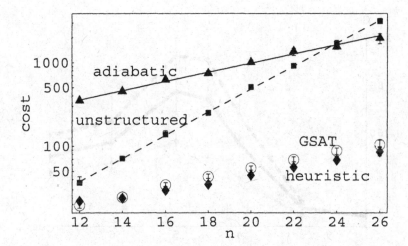

FIGURE 2 Log plot of median search cost vs. number of variables n for solvable random 3-SAT for the parameters of eq. (15) (diamond), unstructured search (box), GSAT with restarts after $2n$ steps (circle) and adiabatic search with $j = n^2$ (triangle). The error bars show the 95% confidence intervals [480, p. 124] of the medians estimated from the random 3-SAT instances with $m = 4.25n$ (when n is not divisible by 4, half the samples have $m = \lfloor 4.25n \rfloor$ and half have $m = \lceil 4.25n \rceil$). The same instances were solved with each method. We use 1000 instances for each n up to 20, and 500 for larger n. The lines are exponential fits to unstructured search (dashed) and the adiabatic method (solid).

The adiabatic limit gives solution probability $P_{\text{soln}} \to 1$ as $T \to \infty$. Empirically it appears to give good average performance for hard search problems [151] but the question of how rapidly T must grow to achieve this limit remains open. An example of the adiabatic limit is $\Delta = 1/\sqrt{j}$ and phase functions $\rho(f) = f$, $\tau(f) = 1 - f$. This gives good cost scaling with the number of steps $j = \Omega(n^2)$.

Figure 2 compares the median search costs of these algorithms as a function of the number of variables n. The figure also shows Grover's unstructured search [215] (without prior knowledge of number of solutions [76]) and the conventional heuristic GSAT [467].

The unstructured search cost grows as $\exp(0.32n)$. The exponential fit to the adiabatic method is $\exp(0.13n)$. The growth rate is about the same as that of GSAT. The phase functions of eq. (15) give the lowest median costs.

The discrete adiabatic method, using $\Delta = 1$ and number of steps $j = n$, gives costs similar to the heuristic. For both algorithms, using nonlinear variation of the phase functions with step fraction f gives significantly better performance

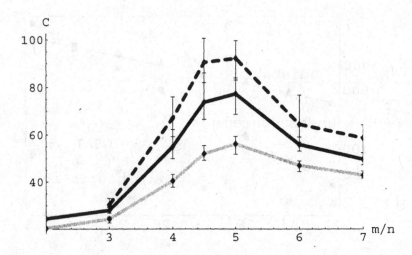

FIGURE 3 Median search costs for solvable random 3-SAT problems with $n = 28$ (dashed), $n = 24$ (black), and $n = 20$ (gray) as a function of clause-to-variable ratio m/n, using at least 100 instances for each point. Error bars show the 95% confidence intervals. The search uses the same algorithm parameters for each problem instance, namely $\Delta = 1$, number of steps $j = n$, and linear varation of the phase functions matching the requirements of the adiabatic theorem, namely $\rho(f) = f$, $\tau(f) = 1 - f$.

than for the linear functions shown here [246], a property also seen with the Hamming-weight problems [508].

As with the $j = O(1)$ case, the number of steps j increasing with n also shows the easy-hard-easy pattern, as illustrated in figure 3 for one choice of algorithm. In this example, the phase choices are the same for each value of α. The cost peak is quite wide for these small problems. This peak also appears with quantum algorithms including partial assignments [248], as arise in classical backtracking searches.

Figure 4 illustrates several properties of the algorithm using eq. (15) for one problem instance. At each step, probability concentrates in states with a fairly small range of costs. Each step shifts the peak in the probability distribution to assignments with fewer conflicts, until a large probability builds up in the solutions. This shift is also seen for other problem instances (with differing final probabilities) and when averaged over many instances.

The variation of amplitudes among states with the same cost is relatively large only in the last few steps of the algorithm and then primarily for higher-cost states for which the amplitudes are small. The shading in figure 4 shows this behavior, indicating the relative deviation of the amplitudes (ratio of standard deviation to mean) for states with the each cost, ranging from white for zero

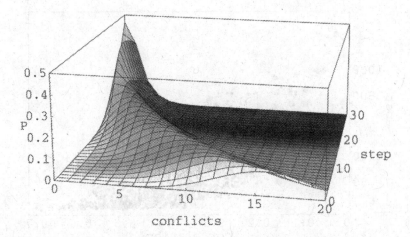

FIGURE 4   Solving a randomly generated 3-SAT problem with $n = 30$ and $m = 127$ clauses using eq. (15). For each step h, the figure shows the probability $P_{\text{conf}}^{(h)}(c)$ in assignments with each number of conflicts. Shading shows the relative deviations of the amplitudes, as described in the text. The small contributions for assignments with $c > 20$ are not included. This instance has 19 solutions.

deviation to black for relative deviations greater than 3. These observations motivate the approximate analysis of section 6.2.

5.2   PROBLEM STRUCTURE AND SEARCH COST

Each step of the algorithm, given in eq. (1), adjusts amplitudes based on the costs associated with the states and mixes them based on their Hamming distances. When cost and solution distance are perfectly correlated, as with the 1-SAT example of section 4, the quantum algorithm performs well. Thus we can expect a structural property of problem instances, namely the correlation between distance between states and their cost difference, to characterize search difficulty: high correlations should correspond to lower costs, on average.

As one example, figure 5 shows the relation between the search cost for the heuristic quantum algorithm (using eq. (15)) and the correlation between cost and distance to the nearest solution for all assignments. GSAT shows a similar relationship.

The adiabatic method provides another structural property relevant for search cost: the minimum energy gap g. The energy gap for step fraction f is the difference between the ground-state energy of $H(f)$ and the energy of the $(S + 1)$th state, where S is the number of solutions. The minimum gap is the smallest gap over the range $0 \leq f \leq 1$. The adiabatic limit requires $T \gg 1/g^2$. With multiple solutions, the distribution and sizes of gaps between successive

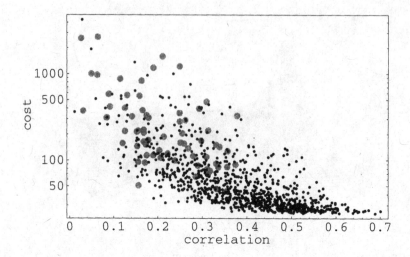

FIGURE 5 Expected search cost for the heuristic quantum method vs. correlation between state cost and distance to nearest solution for 1000 3-SAT instances with $n = 20$ variables and clause-to-variable ratio $\alpha = 4.25$. The large gray points are instances with a single solution.

states up to the $(S+1)$th can also affect performance. Except for simple, highly symmetric problems such as the 1-SAT example of section 4, the scaling behavior of the gap is not known.

Of broader interest for understanding phase transitions in combinatorial search, the minimum energy gap provides an algorithm-independent characterization of search problems. Although directly related to the performance of the adiabatic method [151], the minimum gap g is also relevant for other algorithms. For instance, figure 6 shows high costs for the heuristic (using $T = 1$ and based on eq. (15)) generally correspond to small gaps. GSAT gives a similar plot. These observations suggest the minimum gap is a global property characterizing hard instances for a variety of algorithms. It thus may offer useful insights as an alternative to other such properties, such as the *backbone*, consisting of those variables with the same assigned values in all solutions [477]. Both the minimum gap and backbone are computationally expensive to determine, so they are most significant as theoretical constructs relating problem structure to search cost.

5.3 LONGER RANGE INTERACTIONS FOR AMPLITUDE MIXING

The algorithms discussed so far in this chapter incorporate information about the specific instance to solve only in the cost phase function ρ. As a further application of problem structure to designing quantum algorithms, this section

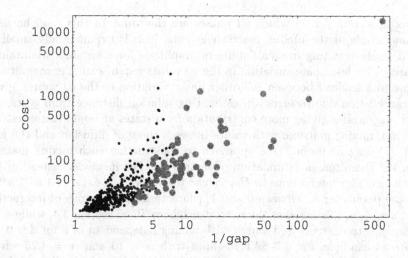

FIGURE 6 Expected search cost for the heuristic quantum method vs. $1/g$ for 500 3-SAT instances with $n = 16$ variables and clause-to-variable ratio $\alpha = 4.25$. The large gray points are instances with a single solution.

briefly examines one approach to adjusting the mixing phase function τ to match the mixing operator to the problem instance.

The mixing matrix in eq. (7) has the phase i^d associated with the mixing matrix elements u_d for all choices of τ. Thus, increasing τ increases the magnitude of the contribution from more distant states, but does not change the variation in phase of the u_d values.

Section 3.2 showed that good performance is possible if distances to the solution can be estimated well. On the other hand, errors in such estimates will make contributions from various distances tend to cancel, leading to less shift of amplitude towards lower-cost states during each step. For example, the phase factor i^d in u_d means an error in estimating distance to the solution by $2, 6, 10, \ldots$ changes the sign of the contribution to the new amplitude in eq. (1). Unfortunately, for problems such as 3-SAT, state costs are not perfectly correlated with solution distance (see fig. 5), so such phase errors in the mixing are inevitable for these algorithms.

One approach to this difficulty is using many steps, each with a small value of Δ, as described in section 3.3. This can be effective, but means that the mixing matrix for each step is close to the identity and that contributions to the amplitude of a state are concentrated among nearby states, which can lead to low performance in cases where solutions tend to be surrounded by high cost states. An alternative is using a mixing matrix in which the phases associated with successive u_d values vary more slowly than i^d. An extreme example is the diffusion matrix of section 3.1, in which all phases are the same. In this case, however, the magnitude of the mixing matrix elements, $|u_d|$, is exponentially small for $d > 0$, again resulting in small shifts in amplitude for each step. Maintaining unitarity with less phase variation in the u_d values requires smaller magnitudes, leading to a tradeoff between smoother phase variation of the u_d values, giving less cancellation due to errors in estimating solution distance from costs, and larger magnitudes giving more contribution from states at larger distances.

Thus, mixing matrices with values between those of diffusion and the form of eq. (7) may be useful. One approach to constructing such mixing matrices is via the Hamiltonian formulation of section 3.4. For instance, instead of just nearest-neighbor interactions in H_0, we can take $(H_0)_{r,s} \propto \delta_{r,s} - (1+a)^{-n} a^{d(r,s)}$ with the parameter a, between 0 and 1, characterizing the range of interaction. If $0 < a \ll 1/n$, this matches the nearest-neighbor H_0 of section 3.4, while $a = 1$ corresponds to unstructured search with mixing independent of d for $d > 0$.

As an example, for a 3-SAT instance with $n = 16$ and $\alpha = 4.25$ with a particularly small minimum gap (about 0.002, compared to the median minimum gap of about 0.5 for such problems), allowing the mixing to depend on a longer-range Hamiltonian with $j = 16$ steps increased the solution probability P_{soln} from 0.0006 to 0.12. Improvement is also seen with other instances with especially small gaps.

While difficult to provide definitive conclusions from these small instances, this additional flexibility in matching the mixing matrix to characteristics of the problem may improve performance. In particular, studies of how state costs vary through the search space to give local minima or plateaus [168, 254, 258] could suggest appropriate choices for the interaction range. Such information may help evaluate other types of quantum algorithms that rely on properties of the cost function throughout the space, such as those using partial assignments [86, 149, 248].

6   APPROXIMATE SCALING BEHAVIOR

As seen in the previous section, simulations for small problems show proper phase choices can give costs comparable to a good conventional heuristic. Unfortunately, these small problem sizes do not adequately address scaling of the cost behavior, particularly whether the quantum algorithms can perform significantly better than classical methods for hard random SAT problems, on average.

Approximate analytical techniques provide a complementary approach. The average properties of random k-SAT successfully help us to understand and improve search methods, both classical [91, 138, 195, 247] and quantum [250]. Quantum algorithms operate with the entire search space at each step, so performance depends on averaged properties of the search states. For simple ensembles, such as random k-SAT, such averages are readily computable.

This section discusses how the properties of random k-SAT provide a qualitative understanding of the phase transition behavior seen with the quantum methods and estimate the algorithm's behavior for large n.

6.1   PROBLEM STRUCTURE

The algorithms in this chapter adjust amplitudes based on the state costs and Hamming distances between them. Thus the selection of appropriate phase functions, and the resulting algorithm performance, depends on the relationship between these quantities for typical problem instances. This section describes this relationship for random k-SAT, and summarizes how its dependence on the number of clauses qualitatively explains the peak in search cost seen with the quantum algorithms.

For random k-SAT with m clauses, the probability an assignment has cost C is a binomial distribution: $P(C) = \binom{m}{C} p^C (1-p)^{m-C}$ where $p = 2^{-k}$ is the probability a single clause conflicts with a given assignment. The expected number of states with cost C is $v(C) = 2^n P(C)$. As one application, if the amplitudes after step h satisfy $\psi_s \propto Z^{c(s)}$ for some constant Z, then the probability of obtaining a state with c conflicts $P_{\text{conf}}^{(h)}(c)$ is

$$P_{\text{conf}}^{(h)}(c) = \frac{P(c)|Z|^{2c}}{(1 - p(1 - |Z|^2))^m} . \tag{16}$$

In particular, $P_{\text{soln}}(h) = P_{\text{conf}}^{(h)}(0)$ is the probability of obtaining a solution.

To relate distances and costs, the probability that two states separated by distance d have costs C and c, respectively, is given by a sum of multinomials depending on the number of clauses conflicting with both states [250]. The corresponding conditional probability $P(c|C, d)$ is peaked for c values close to C when the two states have the same assignments for most variables, that is, when $d \ll n$. This arises from the local nature of the constraints in k-SAT: two states that differ in assignments to only a few variables are very likely to violate many of the same clauses and hence have similar costs. Quantitatively, when n is large, the average cost c for a state at distance d from another state with cost C is

$$\langle c \rangle = \frac{m}{2^k - 1} \left(1 - \chi + (1 - \delta)(2^k \chi - 1) \right) \tag{17}$$

with $\delta \equiv d/n$, the fraction of variables with different values in the two states, and $\chi \equiv C/m$, the fraction of conflicting clauses in the first state. The variance of the distribution for c has a similar expression, proportional to $m(1 - (1 - \delta)^k)$.

Figure 7 is an example of how cost varies with distance from a state with given cost, and gives a qualitative understanding of the underlying cause of the easy-hard-easy behavior for the quantum algorithms. Specifically, since the relative deviation of c/m decreases as $1/\sqrt{m}$, the figure shows the distribution of costs c from the conditional probability $P(c|C, d)$ is narrow for either small

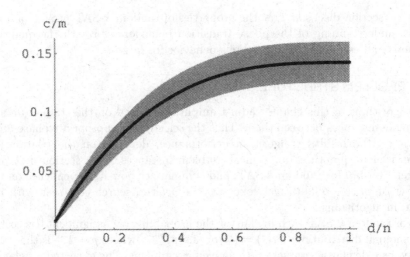

FIGURE 7 Expected fraction of conflicting clauses, $\langle c \rangle /m$, vs. the fraction of variables with different assignments, d/n, for the conditional distribution $P(c|C,d)$ when $n = 100$, $k = 3$, $m = 4n$ and $C = 3$. The gray region shows the extent of the deviation of the distribution: one standard deviation above and below the mean, multiplied by $\sqrt{m}$.

distances d or large numbers of clauses m. The smaller variance gives a stronger correlation between costs and distance, leading to an increased ability to pick phase adjustments to move amplitudes to desired states (as seen in sec. 4).

Underconstrained problems have many solutions, so distance to the nearest solution is typically fairly small. Hence amplitudes need only be shifted a small distance, so steps can mainly mix amplitudes of nearby states (i.e., use relatively small values of the mixing phase function τ, as is also suitable for the single-step method with underconstrained problems [251]). These small distances have high correlations between cost and distance, allowing fairly precise shifts of amplitude towards the lower-cost states and, hence, low overall search costs.

Conversely, overconstrained but solvable problems tend to have just a few solutions and long distances to them from most states. In this case, the increasing number of clauses results in small variance even for large distances, due to the $1/\sqrt{m}$ decrease in relative deviation of the conditional probability distribution $P(c|C,d)$. Thus, we can expect a good ability to shift amplitudes to lower-cost states for overconstrained problems.

Between these extremes we can expect larger search costs because, as shown in figure 7, the deviation grows rapidly with distance when the fraction of variables with different assignments, δ, is small, but more slowly as δ increases. Thus, when the clause-to-variable ratio α is small, we can expect the growth in variance due to increasing distance to outweigh the decrease due to the $1/\sqrt{\alpha}$ factor. As

α increases, $\delta \to 1/2$ when only one solution remains and hence the variance increases slowly due to changes in distance, and the $1/\sqrt{\alpha}$ factor dominates to give an overall decrease. These observations give a qualitative understanding of the cost peak for typical problems with an intermediate number of clauses: relatively long distances to solutions combined with higher variance in the relation between cost and distance. These factors reduce the ability to shift amplitudes reliably towards lower-cost states, giving higher overall search costs.

Using the expression for the relative deviation and estimating typical distances from the expected number of solutions, $\langle S \rangle = 2^n(1 - 2^{-k})^m$, matches this qualitative description with a peak in relative deviations for 3-SAT around a clause-to-variable ratio of $\alpha = 3$. Thus, while by no means a quantitatively accurate identification of the cost peak, the behavior of the conditional probability a state has cost c, given it is at distance d from another state with cost C, $P(c|C,d)$, provides a qualitative understanding of why the easy-hard-easy pattern arises in these quantum search algorithms. This also illustrates the usefulness of structurally simple ensembles such as random k-SAT: since each clause is selected independently at random, the state cost distributions are analytically simple to describe.

6.2 MEAN-FIELD APPROXIMATION

Evaluations of algorithm behavior, such as that of figure 4, show that amplitudes for states with the same number of conflicts are generally quite similar. This observation motivates an analysis based on the behavior of the average amplitude for states with each cost [250]. The resulting approximation corresponds to a *mean-field* approach in statistical physics.

Consider the average amplitude $A_C^{(h)} = \left\langle \psi_s^{(h)} \right\rangle$, with the average taken first over all states s with cost $c(s) = C$ in a problem instance, and then over all random k-SAT instances with given numbers of variables n and clauses m. Simulations show that the probability concentrates in a small range of cost values, as illustrated schematically in figure 8. Let us assume amplitudes for states with the same cost are the same, at least for states whose cost is near the dominant cost value at each step, that is, the peak in $P_{\text{conf}}^{(h)}$ of figure 4. Then eq. (1) becomes

$$A_C^{(h)} \approx \sum_{d,c} u_d^{(h)} e^{-i\rho(h/j,c)} v_d(C,c) A_c^{(h-1)} \tag{18}$$

where $v_d(C,c) = \binom{n}{d} P(d|C,d)$ is the expected number of states with c conflicts at distance d from a state with C conflicts. The dominant costs are close to the average cost associated with the amplitudes, $\langle C \rangle = \sum_C C v(C) |A_C|^2$. We thus expand $A_c \approx A_C Z^{c-C}$ around the average cost, with Z a complex number depending on the step fraction $f = h/j$. This expansion is the same form as the exact expression for the amplitudes given in section 4 for the simple 1-SAT problem.

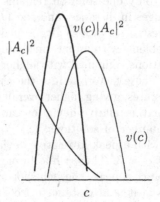

FIGURE 8 Schematic behavior of average amplitudes, on a logarithmic scale, as a function of number of conflicts c. The average number of states with c conflicts, $v(c)$, is sharply peaked around the average number of conflicts $m/2^k$. When the magnitude of the amplitudes decreases rapidly with c, as shown here, the probability in states with c conflicts is also sharply peaked, but at a somewhat lower value, corresponding to the shift towards lower-cost states seen in figure 4. Quantitatively, the values decrease exponentially with n, so the logarithms, shown here, are proportional to n and the relative width of each peak is $O(1/\sqrt{n})$.

For the case of $\Delta = 1/j$ and $j \gg 1$, using this expansion in eq. (9) gives [250]

$$\frac{dZ}{df} = i\left(-\rho Z + \frac{\tau}{2}kF\frac{1 - p(1 - Z)}{1 - p}(1 - Z)\right) \tag{19}$$

where $p = 2^{-k}$ is the probability that a clause conflicts with a given assignment, $\chi = |Z|^2 p/1 - p(1 - |Z|^2)$ is the expected fraction of conflicting clauses, $\langle C \rangle /m$, with this approximation for the amplitudes, and

$$F = \exp\left(-k\alpha(1 - Z)\left(\frac{p(1 - \chi)}{1 - p} - \frac{\chi}{Z}\right)\right).$$

Initially all amplitudes are equal so $Z(0) = 1$.

For $k = 1$ this reduces to the 1-SAT example, eq. (12) with $T = 1$, except for a factor of F due to the random choice of clauses of the ensemble, compared with the situation of section 4, where each clause must involve a distinct variable since the choices are required to give one solution.

With suitable choices for ρ and τ, such as those in eq. (15) for $k = 3$, $\alpha = 4.25$, eq. (19) gives $Z(1) = 0$ thereby predicting that most of the amplitude concentrates in states with the fewest conflicts, that is, solutions if the problem instance is solvable. More precisely, this predicts the solution probability $P_{\text{soln}}(j)$ is, at worst, only polynomially small with proper phase choices. This approximation relies on the decreasing size of the relative variance of the conditional probability $P(c|C,d)$ discussed in section 6.1 and, hence, the number of steps must satisfy $j \gg \sqrt{n}$. Combining these scaling behaviors, the mean-field approximation predicts that the average cost j/P_{soln} grows only polynomially with n for typical random k-SAT instances, with suitable choices of the phase functions depending on the clause-to-variable ratio α. Evaluating the error in this approximate result via simulation is difficult due to the requirements of many states with each cost and small relative deviation in problem structure among states with each cost value, that is, $\sqrt{n} \gg 1$.

The functions of eq. (15) do not have $\rho(0) = 0 = \tau(1)$. Choices for phase functions ρ and τ do exist that both satisfy these conditions for the adiabatic method and give $Z(1) = 0$ from eq. (19). However, empirically they require more steps than the choices of eq. (15).

7   DISCUSSION

This chapter has reviewed several approaches to quantum search. First, unstructured search is the quantum analog of generate-and-test. The probability of finding a solution is close to one after exponentially many steps for hard search problems. Second, the adiabatic method can also guarantee solution probability $P_{\text{soln}} \approx 1$ after sufficiently many steps, with the required number of steps related to an aspect of problem structure, the energy gap, not previously examined in the context of phase transitions. Third, for problems with a strong correlation between cost and distance to solution (such as 1-SAT or highly constrained k-SAT), appropriate phase choices allow solving the problem in $O(1)$ steps for any number of variables. Finally, the heuristic method gives good average performance for hard k-SAT problems based on empirical evaluation, but lacks an exact analysis of performance scaling. An approximate theory modeled on the behavior of the algorithm for 1-SAT suggests the possibility of polynomial scaling of average cost, but the accuracy of this prediction remains an open question. Moreover, even if the algorithm performs well on average, it has no guarantee for specific instances. At any rate, the approximation provides reasonably good choices for the phases, as seen in figure 2.

A number of extensions are possible. First, the amplitude shift of figure 4 means that even if a solution is not found after a trial, the result probably has low cost. Thus, like local classical search methods such as GSAT but unlike unstructured search, the heuristic and adiabatic methods apply directly to combinatorial optimization, that is, finding a minimal conflict state [174]. For example, the shift in amplitudes towards low-cost states is seen in satisfiability problems with no solutions, the traveling salesman problem [252] and graph coloring [149].

Second, the mean-field analysis also applies to other search problem ensembles, provided the probabilities relating problem properties can be determined. This is possible for a variety of commonly studied ensembles such as coloring random graphs. Ensembles of real-world problems lack analytically known probability distributions, but sampling representative instances allows estimating $P(c|C, d)$. Such estimates may even be useful for analytically simple ensembles, allowing some tuning of phase parameters for a particular problem instance.

Third, in common with amplitude amplification [76] and some classical methods [369], the growth of solution probability $P_{\text{soln}}(h)$ with step h during a trial, as seen in figure 4, means stopping a bit before the largest P_{soln} value reduces the expected search cost. More generally, a portfolio [205, 265] of trials with somewhat different parameter values can improve trade-offs between expected costs and their variation among different instances [383].

Fourth, the heuristic can readily incorporate other computationally-efficient properties of the search states as additional arguments to the phase function ρ. One such property, used by conventional heuristics such as GSAT, is how the number of conflicts in a state compares to those of its neighbors. Moreover, in an analogy with quadratically improving conventional heuristics with amplitude amplification [77], we could also evaluate a conventional heuristic, such as GSAT, for a fixed number of steps and use the cost of the resulting state to adjust phases (either instead of or in addition to the cost of the original state). In this case, we would be searching not for a solution state directly but rather for a "good" initial state, from which the conventional heuristic rapidly finds a solution. In fact, using just a few steps of GSAT with random SAT instances shows the same shift towards low-cost states as seen in figure 4, and the resulting solution probability, P_{soln}, is larger. However, for problem sizes amenable to simulation, P_{soln} of the original algorithm is sufficiently large that even if using a few steps of GSAT were able to make $P_{\text{soln}} = 1$, it would not reduce the overall trial cost due to the additional steps involved in evaluating GSAT. Nevertheless, this approach may be useful for larger problem sizes and illustrates the potential trade-off between the cost of the procedure evaluating search state properties and the resulting probability for a solution, which determines the expected number of trials.

An interesting open question is whether the heuristic can benefit from using different parameters and numbers of steps for each trial, as used for amplitude amplification when the number of solutions is not known. The simulations indicate a wide range of performance among different instances with the same numbers of variables and clauses, n and m, even if they have the same number of solutions. This approach would rely on the variation among problem instances not addressed by ensemble averages. Furthermore, the series of low-cost states returned by the unsuccessful trial may also be useful indications of problem structure as another example to apply dynamic adjustments based on algorithm behavior during search [304]. Finally, implementations of structured quantum searches [489] will allow a comparison of how the various algorithms respond to uniquely quantum mechanical sources of error, such as decoherence.

A quantum machine with even a modest number of bits could help address these issues by evaluating algorithm performance beyond the range of classical simulation. This will be particularly useful for more complicated heuristics, using additional problem properties, whose theoretical analysis is likely to be more difficult. Exploring their behavior will identify opportunities for quantum computers to use information available in combinatorial searches to improve performance significantly.

ACKNOWLEDGMENTS

I have benefited from discussions with Wim van Dam. I thank Miles Deegan and the HP High Performance Computing Expertise Center for providing computational resources for the simulations.

CHAPTER 11

Scalability, Random Surfaces, and Synchronized Computing Networks

Zoltan Toroczkai
György Korniss
Mark A. Novotny
Hasan Guclu

1 INTRODUCTION

In most cases, it is impossible to describe and understand complex system dynamics via analytical methods. The density of problems that are rigorously solvable with analytic tools is vanishingly small in the set of all problems, and often the only way one can reliably obtain a system-level understanding of such problems is through direct simulation. This chapter broadens the discussion on the relationship between complexity and statistical physics by exploring how the computational scalability of parallelized simulation can be analyzed using a physical model of surface growth. Specifically, the systems considered here are made up of a large number of interacting individual elements with a finite number of attributes, or local state variables, each assuming a countable number (typically finite) of values. The dynamics of the local state variables are discrete events occurring in continuous time. Between two consecutive updates, the local variables stay unchanged. Another important assumption we make is that the interactions in the underlying system to be simulated have finite range.

Computational Complexity and Statistical Physics, edited by
Allon G. Percus, Gabriel Istrate, and Cristopher Moore, Oxford University Press.

Examples of such systems include: magnetic systems (spin states and spin flip dynamics); surface growth via molecular beam epitaxy (height of the surface, molecular deposition, and diffusion dynamics); epidemiology (health of an individual, the dynamics of infection and recovery); financial markets (wealth state, buy/sell dynamics); and wireless communications or queueing systems (number of jobs, job arrival dynamics).

Often—as in the case we study here—the dynamics of such systems are inherently stochastic and *asynchronous*. The simulation of such systems is nontrivial, and in most cases the complexity of the problem requires simulations on distributed architectures, defining the field of parallel discrete-event simulations (PDES) [186, 367, 416]. Conceptually, the computational task is divided among n processing elements (PEs), where each processor evolves the dynamics of the allocated piece. Due to the interactions among the individual elements of the simulated system (spins, atoms, packets, calls, etc.) the PEs must coordinate with a subset of other PEs during the simulation. For example, the state of a spin can only be updated if the state of the neighbors is known. However, some neighbors might belong to the computational domain of another PE, thus, message passing will be required in order to preserve causality. In the PDES schemes we analyze, update attempts are self-initiated [155] and are independent of the configuration of the underlying system [365, 366]. Although these properties simplify the analysis of the corresponding PDES schemes, they can be highly efficient [342] and are readily applicable to a large number of problems in science and engineering. Further, the performance and scalability of these PDES schemes become independent of the specific underlying system, that is, we learn the generic behavior of these complex computational schemes.

The update dynamics, together with the information sharing among PEs, make the parallel discrete event simulation process a complex dynamical system in itself. In fact, it perfectly fits the type of complex systems we are considering here: the individual elements are the PEs, and their states (local simulated time) evolve according to update events which are dependent on the states of the neighboring PEs.

With the number and size of parallel computers on the rise, the problem of designing efficient parallel algorithms or update schemes becomes increasingly important. In passing, we can mention a few examples of large parallel computers: the 9472-node ASCII Red at Sandia, the 12288-node QCDSP Teraflop Machine at Brookhaven, and the 8192-node IBM ASCII White with 12.3 Teraflops. The 65536-node IBM Blue Gene/L with 360 Teraflops is due for delivery at Livermore as this volume goes to press. And the largest supercomputer ever built is by Nature itself: the brain, which does an immense parallel computing task to sustain the individual. In particular the human brain has 10^{11} PEs (neurons) each with an average of 10^4 synaptic connections, creating a bundle on the order of 10^{15} "wires" jammed into a volume of approximately 1400 cm^3.

The fact that the dynamics of the simulation scheme form a complex system, with properties hard to deduce using classical methods of algorithmic analysis, makes the design of efficient parallel update schemes a challenging problem. In this chapter we present a new approach to analyzing efficiency and scalability for the class of massively parallel conservative PDES schemes [87] by mapping the parallel computational process itself onto a non-equilibrium surface growth model [343]. This allows us to formulate questions of efficiency and scalability in terms of certain topological properties of this non-equilibrium surface. Then, using methods from statistical mechanics, developed some time ago to study the dynamics of such surfaces in a completely different context, we solve the scalability problem of the computational PDES scheme [343, 346]. Similar connections between computational schemes and complex systems behavior have recently been made [457, 478] for rollback-based PDES algorithms [280] and self-organized criticality [24].

The chapter is organized as follows. In the following section we present the problem of scalability in conservative PDES schemes. In section 3 we discuss the scalability of the computational phase and the failure of scalability of the measurement phase of the basic conservative scheme, for regular topologies. We then show how a simple modification of the communication topology (from a regular lattice to a small-world structure) leads to a fully scalable PDES scheme. In section 4 we study the scalability problem on scale-free network topologies, presenting numerical results for Barabási-Albert networks. Section 5 is devoted to conclusions.

2 SCALABILITY OF MASSIVELY PARALLEL DISCRETE-EVENT SIMULATIONS

Since one is interested in the *dynamics* of an underlying complex system, the parallel discrete-event simulation scheme must simulate the "physical time" variable of the complex system. When simulations are performed on a single-processor machine, a single (global) time stream is sufficient to *label* or time-stamp the updates of the local configurations, regardless of whether the dynamics of the underlying system are synchronous or asynchronous. When simulating asynchronous dynamics on distributed architectures, however, each PE generates its own physical, or virtual time, which is the physical time variable of the particular computational domain handled by that PE. Due to the varying complexity of the computation at different PEs, at a given wall-clock instant the simulated, virtual times of the PEs can differ—a phenomenon called *time horizon roughening*. We denote the simulated, or virtual time at PE i measured at wall-clock time t by $\tau_i(t)$. For noninteracting subsystems the wall-clock time t is directly proportional to the (discrete) number of parallel steps simultaneously performed on each PE, also called the number of Monte Carlo steps (MCS) in dynamic Monte Carlo simulations. Without altering the meaning, t will from now on be taken to denote the number of discrete steps performed in the parallel simulation. The set

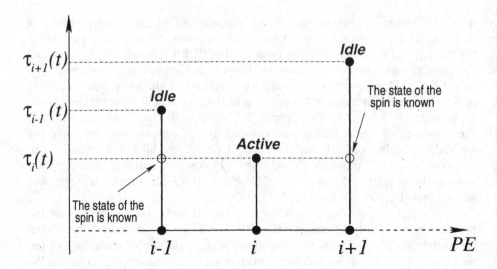

FIGURE 1   A simple diagram to illustrate the conservative PDES scheme for a one-dimensional system with nearest-neighbor interactions.

of virtual times $\{\tau_i(t)\}_{i=1}^n$ forms the *virtual time horizon* of the PDES scheme after t parallel updates.

In conservative PDES schemes [87], a PE can only perform its next update if it can obtain the correct information to evolve the local configuration (local state) of the underlying physical system it simulates, without violating causality. Otherwise, it idles. Specifically, when the underlying system has nearest-neighbor interactions, each PE must check with its "neighboring" PEs (mimicking the interaction topology of the underlying system) to see if those have progressed at least up to the point in virtual time where the PE itself has [365, 366]. Based on the fundamental notion of discrete-event systems that the value of a local state variable remains unchanged between two successive update attempts, the rule above guarantees the causality of the simulated dynamics [365, 366]. A simple illustration of this is given in figure 1. One may consider, for example, a magnetic system as the underlying physical system, where the spins are arranged on the sites of a one-dimensional lattice, and a single spin is handled by a single PE (for more realistic and efficient implementations see Korniss et al. [342], and Lubachevsky [365, 366]). In figure 1, showing the distribution of the virtual simulated times at a given wall-clock instant t, the only PE that can update from the set $\{i-1, i, i+1\}$ is in site i since the states of the neighboring spins at sites $i \pm 1$ are already known. However, PEs $i \pm 1$ cannot update their spin states at wall clock instant t, because the state of the neighboring spin i at *their* simulated times (at τ_{i-1} and τ_{i+1}) is not yet known. In other words PE i can only update at wall-clock instant t if $\tau_i(t) \leq \min\{\tau_{i-1}(t), \tau_{i+1}(t)\}$, that is, its virtual time is a *local minimum* among the virtual times of its neighboring PEs. It is easy to see that the same conclusion holds for arbitrary PE topologies. Let the topology for the communication among the processing elements be symbolized by a graph $G(V, E)$, where V is the vertex set of n nodes and E is the edge set of G. Given a node $i \in V(G)$, we denote by N_i the set of i's nearest neighbors on G. Then, node (PE) i can update its state in the conservative PDES scheme if and only if:

$$\tau_i^{(G)}(t) \leq \min_{j \in N_i}\{\tau_j^{(G)}(t)\} \quad , i = 1, .., n. \tag{1}$$

In the following, the set of (active) nodes obeying condition (1) at time t will be denoted by $A(t)$.

Now we are in a position to formulate the scalability problem of PDES schemes for systems with asynchronous dynamics. For the PDES scheme to be fully scalable, the following two criteria must be met: (i) the virtual time horizon must progress on average at a nonzero rate, and (ii) the typical spread of the time horizon must be finite, as the number of PEs n goes to infinity. When the first criterion is ensured for large enough times t, the simulation is said to be *computationally scalable*. This simply means that when increasing the size of the computation to infinity, while keeping the average computational domain/load constant on a single PE, the simulation will progress at a nonzero rate. However, as we will show below, increasing the system size can cause the *spread* in the time horizon to diverge, severely hindering frequent data collection about the state of the simulated system. Specifically, when one needs to take a measurement of some physical property of the simulated system at (virtual or simulated) physical time τ, we have to *wait*, in wall-clock time, until all the virtual simulated times at all the PEs reach the value τ. Thus in order to collect system-wide measurements from the simulation, we incur a waiting time proportional to the *spread*, or width of the fluctuating time horizon. When condition (ii) is fulfilled for large enough times t, we say that the PDES scheme is *measurement scalable*. For PDES schemes for which the spread diverges with system size, however, the waiting time for the measurements will also diverge, and the scheme is *not* measurement scalable.

The scalability criteria above can be formalized in terms of the properties of the virtual time horizon, $\{\tau_i^{(G)}(t)\}_{i=1}^n$. The average of the time horizon after t parallel steps is:

$$\overline{\tau}^{(G)}(t) = \frac{1}{n}\sum_{j=1}^n \tau_j^{(G)}(t). \tag{2}$$

At a given wall-clock time t the only PEs that can make progress, that is, are not idle, are those with virtual times obeying condition (1). Thus, the rate of progress of the time horizon average becomes:

$$\overline{\tau}^{(G)}(t+1) - \overline{\tau}^{(G)}(t) = \frac{1}{n} \sum_{l \in A(t)} \left[\tau_l^{(G)}(t+1) - \tau_l^{(G)}(t) \right] . \tag{3}$$

The difference in the square brackets on the right-hand side of eq. (3) is the *physical time* elapsed between two consecutive events in the physical domain simulated by the lth PE, and it is determined by the physical process responsible for the stochastic dynamics of the simulated complex system. If we replace the time intervals in square brackets in eq. (3) with their (clearly finite) average value Δ, we obtain that the average progress rate of the time horizon, or average *utilization* $\langle u^{(G)}(t) \rangle = \langle \overline{\tau}^{(G)}(t+1) - \overline{\tau}^{(G)}(t) \rangle$ is proportional to the *number* of non-idling, or active PEs. The average $\langle \cdots \rangle$ is taken over the stochastic event dynamics, assumed to be the same at all sites. For many cases, the Δ factor is independent of n due to the finite range of the interaction in the complex system, so the computational efficiency or average utilization of the simulation can simply be identified with the average density of the active PEs:

$$\langle u^{(G)}(t) \rangle = \frac{\langle |A^{(G)}(t)| \rangle}{n} , \tag{4}$$

where $|A^{(G)}(t)|$ denotes the number of elements of the set $A^{(G)}(t)$. Thus, the PDES scheme is computationally scalable if there exists a *constant* $c > 0$, such that:

$$\langle u^{(G)}(\infty) \rangle = \lim_{\substack{t \to \infty \\ n \to \infty}} \frac{\langle |A^{(G)}(t)| \rangle}{n} > c . \tag{5}$$

The measurement scalability of the PDES scheme is characterized by the spread of the virtual time horizon. Instead of dealing with the actual spread (difference between the maximum and minimum values) we shall consider the average "width" (or variance) of the time horizon defined as:

$$\langle [w^{(G)}]^2(t) \rangle = \frac{1}{n} \sum_{j=1}^{n} \left[\tau_j^{(G)}(t) - \overline{\tau}^{(G)}(t) \right]^2 . \tag{6}$$

A PDES scheme is measurement scalable if there exists a *constant* $M > 0$ such that:

$$\langle [w^{(G)}]^2(\infty) \rangle = \lim_{\substack{t \to \infty \\ n \to \infty}} \frac{1}{n} \sum_{j=1}^{n} \left[\tau_j^{(G)}(t) - \overline{\tau}^{(G)}(t) \right]^2 < M . \tag{7}$$

In reality, the number n of PEs or the simulation time t can never be taken to infinity, so for practical purposes, the scalability is deduced from the scaling behavior of the quantities for long times and for a large number of PEs. The setup presented above is perfectly suited to establishing a mapping between non-equilibrium surface growth models [29] and conservative PDES schemes. We discuss this mapping extensively in the next section.

3   SCALABILITY OF CONSERVATIVE PDES SCHEMES ON REGULAR AND SMALL-WORLD TOPOLOGIES

In many large complex systems the stochastic event dynamics can be characterized by a Poisson-distributed stream. To give one example, in an Ising magnet with single spin-flip Glauber dynamics [342] the spin-flip attempts are Poisson-distributed events. To give another example, in wireless cellular communications the call arrivals obey Poisson statistics [209]. In the following, we restrict ourselves to such Poisson distributed stochastic processes for event dynamics. However, numerical simulations show that our conclusions for scalability hold for a large class of other stochastic distributions as well. The evolution of the virtual time horizon incorporating condition (1) for Poisson asynchrony is given by the equation:

$$\tau_i^{(G)}(t+1) = \tau_i^{(G)}(t) + \eta_i(t) \prod_{j \in N_i} \theta(\tau_j^{(G)}(t) - \tau_i^{(G)}(t)).$$ (8)

Here, $\theta(x)$ is the Heaviside step function and $\eta_i(t)$ is the Poisson-distributed virtual time increment at PE i and time t. These increments are drawn at random, independently of i and t, and independently of the existing time horizon.

3.1   THE BASIC CONSERVATIVE SCHEME ON REGULAR TOPOLOGIES

Next, we consider the *basic* conservative scheme, which is defined on regular, cubic lattice communication topologies, in d dimensions, so that $n = L^d$. For brevity we drop the superscript (G) in the notation for $\tau_i(t)$. In particular, we first illustrate our analysis on the simplest regular topology, that of a regular one-dimensional lattice with periodic boundary conditions, so that G is a ring. Later, we discuss the general, d-dimensional case. The evolution equation on the ring is simply:

$$\tau_i(t+1) = \tau_i(t) + \eta_i(t)\theta(\tau_{i-1}(t) - \tau_i(t))\theta(\tau_{i+1}(t) - \tau_i(t)).$$ (9)

with the boundary conditions $\tau_{n+1} = \tau_n = \tau_0$. The total number of active sites/PEs is thus given by $|A(t)| = \sum_{i=1}^n \theta(\tau_{i-1}(t) - \tau_i(t))\theta(\tau_{i+1}(t) - \tau_i(t))$ so the average utilization (4) becomes:

$$\langle u(L,t) \rangle = \frac{1}{n} \sum_{i=1}^n \langle \theta(\tau_{i-1}(t) - \tau_i(t))\theta(\tau_{i+1}(t) - \tau_i(t)) \rangle .$$ (10)

The average $\langle \cdots \rangle$ is performed over the random variables $\{\eta_i(t')\}_{\substack{i=1,\ldots,L \\ t'=1,\ldots,t}}$, which have an exponential distribution, $\mathbf{Pr}[x < \eta \le x + \delta x] = \int_x^{x+\delta x} dy\, e^{-y}$. In spite of the simple appearance of the dynamics (9), and the exponential (or Poisson) stochastic dynamics at nodes, calculating the average utilization (10) is very

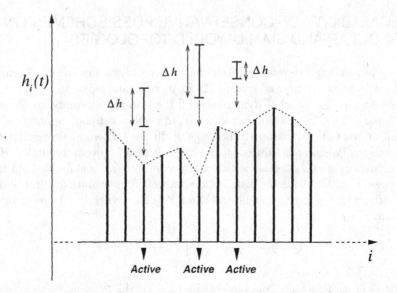

FIGURE 2   A simple surface growth model on a 1-d substrate corresponding to the basic conservative PDES scheme.

difficult. A rigorous proof even for the existence of the lower bound (5) using direct methods is still an open problem.

Here we present a different approach, first mapping the problem to a non-equilibrium surface grown via a molecular beam epitaxy model, where atoms or molecules are deposited from vapors or beams onto the surface. The analogies for the various quantities are as follows: the ith PE is the site i in the substrate; the number of parallel updates t is the number of deposited monolayers; $\tau_i(t)$ is the height $h_i(t)$ at site i and time t; and a virtual time increment of $\eta_i(t)$ at PE i in the tth step corresponds to a material "rod" of length $\eta_i(t)$ deposited onto the surface (see fig. 2). The length of the rod is a Poisson-distributed random variable. During the tth update, the rods are deposited only into *local minima* of the surface. The utilization of the PDES scheme corresponds to the *density* of local minima of the growing surface. Even though the lengths of the rods are independent random variables, the fact that they can only be deposited in local minima will generate lateral correlations into the surface fluctuations, and makes the problem hard to solve exactly. The rods are deposited onto the surface in a parallel update scheme: after all local minima are updated (deposited onto), the time t is incremented by unity. We call the surface growth analog of our basic conservative PDES scheme the massively parallel exponential update (MPEU) model.

Both the utilization (density of minima) and the width of the time horizon are quantities characterizing the fluctuations of the growing surface. The type of fluctuations can be classified into universality classes, each class having distinct statistical properties. Studying the PDES scheme as a surface growth model, we can describe its fluctuations and identify the surface growth universality class to which it belongs. In order to do this, we first introduce the *slope variables*, $\phi_i = \tau_i - \tau_{i-1}$. Provided $\tau_i(t)$ is a local minimum, depositing a rod of length η_i corresponds to taking an amount of η_i from ϕ_{i+1} and adding it to ϕ_i, since $\phi_i(t+1) = \tau_i(t) - \tau_{i-1}(t) + \eta_i(t)$ and $\phi_{i+1}(t+1) = \tau_{i+1}(t) - \tau_i(t) - \eta_i(t)$. Thus, in the *surface of slopes* $\{\phi_i\}_{i=1}^{L}$, the dynamics are those of *biased surface diffusion*, given by the equation:

$$\phi_i(t+1) - \phi_i(t) = \eta_i(t)\,\theta(-\phi_i(t))\,\theta(\phi_{i+1}(t)) - \eta_{i-1}(t)\,\theta(-\phi_{i-1}(t))\,\theta(\phi_i(t)) \quad (11)$$

with the constraint $\sum_{i=1}^{L} \phi_i = 0$ generated by the periodic boundary conditions in the τ variables. In terms of the local slope variables, the expression for the average density of minima or average utilization becomes: $\langle u(L,t) \rangle = \frac{1}{L}\sum_{i=1}^{L} \langle \theta(-\phi_i(t))\theta(\phi_{i+1}(t)) \rangle$. Translational invariance (no node is statistically special) implies $\langle u(L,t) \rangle = \langle \theta(-\phi_i(t))\theta(\phi_{i+1}(t)) \rangle$ for any $i = 1, \ldots, L$. From eq. (9) it follows that $\langle \tau_i(t+1) \rangle - \langle \tau_i(t) \rangle = \langle u(L,t) \rangle$. Therefore, *the average rate of propagation of the MPEU surface is identical to the average utilization of the PDES scheme*. It is also easy to see that in terms of the slope variables it is identical to the average current in the ring.

Next, we perform a naive coarse graining by using the representation $\theta(\phi) = \lim_{\kappa \to 0} \frac{1}{2}[1 + \tanh(\phi/\kappa)]$, and keeping only the terms up to first-order in ϕ/κ. This leads to:

$$\langle \phi_i(t+1) \rangle - \langle \phi_i(t) \rangle = \frac{1}{4\kappa}\langle \phi_{i+1}(t) - 2\phi_i(t) + \phi_{i-1}(t) \rangle - \frac{1}{4\kappa^2}\langle \phi_i(\phi_{i+1} - \phi_{i-1}) \rangle . \quad (12)$$

Strictly speaking, all of the $(\phi/\kappa)^j$, $j = 1, 2, \ldots$ terms are divergent. But by taking the proper continuum limit and introducing an appropriately scaled bias, one can show that the only relevant terms are those appearing in eq. (12). In the continuum limit, one thus obtains for the coarse-grained field:

$$\frac{\partial}{\partial t}\hat{\phi} = \frac{\partial^2}{\partial x^2}\hat{\phi} - \lambda\frac{\partial}{\partial x}\hat{\phi}^2 \quad (13)$$

where λ is a parameter related to the coarse-graining procedure. The nonlinear partial differential equation (13) is known as nonlinear biased diffusion, or the Burgers equation [83]. Returning to the coarse-grained equivalent of the height, or virtual times, $\hat{\tau}$, we obtain via $\hat{\phi} = \partial\hat{\tau}/\partial x$ the Kardar-Parisi-Zhang (KPZ) equation [296]:

$$\frac{\partial\hat{\tau}}{\partial t} = \frac{\partial^2\hat{\tau}}{\partial x^2} - \lambda\left(\frac{\partial\hat{\tau}}{\partial x}\right)^2 . \quad (14)$$

To capture the fluctuations, one typically adds a delta-correlated noise term $\xi(x, t)$, to the right-hand side, conserved for eq. (13), that is, $\int \xi dx = 0$, and non-conserved for eq. (14). It is important to note that we obtained the KPZ equation as a result of a coarse-graining procedure. While this results in the loss of some of the microscopic details for the original growth model on the lattice, eq. (14) with noise added describes the long-wavelength behavior of the MPEU model. Thus, we claim that virtual time horizon for the basic conservative PDES scheme exhibits kinetic roughening and it belongs to the KPZ universality class. Identifying the universality class of a model is one of the main objectives of surface science, and is used extensively to classify fluctuation statistics. Our procedure above indicates that the long-wavelength statistics of the fluctuations of the time horizon for the basic conservative PDES scheme are in fact captured by the nonlinear KPZ equation.

In one dimension a steady state for the surface fluctuations is reached (in the long time limit) for any *finite* system size, and it is governed by the Edwards-Wilkinson (EW) Hamiltonian $H_{EW} \propto \int dx \left(\frac{\partial \hat{\tau}}{\partial x}\right)^2$ (see, e.g., Barabási and Stanley [29]). The corresponding surface is a simple random-walk surface, where the slopes are independent random variables in the steady state. This means that of the four local configurations of slopes around a point (down-up, down-down, up-up, up-down), only one contributes on average to a minimum (down-up), and since they are all equally likely, we conclude that $\langle u_{EW}(L \to \infty, t \to \infty)\rangle = 1/4 = 0.25$. (Zero slopes are statistically irrelevant, since the probability that two virtual times are exactly equal is zero, given that the updates are drawn from a continuous probability distribution.) Our numerical simulations for the MPEU model (see fig. 3(a)) indicate a value of $\langle u(L \to \infty, t \to \infty)\rangle = 0.24641 \pm (7 \times 10^{-6})$, a value close but not identical to that for the simple random walk surface. The reason for the obvious difference is that the coarse-grained version and the original microscopic model are not identical over the whole spectrum of wavelengths of the fluctuations. The coarse-graining procedure preserves the statistics of the long-wavelength modes, but it loses some information on the short-wavelength ones. In particular, the density of minima is heavily influenced by the short wavelengths (by how "fuzzy" the interface is). However, the density of minima cannot vanish in the thermodynamic limit (large n, large t): a zero density of local minima would imply that it is zero on all length scales, which would contradict the fact that it belongs to the EW universality class. The fact that the steady state of the MPEU model belongs to the EW universality class guarantees that the local slopes are *short-range* correlated (fig. 3(c)), and that the finite-size corrections for the density of local minima (average propagation rate of the surface) follow a universal scaling form [350]:

$$\langle u(L, \infty)\rangle \simeq \langle u(\infty, \infty)\rangle + \frac{\text{const.}}{L^{2(1-\alpha)}} . \tag{15}$$

Here α is the roughness exponent (equal to $1/2$ for the EW universality class), characterizing the macroscopic surface-height fluctuations, as described in detail

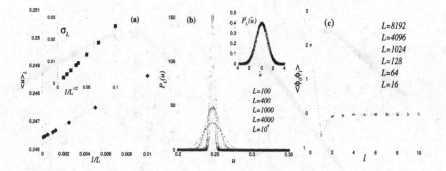

FIGURE 3   (a) Steady state average utilization as a function of the number of PEs L in a one-dimensional ring geometry; (b) The full distribution for the rescaled utilization in the steady state $\tilde{u} = (u(L) - \langle u(L)\rangle)/\sigma_L$, collapsed onto the normal distribution; (c) Slope-slope correlation function.

in the next paragraph. Figure 3 confirms this scaling behavior. Further, calculating the variance in the average utilization in the steady state as a function of system size, $\sigma_L^2 = \langle u^2(L,\infty)\rangle - \langle u(L,\infty)\rangle^2$, we obtain $\sigma_L \propto L^{-1/2}$. These findings suggest that the utilization is a self-averaging macroscopic quantity: its full distribution $P_L(u)$ for large L is a Gaussian (fig. 3(b)).

In the following we show numerical results supporting our claim that the MPEU model belongs to the KPZ universality class. One of the fundamental characteristic quantities strongly influenced by the long-wavelength modes is the average width of the height fluctuations, as given in eq. (6). As the surface grows due to deposition, after an initial transient the width will grow as a power law $\langle w^2(L,t)\rangle \sim t^{2\beta}$ along with the lateral surface correlations $\xi_{\parallel}(L,t) \sim t^{1/z}$, until the correlations reach the system size ($\xi_{\parallel} = L$) at a crossover time $t_\times$ [29]. After the crossover time $t_\times$ (for any finite system L) the surface fluctuations are governed by a steady-state distribution and the width scales as

$$\langle w^2(L,\infty)\rangle \sim L^{2\alpha}. \tag{16}$$

The exponent β is called the *growth exponent*, α is the called *roughness exponent*, and z is called the *dynamic exponent* in the surface growth literature [29]. It is easy to show that the three exponents are not all independent, and in fact $\alpha = z\beta$ [29]. Also, these scaling forms allow one to collapse all the different curves for the width onto a single function in the scaling regime, expressing the *dynamic scaling property* of the width: $\langle w^2(L,t)\rangle = L^{2\alpha} f(t/L^z)$ (f is easy to read off, after comparing it to the scaling behavior). For the KPZ interface, the exact values obtained analytically for the exponents are: $\beta = 1/3$, $\alpha = 1/2$ and $z = 3/2$. Figure 4 shows the scaling properties for the width of the MPEU model, measured numerically. For large system sizes ($L = 10^5$), the values

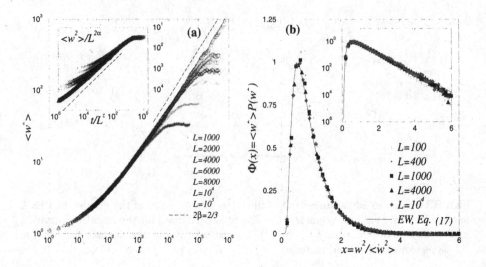

FIGURE 4 (a) The width of the time horizon fluctuations shows dynamical scaling and indicates KPZ universality; (b) The scaling function for the steady-state width distribution follows the scaling function for the EW (one-dimensional KPZ) universality class.

obtained numerically for the exponents, $\beta = 0.326 \pm 0.005$ and $\alpha = 0.49 \pm 0.01$, confirm the KPZ behavior including the dynamical scaling property (inset). Another confirmation for the EW universality class in the steady state comes from measuring the full width distribution $P(w^2)$. For systems belonging to the EW universality class and having the same type of boundary conditions imposed, the width distribution has a universal scaling form [162] $P(w^2) = \frac{1}{\langle w^2 \rangle} \Phi\left(\frac{w^2}{\langle w^2 \rangle}\right)$ with

$$\Phi(x) = \frac{\pi^2}{3} \sum_{n=1}^{\infty} (-1)^{n-1} n^2 e^{-\frac{\pi^2}{6} n^2 x} , \tag{17}$$

for the case of periodic boundary conditions. Figure 4(b) is a confirmation that the MPEU indeed belongs to the steady state of the EW class, implying that the average utilization (density of local minima) approaches a non-zero, finite value in the thermodynamic limit (5) as reflected by eq. (15). Therefore, the basic conservative scheme is *computationally scalable*. For an in-depth and systematic analytical calculation of the density of minima (utilization) for a number of surface growth models (including the EW class) see Toroczkai et al. [501]. The measurement phase of the basic conservative scheme, however, is *not* scalable, as indicated by the power-law divergence of the width in the long-time large L limit (eq. (16)). For higher-dimensional topologies, using universality arguments, the conclusion remains the same: the basic conservative PDES is computationally scalable, but the measurement phase may not be, depending on what is known as the *upper critical dimension* [29] of the surface (see Korniss et al. [344, 345]).

3.2   THE CONSERVATIVE SCHEME ON SMALL WORLD NETWORKS

From the previous section it follows that the average width of the fluctuations scales in the steady state as $\langle w^2(L, t = \infty)\rangle \sim L^{2\alpha} = L$, and thus grows linearly with the system size. This means that the basic conservative PDES scheme is *not* measurement scalable. Standard methods to control the width of the virtual time horizon in a PDES scheme employ windowing techniques [186]. That is, the local simulated time at any PE cannot progress beyond an appropriately chosen and regularly updated "cap," measured from the global minimum of the time horizon [340]. Thus, a PDES scheme with a moving window relies on frequent global synchronizations or communications, which, depending on the architecture, can get costly for large number of PEs. Here we show how to modify the original conservative scheme such that the scheme is also measurement scalable *without* global "intervention" [346].

The divergence of the width of the surface fluctuations is closely related to the fact that the lateral surface correlations also grow with the system size. In particular, for the one-dimensional EW surface in the steady state, for large L (and fixed l)

$$\langle \hat{\tau}_i \hat{\tau}_{i+l}\rangle \propto \xi_{||}(L, \infty) - |l| , \qquad (18)$$

where $\hat{\tau}_i$ are the coarse-grained height fluctuations measured from the mean and $\xi_{||}(L, \infty) \sim L$. Thus, $\langle w^2(L, \infty)\rangle = \langle \hat{\tau}_i^2\rangle \propto \xi_{||}(L, \infty) \sim L$. The "height-height" correlations can be characterized by introducing the structure factor for the heights:

$$S^{(\tau)}(k) = \frac{1}{L}\langle \tilde{\tau}_k \tilde{\tau}_{-k}\rangle \qquad (19)$$

where $k = 2\pi\alpha/L$, $\alpha = 0, 1, 2, \ldots, L-1$ is the wave-vector, and $\tilde{\tau}_k = \sum_{j=0}^{L-1} e^{-ikj} (\tau_j - \overline{\tau})$ is the discrete spatial Fourier transform of the fluctuations of the virtual time horizon. Then

$$\langle \hat{\tau}_i \hat{\tau}_{i+l}\rangle = \frac{1}{L}\sum_k e^{ikl} S^{(\tau)}(k) \qquad (20)$$

and

$$\langle w^2(L, \infty)\rangle = \frac{1}{L}\sum_k S^{(\tau)}(k) . \qquad (21)$$

Since the universality class for the time horizon evolution is EW, it follows that the expected behavior for the steady-state structure factor for small wave-numbers is

$$S^{(\tau)}(k) \propto \frac{1}{k^2} \qquad (22)$$

(see, e.g., eq. (11) in Toroczkai et al. [501]). Indeed, this is also confirmed by

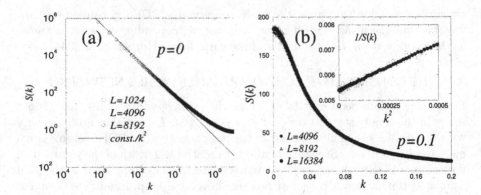

FIGURE 5   Steady-state structure factors for the virtual time horizon for the (a) basic conservative scheme on a regular one-dimensional lattice ($p = 0$) and (b) small-world scheme with $p = 0.1$.

our direct simulation results, shown in figure 5(a). This form of the structure factor implies that there are no length scales other than the lattice constant and the system size, and thus the correlation length and the width diverge in the thermodynamic limit, as can also be seen by evaluating eq. (21) directly.

To de-correlate the surface fluctuations, we modify the communication topology in the following way [346]: for every node i, at the onset of the simulation, we introduce one extra quenched (fixed for a given network realization) random communication link $r(i)$. Together with the existing regular topology, these extra communication links will form a small-world graph [326, 415, 519]. Note that in our specific construction of the small-world network, each node has exactly one random connection and $r(r(i)) = i$, so that there are exactly $L/2$ random links distributed. The updating on PE i will obey the following probabilistically chosen condition:

$$\tau_i \le \begin{cases} \min\{\tau_{i-1}, \tau_{i+1}, \tau_{r(i)}\} & \text{with probability } p \\ \min\{\tau_{i-1}, \tau_{i+1}\} & \text{with probability } 1 - p \end{cases} \tag{23}$$

The PE performs the update (generates the virtual time of the next update or deposits the rod at i in the MPEU surface) only if condition (23) is fulfilled. This means that for sites that would normally be updated within the basic conservative scheme, that is, $\tau_i \le \min\{\tau_{i-1}, \tau_{i+1}\}$, the PE will make an extra check for the condition $\tau_i \le \tau_{r(i)}$ with probability p. The parameter p allows us to tune the scalability properties of the corresponding PDES scheme on the quenched small-world network continuously from the pure basic conservative scheme ($p = 0$) to the "fully" small-world conservative scheme ($p = 1$). These occasional extra checks through the quenched random links are not necessary for the faithfulness of the simulation. Rather, they are used to *synchronize* the PEs in such a way that the fluctuations of the time horizon remain bounded in the limit of infinite system size. Most importantly, as the width is reduced from "infinity" (or some large number proportional to L for a finite number of PEs) to a finite, controlled value, the utilization still remains bounded away from zero.

To support this statement, we first use the same coarse-graining procedure used to derive the KPZ equations, as the continuum counterpart of the MPEU model. For the small-world topology we obtain

$$\frac{\partial \hat{\tau}}{\partial t} = -\gamma(p)\hat{\tau} + \frac{\partial^2 \hat{\tau}}{\partial x^2} - \lambda \left(\frac{\partial \hat{\tau}}{\partial x} \right)^2 + \xi(x,t) \tag{24}$$

with $\gamma(p) = 0$ for $p = 0$, and $\gamma(p) > 0$ for $0 < p \le 1$. This implies that the extra checking along the random links introduces a *strong* relaxation (first term on the right-hand side of eq. (24)) for the long-wavelength modes of the surface fluctuations, resulting in a finite width. A more transparent picture is gained if we look at the steady-state structure factor (19). Restricting our attention to the linear terms in eq. (24) we obtain

$$S^{(\tau)}(k) \propto \frac{1}{\gamma + k^2} . \tag{25}$$

In this approximation, the lateral correlation length $\xi_{||}$ scales as $1/\sqrt{\gamma}$, and remains *finite* (and independent of system size) in the thermodynamic limit for all $p > 0$, that is, for an arbitrary small probability of using the random links. Figure 5(b) shows the structure factor for the small-world network with $p = 0.1$, confirming the prediction of eq. (25) for small wave numbers. Consequently, the height-height correlations decay exponentially

$$\langle \hat{\tau}_i \hat{\tau}_{i+l} \rangle \propto \xi_{||}\, e^{-|l|/\xi_{||}} , \tag{26}$$

and the width remains finite, $\langle w^2(L,\infty) \rangle \sim \xi_{||}$, where $\xi_{||}$ is independent of the system size for all $p > 0$. Further, for the structure factors of the local slopes (the Fourier transform of the slope-slope correlations) one obtains

$$S^{(\phi)}(k) = \frac{1}{L} \langle \tilde{\phi}_k \tilde{\phi}_{-k} \rangle = k^2 S^{(\tau)}(k) \propto \frac{k^2}{\gamma + k^2} = 1 - \frac{\gamma}{\gamma + k^2} . \tag{27}$$

Both terms above yield short-range correlations (delta function for the first term and exponential decay for the second one), thus the slopes remain short-range correlated, resulting in a non-zero density of local minima. Figure 6 shows two snapshots of the virtual time horizons for the basic conservative scheme $p = 0$, and the small-world scheme with $p = 0.1$. Figure 7(a) shows the scaling of the steady-state width with the system size for various p values and figure 7(b) shows the scaling of the average, steady-state utilization with the system size for the same set of p values. Notice that when increasing p (from $p = 0$ to $p = 0.01$),

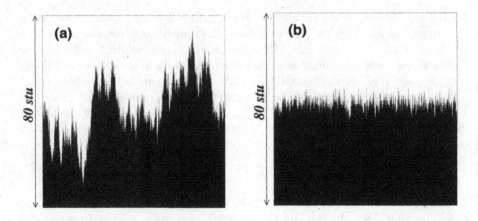

FIGURE 6   Steady-state virtual time horizon snapshots with $L = 10000$ after $t = 10^6$ parallel algorithmic steps (Monte-Carlo sweeps) for the (a) basic conservative scheme ($p = 0$) and (b) small-world scheme $p = 0.1$. Note that the vertical scales are the same in (a) and (b) (plotted in arbitrary simulated time units).

the width instantaneously drops from a linear divergence to a saturated value, while at the same time, the utilization hardly changes. In fact, an infinitesimally small p will make the width bounded, and only at an infinitesimal expense to the utilization. For example, for a hypothetical infinite system, taking $p = 0.01$, the width is reduced from infinity to about 40, while the utilization only from 0.2464 to about 0.246; for $p = 0.1$, the width is further reduced to about 5, while the utilization only to 0.242. By further increasing p, the width further reduces, and at $p = 1$ it is about 1.46, whereas the utilization decreases to 0.141, still clearly bounded away from zero in the thermodynamic limit.

4   SCALABILITY OF THE CONSERVATIVE PDES SCHEME ON SCALE-FREE NETWORK TOPOLOGIES

The internet is a spontaneously grown collection of connected computers. The number of webservers by February 2003 reached over 35 million [414]. The number of PCs in use (internet users) surpassed 660 million in 2002, and it is projected to surpass one billion by 2007 [105]. The idea for using it as a giant supercomputer is rather natural: many computers are in an idle state, running at best some kind of screen-saver software, and the "wasted" computational time is simply immense. Projects such as SETI@home [473] or the GRID consortium [198] are aiming to harness the power lost to screen-savers.

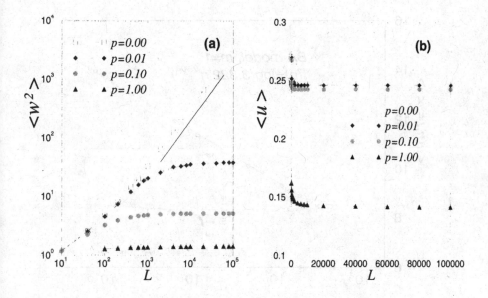

FIGURE 7   (a) The average steady-state width and (b) the utilization for various p values. In addition to ensemble averages over 10 realizations of the random links (solid symbols) a single realization is also shown (open symbols). The solid straight line has a slope of 1/2 and represents the asymptotic one-dimensional KPZ power-law divergence of the width for the basic conservative scheme ($p = 0$).

Most of the problems solved currently with distributed computation on the internet are "embarrassingly parallel" [318], in that the computed tasks have little or no connection to each other: for example, starting the same run with a number of different random seeds, and at the end collecting data to perform statistical averages. However, before more large-scale, complex problems can be solved in real time on the internet, a number of challenges have to be solved, such as the task allocation problem that is complex in itself [457].

Here we ask the following question. *Assuming* that task allocation is resolved and the PE communication topology on the internet is a scale-free network, what are the scalability properties of a PDES scheme on such networks? We present numerical results, for the PDES update scheme, as measured on the Barabási-Albert (BA) model [28, 30] of scale-free networks. The network is created through the stochastic process of preferential attachment: to the existing network of n nodes at time t, the $(n + 1)$th node with m links ("stubs") attaches at time $t + 1$, such that each stub attaches to a node with probability proportional to the existing degree (at t) of the node. We restrict ourselves here to the $m = 1$ case, where the network is a scale-free tree. We have repeated the simulations

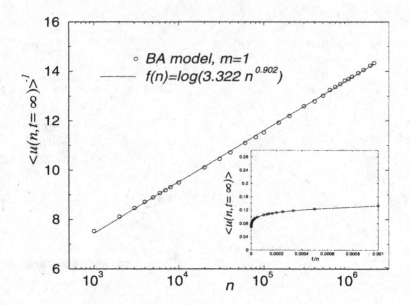

FIGURE 8   Steady-state utilization for the scale-free BA model.

with different m values (up to $m = 10$) and found no significant deviations from our conclusions below—numerical factors are different, but the generic behavior is the same. Once we reach a given number of nodes in the network, we stop the process and use the random network instance to run the MPEU model on top of it, using the evolution (eq. (8)) for the time horizon. While in case of regular topologies, the degree of a node is constant, such as, $P^{(L^d)}(k) = 2d\delta_{k,2d}$ for d-dimensional "square" lattices, for the BA network it is a power law in the asymptotic ($n \to \infty$) limit: $P^{BA}(k) \simeq 2m^2 k^{-3}$. The condition (1) for a site to be updated, namely that its virtual time is a local minimum, is a *local* property. Thus, we expect that the utilization itself will be correlated with local structural properties of the graph, such as the degree distribution.

To get a more detailed picture, we define two more quantities. The first is the *connectivity utilization*

$$u_k(n, t) = \frac{|A_k(t)|}{n}, \tag{28}$$

which is the fraction of active nodes of degree k, and the second is the *relative connectivity utilization*

$$r_k(n, t) = \frac{|A_k(t)|}{n_k}, \tag{29}$$

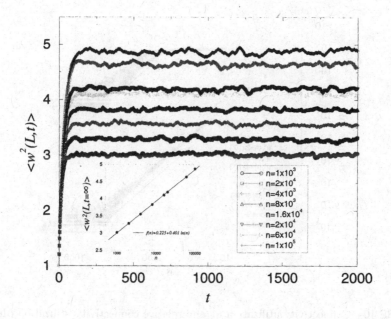

FIGURE 9 Behavior of the time horizon width for the scale-free BA network. The inset shows the scaling of the steady-state width as a function of the system size n. Notice the log-linear scale in the inset.

which is the fraction of nodes that are active and have degree k among the set of all nodes of degree k. From the definitions above, we find the following relations: $\sum_k u_k(n,t) = u(n,t)$ and $\sum_k r_k(n,t)n_k/n = \sum_k r_k(n,t)P^{BA}(k) = \sum_k u_k(n,t) = u(n,t) = \langle r_k(n,t)\rangle_{network}$ at all times, where $\langle \cdots \rangle_{networks}$ is an average over network realizations. Figure 8 shows the steady-state ($t \to \infty$, in the MPEU model on a fixed BA network of n nodes) values of the average utilization as a function of the network size n. The inset in figure 8 is analogous to figure 3(a), which showed the same quantity on a ring. Notice that strictly speaking, the PDES scheme is computationally *non-scalable*. However, an empirical fit suggests that $u^*(n) = \langle u(n,t = \infty) \rangle \simeq \left[\log \left(an^b \right) \right]^{-1}$ with $a \approx 3.322$ and $b = 0.902$, that is, the computation is only logarithmically (or marginally) non-scalable. For a system of $n = 10^3$ nodes we have found a steady-state utilization (for the worst case scenario) of $u^*(10^3) = 0.1328$ (13.3% efficiency), while for a system of $n = 10^6$ nodes, the utilization drops only to $u^*(10^6) = 0.073$ (7.3% efficiency), by less than half of its value! For practical purposes the PDES scheme can be considered computationally scalable, and we will call this type of non-scalability *logarithmic* (or marginal) non-scalability.

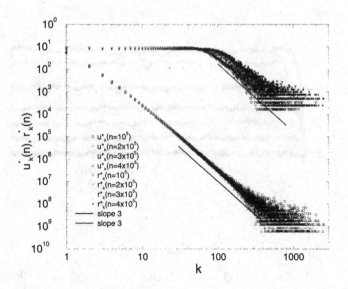

FIGURE 10 Connectivity utilization u_k and relative connectivity utilization (defined in the text) r_k as function of degree. Each data set is obtained after averaging over 200 independent runs.

Figure 9 shows the scaling of the width of the fluctuations for the time horizon as a function of time, and the scaling of its value in the steady state as a function of system size (inset). Notice that while the steady-state width diverges to infinity, it does so only logarithmically, $\langle w^2(n, t = \infty) \rangle \simeq [\log(cn^d)]$ with $c \approx 1.25$ and $d \approx 0.401$. Some specific values are $\langle w^2(10^3, t = \infty) \rangle \approx 3.01$, $\langle w^2(10^5, t = \infty) \rangle \approx 4.78$. This means that the measurement phase of the PDES scheme on a scale-free network is also non-scalable, but only logarithmically, and so for practical purposes the scheme can be considered scalable. Overall, the PDES update scheme has logarithmic (or marginal) non-scalability on scale-free networks. If one examines the connectivity utilization and relative connectivity utilization in the steady state, as shown in figure 10, one finds that to a good approximation $u_k^*(n) \sim k^{-3}$, and $r_k^*(n) = \text{const.} \simeq u^*(n)$ for $k \leq k_\times$ and $r_k^*(n) \sim k^{-3}$ for $k > k_\times$, with $k_\times \sim 1/u^*(n) = \log(an^b) \sim \log n$ being the crossover degree.

5 CONCLUSIONS

We have studied the fundamental scalability problem of conservative PDES schemes where events are self-initiated and have identical distributions on each

PE. First, we considered the scalability of the basic conservative scheme for systems with short-range interactions on regular lattices. By exploiting a mapping between the progress of the simulation and kinetic roughening in non-equilibrium surfaces, we found that while the average progress rate of the PEs $\langle u(\infty, \infty) \rangle$ is a finite *non-zero* value, the spread of the progress of the PEs about the mean $\langle w^2(\infty, \infty) \rangle$ *diverges*. This divergence makes the measurement phase of the algorithm non-scalable. In order to make the measurement part of the simulation scalable as well, we have introduced a small number of quenched random connections between PEs so that the resulting random links on top of the regular short-range connections form a *small-world* connection topology. Invoking the same conservative protocol used at an arbitrarily small (but strictly positive) rate through the random links is sufficient to achieve full scalability: the PEs progress at a non-zero, near-uniform rate *without* requiring global synchronization. This construction of a fully scalable algorithm for simulating large systems with asynchronous dynamics and short-range interactions is an example of the enormous "computational power and synchronizability" [519] that can be achieved by small-world couplings. The suppression of critical fluctuations of the virtual time horizon is also closely related to the emergence of mean-field-like phase transitions and phase ordering in *non-frustrated* interacting systems [34, 197, 256, 257, 316]. In particular, the fluctuations exhibited by the virtual time horizon with small-world synchronization should exhibit very similar characteristics to the fluctuations of the order parameter in the XY spin model on a small-world network [316].

Second, we have studied the scalability properties for a causally constrained PDES scheme hosted by a network of computers where the network is *scale-free* following a "preferential attachment" construction [28, 30]. Here the PEs simply have to satisfy the general criterion eq. (1) in order to advance their local time. Despite some nodes in the network having abnormally high degrees, as a result of the scale-free nature of the degree distribution, we find that the computational phase of the algorithm is only marginally non-scalable. The utilization exhibits slow logarithmic decay as a function of the number of PEs. At the same time, the width of the time horizon diverges logarithmically slowly, rendering the measurement phase of the simulations marginally non-scalable as well. An intriguing question to pursue is how the logarithmic divergence of the surface fluctuations observed here can be related to the collective behavior (in particular, the finite-size effects of the magnetic susceptibility) of Ising ferromagnets on scale-free networks [15, 51, 127, 359] with the same degree distribution.

ACKNOWLEDGEMENTS

Discussions with P. A. Rikvold, B. D. Lubachevsky, Z. Rácz, and G. Istrate are gratefully acknowledged. Zoltan Toroczkai was supported by the Department of Energy under contract W-7405-ENG-36. This research is supported in part by the National Science Foundation, through Grant No. DMR-0113049 and the Research Corporation through Grant No. RI0761.

CHAPTER 12

Combinatorics of Genotype-Phenotype Maps: An RNA Case Study

Christian M. Reidys

1 INTRODUCTION

The fundamental mechanisms of biological evolution have fascinated generations of researchers and remain popular to this day. The formulation of such a theory goes back to Darwin (1859), who in the *The Origin of Species* presented two fundamental principles: genetic variability caused by mutation, and natural selection. The first principle leads to diversity and the second one to the concept of survival of the fittest, where fitness is an inherited characteristic property of an individual and can basically be identified with its reproduction rate. Wright [530, 531] first recognized the importance of genetic drift in evolution in improving the evolutionary search capacity of the whole population. He viewed genetic drift merely as a process that could improve evolutionary search. About a decade later, Kimura proposed [317] that the majority of changes that are observed in evolution at the molecular level are the results of random drift of genotypes. The neutral theory of Kimura does not deny that selection plays a role, but claims that no appreciable fraction of observable molecular change can

Computational Complexity and Statistical Physics, edited by
Allon G. Percus, Gabriel Istrate, and Cristopher Moore, Oxford University Press.

be caused by selective forces: mutations are either a disadvantage or, at best, neutral in present day organisms. Only negative selection plays a major role in the neutral evolution, in that deleterious mutants die out due to their lower fitness.

Over the last few decades, there has been a shift of emphasis in the study of evolution. Instead of focusing on the differences in the selective value of mutants and on population genetics, interest has moved to evolution through natural selection as an abstract optimization problem. Given the tremendous opportunities that computer science and the physical sciences now have for contributing to the study of biological phenomena, it is fitting to study the evolutionary optimization problem in the present volume. In this chapter, we adopt the following framework: assuming that selection acts exclusively upon isolated phenotypes, we introduce the following compositum of mappings

$$\textbf{Genotypes} \longrightarrow \textbf{Phenotypes} \longrightarrow \textbf{Fitness} . \qquad (1)$$

We will refer to the first map as to the genotype-phenotype map and call the preimage of a given phenotype its neutral network. Clearly, the main ingredients here are the phenotypes and genotypes and their respective organization. In the following we will study various combinatorial properties of phenotypes and genotypes for RNA folding maps.

In the context of the RNA toy-world pioneered by Peter Schuster et al. [160, 443, 462, 463, 464], the phenotypes are secondary structures that allow for a mathematical modeling of their corresponding neutral networks as random graphs. Many significant properties of these neutral networks, such as connectivity, density, and path-connectivity are monotonic: they are maintained after adding any number of edges. One may then ask whether the montonic property in question displays a sharp threshold or phase transition—as, for instance, in the classical random graph ensemble $\mathcal{G}_{n,p}$ where *every* monotonic property satisfies a 0-1 law. The application of random graph theory to biology and particularly computational biology is not new. Bollobás and Rasmussen have used directed random graphs [63] to study the evolution of autocatalytic networks. Lynch has analyzed phase transitions [371, 372] in Kauffmann's random Boolean networks used for the modeling of gene regulatory networks. Finally, Frieze et al. have studied optimal sequencing [181, 184] and the ordering of clone libraries [136] using methods and theory of random graphs.

The mapping of RNA sequences to their secondary structures plays an important role in the understanding of evolutionary optimization, as the generic properties of this mapping dictate to a large extent the dynamics of the optimization process itself. Populations of sequences subject to selective pressures, such as virus populations pressured by immune systems, constantly search for new fitter structures and try to realize them. During this search, however, the current "best" phenotype must necessarily be preserved while new mutants simultaneously emerge. In most cases the search process is essentially a "white noise computation," such as point mutations in single stranded RNA, where there is no rational design according to which the mutations occur. Accordingly, the generic structure of folding maps must allow for effective random search. In the case of folding maps from RNA sequences to their secondary structures, we will show that the key feature for enabling effective search by point mutations is a specific type of redundancy. The sequences folding into one specific secondary structure form networks with giant components. As a consequence, some fraction of random point mutations will have virtually no effect on the phenotype; that is, the RNA folds into the same secondary structure and, complimentarily, some fraction of point mutants will fold into new structures. Additionally, we will show that the combinatorics of secondary structures itself guarantees that any two structures can have neutral nets that are close in sequence space. Kimura's neutral theory fits smoothly into the genotype-phenotype map framework, since it reflects the relation between genotypes and phenotypes. Our main goal consists of providing insight into folding maps exhibiting the type of redundancy above and how generic such maps are, as well as investigating additional properties of these maps that are of key relevance to evolutionary optimization.

In the following section we introduce some basic facts about RNA sequences and RNA secondary structures. In section 3 we introduce the notion of compatible sequences with respect to a secondary structure and prove that for any two secondary structures there exists some RNA sequence that is compatible with both of them. This result guarantees the closeness of the corresponding neutral nets. In section 4 we address the actual modeling of preimages. Our approach consists of employing a certain random graph model for the preimages of a secondary structure. As we are interested in the question of how generic certain properties of these preimages are, a random graph model and its 0-1 laws are of particular relevance. We will state and discuss a suite of generic connectivity and path-connectivity results.

2 DEFINITIONS

2.1 RNA

In the following we will consider single-stranded RNA molecules. In viruses and cells RNA acts as a messenger (mRNA), carrying the genetic information from the DNA to the translation apparatus. As transfer RNA (tRNA), it plays the role of an adapter for the synthesis of proteins. Finally, as ribosomal RNA (rRNA), it is an integral part of the ribosome and exhibits catalytic activities in natural polypeptide synthesis [84, 85, 526]. RNA is thus able to serve two purposes: (i) storage of genetic information based on a one-dimensional template that can be read and copied on request, and (ii) catalytic properties as ribozymes that require three-dimensional structures in order to gain efficiency and specificity in processing specific substrates. As demonstrated by Spiegelman, *in vitro* evolution experiments can be applied to selection of RNA molecules that are capable of fast replication [399]. Indeed, replication rates are optimized in serial transfer experiments [144, 284, 452]. In case one wants to optimize properties other than replication, intervention is required making use of special techniques that interfere with natural selection. A well-known example is represented by the SELEX method—standing for *systematic evolution of ligands by exponential enrichment*—which allows the creation of molecules with optimal binding constants [507]. The SELEX procedure is a protocol that isolates high-affinity nucleic acid ligands for a target, such as a protein, from a pool of variant sequences. Multiple rounds of replication and selection exponentially enrich the population of species that exhibits the highest affinity, that is, that fulfills the required task. This procedure thus permits simultaneous screening of highly diverse pools of nucleic acid molecules for different functionalities (for a review, see Ellington [143] and Klug and Famulok [331]). Results from those experiments clearly demonstrate the essential property of RNA molecules: genotype, meaning the RNA sequence, and phenotype, associated with the structure, are combined in one molecule.

Here we will consider RNA sequences of constant length, represented by n-tuples, $(x_1, \ldots, x_n)$, with $x_i \in \mathcal{A}$, $\mathcal{A}$ being a finite alphabet formed by the nucleotides. The basic mutational mechanism is made up of random point mutations that occur with independent probability. This motivates calling two sequences *adjacent* if they differ by exactly one nucleotide. The sequence space with this adjacency relation is referred to as $\mathcal{Q}_\alpha^n$ (the generalized n-cube), where $\alpha = |\mathcal{A}|$. In $\mathcal{Q}_\alpha^n$ each sequence has $(\alpha - 1)n$ neighbors and the maximal (Hamming) distance between two sequences is n.

2.2 SECONDARY STRUCTURES

A secondary structure is a graph whose vertices are the nucleotides of its underlying sequence, and whose edges are base pairs formed among them. For biophysical reasons, one nucleotide can only establish exactly one Watson-Crick bond with another nucleotide. As we will see below, the fact that the edges of a secondary structure are Watson-Crick base pairs implies a number of additional graph properties. Following Waterman [518] we will consider RNA secondary structures over n vertices $\{1, \ldots, n\}$, which we denote by s_n.

A secondary structure is a vertex-labeled graph with an adjacency matrix $A(s_n) = (a_{i,k})_{1 \le i,k \le n}$ such that

- $a_{i,i+1} = 1$ for $1 \le i \le n - 1$;
- for each i there is at most a single $k \ne i - 1, i + 1$ such that $a_{i,k} = 1$; and
- if $a_{i,j} = a_{k,l} = 1$ and $i < k < j$ then $i < l < j$.

We call an edge $\{i, k\}$, $|i - k| \ne 1$ a *base pair*. A vertex i connected only to $i - 1$ and $i + 1$ is called *unpaired*.

The enumeration of secondary structures has been studied in detail in a series of excellent papers by Waterman et al. [263, 456]. A particular result from asymptotic combinatorics on secondary structures—with certain restrictions, such as minimum helix length—is that their number asymptotically becomes $O(a^n)$ with $a < 2$ [241]. This result immediately implies that there are structures having preimages of exponential size. The RNA model allows, moreover, several generic choices for the fitness assignment, for example using the thermodynamic stability and the degradation constant of the corresponding secondary structure.

3 SECONDARY STRUCTURES AND COMPATIBLE SEQUENCES

In this section we introduce the notion of compatible sequences with respect to a secondary structure. While Waterman et al. have extensively studied the combinatorics of secondary structures, their compatible sequences play a central role in the understanding of the mapping between RNA sequences and their structures. Theorem 3.1 below is central for evolutionary optimization as it guarantees the existence of at least one sequence that is compatible with any two given secondary structures. This fundamental property of secondary structures has been used, for example, in the *Science* publication "One Sequence Two Ribozymes," [461] in which the authors construct a sequence that can assume either of two ribozyme folds and catalyze the two respective reactions.

Let us now introduce compatible sequences. We call a sequence (x_i) compatible with respect to a secondary structure, s_n, if and only if for all $a_{i,k}$ with $a_{i,k} = 1$ and $k \neq i - 1, i + 1$, the nucleotides x_i and x_k can in principle form a Watson-Crick base pair.

In terms of combinatorics, the uniqueness property of the Watson-Crick base pairs of an RNA secondary structure corresponds to an involution (an operator of period 2), viewing the base pairs as transpositions within the symmetric group S_n [442, 443]. Now, any two involutions form a dihedral group that, in our situation, acts upon the nucleotides regularly and whose orbits are either even-length cycles or lines, as illustrated in figure 1.

Theorem 3.1 (Reidys et al. [443]). *Let s_n^1, s_n^2 be two secondary structures with the sets of compatible sequences $C(s_n^1)$, $C(s_n^2)$. Then*

$$C(s_n^1) \cap C(s_n^2) \neq \varnothing . \tag{2}$$

Accordingly, for any two secondary structures there exists at least one sequence that could, in principle, realize both. We will call such a sequence bicompatible with respect to the pair of structures. From this we can conclude that their corresponding neutral networks come relatively close in sequence space.

At this point we may speculate that populations performing evolutionary search by point mutations are capable of switching between any two networks. This speculation turns out to be not entirely correct but has, however, led to some

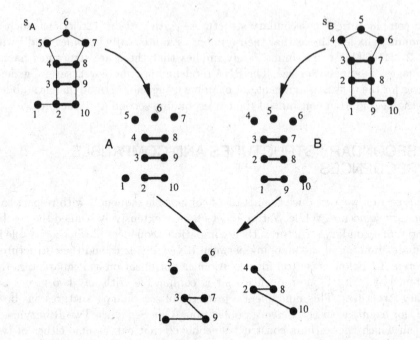

FIGURE 1 The key idea in theorem 3.1: any two involutions yield either non-closed paths or loops of even length. The two secondary structures s_A and s_B are decomposed into their paired and unpaired regions (see also fig. 2) yielding two graphs of identical order, A and B. Finally, the edge sets of these graphs are joined, resulting in the graph shown at the bottom. One will always find a sequence that is compatible with this graph. We may then conclude—for instance, by taking a segment composed of pairs of complementary nucleotides—that for any two secondary structures there exists at least one sequence compatible with both structures.

understanding of the transition phenomenon [165, 465, 520]. In fact, the group action above suggests the definition of a distance measure between secondary structures [442] from which the probability of a transition can be computed. Structural similarity thus plays an important role in the transition phenomenon.

4   NEUTRAL NETWORKS

4.1   MODELLING NEUTRAL NETWORKS VIA RANDOM GRAPHS

In the following we will model the preimage of a given structure as a random graph. The main motivation is that folding maps will always vary as a function of their underlying biophysical parameters. Hence "generic properties" of classes of maps are of particular interest. We will restrict ourselves to RNA secondary structures as phenotypes but, in principle, an analogous construction can be obtained for random structures, a more general class of phenotypes. The random graph model is constructed in the following two steps:

1. *Creating two new cubes.* One first determines the set of sequences $C(s_n)$ that are compatible with the given structure s_n. Each compatible sequence is decomposed into an unpaired and a paired segment, consisting of all unpaired and paired nucleotides respectively, as shown in figure 2. While the unpaired segment (of length n_u) is simply again a sequence of a sequence space of reduced dimensionality, the paired segment (of length n_p) is interpreted as a sequence over the alphabet of base pairs. For example, a paired segment in the case of the biophysical $\{A, U, G, C\}$-alphabet would have $\{(A-U), (U-A), (G-C), (C-G), (G-U), (U-G)\}$ as its new alphabet, that is, an alphabet of size 6. Accordingly, the set $C[s_n]$ of compatible sequences can be written as

$$C[s_n] = \mathcal{Q}_\alpha^{n_u(s_n)} \times \mathcal{Q}_\beta^{n_p(s_n)} . \tag{3}$$

2. *Randomization.* We now proceed by selecting the unpaired and paired segments with independent probabilities λ_u and λ_p. Accordingly, each compatible sequence is selected with probability $\lambda = \lambda_u \lambda_p$. Interestingly, it is not difficult to determine λ_u and λ_p for RNA folding maps by introducing the corresponding mutations systematically and then folding the mutants.

From the biophysical point of view, there is a significant difference between λ_u and λ_p: in the case of a $\{G, C\}$-alphabet a point mutant is produced with probability p and a base pair mutation occurs with probability p^2. From the combinatorial perspective, however, up to an isomorphism there is none. The selection processes of the unpaired and paired segments both take place in generalized n-cubes, and accordingly, we may formulate our results only for generalized n-cubes. It is worth pointing out that the random graph model above does not aim *a priori* to construct particular neutral networks, but to identify generic properties of the probability space formed by all neutral networks. In this sense, the present model follows an approach that is very natural in statistical physics.

In the following, we will denote a probability measure by μ_n where n refers to some index of the corresponding probability space Ω_n (here: a random graph). A random variable is a mapping $X : \Omega \to \mathbb{Z}$. Let P_n be some property or event in Ω_n. We then write that P_n holds *asymptotically almost surely* (a.a.s.) if $\lim_{n \to \infty} \mu_n \{P_n\} = 1$.

The random graph model. Let $\mathcal{Q}_\alpha^n$ be a generalized n-cube over an alphabet of length α. Let Γ_n be a subgraph of $\mathcal{Q}_\alpha^n$ and $\mu_n \{\Gamma_n\} = \lambda_n^{|\Gamma_n|}(1 - \lambda_n)^{\alpha^n - |\Gamma_n|}$. Then we call $\mathcal{Q}_{\alpha, \lambda_n}^n$ the random induced subgraph model.

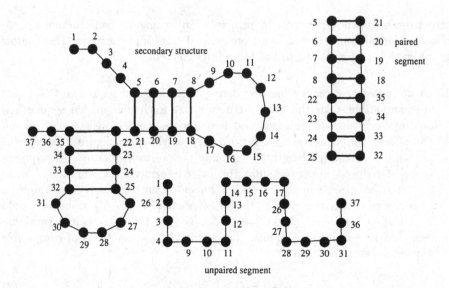

FIGURE 2 Decomposing a compatible sequence into the unpaired and paired segments. Note that the resulting alphabet over which the paired segment is considered is, in general, different from the alphabet of the unpaired nucleotides. In the case of Watson-Crick base pairing rules we obtain for the biophysical $\{A, U, G, C\}$-alphabet of size 4 the alphabet $\{(A - U), (U - A), (G - C), (C - G), (G - U), (U - G)\}$ of size 6.

4.2 GIANT COMPONENTS AND CONNECTIVITY

In the following, we will analyze generic properties of $\mathcal{Q}^n_{\alpha, \lambda_n}$, all of which deal with connectivity. The idea will be to let the picking probability, λ, gradually increase. Let us start our investigations with the probability $\lambda = O(\log n/n)$.

It is beyond the scope of this chapter to present full proofs of our results. Instead we will discuss and outline the proofs, and present the main ideas. For details, the reader is referred to the papers by Reidys and Stadler [441] and Reidys [440]. The proof of theorem 4.1 in [441] is inspired by the paper of Ajtai, Komlós, and Szemerédi [11] but differs significantly in the estimation of the respective vertex boundaries. While Ajtai et al. rely on Harper's isoperimetric inequality [225] for estimating the edge boundary, a completely new method has to be employed in order to estimate the vertex boundary. The proof of theorem 4.2 in Reidys and Stadler [441] is completely different from the proof of the classical result for $\mathcal{Q}^2_{2,p}$, which localizes the connectivity threshold at $p = 1/2$. Our proof is entirely constructive and additionally allows for the development of algorithms connecting two sequences on a neutral network above the threshold.

Theorem 4.1. *Let $C_n^{(1)}$ be the largest component of a $\mathcal{Q}_\alpha^n$-subgraph Γ_n. Then there exists a constant $c > 0$ such that for $\lambda_n \geq \frac{c \log n}{n}$,*

$$|C_n^{(1)}| \sim |\Gamma_n| \qquad \text{a.a.s.}$$

The existence of this giant component is proven indirectly in two steps.

1. One shows that a.a.s. any vertex of a random graph is contained in a component of at least size n^h, for some natural number h. That is, given a picking probability $\lambda_n = O(\log n / n)$, the random graph is composed almost entirely of connected components of polynomial size, where the degree of the polynomial is arbitrarily high. The idea to prove this involves estimating the vertex-boundary of subsets of n-cube vertices and computing the mean of all such components. Step 1 can be proven exclusively using the fact that n-cubes are Cayley graphs over Z_α^n, Z_α being the cyclic group of order α.
2. From step 1 we know that the random graph is composed almost exclusively of connected components of at least polynomial size, and potentially many of these. Clearly, if there exist at least two such components, then there must be a bipartition of the set of all components such that no edge connects the two parts. We show that the probability of such a bipartition existing, formed by two sets of vertices of the same order, tends to 0. Thus, the size of the second-largest component can be at most subpolynomial in n.

It is important to note that our argument proves the existence of a giant component indirectly. The proof of theorem 4.1 gives no clue as to how to construct a path between two vertices, and, moreover, as to how long such a path might be. The explicit construction of (short) paths between vertices of neutral networks would, therefore, be of particular interest and would lead to a deeper understanding of how likely such a path would be realized in an evolutionary search. We address this question by studying paths and distances in generalized n-cubes in theorem 4.3 below.

Let us next analyze connectivity of generalized n-cubes. We now assume a constant probability $\lambda > 0$.

Theorem 4.2. *In the random graph $\mathcal{Q}_{\alpha,\lambda}^n$ the probability $\lambda^* = 1 - \sqrt[\alpha-1]{\alpha^{-1}}$ is the threshold value for connectivity. That is, a.a.s. no random graph is connected for $\lambda < \lambda^*$ and a.a.s. every random graph is connected for $\lambda > \lambda^*$.*

Let P, Q be arbitrary vertices of the random graph. As will be seen for theorem 4.3, we can reduce the case to P, Q having finite Hamming distance. For $\lambda > \lambda^*$, one then shows that any vertex has an arbitrary finite number of neighbors in the random graph. Using these neighboring vertices one proceeds analogously to the proof of theorem 4.3 below. To prove that λ^* is a threshold value, we show that there exist isolated vertices when $\lambda < \lambda^*$. This can be proven by considering the random variable counting the isolated vertices, Y. It is clear that Y has mean $\mu = \lambda \, \alpha^n \, (1 - \lambda)^{(\alpha-1)n}$ and for finite μ one can show that Y becomes Poisson-distributed in the limit of large n. From this we can conclude that a.a.s. for $\lambda < \lambda^*$ and arbitrary natural number ℓ, there are at least ℓ isolated vertices in the random graph.

4.3   DISTANCES

As we have seen, theorem 4.1 does not provide insight into the path structure of the giant component. Theorem 4.2 on the other hand is proven constructively, but only works for constant λ. In this section we present a framework that allows us to bound the length of shortest paths between two $\mathcal{Q}_\alpha^n$ vertices for the probability $\lambda_n \geq n^{-a}$ with $0 \leq a < 1/2$.

In the following, we write Γ instead of Γ_n. Intuitively, our result guarantees the a.a.s. existence of very short paths between any two Γ-vertices. Technically this fact is a little delicate to express in probabilistic language, since it is impossible to have terms like a.a.s. as a predicate of a property in a probability space. Our strategy will be to use conditional probabilities in the statement of the result. The main question is how the distance $d_\Gamma(P,Q)$ between two vertices P, Q in a random graph Γ relates to the distance $d_{\mathcal{Q}_\alpha^n}(P,Q)$ between P, Q in $\mathcal{Q}_\alpha^n$, which is known to be very small. Let us denote the least integer greater or equal to c by $\lceil c \rceil$.

Theorem 4.3. *Let* $0 \leq a < 1/2$, $k = \lceil \frac{1+3a}{1-2a} \rceil$ *and* $p_n = n^{-a}$. *Then for any two vertices* $P, Q \in \mathcal{Q}_\alpha^n$ *we have* $d_\Gamma(P,Q) < [2k+3]d_{\mathcal{Q}_\alpha^n}(P,Q)$ *a.a.s. conditional on* $P, Q \in \Gamma$, *and for any constant* $p > 0$ *we have* $d_\Gamma(P,Q) \leq 7d_{\mathcal{Q}_\alpha^n}(P,Q)\} = 1$.

Essentially, theorem 4.3 means that for probabilities larger than $1/\sqrt{n}$ and in the limit of large sequence length, the distance between almost all pairs of vertices is, up to a constant factor, equal to their distance in the n-cube itself. One consequence of this result is that the distances between sequences on a neutral network are surprisingly small. The diffusion process, performed by the error-prone relication of haploid RNA sequences in the course of their evolutionary optimization, enables visiting every region of the neutral network.

The main idea for the proof of theorem 4.3 is as follows: from two different $\mathcal{Q}_\alpha^n$-vertices (sequences) one tries to branch *simultaneously*, that is, by performing successively identical point-mutations on the sequences in positions where P and Q do not differ, into some kth sphere centered at P and Q, respectively. The trick with respect to the simulaneous mutations consists of being able to guarantee that the resulting pairs of sequences have the same distance as P and Q. We then have to show that there are sufficiently "many" of these pairs in the kth sphere and that the collection of their associated paths connecting them is vertex disjoint. This is illustrated in figure 3.

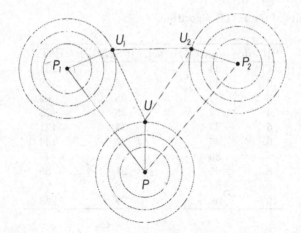

FIGURE 3 The branching process with initial vertex P in an $(n - m)$-cube can be considered by lifting as a simultaneous branching process in an n-cube initialized at the two vertices P_1, P_2. By concatenation, any point U of the branching process yields two points U_1, U_2 in the n-cube. The key feature of this construction is that any two points reached by the simultaneous branching have *constant* distance m, and for increasingly high Hamming distances, more and more such pairs are constructed.

4.4   AN ALGORITHM

Let s_n be a secondary structure. The proof of theorem 4.3 motivates the algorithm *PATH*, which tries to determine short paths on the neutral network of s_n. The algorithm works in $C[s_n] \cong \mathcal{Q}_\alpha^{n_u(s_n)} \times \mathcal{Q}_\beta^{n_p(s_n)}$. The *input* of *PATH* consists of (i) a secondary structure, s_n, and (ii) two $\mathcal{Q}_\alpha^n$-vertices P, Q that map into s_n. Its *output* is the length of a $C[s_n]$-path connecting P and Q on the neutral network of s_n if the algorithm finds one of length $\leq 11\, d_{C[s_n]}(P, Q)$, and "$-$" otherwise. *PATH* can be sketched as follows:

1. Write P, Q in the form (cf. eq. (3))

$$(\xi_1, \ldots, \xi_{n_u}, (\eta_1, \eta'_1), \ldots, (\eta_{n_p}, \eta'_{n_p})),$$

   where $\xi_l < \xi_{l+1}$, $l \in \mathbb{N}_{n_u-1}$, $\eta_i < \eta'_i$, $i \in \mathbb{N}_{n_p}$ and $\eta_j < \eta_{j+1}$, $j \in \mathbb{N}_{n_p-1}$

2. Construct a $C[s_n]$-path, $\pi(P, Q) = (P, V_1, \ldots, V_\ell, Q)$, from P to Q successively replacing ξ_i^P by ξ_i^Q and then $(\eta_i^P, \eta_i'^P)$ by $(\eta_i^Q, \eta_i'^Q)$ according to the ordering given in step 1

3. For $1 \leq i \leq \ell$, try to find a vertex $G_i \in \mathcal{B}_3(V_i)$ which maps to s_n and store the family $(P, G_1, \ldots, G_\ell, Q)$

4. Try to connect the pairs of vertices (P, G_1), (G_ℓ, Q) and (G_i, G_{i+1}), $1 \leq i \leq \ell - 1$. This is done using (a) the branching process shown in figure 3

TABLE 1   Results of the PATH algorithm.

(i)	$d_{\mathcal{Q}_\alpha^n}(\sigma_{76}^*, \sigma_{76}^{(i)})$	$d_{C[s_{76}^*]}(\sigma_{76}^*, \sigma_{76}^{(i)})$	$PATH$
1	34	28	131
2	39	28	98
3	37	25	62
4	74	28	73
5	37	34	121
6	34	27	144
7	39	24	43
8	35	21	35
9	34	18	94
10	39	29	43

with concentric sphere $k \leq 3$, and (b) families of independent paths that are employed in the proof of theorem 4.3.

We finally present some results of $PATH$ [171]. As the underlying map from sequence to structure, we use the bio-physical folding algorithm RNAfold [242]. As the input secondary structure we select the tRNA

$$s_{76}^* = ((((((((.(((.(((((\ldots\ldots))))).(((((.(\ldots\ldots)))))\ldots\ldots(((.(\ldots\ldots))))))))))))))\ldots.$$

where "(" and ")" represent paired bases and "." represents an unpaired base. We take the natural RNA-sequence σ_{76}^*:

$$GCGGAUUU\,AGCUC\,AG\ddag\ddag GGGAG\,AGC\ddag CC\,AG\,ACUG\,AA\ddag$$
$$AUCUGG\,AG\ddag U\,CCUGUG\ddag\ddag CG\,AUCC\,AC\,AG\,AAUU\,CGC\,ACC\,A,$$

where "$\ddag$" denotes a *special base* that is kept fixed. Using the algorithm RNAinverse [242] we determine a set of sequences, $\sigma_{76}^{(i)}$, $i = 1, \ldots, 10$ of the neutral network of s_{76}^*. We then use s_{76}^*, σ_{76}^* and $\sigma_{76}^{(i)}$ as input for $PATH$. Preliminary data indicate that the success rate of $PATH$ for $n = 76$ is approximately 50%. We present some data in table 1.

5 CONCLUSION

We have investigated folding maps from RNA sequences to their secondary structures. We have first shown that the combinatorics of the structures themselves allows for sequences that are compatible with two given structures. This intersection result for the corresponding sets of compatible sequences indicates that secondary structures as phenotypes can be searched effectively by point mutations. We have then modeled the preimage (neutral network) of a secondary structure via random subgraphs of (generalized) n-cubes, proving that there exists a 0-1 law for connectivity and establishing probabilities above which giant components in these neutral networks exist.

Random graph theory not only provides insight into the structure of neutral nets of RNA secondary structures but also contributes on a conceptual level to the understanding of evolutionary optimization. We have studied short paths in neutral networks, which are of key importance for the dynamics of the optimization process. We have shown that the shortest path between two sequences on a neutral network is longer only by a constant factor than the shortest path between these sequences in the n-cube itself. Finally, we have presented an algorithm that computes the length of these paths in the neutral network of the tRNA structure.

In this context, it is of interest to note that Grüner et al. have performed [217, 218] an exhaustive folding of GC sequences of lengths 30, according to a minimum free energy folding algorithm, into their corresponding secondary structures. This study allows the comparison of the probabilistic results on the structure of neutral networks with those of biophysical folding maps. One particular finding is that the existence of certain structural motifs (at this sequence length) can cause a multi-partition of the corresponding neutral network into distinct components, since the preservation of these motifs induces a certain bias in the sequences of the corresponding neutral network. As the probabilistic model is based on a uniform picking probability, the findings above were anticipated. However, at this point it is not obvious whether or not this phenomenon will persist for significantly longer sequences, as the dimensionality of the n-cube increases.

CHAPTER 13

Towards a Predictive Computational Complexity Theory for Periodically Specified Problems: A Survey

Harry B. Hunt III
Madhav V. Marathe
Daniel J. Rosenkrantz
Richard E. Stearns

1 INTRODUCTION

The preceding chapters in this volume have documented the substantial recent progress towards understanding the complexity of *randomly* specified combinatorial problems. This improved understanding has been obtained by combining concepts and ideas from theoretical computer science and discrete mathematics with those developed in statistical mechanics. Techniques such as the cavity method and the replica method, primarily developed by the statistical mechanics community to understand physical phenomena, have yielded important insights into the intrinsic difficulty of solving combinatorial problems when instances are chosen randomly. These insights have ultimately led to the development of efficient algorithms for some of the problems.

A potential weakness of these results is their reliance on random instances. Although the typical probability distributions used on the set of instances make the mathematical results tractable, such instances do not, in general, capture the realistic instances that arise in practice. This is because practical applications of

Computational Complexity and Statistical Physics, edited by
Allon G. Percus, Gabriel Istrate, and Cristopher Moore, Oxford University Press.

graph theory and combinatorial optimization in CAD systems, mechanical engineering, VLSI design, transportation networks, and software engineering involve processing large but regular objects constructed in a systematic manner from smaller and more manageable components. Consequently, the resulting graphs or logical formulas have a regular structure, and are defined systematically in terms of smaller graphs or formulas. It is not unusual for computer scientists and physicists interested in worst-case complexity to study problem instances with regular structure, such as lattice-like or tree-like instances. Motivated by this, we discuss periodic specifications as a method for specifying regular instances. Extensions of the basic formalism that give rise to *locally random but globally structured* instances are also discussed. These instances provide one method of producing random instances that might capture the structured aspect of practical instances. The specifications also yield methods for constructing *hard* instances of satisfiability and various graph theoretic problems, important for testing the computational efficiency of algorithms that solve such problems.

Periodic specifications are a mechanism for succinctly specifying combinatorial objects with highly regular repetitive substructure. In the past, researchers have also used the term *dynamic* to refer to such objects specified using periodic specifications (see, for example, Orlin [419], Cohen and Megiddo [103], Kosaraju and Sullivan [347], and Hoppe and Tardos [260]). However, since "dynamic" has also been used by researchers to mean other things, we have elected to use periodic specifications in the rest of the chapter to avoid ambiguity. The kinds of objects considered here include graphs, logical formulas, and systems of equations/constraints. These specifications arise naturally in engineering and VLSI designs, as well as in scheduling and routing models for airline industry. They have been studied for over 40 years, since the work of Ford and Fulkerson on dynamic network flows [163, 164] and extensively thereafter [103, 104, 245, 260, 274, 276, 347, 379, 380, 419, 420, 421]. In this chapter, we survey a number of results on the complexity and efficient approximability of problems, for periodically specified objects. We also propose several new extensions of the basic formalism that may be of interest to researchers studying phase transition phenomena for combinatorial problems.

Generally speaking, periodic specifications are extensions of the standard specifications used to represent combinatorial objects. An example of a standard specification for satisfiability problems on Boolean formulas is the conjunctive normal form, where the formula is represented as a set of clauses, with each clause being a set of literals. For problems in graph theory, a standard specification of the graph is the adjacency list representation or the adjacency matrix representation of the edges in the graph. Periodic specifications can represent succinctly—and in a space-efficient way—certain kinds of objects with highly regular structure. For example, consider a graph G_n consisting of a simple path with n vertices. At best, the standard specification represents G_n by each of its vertices and edges separately, and is thus of size $\Theta(n)$. In contrast, G_n can be specified succinctly by a *one-dimensional periodic finite graph specification* with

$O(\log n)$ symbols, by replicating a single edge (u, v) n times, and specifying that for $1 \leq i \leq (n-1)$, the ith copy of v is connected to the $(i+1)$th copy of u. Thus, the periodic specification of G_n results in exponential savings in space as compared to the standard specification of G_n. The simple example shows that, for all $n \geq 1$, periodic specifications of size $\Theta(n)$ can represent certain objects of size $2^{\Omega(n)}$, any of whose standard specifications are also of size $2^{\Omega(n)}$. Typically, the complexity of solving a problem is measured in terms of the size of the specifications of the problem's instances. This suggests that complexity of problems can be different depending on whether the instances are specified periodically, or are specified standardly. That is indeed true. For example, assuming NP$\neq$PSPACE, the 3-coloring problem for graphs, is NP-complete when graphs are specified by standard specifications such as adjacency matrices or adjacency lists [191]. On the other hand, it is PSPACE-complete when graphs are specified by the *one-dimensional infinite periodic specifications* of Orlin [419]. In contrast, however, the 2-coloring problem for graphs is solvable in polynomial time, *even* when instances are specified by one-dimensional infinite periodic specifications. Such results lead us to investigate the complexity and efficient approximability of solving graph theoretic, combinatorial, and algebraic problems, when instances are periodically specified.

In this chapter, for demonstration purposes, we focus mainly on periodically specified constraint satisfaction problems. Previously, constraint satisfaction problems with instances specified using standard specifications have been used to model a number of problems in such areas as automated reasoning, computer-aided design [219], computer-aided manufacturing [220], machine vision [220], database, robotics, integrated circuit design [219, 220], computer architecture, and computer network design. See Gu et al. [220] for a recent survey. In addition, constraint satisfaction problems have served as a rich collection of base problems, for proving NP-hardness, #P-hardness, APX-hardness, and a number of similar properties for numerous combinatorial problems (see Garey and Johnson [191], Schaefer [455], and Papadimitriou [423]). Here we outline how, analogously, periodically specified constraint satisfaction problems are useful in modeling problems arising in practical applications and serve as base problems for proving both easiness and hardness results for periodically specified combinatorial, logical, and algebraic problems. The results outlined here enable the development of a *predictive* complexity theory for periodically specified problems (section 7).

There are two main reasons why a discussion of periodically specified problems is of interest in the context of the relationship between computational complexity and statistical physics. First, periodically specified problems are an algebraic generalization of tiling problems (see section 8) and thus provide a natural parametric class of lattice-like structured problem instances. Lattice-like structured problems have been a topic of active research by physicists and computer scientists in the context of designing "hard" instances for heuristics solving satisfiability and graph problems [6]. Second, as we discuss in section 9, it is possible to define random periodically specified graphs and formulas. Such instances are locally random but globally structured, and provide parametrized classes of random finite and infinite satisfiability and graph problems. Random graph and satisfiability problems and questions related to their phase transitions have been an active topic of recent research, as seen throughout this volume. Random periodically specified satisfiability and graph problems are introduced here in the hope that their study will provide interesting insights into the phase transitions associated with combinatorial problems.

The rest of the chapter is organized as follows. Section 2 consists of examples illustrating how periodic specifications can *naturally* model a number of realistic problems. Section 3 outlines the basic definitions of periodically specified graphs and formulas, as well as simple variants of the main formalism. Section 4 consists of several broader extensions of the basic formalism of periodic specifications and the objects they specify. We also illustrate several situations where these extensions are likely to occur. Section 5 contains a brief description of the techniques developed for obtaining both easiness and hardness results for periodically specified problems. We also argue how these techniques form the basis for developing a *predictive complexity theory* for periodically specified problems: informally, we illustrate that many reductions between standardly specified problem instances can be translated mechanically into efficient reductions for the corresponding periodically specified problems. Section 7 outlines the complexity theoretic implications of the general results for periodically specified problems. Section 8 argues that periodically specified constraint satisfaction problems can be used as alternatives to tiling problems for proving bounds on complexity. Finally, section 9 presents concluding remarks and directions for future work.

2   MOTIVATION

Formally, a *one-dimensional finite periodic graph specification* $\Gamma(G(V, E), M)$ consists of (1) a finite directed labeled graph $G(V, E)$ called the *static graph* of the specification, each of whose edges is labeled by a non-negative integer, together with (2) a non-negative integer M. The finite directed graph $G^M(V^M, E^M)$ *specified* by $\Gamma(G(V, E), M)$ is defined as follows. V^M consists of $M + 1$ distinct copies of each vertex $v \in V$, denoted $v_0, \ldots, v_M$, respectively. E^M consists of $M - l + 1$ distinct copies of each edge $(u, v) \in E$ labeled with $l \leq M$, namely (u_r, v_{r+l}) for all $0 \leq r \leq M - l$. M is called the range or the span of the specification. A k-*dimensional periodic graph specification* is defined analogously for $k \geq 2$, except now all edges are labeled by k-tuples of non-negative integers, M is a k-tuple of non-negative integers. Examples of a *one-* and a *two-dimensional periodic graph specification* and the graphs they specify are given in figures 1 and 2. These concepts can be extended to define 1-, 2- and k-dimensional periodic graph specifications that are *infinite* in some of their k-dimensions. They can also be extended quite naturally to define one-, two- and k-dimensional periodically specified formulas and systems of equations/constraints. See section 3 for formal definitions.

Periodically specified graphs and logical formulas occur naturally when modeling practical problems in VLSI design, transportation science, and program optimization. We discuss four examples that illustrate the range of applications. Many others can be found [104, 244, 260, 302, 358, 377, 379, 380, 419, 420, 421, 423, 437].

- *Routing.* The *tramp steamer problem* is discussed by Orlin [420]. Consider a steamer that visits n distinct ports. Traveling from port u to port v takes t_{uv} days and earns a profit of p_{uv} dollars, and both the transit time and the profit are independent of the starting time for the trip. The objective is to determine an infinite-horizon tour that maximizes the average daily profit. The static graph has n nodes, one for each port, and for each pair u, v of distinct nodes there is an arc with transit time t_{uv} and unit cost $-p_{uv}$. The upper and lower bounds on arc flows are 1 and 0, respectively, and the throughput is restricted to 1, representing the steamer. Formulating the problem with this static network, Dantzig, Blattner, and Rao [115] observed that each basic solution to the tramp steamer problem is a flow around a *circuit*, which is a simple directed cycle. Each circuit induces an infinite-horizon tour. Ports are traveled in the order that they appear on the circuit and the average daily cost is the ratio of the cost of traveling the circuit to the transit time. Thus, an optimal circuit has the minimum cost-to-time ratio and induces an optimal tour.

- *Network scheduling and dynamic network flows.* Applications of dynamic network flow problems arise when one wishes to model transit time on edges. The following example is from Hoppe and Tardos [260]. We are given a directed graph $G(V, E)$ with sources, sinks, non-negative edge capacities c_{uv} and transit times t_{uv} for each edge $(u, v) \in E$. Time is assumed discrete here. In a feasible dynamic flow, at most c_{uv} units of flow can enter edge (u, v) at each integer time step. The flow leaving u along edge (u, v) at time θ reaches the other endpoint v at time $\theta + t_{uv}$. For example, an edge with capacity 2 and transit time 3 can accept 2 units of flow at any given time step, for a total of up to 6 units of flow on the edge at any time. The *quickest transshipment* problem is defined by a dynamic network with a set of sources and sinks; each source has a specified supply of flow and each sink has a specified demand, with the standard assumption that total supply equals total demand. The problem is to find a way to schedule the flow so that each source and sink sends and receives the specified amount of flow in a *minimum amount of time.*

The problem of finding a feasible and quickest dynamic flow in dynamic networks reduces to finding "usual static flow" in time-expanded graphs, following the periodic specification above. Formally, for a given time horizon T, we construct a time expanded network $G(T) = (V(T), E(T))$ as follows: Each vertex

$v \in V$ has $T + 1$ copies in $V(T)$, denoted by $v(i)$, $0 \leq i \leq T$. Each edge $(u, v) \in E$ has $T - t_{uv} + 1$ copies in $E(T)$, each with capacity c_{uv} and denoted by $(u(\theta), v(\theta + t_{uv}))$ with the provision that such edges exist if both end points are within the time horizon bounds, that is, $0 \leq \theta \leq T - t_{uv}$. In addition, we add holdover edges $(u(\theta), v(\theta + 1))$ with infinite capacity, representing flow that remains at a given node over a time step. An *infinite-horizon dynamic flow* is a static flow in the infinite time-expanded dynamic network. Note that the time-expanded dynamic network is essentially a periodically specified graph with additional holdover edges, and the infinite version corresponds similarly to an infinite periodically specified graph. The single-source and single-sink version of the problem was originally defined by Ford and Fulkerson [164]; the work of Hoppe and Tardos extends it to the multi-source and multi-sink case. Note that as specified, since the numbers are given in binary, we have infinite graphs in which the end points of an edge can be exponentially far apart in time. Recently, Fleischer [161] gave a faster algorithm for the quickest trans-shipment problem when the transit times are zero. Periodic specifications that allow us to specify such "long edges" are called *wide specifications*.

The quickest transshipment problem and its variants have a number of applications. One such application is to find the quickest way to evacuate a building in emergencies. Another application arises in network scheduling problems where there is a transit cost for moving jobs from one processor to another: the goal is to minimize the make-span of the schedule. See Hoppe and Tardos [260] for a detailed discussion of these applications. A related problem that can be cast in much the same terms is to find the *quickest path in a temporal network*; that is, the fastest way to reach a destination from a source when travel times on edges change over time.

- *Phase space properties of discrete dynamical systems.* One-dimensional cellular automata consist of a sets of vertices placed on a one-dimensional grid. Each vertex has an associated Boolean function that depends on the Boolean values associated with adjacent vertices. The system evolves synchronously: at each time step, the automata corresponding to nodes synchronously update their state using the Boolean transition function that takes as input the values stored at the vertex and at its neighbors. A two-dimensional periodic specification can easily be seen to represent the dynamic changes in the configuration of finite one-dimensional cellular automata over time, where the second dimension represents time [528]. Using this representation, the configuration reachability problem for a finite one-dimensional cellular automata is simply the circuit value problem for periodically specified circuits. Thus, periodic specifications provide a succinct method for representing the phase spaces of cellular automata and finite discrete dynamical systems.

- *Parallel programming.* The following problem was introduced in Iwano and Steiglitz [276]; more efficient algorithms were given by Kosaraju and Sullivan [347], and by Cohen and Megiddo [104]. An essentially similar problem was first considered by Karp, Miller, and Winograd [302]. The problem arises in the implementation of regular iterative algorithms on systolic arrays. We are given n functions $F_1, F_2, \ldots, F_n$, on the k-dimensional integer lattice defined recursively as follows:

$$F_u(z) = \psi_u(F_1(z - w_{u1}), \ldots, F_n(z - w_{un})).$$

Here, the w_{uv}'s are integer vectors. In order for the functions to be well-defined it is necessary and sufficient that no cycle have a total vector weight that is non-negative. This fundamental problem also arises while implementing simulations on parallel computers. A closely related problem arises in the context of the design of memory-efficient simulations of iterative programs consisting of **for** loops [243, 244, 358]. We can model the problem as follows. We have a static graph consisting of n vertices, one corresponding to each function. Each directed edge (u, v) has an integer weight w_{uv} on it, denoting the dependency of $F_u(z)$ on $F_v(z - w_{uv})$. The expanded graph is constructed by placing a copy of each vertex in the static graph at the lattice point in $\mathbb{N}^k$. The vertex corresponding to F_u at lattice point z is connected by a directed edge to the vertex corresponding to F_v at lattice point $(z - w_{uv})$. The problem is to find if the *expanded infinite graph* has a directed cycle. Note that we seek to find a cycle in the expanded graph as opposed to the static graph. Cohen and Megiddo give a strongly polynomial algorithm for detecting cycles in such expanded infinite graphs. Note also that w_{uv} is given in binary: this makes the problem substantially harder, since as in the dynamic network flow problem, the vertices of a cycle can now span time periods that are exponentially apart.

3   PRELIMINARY DEFINITIONS

Basic definitions are used in algebra, graph theory, computational complexity, dynamical systems, and approximation algorithms [23, 54, 373, 423, 447, 525, 528]. We have already defined *one-dimensional finite periodic graph specifications* and the *finite graphs* they specify. Here we discuss related concepts that yield variant periodic specifications.

3.1   PERIODICALLY SPECIFIED GRAPHS

Definition 1. *Let the static graph $G(V, E)$ be a finite undirected graph such that each edge (u, v) has an associated non-negative integer weight t_{uv}. The two-way infinite graph $G^{\mathbb{Z}}(V^{\mathbb{Z}}, E^{\mathbb{Z}})$ is defined as follows. $V^{\mathbb{Z}}$ and $E^{\mathbb{Z}}$ are multiple copies of the vertex and edge set:*

1. $V^{\mathbb{Z}} = \{v(i) \mid v \in V \ and \ i \in \mathbb{Z}\}$

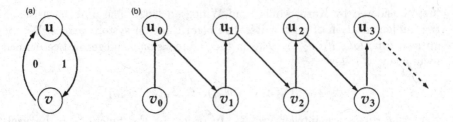

FIGURE 1   (a) The static graph with one-dimensional integer vectors associated with each edge. (b) Part of the one-way infinite graph it represents.

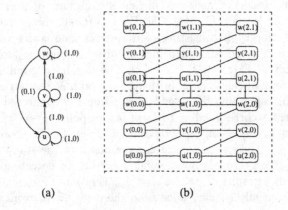

FIGURE 2   (a) The static graph with two-dimensional integer vectors associated with each edge. (b) The graph $G^{2,1}$ specified by $\Gamma(G, 10, 01)$.

2. $E^{\mathbb{Z}} = \{(u(i), v(i + t_{uv})) \mid (u, v) \in E$, t_{uv} is the weight associated with the edge (u, v) and $i \in \mathbb{Z}\}$

A one-dimensional two-way infinite periodic specification, or $(\mathbb{Z})$W-specification, is given by $\Gamma(G(V, E))$ and specifies the graph $G^{\mathbb{Z}}(V^{\mathbb{Z}}, E^{\mathbb{Z}})$.

Γ is said to be a narrow specification, or $(\mathbb{Z})$N-specification, if $\forall (u, v) \in E$, $t_{uv} \in \{0, 1\}$. This implies that $\forall (u(p), v(q)) \in E^{\mathbb{Z}}, |p - q| \leq 1$. ∎

Note that if we replace $\mathbb{Z}$ by $\mathbb{N}$ in definition 1, we obtain *one-way* infinite periodic specifications and the graphs they define. It may be useful to imagine a narrow periodically specified graph $G^{\mathbb{Z}}$ as being obtained by placing a copy of the vertex set V at each lattice point on the x-axis (or the timeline), and joining vertices placed on neighboring lattice (time) points in the manner specified by the edges in E.

Definition 2. *Let $G(V, E)$ denote a static graph. Let $G^{\mathbb{Z}}(V^{\mathbb{Z}}, E^{\mathbb{Z}})$ denote the two-way infinite $(\mathbb{Z})$N-specified graph as in definition 1. Let $M \geq 0$ be an integer specified using binary numerals. Let $G^M(V^M, E^M)$ be the subgraph of $G^{\mathbb{Z}}(V^{\mathbb{Z}}, E^{\mathbb{Z}})$ induced by the vertices $V^M = \{v(i)|v \in V \text{ and } 0 \leq i \leq M\}$. A one-dimensional finite periodic specification, or (B)N-specification, is given by $\Gamma(G(V, E), M)$ and specifies the graph G^M.* ∎

It is important to observe that M is specified using binary notation. If we use unary notation, then we denote such specifications as (U)N-specifications. The size of the (B)N-specification $\Gamma(G(V, E), M)$ is given by size$(\Gamma) = |V| + |E| + \text{bits}(M)$, where bits$(M)$ is the number of bits in the numeral M. (Note that in the rest of the chapter we use M to denote both integer and binary representation; its intended meaning will be clear from context.) An example of a periodic specification and the associated graph appears in figure 1.

It is easy to extend the definition above to define two-dimensional periodic specifications and associated graphs. As before we have a static graph, but now for each edge (u, v) we have a two-dimensional label (l, b). The *two-dimensional four-way infinite periodically specified graph* $G^{\mathbb{Z},\mathbb{Z}}(V^{\mathbb{Z},\mathbb{Z}}, E^{\mathbb{Z},\mathbb{Z}})$ is defined as follows: $V^{\mathbb{Z},\mathbb{Z}} = \{v(i,j) \mid v \in V \text{ and } i, j \in \mathbb{Z}\}$, and $E^{\mathbb{Z},\mathbb{Z}} = \{(u(i,j), v(i + l, j + b) \mid (u, v) \in E(i, j) \text{ and } i, j \in \mathbb{Z}\}$. For narrow periodic specifications this is called the $(\mathbb{Z},\mathbb{Z})$N-specification. For a non-negative integer vector (M, N), the *two-dimensional finite periodically specified graph* $G^{M,N}(V^{M,N}, E^{M,N})$ is the subgraph of $G^{\mathbb{Z},\mathbb{Z}}(V^{\mathbb{Z},\mathbb{Z}}, E^{\mathbb{Z},\mathbb{Z}})$ induced by the vertices $V^{M,N} = \{v(i,j) \mid v \in V \text{ and } 0 \leq i \leq M, 0 \leq j \leq N\}$. As mentioned previously, the method of representation used to specify M and N yields various kinds of specifications: when they are binary numerals, this results in the (B,B)N-specification. An example of such a periodic specification and its associated graph appears in figure 2. It is easy to extend the definitions above to obtain $G^{N,\mathbb{Z}}(V^{N,\mathbb{Z}}, E^{N,\mathbb{Z}})$, $G^{\mathbb{Z},N}(V^{\mathbb{Z},N}, E^{\mathbb{Z},N})$, and $G^{N,N}(V^{N,N}, E^{N,N})$ as well. Similarly, one can define variants where one of the dimensions is finite while the other dimension is infinite. For example $G^{M,\mathbb{Z}}(V^{M,\mathbb{Z}}, E^{M,\mathbb{Z}})$, is a graph in which the x-dimension has a span represented by M while the graph is infinite in both directions along the y-axis.

Periodically specified logical formulas can be defined in a similar manner. An example of periodically specified Boolean formulas is as follows.

Example 1. *Let $U = \{x(t), x(t+1), y(t), y(t+1), z(t), z(t+1)\}$ be a set of static variables. Let C be a set of static clauses given by $[x(t) \vee \overline{y}(t) \vee z(t)] \wedge [\overline{x}(t+1) \vee z(t)] \wedge [z(t+1) \vee y(t)]$. Let $F = (U, C, 3)$ be a (B)N-specification. Then F specifies the 3-CNF formula $F^3(U^3, C^3)$ given by*

$$\left([x(0) \vee \overline{y}(0) \vee z(0)] \wedge [\overline{x}(1) \vee z(0)] \wedge [z(1) \vee y(0)] \right) \bigwedge$$

$$\left([x(1) \vee \overline{y}(1) \vee z(1)] \wedge [\overline{x}(2) \vee z(1)] \wedge [z(2) \vee y(1)] \right) \bigwedge$$

$$\left(\, [x(2) \vee \overline{y}(2) \vee z(2)] \wedge [\overline{x}(3) \vee z(2)] \wedge [z(3) \vee y(2)] \, \right) \bigwedge$$
$$[x(3) \vee \overline{y}(3) \vee z(3)] \, . \qquad\qquad \blacksquare$$

It is easy to see that the basic formalism is quite rich: one can define many different combinatorial objects, including graphs, logical formulas, systems of equations, and inequalities.

3.2   TYPES OF PERIODIC SPECIFICATIONS

Different kinds of periodic specifications can be obtained either by changing the basic definition of the specifications or the algorithm used to construct the expanded object. We discuss this briefly.

- *Dimension.* The number of dimensions in which the expansion is carried out can be varied, e.g., 1-, 2-, or k-dimensions.
- *Finite vs. infinite object.* For finite objects, we can specify the bounds either in *unary* (U) or *binary* (B) notation for specifying the range M and N. For infinite objects we have two options: one-way infinite objects, represented by natural numbers N, or two-way infinite objects, represented by integers $\mathbb{Z}$. Note that one dimension can be finite while another is infinite. If an object is infinite, it can be infinite in any of its dimensions.
- *Narrow vs. wide specification.* Most generally, in the case of narrow specifications, the weights on the edges of the static graph (or the difference between the indices of the static variables) are specified in unary. For wide specifications, they are specified in binary. We denote narrow specifications with the letter N, and wide specifications with the letter W. When we have more than one dimension, edges for certain dimensions may be specified in unary and for others in binary. In the case of narrow specifications, intuitively, vertices having an edge are not too far apart (in terms of the distance in index space). For wide specifications, two vertices that are exponentially far apart can have an edge between them.
- *Boundary conditions.* We can allow initial or final boundary conditions— explicit assignments to the variables at the beginning or at the end. In case we have more than 1-dimension, we could allow boundary conditions for a subset of the dimensions. We use the suffix (BC) to denote a specification with boundary conditions. As described here, the concept only applies to Boolean formulas: an extension to graphs is possible, but more problem-dependent.

In the interest of simplifying notation, we specify the dimension and the finite vs. infinite nature implicitly. Note that in the computational complexity literature, these are often specified explicitly with a prefix such as 1-, 2-, to indicate dimension followed by an F or I to indicate finite or infinite. A letter P often appears as well to indicate that the specification is periodic. Thus, for example, the $(\mathbb{Z},\mathbb{Z})$N-specification is more fully written out as 2-I$(\mathbb{Z},\mathbb{Z})$PN, and the (B)N-specification as 1-F(B)PN.

Technically, some of the variants discussed above refer to specifications while others refer to the algorithms used to construct the expanded object. In other words, we are talking about both the specification (syntax) and the specified object (semantics). This distinction is important, although for the most part, it can be understood from the context. We omit the formal definitions of these extensions.

Let Π be a problem whose instances are specified using one of the standard specifications in the literature. For example, instances of CNF satisfiability problems are specified by CNF formulas and by sets of clauses, each clause being a set of literals. Let α be one of the periodic specifications. Then we use α-Π to denote the problem Π when instances are specified using periodic specification α. For example, one-dimensional finite narrow periodic 3-SAT (denoted by (B)N-3-SAT, or more fully as 1-F(B)PN-3-SAT) is the problem of determining if a one-dimensional finite narrow periodically specified 3-CNF formula is satisfiable.

4   EXTENSION OF THE BASIC FORMALISM

The extensions outlined in section 3.2 are straightforward. We now discuss four other extensions that are somewhat less straightforward. The first extension concerns periodically specified constraint satisfaction problems, the second describes a different algorithm for constructing the expanded graph, the third concerns how to define satisfiable formulas, and the fourth describes how to define quantified formulas using periodic specifications. Note that these extensions change one or more of the basic elements used to define periodic specifications and the associated graphs, formulas or system of equations.

4.1   PERIODICALLY SPECIFIED CONSTRAINT SATISFACTION PROBLEMS

Let D be an arbitrary nonempty set (not necessarily finite); C a finite set of constant symbols denoting elements of D; and S an arbitrary finite set of finite-arity relations on D. An S-clause is a relation in S applied to variables on elements in D. An S-formula is a finite nonempty conjunction of S-clauses. We denote the problem of determining the satisfiability of finite conjunctions of S-clauses by SAT(S). The corresponding problems including (B)N-SAT(S) and (B,B)N-SAT(S) are defined analogously. We give a simple example to illustrate the one-dimensional case.

Example 2. *Let $D = \{0,1\}$, i.e., we have a Boolean domain. Let $S = \{\text{XOR}(\alpha,\beta),$ $\text{XNOR}(\alpha,\gamma)\}$, be the set of relations on D, where $\text{XNOR}(\alpha,\beta) \equiv \text{NOTXOR}(\alpha,\beta)$.*

Let $V = \{w, x, y, z\}$ be the set of variables and the S-clauses be given by $P = $ XOR(x, y), XOR$(\overline{w}, y)$ and XNOR(y, z). Let $F(V, P)$ be an instance of the SAT(S) problem given by

$$F(V, P) = \text{XOR}(x, y) \wedge \text{XOR}(\overline{w}, y) \wedge \text{XNOR}(y, \overline{z}).$$

Then F is TRUE with $x = 0, y = 1, z = 0, w = 1$. Now let $U = \{w, x, y, z\}$ be a set of static variables and $H = (U, C, 2)$ an instance of (B)N-SAT(S) with the set S above, where C is given as

$$C = \text{XOR}(x(0), y(1)) \wedge \text{XOR}(\overline{w}(0), y(0)) \wedge \text{XNOR}(y(0), \overline{z}(1)).$$

Then $H^2(U^2, C^2)$ is the expanded SAT(S) formula given by

$$\left[\text{XOR}(x(0), y(1)) \wedge \text{XOR}(\overline{w}(0), y(0)) \wedge \text{XNOR}(y(0), \overline{z}(1)) \right] \bigwedge$$

$$\left[\text{XOR}(x(1), y(2)) \wedge \text{XOR}(\overline{w}(1), y(1)) \wedge \text{XNOR}(y(1), \overline{z}(2)) \right] \bigwedge$$

$$\text{XOR}(\overline{w}(2), y(2)). \quad \blacksquare$$

4.2   RULES FOR CONSTRUCTING EXPANDED GRAPHS

Our original definition of time expanded graphs used certain specific semantics for interpreting the meaning of edge weights. There are other ways to construct expanded networks. We illustrate this via an example in epidemiology.

The *contact graph* is constructed as follows. Let V be a set representing a population; consider a complete graph G on V. Each edge $e \in E$ of G consist of a list of time intervals $L_1^e, L_2^e, \ldots$. Each $L_i^e = [a_i^e, b_i^e]$, where a_i and b_i are integers and we assume that $a_i^e > b_{i-1}^e$. The semantics of the lists are simple: they give the time ranges when the two people were in contact. These graphs can model certain time-varying phenomena. Let us first consider a simple version of this [305].

Definition 3. *A temporal network is an undirected graph $G(V, E)$ in which each edge has a time label $\lambda(e)$ representing the time when the two end nodes of the edge come in contact (or communicate). In general, each edge can have multiple labels capturing the fact that the nodes can come in contact more than once. A path P in G is time respecting if the labels on the edges of the path are non-decreasing.* $\blacksquare$

A time-expanded temporal network is constructed as follows. Assume for the present purposes that we have only one label per edge, with $\lambda_{min}(e)$ being the minimum value and $\lambda_{max}(e)$ the maximum value. A copy of the vertices in G are placed at each discrete time step t between $\lambda_{min}(e)$ and λ_{max}. A copy of the node $v(t)$ is joined to $v(t+1)$ by a directed edge. An edge (u, v) in G with label

λ is replaced by directed edges between the copies of the vertices at time λ, that is, between $(v(\lambda), w(\lambda))$ and $(w(\lambda), v(\lambda))$. Finding a critical path from $v(t)$ to $w(t + x)$ is merely finding a path in this time-expanded network between these two nodes. This representation can also be extended easily to the case in which edges have multiple labels. A more interesting situation arises when a person is infected by a communicable disease at time t and then becomes non-contagious at some other time $t + x$. This can also be represented quite easily using the formalism discussed above.

Note the difference between how an edge is added to time-expanded temporal networks and to expanded periodic graphs. The representation above is used commonly for routing in networks with time-dependent edge delay functions. The basic idea is quite general: it allows us to define rules for specifying how to add edges in the temporal networks on the basis of the static network. Also note that the procedure for constructing time-expanded temporal networks can be combined with the procedure for constructing expanded periodic networks.

4.3 SEMANTICS OF SATISFACTION

Recall that a periodically specified CNF formula was said to be satisfiable if and only if all the clauses in the expanded formula can be made TRUE. In other words, $F^M(U^M, C^M)$ is said to be satisfiable iff $\forall i, 0 \leq i \leq M$, $C(i)$ is satisfiable. This suggests a generalization allowing us to write a quantified formula consisting of i and basic integer inequalities. For instance, we could say that $F^M(U^M, C^M)$ is satisfiable iff

$$\forall i, \ L \leq i \leq U, \ C(i) \ \text{is satisfiable}.$$

Such an extension lets us, in a natural way, relate periodic satisfiability problems to satisfiability problems for temporal logics [19, 476] and, in general, to reasoning about any temporal phenomenon, such as questions in epidemic modeling and ad hoc wireless networks.

4.4 PERIODICALLY SPECIFIED QUANTIFIED FORMULAS

As a final extension, let us consider periodic Boolean formulas where not all the variables necessarily are existentially quantified. Quantified formulas have been well studied in the literature. We consider periodically specified quantified formulas. We have a static formula as before, but now each variable template used in the static clause is either existentially or universally quantified. The semantics we use in our expanded formula are that all copies of the variable have the same associated quantifier. For example, let F be a static formula given by

$$F = \forall x \ \exists y \ \forall z \ ([x(0) \vee y(1)] \wedge [y(0) \vee \overline{z}(0)]) .$$

Then the expanded formula $F^{\mathbb{N}}(U^{\mathbb{N}}, C^{\mathbb{N}})$ is given by:

$$\forall x(0), \forall x(1) \ldots \exists y(0), \exists y(1) \ldots \forall z(0), \forall z(1) \ldots \bigwedge_{t \in \mathbb{N}} ([x(t) \vee y(t+1)] \wedge [y(t) \vee \overline{z}(t)]) .$$

5 TECHNIQUES: HARDNESS AND EASINESS RESULTS

We now discuss how to combine four concepts: (i) local transformations (possibly augmented with fixed size *enforcers*), (ii) relational representability, (iii) *simultaneous* reductions based on local transformation, and (iv) *lifting* of simultaneous reductions based on local transformation to characterize relative complexities, or efficient approximability of various periodically specified problems. In conjunction with certain translation results (algorithms to transform periodic specifications of logical formulas into other succinct specifications of the same logical formula, up to a renaming), discussed in Hunt et al. [266] and Marathe et al. [378, 377], we also get as a corollary unified complexity results for problems specified using other succinct specifications. We discuss each of these techniques in some detail below. The ideas form a first step towards building a predictive complexity theory of periodically specified problems. We explain this further in subsequent sections. The theory is similar in spirit to very general results presented by Bálcazar, Lozano, and Toran [26] on the complexity of problems when they are encoded using circuits. However, the circuit model is a complexity theoretic model. The approach does not naturally model real-life problems, and the corresponding results do not hold for problems specified using periodic specifications. See Marathe et al. [378, 379, 380] for additional discussion on this topic.

5.1 LOCAL TRANSFORMATIONS

Reductions by local transformation have been used extensively in the literature (see Garey and Johnson [191]). The first step in formalizing this concept is to separate the concept of replacement from that of reduction. Transformation using local replacement constructs target instances from source instances by replacing each object (clause/variable in a formula) by a collection of objects (conjunction of clauses) in the target instance. A schematic diagram of this is shown in figure 3.

For the purposes of this chapter, it suffices to observe that the *local* transformations from a problem SAT(S) to a problem SAT(T) used here are of the following two kinds:

1. *Simple-local (SL) transformations.* Let $F = C_1 \wedge \ldots \wedge C_n$ where the C_i are S-clauses. Then, the T-formula $F' = \mathcal{R}(F)$ equals $C'_1 \wedge \ldots \wedge C'_n$, such that the following holds:
   (a) Each C'_i is a fixed conjunction of T-clauses depending only upon the relation C_i.
   (b) The variables of C'_i are the variables of C_i plus *new* variables *local* to the clauses of C'_i.
2. *Simple-local-enforcer (SLE) transformations.* Let F be defined as in 1 immediately above. Then, the T-formula $F' = \mathcal{R}(F)$ equals $C'_0 \wedge C'_1 \wedge \ldots \wedge C'_n$, such that the following holds:

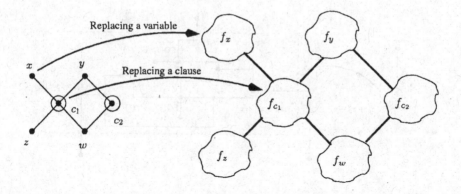

FIGURE 3   A schematic diagram illustrating the concept of local transformation.

(a) C_0' is a fixed T-formula, called the *enforcer*, the variables of which are called the *enforcer* variables.
(b) The clauses C_i' satisfy 1a and 1b, *except* that their variables can include *enforcer* variables.

For a simple demonstration of a local transformation, we first define the following problems. 1IN3-SAT is the problem of determining whether a 3-CNF formula has a satisfying assignment where exactly *one* literal in each clause is satisfied. 1EX3-SAT is the same problem but on a CNF formula in which each clause contains exactly 3 literals. We now give an example of an SL-transformation of 3-SAT to 1EX3-SAT.

Example 3. *Consider a transformation of an instance F of 3-SAT to an instance F' of 1EX3-SAT. Each clause $C_j = (z_p \vee z_q \vee z_r)$ of F is transformed into a set of clauses C_j' of F' given by: $C_j' = \text{EO}(z_p, u^j, v^j) \wedge \text{EO}(\overline{z_q}, u^j, w^j) \wedge \text{EO}(v^j, w^j, t^j) \wedge \text{EO}(\overline{z_r}, v^j, x^j)$. $\text{EO}(x, y, z)$ is a logical relation that takes the value of TRUE when exactly one of x, y, z is TRUE, and takes the value of FALSE otherwise. Here u^j, v^j, w^j, t^j and x^j are new variables local to C_j'. It is easy to see that this is an SL-transformation. The transformation is shown in figure 4.* ■*

Note that the definitions of SL- and SLE- transformations are fully syntactic in nature, since they do *not* require such transformations to be reductions. Essentially all the reductions discussed here are by SL- or SLE-transformations. Local replacements have a number of desirable properties. First, it is straightforward to show the following:

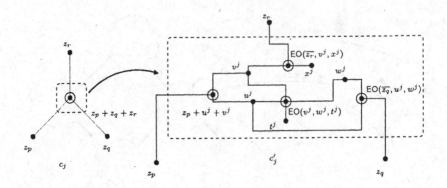

FIGURE 4   Figure showing how to replace a single clause in an instance of 3-SAT by a set of clauses to obtain an instance of 1IN3-SAT.

Proposition 5.1. *SL- and SLE-transformations are ultra-efficient, in the sense that they are reductions on multiple tape deterministic Turing machines that are simultaneously $O(n \log n)$ time-, linear size-, and $O(\log n)$ intermediate space-bounded.* ∎

Second, they simultaneously preserve a number of both semantic and structural properties of instances. By structure of instances we mean the graph-theoretic structure as well as the structure of its specification. Third, they are extremely efficient in terms of the resources used, and preserve power and polynomial indices [487, 488].

5.2   RELATIONAL REPRESENTABILITY

For local replacement based transformations to be useful as reductions, we need the notion of relational representability. Let S and T be sets of relations/algebraic constraints on a common domain D. Relational representability formalizes the intuitive concept that the relations in S are *expressible* (or, extending the terminology from Schaefer [455], *representable*) by finite conjunctions of the relations in T. This is formalized in Definition 4 below:

Definition 4.

1. *We denote by $Rep(S)$ the set of all finite-arity relations on a non-empty set D logically equivalent to finite existentially quantified conjunctions of relations/algebraic constraints in S applied to variables.*
2. *We say that a set of relations S is representable by a set of relations/algebraic constraints T if and only if $S \subset Rep(T)$.*

Example 4. *Let* $S = \{XOR(\alpha, \beta)\}$ *and* $T = \{XNOR(\alpha, \beta)\}$. *Clearly,* $XOR(x, y) \equiv XNOR(x, z) \wedge XNOR(y, \overline{z})$ *Thus each* S*-clause can be represented by a conjunction of* T*-clauses. The same holds for* S*-formulas. For example,*

$$XOR(x, y) \wedge XOR(x, w) \equiv XNOR(x, z) \wedge XNOR(y, \overline{z}) \wedge XNOR(x, z_1)$$
$$\wedge XNOR(w, \overline{z_1}) . \quad \blacksquare$$

Variants of the concepts of definition 4 on the *relative representability* of ordered-pairs (S, T) of sets of *relations*, henceforth denoted collectively by *relational representability*, are well known, especially in mathematical logic. Previously in complexity theory, *relational representability* as used here and the individual constraint satisfaction problems studied have usually been restricted to finite sets S of finite-arity relations on *finite* sets D, generally the set $\{0, 1\}$. In contrast, the results discussed here apply to *both* finite and infinite domains and sets of relations/constraints.

Transformations that preserve a semantic property of interest are called reductions. To show this usually requires one to use some form of relational representability. For example, reductions that preserve decision complexity are simply called "reductions" in the literature. Reductions that preserve the number of solutions are known as parsimonious reductions. Several approximation-preserving reductions have been studied in the literature, including L-reductions that preserve polynomial time approximation schemes and A-reductions that preserve the approximation ratio. Given the concepts above, it is intuitively clear how to go about constructing reductions based on local transformations. The concept of relational representability must be modified when we wish to construct local transformations that also preserve other semantic properties. For example, number-preserving relational representability is a special form of relational representability that also preserves the number of solutions. The variants of relational representability used to construct A-reductions and L-reductions are a bit more subtle and do not necessarily have to be a decision-preserving transformation. Approximation-preserving versions of relational representability are also called *implementations* in Creignou [111] and Creignou et al. [113]. We will have more to say about this in the next section.

5.3   SIMULTANEOUS REDUCTIONS BASED ON LOCAL TRANSFORMATIONS

In general, it is easy to see that a local transformation preserving one type of semantic property does not necessarily preserve another type of semantic property. In fact, under standard complexity theoretic assumptions, designing a (local) transformation that simultaneously preserves more than one semantic property is not always possible. For example, consider the two widely studied problems 3-SAT and 2-SAT. The problem 3-SAT is NP-hard and 2-SAT is polynomial time solvable [191]. On the other hand, both MAX-3-SAT and

MAX-2-SAT are APX-hard, that is, unless P = NP they cannot have a poly-nomial time approximation scheme. Therefore, a natural question to ask in this context is: when can we design single transformations that are *simultaneously* decision-preserving, number-preserving, and approximation-preserving? We have found that for a large class of algebraic problems, it is indeed possible to devise such transformations: we call them *simultaneous reductions* [113, 267, 268, 310]. Moreover, most of these are based on local transformations. For example, a (parsimonious + A + L)-reduction is a reduction that is simultaneously a parsi-monious reduction, an A-reduction and an L-reduction. Simultaneous reductions have the advantage that they simultaneously preserve a variety of semantics and the structure of instances. By structure of instances we usually mean the variable-clause interaction graph structure and the structure of the specification used to specify the problem. The existence for a wide class of natural algebraic problems of simultaneous reductions based on local transformations is a bit surprising.

For example, we can show that there is a local transformation from the problem 3-SAT to the problem 1IN3-SAT that is simultaneously a (decision + parsimonious + A + L)-reduction. Consequently, using the known results on the complexity of 3-SAT and its variants, we *simultaneously* obtain the follow-ing: 1IN3-SAT is NP-hard, #-1IN3-SAT is #P-complete, MAX-1IN3-SAT is APX-complete and MAX-DONES-1IN3-SAT is MAX-Π_1-complete (MAX-DONES-1IN3-SAT is the problem of finding a satisfying 1IN3-SAT assignment maximizing the total number of variables set to TRUE). These constitute results on the complexity of 1IN3-SAT for standardly specified instances. As discussed in the next section, the transformation can be translated to obtain the rela-tive hardness of the periodically specified 1IN3-SAT problem and its variants, showing notably that one-dimensional finite narrow periodic 1IN3-SAT ((B)N-1IN3-SAT) is PSPACE-hard.

Simultaneous reductions based on local transformations induce natural equiv-alence classes of combinatorial problems. Obtaining general techniques showing when two problems are in the same equivalence class is an interesting direction for future research.

5.4   PUTTING IT ALL TOGETHER: LIFTING OF SIMULTANEOUS REDUCTIONS BASED ON LOCAL TRANSFORMATIONS

How does one prove complexity bounds for periodically specified problems? Our approach consists of two natural steps and builds on the concept of simultaneous reductions based on local replacement, as laid out in preceding sections.

First, by direct reductions from Turing machines, we characterize the com-plexity of a number of basic CNF satisfiability problems when specified peri-odically. The proof technique used is fairly generic; results characterizing the complexity of these satisfiability problems when the underlying periodic spec-ifications change can thus be obtained directly. For example, we prove that two-dimensional finite narrow periodic 3-SAT with explicit boundary conditions for both dimensions ((B,B)N(BC)-3-SAT) is NEXPTIME-complete. This proof together with a few simple observations shows that one-dimensional finite narrow periodic 3-SAT ((B)N-3-SAT) is PSPACE-complete, and that two-dimensional narrow periodic 3-SAT with one dimension finite and specified in binary and the other dimension two-way infinite in one direction ((B,$\mathbb{Z}$)N-3-SAT) is EXPSPACE-complete. A summary of our results for 3-SAT as well as for the two problems 3-HornSAT and CLIQUE appears later in table 2.

Second, we show that efficient reductions involving *local replacement* (possibly augmented with fixed-size enforcers) [191] including the problems 3-SAT, 1IN3-SAT, NAE3-SAT, to a problem Π can be extended to obtain efficient reductions from the problems α-3-SAT, α-1IN3-SAT, α-NAE3-SAT, to the problem α-Π. These problems include most of the basic problems in Karp [299], Garey and Johnson [191], as well as several basic P-complete problems [283]. An important property of our reductions is that they preserve the underlying specifications. *We note that the same reduction works when the specification α is changed,* thus avoiding the need for devising a new reduction for each result.

The idea, in fact, applies to simultaneous reductions based on local replacement. In other words, given a simultaneous reduction $\mathcal{R}$ from Π_1 to Π_2 that is based on local transformations, there is an efficient algorithm that takes as input $\mathcal{R}$ and an instance of the problems α-Π_1 and α-Π_2 (recall that α denotes a periodic specification), and constructs a transformation $\mathcal{R}'_\alpha$ such that $\mathcal{R}'_\alpha$ is an efficient reduction between α-Π_1 and α-Π_2. We call this *lifting* the reduction: transforming the static formulas into another static graph so as to obtain the needed correspondence between the expanded formulas. Lifting can be thought of as a compiler. It takes a known local transformation between two standardly specified problems and constructs a new transformation between their periodic counterparts in such a way that the semantics of transformation are preserved. Our idea, then, is to lift the known reduction from 3-SAT to problem Π when the instance is specified using standard specifications, and thus obtain a suitable reduction from α-3-SAT to the problem α-Π. In algebraic terms, the process can be seen in the form of the following *commutative diagram*:

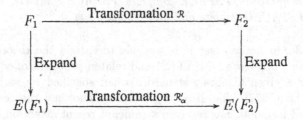

An example of this general technique of lifting is given below.

Theorem 5.1. *Let S and T be finite sets of finite-arity relations on a (possibly infinite) nonempty set D. Let α be one of the following periodic specifications: (B)N, (Z)N, (B,B)N, (B)W, ...} Then, if $S \subset Rep(T)$, the problem SAT(S) is reducible by a local replacement $\mathcal{R}$ to the problem SAT(T). Moreover, the transformation $\mathcal{R}$ can be extended to transformations $\mathcal{R}'_\alpha$ of the problems α-SAT(S) to α-SAT(T) such that the following hold:*

1. *Both transformations $\mathcal{R}$ and $\mathcal{R}'_\alpha$ are $O(n \log n)$ time-, $O(\log n)$ space-, and $O(n)$ size-bounded.*
2. *Both transformations $\mathcal{R}$ and $\mathcal{R}'_\alpha$ are decidable in parallel logarithmic time using only $O(n)$ processors.*
3. *Both transformations $\mathcal{R}$ and $\mathcal{R}'_\alpha$ preserve bandwidth, treewidth, and pathwidth of instances.*
4. *If the transformation $\mathcal{R}$ is a parsimonious reduction, then so is the transformation $\mathcal{R}'_\alpha$.*
5. *If the transformation $\mathcal{R}$ is an A- or L- reduction, then so is the transformation $\mathcal{R}'_\alpha$.*
6. *If the transformation $\mathcal{R}$ is a metric reduction, then so is the transformation $\mathcal{R}'_\alpha$.*
7. *If the transformation $\mathcal{R}$ preserves strong planarity, then so does the transformation $\mathcal{R}'_\alpha$.*

∎

As one example of theorem 5.1, we can show the following very general result. The theorem shows that as long as SAT(S), is NP-complete when instances are specified using standard specifications, it becomes hard for the appropriate complexity class when instances are specified using periodic specifications.

Theorem 5.2. *Let D be a finite nonempty set. Let S be a finite set of finite-arity relations on D such that $Rep(S) =$ **Boolean Relations**. Then, the problems (B)N-SAT(S), (Z)N-SAT(S), (B,B)N-SAT(S), (B)W-SAT(S) and (N,N)N-SAT(S) are, respectively, PSPACE-complete, PSPACE-complete, NEXPTIME-complete, EXPSPACE-complete and undecidable.* ∎

As an aside, in many cases it is possible to extend the theorem above to obtain *dichotomy theorems* for SAT(S) and related problems of equational satisfiability over a given algebraic structure when specified by variant periodic specifications [376, 377]. The discovery of such dichotomy theorems, for standardly specified formulas, has received significant recent attention in the literature [113, 310, 455].

Finally, we note that using the complexity theoretic results for periodic constraint satisfaction problems, we can characterize the complexity of a number of combinatorial problems when specified using periodic specifications.

6 TECHNIQUES: EASINESS RESULTS

Next, we discuss various methods by which easiness results can be obtained for periodically specified problems. We first consider methods by which exact polynomial time algorithms can be obtained for such problems. We then discuss how this idea can be extended to obtain approximation algorithms for "hard" problems.

6.1 POLYNOMIAL TIME ALGORITHMS

Almost all the polynomial time algorithms for periodically specified problems use the idea of periodic certificates. The basic idea is that if the given problem has a solution, then it has a periodic solution with a small period. Once this is established, the problem reduces to finding a solution on a polynomially sized instance that is a function of the periodicity of the solution. We explain the idea in the case of a specific kind of satisfiability problem.

A logical relation R is said to be *weakly negative* if $R(x_1, x_2, \ldots)$ is logically equivalent to some CNF formula having at most one unnegated variable in each conjunct. A weakly negative formula F is one in which each conjunct is weakly negative. The problem of deciding if a weakly negative formula is satisfiable is called *Horn satisfiability* or HornSAT: this problem has been discussed in chapter 9. The problem 3-HornSAT is the restriction of HornSAT to clauses containing no more than three literals. The problem $(\mathbb{Z})$N-HornSAT is the problem of deciding whether a one-dimensional two-way infinite periodically specified weakly negative formula is satisfiable. Here is a simple algorithm for solving the problem.

The algorithm works on the static formula F representing $F^{\mathbb{Z}}$ and is based on the following two observations. The first observation is that if there is a clause with only one literal, all copies of the corresponding variable must have the same value. For instance, if there is a clause consisting of the single literal $\overline{x_i(t+1)}$, then all copies of variable x_i have to be set to FALSE. The second observation is that after simplifying the set of clauses as much as possible on the basis of the first observation, every remaining clause has either no literals or more than one literal. Weak negativity implies that each clause with more than one literal contains at least one negative literal, so setting all remaining variables to FALSE will satisfy all such clauses. Since each simplification of the set of clauses based on the first observation assigns a value to a variable in the static formula that has not previously been assigned a value, the algorithm will terminate in polynomial time. When the algorithm terminates, either we are left with no clauses (in which case the formula is satisfiable by the discussion above) or we obtain a contradiction.

Note that if the expanded formula $F^{\mathbb{Z}}$ for the given instance F of $(\mathbb{Z})$N-HornSAT is satisfiable, then there exists a satisfying assignment assigning the same value to all copies of a given variable in the static formula.

Other researchers [103, 104, 243, 244, 260, 275, 276, 302, 338, 420, 421] have given efficient algorithms for solving problems such as determining strongly connected components, testing for existence of cycles, finding minimum cost paths between a pair of vertices, bipartiteness, planarity, quickest transshipment, and minimum cost spanning forests for periodically specified graphs. One particular problem that has received a lot of attention is that of detecting cycles in periodic graphs [104, 276, 302, 347]. Currently, the best known algorithm for this problem is by Cohen and Megiddo [104] and works even in the case of wide specifications. In Marathe et al. [377, 378], we gave polynomial time algorithms for various satisfiability problems when instances are specified using variant one-dimensional narrow periodic specifications. Interestingly, most of the results above are for one-dimensional periodically specified graphs. Höfting and Wanke [243, 244] and Wanke [516] have considered (finite/infinite) periodically specified (toroidal) graphs when the dimension in which the graph is replicated is given as part of the instance. In general, their results show that very simple problems become computationally intractable. On the other hand, certain problems are still solvable in polynomial time. As an example [243], polynomial time algorithms are obtained for solving path problems when the static graph is strongly connected or has a constant number of strongly connected components. The results rely crucially on the polynomial time solvability of solving linear Diophantine equations (integer linear equations with integral solutions). Finding polynomial time algorithms for two-dimensional narrow and one-dimensional wide periodically specified problems is an interesting direction for future research.

We finally discuss the notion of real-time certificates proposed by Orlin [419]. Here, instead of finding the solution for the complete expanded instance, we seek to find the solution for the first i periods in time that is polynomial in i and the instance representation. Unfortunately, as shown in Orlin [419], this does not make the problem any easier: all the problems for which he shows PSPACE-hardness results continue to be PSPACE-hard even when we wish to find a real-time solution.

6.2   APPROXIMATION ALGORITHMS

As we have seen, problems tend to become harder when specified succinctly using periodic specifications. Given the hardness results for solving the problems exactly when periodically specified, we investigate the existence of polynomial time approximation algorithms for these problems. We present a uniform approach for developing efficient approximation algorithms, as well as schemes for a number of optimization problems when specified using one- or two-dimensional finite, narrow, periodically specified problems. For the rest of the section, let α be one of the periodic specifications:

- (B)N: one-dimensional finite narrow periodic specifications,

- (B)N(BC): one-dimensional finite narrow periodic specifications with explicit boundary conditions,
- (B,B)N: two-dimensional finite narrow periodic specifications, and
- (B,B)N(BC): two-dimensional finite narrow periodic specifications with explicit boundary conditions in both dimensions.

It is important to understand what is meant by a *polynomial time approximation algorithm* for a problem Π, when Π's instances are specified by one of the periodic specifications α. We illustrate this by an example:

Example 5. *Consider the maximum independent set problem, when graphs are specified by* (B,B)N-*specifications. We provide efficient algorithms for the following versions of the* approximate maximum independent set problem:

1. Approximation problem: *compute the size of a near-maximum independent set in G.*
2. Query problem: *given any vertex v of G, determine whether v belongs to the approximate independent set so computed.*
3. Construction problem: *output a* (B,B)N-*specification of the set of vertices in the approximate independent set.*
4. Output problem: *output the approximate independent set computed.*

We require that algorithms for versions 1, 2, and 3 above run in time polynomial in the size of the (B,B)N-*specification rather than in the size of the graph obtained by expanding the specification. The algorithm for version 4 should run in time polynomial (ideally linear) in the size of the expanded graph but use space which is polynomial (ideally linear) in the size of the periodic specification.* ∎

The requirements above are a natural extension of the requirements imposed on approximation algorithms when instances are specified using standard specifications. This can be seen as follows for graph problems, and a similar argument holds for satisfiability problems. When instances are specified using standard specifications, the number of vertices is polynomial in the size of the description. Given this, any polynomial time algorithm to determine if a vertex v of G is in the approximate maximum independent set can be modified easily into a polynomial time algorithm that lists all the vertices of G in the approximate maximum independent set. For an optimization problem or a query problem, our algorithms use space and time that are low-level polynomials in the size (η) of the periodic specification and thus $O(\text{poly} \log \eta)$ in the size of the graph. Moreover, when we need to output, for example, the subset of vertices, or the subset of edges, corresponding to a vertex cover, or maximal matching, in the expanded graph, our algorithms take essentially the same time but substantially less (often exponentially less) space than algorithms that work directly on the expanded graph. It is important to design algorithms that work directly on the periodic specifications by exploiting the regular structure of the underlying graphs, because graphs resulting from expansions of given periodic descriptions are frequently too large to fit into the main memory of a computer. Hence, standard algorithms designed for flat graphs are impractical for periodically specified graphs.

We outline how to obtain approximation algorithms satisfying the performance requirements above for a number of problems, including problems Π in table 1, when instances are given by (B)N-, (B)N(BC)-, (B,B)N-, (B,B)N(BC)-specifications.

The basic technique consists of two main steps. First, by an extension of ideas in Baker [25] we show that for each fixed finite set S there is a polynomial time approximation algorithm as well as a scheme for planar instances (corresponding bipartite graphs are planar), for the problems MAX-SAT(S) specified periodically using one of the specifications mentioned earlier in the section. Next, we show that a number of important classes of problems, when specified periodically, can be reduced in an approximation-preserving way to appropriate problems MAX-SAT(S) specified using the same type of periodic specifications. We call these *structure preserving* L-reductions. This step uses the concept of simultaneous reductions outlined earlier.

Let us elaborate a bit more on the first step. The idea behind our approximation algorithms involves the conversion of solutions obtained from a *local* algorithm on small sub-grids to a solution of the *global* problem. The method of partial expansion involves the application of a divide and conquer algorithm iteratively by considering different subsets of the given graph, solving each subset with a local algorithm, constructing a global solution and finally choosing the best solution among these iterations as the solution to Π. The method can be seen as an extension of the shifting strategy devised by Baker [25] for finding efficient approximation algorithms to several combinatorial problems.

We illustrate the idea by discussing our polynomial time approximation scheme (PTAS) for the *maximum independent set* problem. Recall that an approximation algorithm for an optimization problem Π provides a *performance guarantee* of ρ if, for every instance I of Π, the value returned by the approximation algorithm is within a factor ρ of the optimal value for I. A PTAS for problem Π is a family of algorithms $\mathcal{F}$ such that for any fixed $\epsilon > 0$ there is a polynomial time algorithm $A \in \mathcal{F}$ that for all $I \in \Pi$ returns a solution within a factor $(1 + \epsilon)$ of the optimal value for I.

Consider a (B,B)N-specification of a graph G, and an integer $l > 1$. To begin with, for each i, $0 \leq i \leq l$, partition the graph G into k disjoint sets $G_1, \ldots, G_k$ by removing vertices with horizontal coordinates congruent to $i \mod (l+1)$. For each subgraph G_p, $1 \leq p \leq k$, we find an independent set of size at least $l/l+1$ times the optimal value of the independent set in G_p. The independent set for this partition is simply the union of independent sets for each of G_p. By an averaging argument, it follows that the partition yielding the largest solution value contains at least $(l/l+1)^2 OPT(G)$ nodes, where $OPT(G)$ denotes the value of the maximum independent set in G. (For simplicity, we use a symbol to denote a set as well as its cardinality: the intended meaning will be clear from context.)

It is important to note that the size of the graph we are dealing with is, in general, exponential in the size of the specification. Hence, a naive application of the idea above will lead to algorithms that take an exponential amount of time. However, the regular structure of the graph allows us to solve the problems considered here in time polynomial in the size of the specification. The key observation is that for each iteration, although the total number of subproblems to be considered is exponential, they can be divided into a small number of equivalence classes. Moreover, it is easy to compute in polynomial time the number of elements in each equivalence class. Combining these two observations immediately yields the desired results.

Theorem 6.1. *For each fixed $l \geq 1$, and for each of the problems Π listed in table 1, the problem α-Π, has a polynomial time approximation algorithm with performance guarantee $(l + 1/l)^2 \cdot FBEST_\Pi$ and running time $O(RT_\Pi(l^2|G|))$. Here, $FBEST_\Pi$ denotes the best-known performance guarantee of an algorithm for the problem Π for non-succinctly specified instances, $RT_\Pi(n)$ denotes the running time of the algorithm with input size n guarantees the performance of $FBEST_\Pi$ for the problem Π and $|G|$ denotes the size of the specification.* ∎

In fact, we can show that the theorem holds for most problems α-Π such that Π is in syntactic MAX-SNP.

As an example, using recent results in Goemans and Williamson [199], we find that for all $\epsilon > 0$, the problems (B,B)N-, (B,B)N(BC)-, (B,B)N- and (B)N-MAX-2-SAT have a PTAS that outputs solutions within a factor of $(1 + \epsilon)1.137$ of an optimal solution. As a corollary of theorem 6.1, using recent non-approximability results [21] we get the following:

Theorem 6.2. *For all the problems Π listed in table 1, the problems α-Π have a PTAS if and only if $P = NP$.* ∎

A second result following from the proof of theorem 6.1 is as follows.

Theorem 6.3. *For all the problems Π listed in table 1, the problems α-Π have a PTAS when restricted to planar instances.* ∎

We can show that many of these problems remain NEXPTIME-complete, even when restricted to planar instances.

The general approximation algorithms and schemes for the problems MAX-SAT(S) are an attempt to answer the fundamental question: which "hard" periodically specified optimization problems have efficient approximations? In this

TABLE 1 Performance guarantee results for optimization problems corresponding to problems specified using (B,B)N-specifications. All these problems can be shown to be **NEXPTIME**-hard using the method outlined in this chapter. Similar results hold for problems specified using (B,B)N(BC)-specifications. The symbol b denotes the degree bound and the symbol p denotes the maximum arity of a relation in S. Approximation results for the standard case for arbitrary and planar instances can be found in Ausiello et al. [23].

Problem	(B,B)N Specifications		Standard Specifications	
	Planar	Arbitrary	Planar	Arbitrary
MAX-3-SAT	$(\frac{l+1}{l})^3$	$(\frac{l+1}{l})^2 \cdot 4/3$	$(\frac{l+1}{(l})$	$4/3$
MAX-SAT(S)	$(\frac{l+1}{l})^3$	$(\frac{l+1}{l})^2 \cdot 2^p$	$(\frac{l+1}{(l})$	2^p
MIN-VERTEX-COVER	$(\frac{l+1}{l})^3$	$(\frac{l+1}{l})^2 \cdot 2$	$(\frac{l+1}{l})$	2
MAX-INDEPENDENT-SET	$(\frac{l+1}{l})^3$	$(\frac{l+1}{l})^2 \cdot b$	$(\frac{l+1}{l})$	b
MIN-DOMINATING-SET	$(\frac{l+1}{l})^3$	$(\frac{l+1}{l})^2 \cdot b$	$(\frac{l+1}{l})$	$\log b$
MAX-EDGE-DOMINATING-SET	$(\frac{l}{l-1})^3$		$(\frac{l}{l-1})$	2
MAX-PARTITION-INTO-TRIANGLES	$(\frac{l+1}{l})^3$	$(\frac{l+1}{l}) \cdot 3$	$(\frac{l+1}{l})$	3
MAX-H-MATCHING	$(\frac{l+1}{l})^3$	$(\frac{l+1}{l}) \cdot (|V_H|/2 + \epsilon)$	$(\frac{l+1}{l})$	$(|V_H|/2 + \epsilon)$
MAX-CUT	$(\frac{l+1}{l})^2$	$(\frac{l+1}{l}) \cdot 1.137$	polynomial	1.137

direction, the general theory developed here and discussed above provides a sufficient condition:

> Periodically specified graph and other optimization problems have an ϵ-approximation algorithm (or PTAS) when the semantics of the problem can be described by a SAT(S) formula in such a way that the formula interaction graph inherits the structure of the graph.

In recent years there has been significant interest [23, 113, 269, 309] in providing syntactic characterizations of optimization problems in an attempt to provide a uniform framework for solving such problems. Our results provide a syntactic (algebraic) class of problems, namely, MAX-SAT(S) whose closure under L-reductions and other appropriate approximation-preserving reductions define one such characterization for problems that have an ϵ-approximation (or PTAS). The algebraic model (characterization) is general enough to express the optimization version of: (i) the generalized satisfiability problems of Schaefer [455]; (ii) feasibility of systems of linear equations over a variety of algebraic structures; (iii) a class of nonlinear optimization problems; and (iv) several well-known graph theoretic problems. We refer the reader to Hunt et al. [269] and Khanna and Motwani [309] for more details.

The approximation algorithms have three desirable features: they are conceptually simple, they apply to large classes of problems Π and they apply to problems specified using any of the periodic specifications considered here. The polynomial time approximation algorithms for *natural* (as opposed to specifically constructed) NEXPTIME-hard problems yield a large class of problems for which there is a proven exponential—and possibly doubly exponential—gap between the time complexities of finding exact and approximate solutions. Previous non-approximability results have show that many optimization problems are NP-hard or PSPACE-hard to approximate beyond a certain factor. While those hardness results point out that it is *unlikely* in general to find "good" polynomial time approximation algorithms, the possibility is not ruled out. The results presented here, on the other hand, show a *provable* gap between approximation and decision versions of the problem. To see this, note that the decision problems are NEXPTIME-complete, and hence require *at least* 2^{cn} steps—and *possibly* $2^{2^{cn}}$ steps—to solve, assuming NEXPTIME $\neq$ DEXPTIME.

The study of approximation algorithms for NP-hard optimization problems has received a great deal of attention [23]. In contrast, efficient approximability of PSPACE-, NEXPTIME-hard problems has been considered only very recently. We refer the reader to Condon [106], Feigenbaum [154], and Marathe [376] for survey articles and Agarwal and Condon [10], Condon [107, 108], Hunt et al. [266], and Marathe et al. [379, 380] for related results. The NEXPTIME-hardness results for periodically specified problems show that the very regular structure of problem instances does *not* suffice to make problems easy. But the efficient approximation algorithms and schemes developed here show the following:

> The very regular structures of problem instances specified by the periodic specifications does make many of the basic problems approximable.

Interestingly, approximating many of the optimization problems considered here when instances are specified using *small circuit specifications* [26, 426] can be shown to be NEXPTIME-hard by extensions of the arguments in Arora et al. [21]. Thus, our results highlight an important difference between problems specified using multiple-dimension finite periodic specifications and small circuit specifications.

7 COMPLEXITY THEORETIC INSIGHTS

We briefly discuss certain complexity theoretic implications of the results summarized in the preceding sections. Additional discussion can be found in Hunt et al. [267, 268] and Marathe et al. [376, 380].

7.1   PREDICTIVE COMPLEXITY THEORY

Simultaneous local reductions and their lifts allow us to relate the computational complexities of variant combinatorial problems in a very strong sense. For example, we can show the following.

Theorem 7.1. *The problem* 3-SAT *is* (decision+parsimonious+A+L)-*reducible by local replacement to* EM-SAT, *the restriction of* 1EX3-SAT *to formulas having no negated literals. This together with the known results about* 3-SAT *and its periodically specified variants directly implies that:*

1. EM-SAT *is NP-complete*
2. MAX-EM-SAT *is APX-complete*
3. #-EM-SAT *is #P-complete*
4. *It is NP-hard to approximate* MAX-DONES-EM-SAT *beyond a factor* n^ϵ
5. (B)N-EM-SAT *is PSPACE-complete,* (B)W-EM-SAT *is EXPSPACE-complete and* (B,B)N-EM-SAT *is NEXPTIME-complete*
6. (B)N-MAX-EM-SAT *does not have a PTAS unless* $P = NP$
7. *It is PSPACE-hard to approximate* (B)N-MAX-DONES-EM-SAT *beyond a factor* n^ϵ

∎

   This is a step towards developing a predictive complexity theory for periodically specified problems. The predictive aspect implies that the relationship between problems specified using standard specifications and the way it was derived is sufficient to deduce the relationship between the corresponding periodically specified problems. In other words, (i) a single transformation can serve to simultaneously relate the complexity of several variants of a standard problem (e.g., decision, counting, optimization), and (ii) sufficient conditions on the reductions between standardly specified problems can be used to predict the relationships between the corresponding periodically specified problems. The general technique presented here *simultaneously* applies to a large collection of problems α-SAT(S) when one varies (i) the periodic specification, (ii) the set S, and (iii) the objective function. Moreover, it applies for obtaining easiness as well as hardness results.

7.2   NATURAL MORPHISMS FOR COMPUTATIONAL COMPLEXITY

The results discussed in this chapter show in a number of cases—and strongly suggest in others—that *strongly-local reducibility* degrees for constraint satisfaction problems are preserved, when problems in P or in NP are generalized to periodically specified and to infinite recursive versions of these problems. In contrast, this is *not* true for *polynomial time reducibility* degrees. (Following Ladner [352], polynomial degrees are equivalence classes of languages or sets induced

TABLE 2 Table summarizing how the complexity of three basic problems changes when the periodic specification is changed. Note that the complexity of 3-SAT and 3-HornSAT$_C$ changes drastically while the complexity of CLIQUE remains unchanged.

Problems	Flat Specifications (boundary conditions) (U,U)N-specifications	2-D Periodic Specifications (boundary conditions) (N,N)N-specifications
3-SAT	NP-complete	undecidable
3-HornSAT$_C$	P	undecidable
CLIQUE	NP-complete	NP-complete

by polynomial time reducibility.) Indeed, Marathe et al. [380] have shown that the problems 3-SAT and 3-HornSAT$_C$ (weakly negative SAT when clauses can contain variables as well as constants) are *polynomial time inter-reducible*, when specified by several different kinds of succinct specifications. For example, they are both PSPACE-complete, both EXSPACE-complete, and even both undecidable, for certain specifications. In contrast, for other kinds of succinct specifications, such as two-dimensional periodic narrow finite specifications, 3-SAT is NEXPTIME-hard but 3-HornSAT$_C$ is DEXPTIME-hard. Interestingly, for each of these specifications the problem CLIQUE remains in NP. These results are summarized in table 2.

Thus, the results show that the specific method of constructing infinitary versions of standardly specified problems considered in Freedman [173] cannot be used to resolve the P versus NP question. In fact, our results suggest that many other infinitary extensions of combinatorial problems cannot be used to resolve the P versus NP question either, since they also fail to distinguish versions of certain basic NP- and P-complete problems. In other words, equivalence classes (degrees) induced by polynomial time or Turing reducibility are *not invariant*, across variant periodic specifications. In contrast, the results in Marathe et al. [380] and Hunt et al. [267, 268] show that local transformation-based (simultaneous) reductions and the degrees induced by such reductions may be the natural *morphisms* for complexity theory.

In addition, *none* of the very general structural extension properties discussed here for *strongly-local reductions*, hold for *simultaneous* linear time-, linear size-, and $O(\log n)$ space- bounded reductions. (To see this, just observe that a suitably $\Theta(n^2)$-padded version of 3-SAT is *simultaneously* linear time-, linear size-, and $O(\log n)$-space-bounded reducible to the problem CLIQUE, which remains NP-complete for various periodic specifications.)

Additional evidence for this is provided by the fact [267] that the *strongly-local reductions* as defined here are actually algebraic morphisms, or crypto-morphisms as defined in Birkhoff [54]. Given the central importance of the proper definition of morphisms in many areas of modern mathematics including topology, algebra, and dynamical systems, it seems reasonable to conjecture that a successful relation of the P versus NP question to other areas of mathematics—as alluded to in Freedman [172, 173]—will require appropriate definitions of *morphism* possessing *good* preservation properties with respect to various classes of instance specifications. This may turn out to be an important implication of the results discussed here and in Hunt et al. [267, 268] and Marathe et al. [376, 380].

Interestingly, constructing infinitary versions of standardly specified problems has been used successfully for showing that certain optimization problems do not belong to the class syntactic MAX-SNP: a class defined syntactically using an existential second-order formula [240]. The elegant results of Hirst and Harel [240] use an idea very similar to the one proposed in Freedman [172] to achieve this.

8   PERIODIC SATISFIABILITY FOREVER

The title of this section is influenced by papers of Savelsberg and van Emde Boas [454], van Emde Boas [509], and Harel [224]. They, as well as other authors [48, 82, 206], have elegantly articulated the use of tiling or domino problems for obtaining lower bounds, especially for decision problems for various logical theories. Here, we present several advantages of using periodically specified satisfiability problems over the use of domino problems in proving *both* hardness and easiness results.

Domino problems were introduced by Wang [515] and Büchi [82] and have been studied extensively in the literature [224, 454, 509]. Usually a *domino system* is described as a finite set of *tiles* or *dominoes*, each tile being of a fixed shape (e.g., unit square) with a fixed orientation and colored edges. We have an unlimited supply of copies of every tile. Technically, if one arbitrarily shapes tiles, then one does not need colors and vice-versa. A *domino problem* asks whether it is possible to tile a prescribed subset of the Cartesian plane with elements of a given domino system, such that adjacent tiles have matching colors on their common edges. There may also be certain constraints on the tiles that are allowed at specific places, such as the origin.

1. Quoting Harel [224]: *"Since all domino problems owe their complexity to the correspondence with Turing machine computations and since this correspondence applies to non-deterministic models as well, domino problems can apparently not distinguish between deterministic and non-deterministic classes."* In contrast, the hardness results for periodically specified generalized CNF satisfiability problems include complete problems for the deterministic classes P, DSPACE(n), DEXPTIME, DEXPSPACE(n), etc. For example, when instances are specified periodically with explicit boundary conditions, the hardness results for 3-HornSAT$_C$ imply that exactly analogous hardness results hold for the monotone circuit value problem, when instances are periodically

specified with boundary conditions. The last result can be used to prove that a number of P-complete problems become DSPACE(n)-, DEXPTIME-, or DEXPSPACE-complete when periodically specified. One such problem is linear programming feasibility.

2. It is natural to consider periodically specified formulas with clauses containing variables defined at times $t, t + c_1, t + c_2$, etc, where c_1 and c_2 are integers specified using binary numerals. Following Orlin [419], we say that such periodic specifications are *wide*. As stated earlier, periodic specifications only containing clauses in which all the variables are defined at times $t, t + 1$ and $t - 1$ are called *narrow*. In contrast, domino problems are based on adjacency, and thus, are intrinsically narrow. (It is, of course, possible to define consistency relationships between tiles that are far apart, but in general, this is not natural.) The hardness results for wide, periodically specified satisfiability problems imply exactly analogous results for a number of problems specified using wide periodic specifications. Furthermore, these results show that there can be a significant difference between the complexities of the narrow and wide periodically specified versions of the same problem.

3. As mentioned earlier, efficient local simultaneous reductions to/from the problems 3-SAT, NAE3-SAT, 2-SAT can be extended to efficient approximation preserving reductions to/from 3-SAT, NAE3-SAT, 2-SAT, when instances are specified by various kinds of periodic specifications considered here. These reductions, taken together with the easiness/hardness results, imply analogous easiness/hardness results for a number of variant problems for periodically specified problems in graph theory and logic. Developing analogous theory using tiling problems, although plausible, appears to be much more cumbersome.

This is not to say that tiling problems are not useful starting points, nor does it imply that they are not interesting. The simplicity of tiling problems certainly makes them a natural starting point for proving lower bounds.

9 CONCLUSIONS AND FUTURE WORK

We have discussed instances of graph and satisfiability problems created in natural and simple ways: namely, by repeating a single graph or formula in a multidimensional grid and then connecting vertices placed at given grid points to vertices placed at neighboring grid points. The size of large objects created in this way can be exponential, or even infinite, in the *size* of the object being replicated. In spite of the simple repetitive nature of the constructed object, the difficulty in solving certain NP-complete problems blows up with the size of the object being specified. Thus, several of these problems are NEXPTIME-complete or even undecidable when complexity is measured in the size of the original (periodic) description. However, at the same time, the simple repetitive nature enables us to design efficient polynomial time approximation algorithms with good performance guarantees *even when* complexity is measured in the size of the periodic specification. The complexity of approximation algorithms remains polynomial in the size of the description. Thus we have a striking contrast: problems that are NEXPTIME-complete to solve exactly can be efficiently approximated in polynomial time.

The fact that there is an exponential gap between solving the problem exactly and approximately for such succinctly specified objects may prove to be useful in trying to tackle other questions in complexity theory. For example, the results obtained in this chapter raise the possibility of proving the recent non-approximability results *without* using the machinery of interactive proof systems [21, 23]. Obtaining formal proofs that this is not possible is an equally interesting direction for future research.

The simplicity of the graph or formula obtained in the proof of theorem 5.2 makes it a good candidate for being specified using other kinds of succinct and recursive descriptions. In particular, it can be specified using graph construction representation (GCR) specifications [189, 190] and by the recursive specifications of Beigel and Gasarch [42]. This shows that natural problems specified using the GCR model are NEXPTIME-hard to solve and problems specified by very simple recursive graphs are undecidable. The GCR model is generally acknowledged as a natural and useful way of describing large real-world objects such as circuits and VLSI designs.

We have outlined a collection of techniques that are a step towards developing a predictive complexity theory for periodically specified problems. These ideas are in fact much more general; we believe that they can be used to develop a predictive complexity theory of succinctly specified problems. We refer the reader to Hunt et al. [267, 268] and Marathe [376] for additional details. Further general results for characterizing the approximability of PSPACE-hard and NEXPTIME-hard periodically specified problems is an interesting direction for future research. As an example, it is an open question if a dichotomy theorem such as the one for MAX-SAT(S) exists for the one-dimensional, finite, wide, periodically specified MAX-SAT(S) problem. We conclude with a brief discussion of two topics currently under investigation.

9.1 PERIODICALLY SPECIFIED RANDOM CONSTRAINT SATISFACTION PROBLEMS

Recently there has been substantial interest in understanding the phenomenon of phase transitions in satisfiability problems. See Istrate [270], Kirkpatrick and Selman [319], and Monasson et al. [406] for more details on the subject. Here we propose a method to construct random instances of periodic constraint satisfaction problems. Similar models can be given for periodically specified random graphs and other combinatorial objects. The model presented here is proposed in the hope that it will provide a hierarchy of locally random but globally structured instances of constraint satisfaction problems whose worst-case complexity is, for example, NP-hard, PSPACE-hard, or NEXPTIME-hard.

Recall that a periodic specification of a constraint satisfaction problem consists of two different parts: the static formula and the rule used to expand it. A natural way to construct a random instance is to construct a random instance of the static formula. For this, we have the four literals $x_i(t), \overline{x_i(t)},$ $x_i(t+1), \overline{x_1(t+1)}$ for each variable x_i. Call this the set X. We can now construct a random static 3-CNF formula as is done for standardly specified instances: namely, for each clause the three literals appearing in it are chosen uniformly at random from X (we ignore the technicalities of whether these literals are chosen with or without replacement). Note that as constructed, the static formulas can yield finite as well as infinite formulas depending on the particular periodic specification. It would be of interest to investigate the similarities (and differences) between the phase transition behavior of such finite and infinite formulas. The formalism is very rich and can be extended to construct other constraint satisfaction problems. It can also be applied to periodic specifications of higher dimensional objects. Defining wide specifications is more subtle. In such a case, we might decide to choose the index of difference at random.

We reiterate that an interesting aspect of such formulas is that they are *locally random but globally structured*; that is, the set of clauses in two consecutive grid points is chosen randomly, but this random set is repeated by a simple replication rule. Furthermore, note that we do not have to study exponentially large instances: specifying the range in unary yields a polynomially sized formula. By observing the proof given by Cook [191], it is easy to see that even such formulas are NP-hard to decide in the worst case. Investigating the phase transition behavior of such formulas is an interesting direction for further research.

9.2 LATTICE-LIKE INSTANCES FOR SATISFIABILITY PROBLEMS

There has been substantial interest in generating structured and random instances of satisfiability to test the efficacy of the SAT solvers proposed in the literature [6, 303]. In this context, physicists have long studied and developed methods inspired by statistical mechanics for understanding physical phenomena on lattice-like structures. Recently, methods inspired by statistical mechanics have also been proposed to solve constraint satisfaction problems, as has been seen in chapter 4. Periodically specified random constraint satisfaction problems, graph problems, and feasibility of system of linear/nonlinear inequalities are in a parametrized class of *lattice structured* problems and thus might serve as test cases for physics-inspired methods for solving such problems. The value of the formalism lies in the fact that one can construct a large number of variant problems by specifying a simple set of parameters. In addition, work done on quasi-group completion and related Latin square completion methods can be viewed as special instances of periodic satisfiability problems. One way to see this is that a Latin square completion method often starts with a consistent tiling of the grid and then randomly punches holes or, stated alternatively, removes some of the tiles. It then presents this satisfiable instance to SAT solvers. In view of the discussion on tiling and its relationship to periodic satisfiability problems, it is clear that periodic satisfiability problems offer a rich parameterized class of such instances. More interestingly, the method yields hard instances of higher complexity classes such as PSPACE and NEXPTIME. Such instances might be significant, given the close correspondence of periodically specified satisfiability problems to problems in temporal logics.

To see the close similarity of periodically specified formulas to Latin square completion methods for specifying satisfiable formulas, consider an alternate definition of periodically specified formulas proposed by Freedman [172, 173]. As an example, the infinite version of 3-SAT in Freedman [172] is obtained as follows: take a finitely generated group $\mathcal{G}$ and a subgroup $\mathcal{H}$ of $\mathcal{G}$, of finite index. The elements of $\mathcal{G}$ are our alphabet and a literal is a symbol g or $\overline{g} \in \mathcal{G}$. An instance of 3-SAT is specified as a conjunction of clauses of the form $(g'_1 \vee g'_2 \vee g'_3)$, where g'_i, $1 \leq i \leq 3$ denotes either a negated or an unnegated literal. Thus a 3-CNF formula will be given as $F = \bigwedge_{j=1}^{m}(g'_{1,j} \vee g'_{2,j} \vee g'_{3,j})$. The infinite instance is now created as follows:

$$F^{\mathbb{Z}} = \bigwedge_{h \in \mathcal{H}} \bigwedge_{j=1}^{m}((hg)'_{1,j} \vee (hg)'_{2,j} \vee (hg)_{3,j}).$$

Freedman considers the special cases $\mathcal{G} = \mathbb{Z}$ and $\mathcal{G} = \mathbb{Z} \oplus \mathbb{Z}$. In the latter case, he effectively considers four-way, infinite, wide formulas with periods (p_1, p_2) and thus $\mathcal{H} = \{(n_1 p_1, n_2 p_2) \mid n_1, n_2 \in \mathbb{Z}\}$. Assuming natural representations of integers, it is easy to see that these special cases are simply one-dimensional, two-way, infinite, wide periodic specifications and two-dimensional four-way infinite, wide, periodic wide specifications, denoted as $(\mathbb{Z})W$ and $(\mathbb{Z},\mathbb{Z})W$-specifications respectively. The $(\mathbb{Z},\mathbb{Z})N$-specifications considered here can be easily seen to be special cases with $p_1 = p_2 = 1$. Using the close correspondence between tilings and periodic formulas, it is now possible to generate satisfiable formulas with periodic solutions as well as satisfiable formulas that do not have periodic solutions. See Freedman [172] and Grunbaum and Shephard [216] for more details.

ACKNOWLEDGMENTS

We thank the editors for inviting us to include our results in this volume. We thank the referees and the editors of the volume for a careful reading of the manuscript and suggesting changes that have substantially improved the readability of the text. We thank S. Arora, A. Condon, J. Feigenbaum. D. Harel, G. Istrate, T. Lengauer, J. Orlin, V. Radhakrishnan, S. Ravi, S. Shukla, M. Sudan, and E. Wanke for valuable discussions and comments. The work presented here was partly motivated by the questions raised in Orlin [419] and Freedman [173].

Bibliography

1. Achlioptas, D. "Lower Bounds for Random 3-SAT via Differential Equations."
   Theor. Comp. Sci. 265 (2001): 159–186.
2. Achlioptas, D. "Setting Two Variables at a Time Yields a New Lower Bound
   for Random 3-SAT." In *Proceedings of the 32nd Annual ACM Symposium on
   Theory of Computing (STOC'00)*, 28–37. New York: ACM Press, 2000.
3. Achlioptas, D., and C. Moore. "The Asymptotic Order of the Random k-SAT
   Threshold." In *Proceedings of the 43rd Annual IEEE Symposium on Foundations of Computer Science (FOCS'02)*, 779–788. IEEE Computer Society,
   2002.
4. Achlioptas, D., and Y. Peres. "The Threshold for Random k-SAT is $2^k \ln 2 -
   O(k)$." In *Proceedings of the 35th Annual ACM Symposium on Theory of
   Computing (STOC'03)*, 223–231. New York: ACM Press, 2003.
5. Achlioptas, D., and G. B. Sorkin. "Optimal Myopic Algorithms for Random
   3-SAT." In *Proceedings of the 41st Annual Symposium on Foundations of
   Computer Science (FOCS'00)*, 590–600. IEEE Computer Society, 2000.

6. Achlioptas, D., C. Gomes, H. Kautz, and B. Selman. "Generating Satisfiable Problem Instances." In *Proceedings of the 17th National Conference on Artificial Intelligence (AAAI'00)*, 256–261. Menlo Park, CA: AAAI Press, 2000.

7. Achlioptas, D., A. Chtcherba, G. Istrate, and C. Moore. "The Phase Transition in 1-in-k SAT and NAE 3-SAT." In *Proceedings of the 12th Annual ACM-SIAM Symposium on Discrete Algorithms (SODA'01)*, 721–722. New York: ACM Press, 2001.

8. Achlioptas, D., L. M. Kirousis, E. Kranakis, and D. Krizanc. "Rigorous Results for Random $(2 + p)$-SAT." *Theor. Comp. Sci.* 265 (2001): 109–129.

9. Achlioptas, D., P. Beame, and M. Molloy. "A Sharp Threshold in Proof Complexity." In *Proceedings of the 33rd Annual ACM Symposium on Theory of Computing (STOC'01)*, 337–346. New York: ACM Press, 2001.

10. Agarwal, S., and A. Condon. "On Approximation Algorithms for Hierarchical MAX-SAT." *J. Algorithms* 26 (1998): 141–165.

11. Ajtai, M., J. Komlós, and E. Szemerédi. "Largest Random Component of a k-Cube." *Combinatorica* 2 (1982): 1–7.

12. Akahori, J. "Asymptotics of Hedging Errors in a Slightly Incomplete Discrete Market: A Noise-Sensitive Example." Preprint, 2002.
http://www.ritsumei.ac.jp/se/~akahori/papers/pp/slightly_incomplete.pdf (accessed September 27, 2005).

13. Aldous, D. "The Harmonic Mean Formula for Probabilities of Unions: Applications to Sparse Random Graphs." *Discrete Math.* 76 (1989): 167–176.

14. Alekhnovich, M., and E. Ben-Sasson. "Linear Upper Bounds for Random Walk on Small Density Random 3-CNFs." In *Proceedings of the 44th Annual Symposium on Foundations of Computer Science (FOCS'03)*, 352–361. IEEE Computer Society, 2003.

15. Aleksiejuk, A., J. A. Holyst, and D. Stauffer. "Ferromagnetic Phase Transition in Barabási–Albert Networks." *Physica A* 310 (2002): 260–266.

16. Alexander, S., and P. Pincus. "Phase Transitions of Some Fully Frustrated Models." *J. Phys. A: Math. Gen.* 13 (1980): 263–273.

17. Alon, N., and J. Spencer. *The Probabilistic Method.* New York: John Wiley & Sons, 1992.

18. Alon, N., I. Dinur, E. Friedgut, and B. Sudakov. "Graph Products, Fourier Analysis and Spectral Techniques." *Geom. Funct. Anal.* 14 (2004): 913–940.

19. Alur, R., and T. Henzinger. "A Really Temporal Logic." *J. ACM* 41 (1994): 181–204.

20. Arora, S., and S. Safra, "Probabilistic Checking of Proofs: A New Characterization of NP." *J. ACM* 45 (1998): 70–122.

21. Arora, S., C. Lund, R. Motwani, M. Sudan, and M. Szegedy. "Proof Verification and Intractability of Approximation Problems." *J. ACM* 45 (1998): 501–555.

22. Arrow, K. "A Difficulty in the Theory of Social Welfare." *J. Pol. Econ.* 58 (1950): 328–346.

23. Ausiello, G., P. Crescenzi, G. Gambosi, V. Kann, A. Marchetti-Spaccamela, and M. Protasi. *Complexity and Approximation: Combinatorial Optimization Problems and Their Approximability Properties.* Berlin: Springer-Verlag, 1999.

24. Bak, P., C. Tang, and K. Wiesenfeld. "Self-Organized Criticality: An Explanation of the 1/f Noise." *Phys. Rev. Lett.* 59 (1987): 381–384.

25. Baker, B. S. "Approximation Algorithms for NP-Complete Problems on Planar Graphs." *J. ACM* 41 (1994): 153–180.

26. Bálcazar, J. L., A. Lozano, and J. Toran. "The Complexity of Algorithmic Problems for Succinct Instances." In *Computer Science*, ed. R. Baeza-Yates, 351–377. New York: Plenum Press, 1992.

27. Baptista, L., and J. P. Marques-Silva. "Using Randomization and Learning to Solve Hard Real-World Instances of Satisfiability." In *Proceedings of the Sixth International Conference on Principles and Practice of Constraint Programming (CP 2000)*, ed. R. Dechter, 489–494. Lecture Notes in Computer Science, vol. 1894. Berlin: Springer-Verlag, 2000.

28. Barabási, A. L., and R. Albert. "Emergence of Scaling in Random Networks." *Science* 286 (1999): 509–512.

29. Barabási, A.-L., and H. E. Stanley. *Fractal Concepts in Surface Growth.* Cambridge, UK: Cambridge University Press, 1995.

30. Barabási, A. L., R. Albert, and H. Jeong. "Mean-Field Theory for Scale-Free Random Networks." *Physica A* 272 (1999): 173–187.

31. Barahona, F. "On the Computational Complexity of Ising Spin Glass Models." *J. Phys. A* 15 (1982): 3241–3253.

32. Barahona, F., R. Maynard, R. Rammal, and J. P. Uhry. "Morphology of Ground States of Two-Dimensional Frustration Model." *J. Phys. A: Math. Gen.* 15 (1982): 673–699.

33. Barg, A. "Complexity Issues in Coding Theory." In *Handbook of Coding Theory*, vol. 1, ed. V. S. Pless and W. C. Huffman, 649–754. Amsterdam: Elsevier Science, 1998.

34. Barrat, A., and M. Weigt. "On the Properties of Small-World Network Models." *Eur. Phys. J. B* 13 (2000): 547–560.

35. Barthe, F., P. Cattiaux, C. Roberto. "Interpolation Inequalities between Exponential and Gaussian, Orlicz Hypercontractivity and Applications to Isoperimetry." *Revista Mat. Iberoamericana* (2005): to appear.

36. Barthel, W., A. Hartmann, and M. Weigt. "Solving Satisfiability Problems by Fluctuations: An Approximate Description of the Dynamics of Stochastic Local Search Algorithms." *Phys. Rev. E* 67 (2003): 066104.

37. Bauer, M., and O. Golinelli. "Core Percolation in Random Graphs: A Critical Phenomena Analysis." *Eur. Phys. J. B* 24 (2001): 339–352.

38. Bauke, H., S. Mertens, and A. Engel. "Phase Transition in Multiprocessor Scheduling." *Phys. Rev. Lett.* 90 (2003): 158701.

39. Beame, P., R. Karp, T. Pitassi, and M. Saks. "The Efficiency of Resolution and Davis-Putnam Procedures." *SIAM J. Comp.* 31 (2002): 1048–1075.

Preliminary version in *Proceedings of the 30th Annual ACM Symposium on Theory of Computing (STOC'98)*, 561–571. New York: ACM Press, 1998.

40. Beckner, W. "Inequalities in Fourier Analysis." *Ann. Math.* 102 (1975): 159–182.

41. Beeri, C., and P. A. Bernstein. "Computational Problems Related to the Design of Normal Form Relational Schemas." In *ACM Trans. Database Systems (TODS'79)*, 30–59. New York: ACM Press, 1979.

42. Beigel, R., and W. I. Gasarch. "On the Complexity of Finding the Chromatic Number of Recursive Graphs: Parts I and II." *Ann. Pure. Appl. Logic* 45 (1989): 1–38; 227–247.

43. Bellare, M., O. Goldreich, and M. Sudan. "Free Bits, PCPs, and Non-approximability—Towards Tight Results." *SIAM J. Comp.* 27 (1998): 804–915.

44. Benjamini, I., G. Kalai, and O. Schramm. "First Passage Percolation has Sublinear Distance Variance." *Ann. Probab.* 31 (2003): 1970–1978.

45. Benjamini, I., G. Kalai, and O. Schramm. "Noise Sensitivity of Boolean Functions and Applications to Percolation." *Publ. I.H.E.S.* 90 (1999): 5–43.

46. Ben-Or, M., and N. Linial. "Collective Coin Flipping." In *Randomness and Computation*, ed. S. Micali, 91–115. New York: Academic Press, 1990.

47. Berg, B. A., U. E. Hansmann, and T. Celik. "Ground-State Properties of the Three-Dimensional Ising Spin Glass." *Phys. Rev. B* 50 (1994): 16444–16452.

48. Berger, R. "The Undecidability of the Domino Problem." *Mem. Amer. Math. Soc.* 66 (1966).

49. Berlekamp, E. R., R. J. McEliece, and H. C. A. van Tilborg. "On the Inherent Intractability of Certain Coding Problems." *IEEE Trans. Inf. Theory* 24 (1978): 384–386.

50. Bernstein, A. J. "Maximally Connected Arrays on the *n*-Cube." *SIAM J . Appl. Math.* 15 (1967): 1485–1489.

51. Bianconi, G. "Mean Field Solution of the Ising Model on a Barabási–Albert Network." *Phys. Lett. A* 303 (2002): 166–168.

52. Bieche, L., J. P. Uhry, R. Maynard, and R. Rammal. "On the Ground States of the Frustration Model of a Spin Glass by a Matching Method of Graph Theory." *J. Phys. A: Math Gen.* 13 (1980): 2553–2576.

53. Binder, K., and D. W. Herrmann. *Monte Carlo Simulation in Statistical Physics.* Berlin: Springer-Verlag, 1988

54. Birkhoff, G. *Lattice Theory*, 3d ed. Providence, RI: American Mathematics Society, 1966.

55. Biroli, G., and R. Monasson. "From Inherent Structures to Pure States: Some Simple Remarks and Examples." *Europhys. Lett.* 50 (2000): 155–161.

56. Biroli, G., R. Monasson, and M. Weigt. "A Variational Description of the Ground State Structure in Random Satisfiability Problems." *Eur. Phys. J. B* 14 (2000): 551–568.

57. Boettcher, S. Personal communication.

58. Boettcher, S., and M. Grigni. "Jamming Model for the Extremal Optimization Heuristic." *J. Phys. A* 35 (2002): 1109–1123.

59. Boettcher, S., and A. G. Percus. "Extremal Optimization at the Phase Transition of the Three-Coloring Problem." *Phys. Rev. E* 69 (2004): 066703.

60. Boettcher, S., and A. G. Percus. "Nature's Way of Optimizing." *Art. Intel.* 119 (2000): 275–286.

61. Boettcher, S., and A. G. Percus. "Optimization with Extremal Dynamics." *Phys. Rev. Lett.* 86 (2001): 5211–5214.

62. Bollobás, B. *Random Graphs*, 2d ed. Cambridge, UK: Cambridge University Press, 2001.

63. Bollobás, B., and S. Rasmussen. "First Cycles in Random Directed Graph Processes." *Discrete Math.* 75 (1989): 55–68.

64. Bollobás, B., and O. Riordan. "The Critical Probability for Random Voronoi Percolation in the Plane is 1/2." arXiv.org E-print Archive, Cornell University Library, 2004. http://arxiv.org/abs/math.PR/0410336 (accessed September 27, 2005).

65. Bollobás, B., and O. Riordan. "A Short Proof of the Harris-Kesten Theorem." arXiv.org E-print Archive, Cornell University Library, 2004. http://arxiv.org/abs/math.PR/0410359 (accessed September 27, 2005).

66. Bollobás, B., and A. Thomason. "Threshold Functions." *Combinatorica* 7 (1987): 35–38.

67. Bollobás, B., C. Borgs, J. T. Chayes, J. H. Kim, and D. B. Wilson. "The Scaling Window of the 2-SAT Transition." *Rand. Struct. & Algorithms* 18 (2001): 201–256.

68. Bonami, A. "Etude des Coefficients Fourier des Fonctiones de $L^p(G)$." *Ann. Inst. Fourier* 20 (1970): 335–402.

69. Boppana, R. "The Average Sensitivity of Bounded Depth Circuits." *Inf. Proc. Lett.* 63 (1997): 257–261.

70. Boppana, R. "Threshold Functions and Bounded Depth Monotone Circuits." In *Proceedings of the 16th Annual ACM Symposium on Theory of Computing (STOC'84)*, 475–479. New York: ACM Press, 1984.

71. Borgs, C., J. Chayes, and B. Pittel. "Phase Transition and Scaling Window for the Integer Partitioning Problem." *Rand. Struct. & Algorithms* 19 (2001): 247–288.

72. Borgs, C., J. T. Chayes, S. Mertens, and B. Pittel. "Phase Diagram for the Constrained Integer Partitioning Problem." *Rand. Struct. & Algorithms* 24 (2004): 315–380.

73. Bourgain, J. "On Sharp Thresholds of Monotone Properties, Appendix to E. Friedgut. "Sharp Thresholds of Graphs Properties, and the k-SAT Problem."" *J. Amer. Math. Soc.* 12 (1999): 1017–1054.

74. Bourgain, J., and G. Kalai. "Influences of Variables and Threshold Intervals under Group Symmetries." *Geom. Funct. Anal.* 7 (1997): 438–461.

75. Bourgain, J., J. Kahn, G. Kalai, Y. Katznelson, and N. Linial. "The Influence of Variables in Product Spaces." *Israel J. Math.* 77 (1992): 55–64.

76. Boyer, M., G. Brassard, P. Høyer, and A. Tapp. "Tight Bounds on Quantum Searching." In *Proceedings of the Workshop on Physics and Computation (PhysComp'96)*, 36–43. Cambridge, MA: New England Complex Systems Institute, 1996.

77. Brassard, G., P. Høyer, and A. Tapp. "Quantum Counting." In *Proceedings of the 25th International Colloquium on Automata, Languages, and Programming (ICALP'98)*, ed. K. Larsen, 820–831. Berlin: Springer, 1998.

78. Braunstein, A., R. Mulet, A. Pagnani, M. Weigt, and R. Zecchina. "Polynomial Iterative Algorithms for Coloring and Analyzing Random Graphs." *Phys. Rev. E* 68 (2003): 036702.

79. Braunstein, A., M. Mézard, and R. Zecchina. "Survey Propagation: An Algorithm for Satisfiability." *Rand. Struct. & Algorithms* 27 (2005): 201–226.

80. Broadbent, S. R., and J. M. Hammersley. "Percolation Processes: I. Crystals and Mazes." *Proc. Cambridge Phil. Soc.* 53 (1957): 629–641.

81. Broder, A. Z., A. Frieze, and E. Upfal. "On the Satisfiability and Maximum Satisfiability of Random 3-CNF Formulas." In *Proceedings of the 4th Annual ACM-SIAM Symposium on Discrete Algorithms (SODA'93)*, 322–330. New York: ACM Press, 1993.

82. Büchi, J. R. "Turing Machines and the Entscheidungsproblem." *Math. Ann.* 148 (1962): 201–213.

83. Burgers, M. *The Nonlinear Diffusion Equation*. Boston: Riedel, 1974.

84. Cech, T. R. "RNA As An Enzyme." *Sci. Am.* 255(5) (1986): 64–75.

85. Cech, T. R. "Self-Splicing RNA: Implications for Evolution." *Intl. Rev. Cytology* 93 (1985): 3–22.

86. Cerf, N. J., L. K. Grover, and C. P. Williams. "Nested Quantum Search and NP-Complete Problems." *Applicable Algebra in Engineering, Communication and Computing* 10 (2000): 311–338.

87. Chandy, K. M., and J. Misra. "Asynchronous Distributed Simulation via a Sequence of Parallel Computations." *Comm. ACM* 24 (1981): 198–206.

88. Chao, M. T., and J. Franco. "Probabilistic Analysis of a Generalization of the Unit-Clause Literal Selection Heuristics for the k-Satisfiability Problem." *Inf. Sci.* 51 (1990): 289–314.

89. Chao, M. T., and J. Franco. "Probabilistic Analysis of Two Heuristics for the 3-Satisfiability Problem." *SIAM J. Comp.* 15 (1986): 1106–1118.

90. Chayes, J. T., L. Chayes, D. S. Fisher, and T. Spencer. "Finite-Size Scaling and Correlation Length for Disordered Systems." *Phys. Rev. Lett.* 57 (1986): 2999–3002.

91. Cheeseman, P., B. Kanefsky, and W. M. Taylor. "Where the *Really* Hard Problems Are." In *Proceedings of the Twelfth International Joint Conference on Artificial Intelligence (IJCAI'91)*, ed. J. Mylopoulos and R. Rediter, 331–337. San Mateo, CA: Morgan Kaufmann, 1991.
Morgan Kaufmann, 1991.

92. Cheung, H.-F., and W. L. McMillan. "Equilibrium Properties of a Two-Dimensional Random Ising Model with a Continuous Distribution of Interactions." *J. Phys. C: Solid State Phys.* 16 (1983): 7027–7032.

93. Chung, S.-Y., G. D. Forney, Jr., T. J. Richardson, and R. Urbanke. "On the Design of Low-Density Parity-Check Codes within 0.0045 dB of the Shannon Limit." *IEEE Comm. Lett.* 5 (2001): 58–60.

94. Chvátal, V., and B. Reed. "Mick Gets Some (the Odds are on His Side)." In *Proceedings of the 32nd Annual IEEE Symposium on Foundations of Computer Science (FOCS'92)*, 620–627. IEEE Computer Society, 1992.

95. Chvátal, V., and E. Szemerédi. "Many Hard Examples for Resolution." *J. ACM* 35 (1988): 759–768.

96. Coarfa, C., D. D. Demopoulos, A. San Miguel Aguirre, D. Subramanian, and M. Y. Vardi. "Random 3-SAT: The Plot Thickens." In *Proceedings of the Sixth International Conference on Principles and Practice of Constraint Programming (CP 2000)*, ed. R. Dechter, 143–159. Lecture Notes in Computer Science, vol. 1894. Berlin: Springer-Verlag, 2000.

97. Cocco, S., and R. Monasson. "Analysis of the Computational Complexity of Solving Random Satisfiability Problems using Branch and Bound Search Algorithms." *Eur. Phys. J. B* 22 (2001): 505–531.

98. Cocco, S., and R. Monasson. "Exponentially Hard Problems are Sometimes Polynomial, A Large Deviation Analysis of Search Algorithms for the Random Satisfiability Problem, and Its Application to Stop-and-Restart Resolutions." *Phys. Rev. E* 66 (2002): 037101.

99. Cocco, S., and R. Monasson. "Restarts and Exponential Acceleration of the Davis-Putnam-Loveland-Logemann Algorithm. A Large Deviation Analysis of the Generalized Unit Clause Heuristic for Random 3-SAT." *Ann. Math. & Art. Intel.* 43 (2005): 153–172.

100. Cocco, S., and R. Monasson. "Trajectories in Phase Diagrams, Growth Processes and Computational Complexity: How Search Algorithms Solve the 3-Satisfiability Problem." *Phys. Rev. Lett.* 86 (2001): 1654–1657.

101. Cocco, S., O. Dubois, J. Mandler, and R. Monasson. "Rigorous Decimation-Based Construction of Ground Pure States for Spin Glass Models on Random Lattices." *Phys. Rev. Lett.* 90 (2003): 047205.

102. Coffman, E., and G. S. Lueker. *Probabilistic Analysis of Packing and Partitioning Algorithms.* New York: John Wiley & Sons, 1991.

103. Cohen, E., and N. Megiddo. "Recognizing Properties of Dynamic Graphs." In *Applied Geometry and Discrete Mathematics, The Victor Klee Festschrift*, ed. P. Gritzmann and B. Strumfels, 135–146. New York: ACM, 1991.

104. Cohen, E., and N. Megiddo. "Strongly Polynomial-time and NC Algorithms for Detecting Cycles in Dynamic Graphs." *J. ACM* 40 (1993): 791–830.

105. Computer Industry Almanac Inc. Home Page. http://www.c-i-a.com/ (accessed September 27, 2005).

106. Condon, A. "Approximate Solutions to Problems in PSPACE." *ACM SIGACT News* 26(2) (1995): 4–13.

107. Condon, A., J. Feigenbaum, C. Lund, and P. Shor. "Probabilistically Checkable Debate Systems and Approximation Algorithms for PSPACE-Hard Functions." *Chicago J. Theor. Comp. Sci.* (1995): Article no. 4.

108. Condon, A., J. Feigenbaum, C. Lund, and P. Shor. "Random Debaters and the Hardness of Approximating Stochastic Functions." *SIAM J. Comp.* 26 (1997): 369–400.

109. Cook, S. "The Complexity of Theorem-Proving Procedures." In *Proceedings of the 3rd Annual ACM Symposium on Theory of Computing (STOC'71)*, 151–158. New York: ACM Press, 1971.

110. Crawford, J. M., and L. D. Auton. "Experimental Results on the Crossover Point in Random 3-SAT." *Art. Intel.* 81 (1996): 31–57.

111. Creignou, N. "A Dichotomy Theorem for Maximum Generalized Satisfiability Problems." *J. Comp. Syst. Sci.* 51 (1995): 511–522.

112. Creignou, N., and H. Daudé. "Satisfiability Threshold for Random XOR-CNF Formulae." *Discrete Appl. Math.* 96/97 (1999): 41–53.

113. Creignou, N., S. Khanna, and M. Sudan. "Complexity Classifications of Boolean Constraint Satisfaction Problems." *SIGACT News* 32(4) (2001): 24–33.

114. Cugliandolo, L. F. "Dynamics of Glassy Systems." Lecture notes, Les Houches, July 2002. arXiv.org E-print Archive, Cornell University Library, 2002. http://arxiv.org/abs/cond-mat/0210312 (accessed September 27, 2005).

115. Dantzig, G., W. Blattner, and M. Rao. "Finding a Cycle in a Graph with Minimum Cost to Time Ratio with Application to a Ship Routing Problem." In *Theory of Graphs: International Symposium*, ed. P. Rosenstieh, 77–84. New York: Gordon and Breach, 1967.

116. Darling, R. W. R., and J. R. Norris. "Structure of Large Random Hypergraphs." *Ann. Appl. Prob.* 15 (2005): 125–152.

117. Davis, M., and H. Putnam. "A Computing Procedure for Quantification Theory." *J. ACM* 7 (1960): 201–215.

118. Davis, M., G. Logemann, and D. Loveland. "A Machine Program for Theorem Proving." *Comm. ACM* 5 (1962): 394–397.

119. Dean, D. S. "Metastable States of Spin Glasses on Random Thin Graphs." *Eur. Phys. J. B* 15 (2000): 493–498.

120. Derrida, B., Y. Pomeau, G. Toulouse, and J. Vannimenus. "Fully Frustrated Simple Cubic Lattices and the Overblocking Effect." *J. Physique* 40 (1979): 617–626.

121. De Simone, C., M. Diehl, M. Jünger, P. Mutzel, G. Reinelt, and G. Rinaldi. "Exact Ground States of Ising Spin Glasses: New Experimental Results with a Branch-and-Cut Algorithm." *J. Stat. Phys.* 80 (1995): 487–496.

122. De Simone, C., M. Diehl, M. Jünger, P. Mutzel, G. Reinelt, and G. Rinaldi. "Exact Ground States of Two-Dimensional $\pm J$ Ising Spin Glasses." *J. Stat. Phys.* 84 (1996): 1363–1371.

123. Deutsch, D. "Quantum Theory, the Church-Turing Principle and the Universal Quantum Computer." *Proc. Roy. Soc. Lond. A* 400 (1985): 97–117.

124. Devlin, K. *The Millenium Problems: The Seven Greatest Unsolved Mathematical Puzzles of our Time.* New York: Basic Books, 2002.

125. Dinur, I., and S. Safra. "On the Hardness of Approximating Minimum Vertex Cover." *Ann. Math.* 162 (2005): 439–486. Preliminary version in *Proceedings of the 34th Annual ACM Symposium on Theory of Computing (STOC'02)*, 33–42. New York: ACM Press, 2002.

126. DiVincenzo, D. P. "Quantum Computation." *Science* 270 (1995): 255–261.

127. Dorogovtsev, S. N., A. V. Goltsev, and J. F. F. Mendes. "Ising Model on Networks with an Arbitrary Distribution Of Connections." *Phys. Rev. E* 66 (2002): 016104.

128. Dowling, W. F., and J. H. Gallier. "Linear-Time Algorithms for Testing the Satisfiability of Propositional Horn Formulae." *J. Logic Programming* 1 (1984): 267–284.

129. Dubois, O. "Upper Bounds on the Satisfiability Threshold." *Theor. Comp. Sci.* 265 (2001): 187–197.

130. Dubois, O., and Y. Boufkhad. "A General Upper Bound for the Satisfiability Threshold of Random *r*-SAT Formulae." *J. Algorithms* 24 (1997): 395–420.

131. Dubois, O., and J. Mandler. "The 3-XORSAT Threshold." In *Proceedings of the 43rd Annual IEEE Symposium on Foundations of Computer Science (FOCS'02)*, 769–778. IEEE Computer Society, 2002.

132. Dubois, O., Y. Boufkhad, and J. Mandler. "Typical Random 3-SAT Formulae and the Satisfiability Threshold." In *Proceedings of the 11th Annual ACM-SIAM Symposium on Discrete Algorithms (SODA'00)*, 126–127. New York: ACM Press, 2000.

133. Dubois, O., R. Monasson, B. Selman, and R. Zecchina, eds. "Phase Transitions in Combinatorial Problems." *Theor. Comp. Sci.* 265 (2001): 1.

134. Dubois, O., Y. Boufkhad, and J. Mandler. "Typical Random 3-SAT Formulae and the Satisfiability Threshold." Report TR03-007, Electronic Colloquium on Computational Complexity, 2003.

135. Duchet, P. "Hypergraphs." In *Handbook of Combinatorics*, ed. R. Graham, M. Grötschel, and L. Lovász. Amsterdam: Elsevier Science, 1995.

136. Dyer, M. E., A. M. Frieze, and S. Suen. "Ordering Clone Libraries in Computational Biology." *J. Comp. Biol.* 2 (1995): 207–218.

137. Eastman, W. L. "Linear Programming with Pattern Constraints." Ph.D. thesis, Computation Laboratory, Harvard University, Cambridge, MA, 1958.

138. Edelkamp, S., and R. E. Korf. "The Branching Factor of Regular Search Spaces." In *Proceedings of the 15th National Conference on Artificial Intelligence (AAAI'98)*, 299–304. Menlo Park, CA: AAAI Press, 1998.

139. Edmonds, J. "Maximum Matchings and a Polyhedron with 0,1-Vertices." *J. Res. Nat'l. Bureau of Standards (Section B)* 69B (1965): 125–130.

140. Edmonds, J. "Paths, Trees and Flowers." *Canad. J. Math.* 17 (1965): 449–467.

141. Edwards, S. F., and P. W. Anderson. "Theory of Spin Glasses." *J. Phys. F: Metal Phys.* 5 (1975): 965–974.

142. Ein-Dor, L., and R. Monasson. "The Dynamics of Proving Uncolorability of Large Random Graphs: I. Symmetric Coloring Heuristic." *J. Phys. A: Math. Gen.* 36 (2003) 11055-11067.

143. Ellington, A. D. "Aptamers Achieve the Desired Recognition." *Curr. Biol.* 4 (1994): 427–429.

144. Ellington, A. D., and J. W. Szostak. "*In Vitro* Selection of RNA Molecules that Bind Specific Ligands." *Nature* 346 (1990): 818–822.

145. El Maftouhi, M., and W. Fernandez de la Vega. "On Random 3-SAT." *Comb. Prob. & Comp.* 4 (1995): 190–195.

146. Engel, A., and C. van den Broeck. *Statistical Mechanics of Learning.* Cambridge, UK: Cambridge University Press, 2001.

147. Erdős, P., and A. Rényi. "On the Evolution of Random Graphs." *Publ. Math. Inst. Hung. Acad. Sci.* 5 (1960): 17–61.

148. Erdős, P., and A. Rényi. "On Random Graphs I." *Publ. Math. Debrecen* 6 (1959): 290–297.

149. Fabrikant, A., and T. Hogg. "Graph Coloring with Quantum Heuristics." In *Proceedings of the 18th National Conference on Artificial Intelligence (AAAI'02)*, 22–27. Menlo Park, CA: AAAI Press, 2002.

150. Falik, D., and A. Samorodnitsky. "A Combinatorial Proof for a Theorem of Kahn, Kalai, and Linial and Some Applications." Preprint, 2005.

151. Farhi, E., J. Goldstone, S. Gutmann, J. Lapan, A. Lundgren, and D. Preda. "A Quantum Adiabatic Evolution Algorithm Applied to Random Instances of an NP-Complete Problem." *Science* 292 (2001): 472–476.

152. Feddersen, T., and W. Pesendorfer. "Convicting the Innocent: The Inferiority of Unanimous Jury Verdicts under Strategic Voting." *Amer. Pol. Sci. Rev.* 92 (1998): 23–35.

153. Feige, U. "A Threshold of ln n for Approximating Set Cover." *J. ACM* 45 (1998): 634–652.

154. Feigenbaum, J. "Games, Complexity Classes and Approximation Algorithms." Invited talk at the *International Congress on Mathematics,* Berlin, 1998.

155. Felderman, R. E., and L. Kleinrock. "Bounds and Approximations for Self-Initiating Distributed Simulation without Lookahead." *ACM Trans. Model. Comp. Simul.* 1 (1991): 386–406.

156. Fernandez de la Vega, W. "On Random 2-SAT." Unpublished manuscript, 1992.

157. Ferreira, F., and J. Fontanari. "Probabilistic Analysis of the Number Partitioning Problem." *J. Phys. A* 31 (1998): 3417–3428.

158. Feynman, R. P. *Feynman Lectures on Computation.* Reading, MA: Addison-Wesley, 1996.

159. Fisher, M. E. "The Theory of Equilibrium Critical Phenomena." *Rep. Prog. Phys.* 30 (1967): 615–730.

160. Flamm, C., I. L. Hofacker, and P. F. Stadler. "RNA *In Silico:* The Computational Biology of RNA Secondary Structures." *Adv. Compl. Syst.* 2 (1999): 65–90.

161. Fleischer, L. "Faster Algorithms for Quickest Transshipment Problem with Zero Transit Time." *SIAM J. Optimization* 12 (2001): 18–35.

162. Foltin, G., K. Oerding, Z. Rácz, R. L. Workman, and R. K. P. Zia. "Width Distribution for Random-Walk Interfaces." *Phys. Rev. E* 50 (1994): R639–R642.

163. Ford, L. R., and D. R. Fulkerson. "Constructing Maximal Dynamic Flows from Static Flows." *Oper. Res.* 6 (1958): 419–433.

164. Ford, L. R., and D. R. Fulkerson. *Flows in Networks*, 419–433. Princeton, NJ: Princeton University Press, 1958.

165. Forst, C. V., C. M. Reidys, and J. Weber. "Evolutionary Dynamics and Optimization: Neutral Networks as Model Landscapes for RNA Secondary Structure Landscapes." In *Advances in Artificial Life, Third European Conference on Artificial Life (ECAL 1995)*, ed. F. Morán, A. Moreno, J. J. Merelo Guervós, and P. Chacón, 128–147. Lecture Notes in Artificial Intelligence, vol. 929. New York: Springer Verlag, 1995.

166. Franco, J. "Probabilistic Analysis of the Pure Literal Heuristic for the Satisfiability Problem." *Ann. Oper. Res.* 1 (1984): 273–289.

167. Franco, J., and M. Paull. "Probabilistic Analysis of the Davis-Putnam Procedure for Solving the Satisfiability Problem." *Discrete Appl. Math.* 5 (1983): 77–87.

168. Frank, J., P. Cheeseman, and J. Stutz. "When Gravity Fails: Local Search Topology." *J. Art. Intel. Res.* 7 (1997): 249–281.

169. Franz, S., M. Leone, A. Montanari, and F. Ricci-Tersenghi. "The Dynamic Phase Transition for Decoding Algorithms." *Phys. Rev. E* 66 (2002): 046120.

170. Franz, S., M. Leone, F. Ricci-Tersenghi, and R. Zecchina. "Exact Solutions for Diluted Spin Glasses and Optimization Problems." *Phys. Rev. Lett.* 87 (2001): 127209.

171. Fraser, S. M. Private communication, 1997.

172. Freedman, M. "*k*-SAT on Groups and Undecidability." In *Proceedings of the 30th Annual ACM Symposium on Theory of Computing (STOC'98)*, 572–576. New York: ACM Press, 1998.

173. Freedman, M. "Limits, Logic and Computation." *PNAS* 95 (1998): 95–97.

174. Freuder, Eugene C., and Richard J. Wallace. "Partial Constraint Satisfaction." *Art. Intel.* 58 (1992): 21–70.

175. Friedgut, E. "Boolean Functions with Low Average Sensitivity Depend on Few Coordinates." *Combinatorica* 18 (1998): 27–35.

176. Friedgut, E. "Hunting for Sharp Thresholds." *Rand. Struct. & Algorithms.* 26(1-2) (2005): 37–51.

177. Friedgut, E. "Sharp Thresholds of Graph Properties, and the *k*-SAT Problem." *J. Amer. Math. Soc.* 12 (1999): 1017–1054.

178. Friedgut, E., and G. Kalai. "Every Monotone Graph Property Has a Sharp Threshold." *Proc. Amer. Math. Soc.* 124 (1996): 2993–3002.

179. Friedgut, E., J. Kahn, and A. Wigderson. "Computing Graph Properties by Randomized Subcube Partitions." In *Randomization and Approximation*

Techniques in Computer Science, 6th International Workshop (RANDOM 2002), 105–113. Berlin: Springer-Verlag, 2002.

180. Frieze, A. M. "On the Independence Number of Random Graphs." *Discrete Math.* 81 (1990): 171.

181. Frieze, A. M., and B. V. Halldórsson. "Optimal Sequencing by Hybridization in Rounds." *J. Comp. Biol.* 9 (2002): 355–369.

182. Frieze, A., and S. Suen. "Analysis of Two Simple Heuristics on a Random Instance of k-SAT." *J. Algorithms* 20 (1996): 312–335.

183. Frieze, A., and N. C. Wormald. "Random k-SAT: A Tight Threshold for Moderately Growing k." In *Proceedings of the 5th International Symposium on the Theory and Applications of Satisfiability Testing (SAT 2002)*, 1–6. University of Cincinnati, 2002. Available at http://gauss.ececs.uc.edu/Conferences/SAT2002/sat2002list.html (accessed September 27, 2005).

184. Frieze, A. M., F. P. Preparata, and E. Upfal. "Optimal Reconstruction of a Sequence from Its Probes." *J. Comp. Biol.* 6 (1999): 361–368.

185. Fu, Y. "The Use and Abuse of Statistical Mechanics in Computational Complexity." In *Lectures in the Sciences of Complexity*, ed. D. L. Stein, 815–826. Santa Fe Institute Studies in the Sciences of Complexity Series, vol. 1. Reading, MA: Addison-Wesley, 1989.

186. Fujimoto, R. "Parallel Discrete Event Simulation." *Commun. ACM* 33 (1990): 30–53.

187. Galambos, J. *The Asymptotic Theory of Extreme Order Statistics*. Malabar, Florida: Robert E. Krieger Publishing Co., 1987.

188. Gallager, R. G. *Low Density Parity-Check Codes*. Cambridge, MA: MIT Press, 1963.

189. Galperin, H. "Succinct Representation of Graphs." Ph.D. thesis, Princeton University, 1982.

190. Galperin, H., and A. Wigderson. "Succinct Representation of Graphs." *Information and Control* 56 (1983): 183–198.

191. Garey, M. R., and D. S. Johnson. *Computers and Intractability. A Guide to the Theory of NP-Completeness*. New York: W.H. Freeman, 1997 .

192. Gasper, G., and M. Rahman. *Basic Hypergeometric Series*, 2d ed. Encyclopedia of Mathematics and Its Applications, vol. 96. Cambridge, UK: Cambridge University Press, 2004.

193. Gazmuri, P. G. "Independent Sets in Random Sparse Graphs." *Networks* 14 (1984): 367–377.

194. Gent, I. P., and T. Walsh. "Phase Transitions and Annealed Theories: Number Partitioning as a Case Study." In *Proceedings of ECAI-96*, ed. W. Wahlster, 170–174. New York: John Wiley & Sons, 1996.

195. Gent, I. P., E. MacIntyre, P. Prosser, and T. Walsh. "The Constrainedness of Search." In *Proceedings of the 13th National Conference on Artificial Intelligence (AAAI'96)*, 246–252. Menlo Park, CA: AAAI Press, 1996.

196. Gent, I., H. van Maaren, and T. Walsh, eds. *SAT2000: Highlights of Satisfiability Research in the Year 2000.* Frontiers in Artificial Intelligence and Applications, vol. 63. Amsterdam: IOS Press, 2000.

197. Gitterman, M. "Small-World Phenomena in Physics: The Ising Model." *J. Phys. A* 33 (2000): 8373–8381.

198. Global Grid Forum. Home Page. http://www.gridforum.org (accessed September 27, 2005).

199. Goemans, M. X., and D. P. Williamson. ".878 Approximation Algorithms for MAX CUT and MAX 2SAT." In *Proceedings of the 26th Annual ACM Symposium on Theory of Computing (STOC'94)*, 422–431. New York: ACM Press, 1994.

200. Goemans, M. X., and D. P. Williamson. "Improved Approximation Algorithms for Maximum Cut and Satisfiability Problems using Semidefinite Programming." *J. ACM* 42 (1995): 1115–1145.

201. Goerdt, A. "A Threshold for Unsatisfiability." In *Proceedings of the 17th Symposium on Mathematical Foundations of Computer Science (MFCS'92)*, ed. I. M. Havel and V. Koubek, 264–274. Lecture Notes in Computer Science, vol. 629. Berlin: Springer-Verlag, 1992.

202. Goerdt, A. "A Threshold for Unsatisfiability." *J. Comp. Syst. Sci.* 53 (1996): 469–486.

203. Goldberg, A. "On the Complexity of the Satisfiability Problem." Courant Computer Science Report No. 16, New York University, 1979.

204. Goldberg, A., P. W. Purdom, and C. A. Brown. "Average Time Analyses of Simplified Davis-Putnam Procedures." *Inf. Proc. Lett.* 15 (1982): 72–75.

205. Gomes, C. P., and B. Selman. "Algorithm Portfolio Design: Theory vs. Practice." In *Proceedings of the 13th Conference on Uncertainty in Artificial Intelligence (UAI'97)*, ed. D. Geiger and P. Shenoy, 190–197. San Francisco: Morgan Kaufmann, 1997.

206. Grädel, E. "Domino Games and Complexity." *SIAM J. Comp.* 19 (1990): 787–804.

207. Graham, B. T., and G. R. Grimmett. "Influence and Sharp Threshold Theorems for Monotonic Measures." arXiv.org E-print Archive, Cornell University Library, 2005. http://www.arxiv.org/abs/math.PR/0505057 (accessed September 27, 2005).

208. Graham, R., O. Patashnik, and D. E. Knuth. *Concrete Mathematics: A Foundation for Computer Science*, 2d ed. Reading, MA: Addison-Wesley, 1994.

209. Greenberg, A. G., B. D. Lubachevsky, D. M. Nicol, and P. E. Wright. "Efficient Massively Parallel Simulation of Dynamic Channel Assignment Schemes for Wireless Cellular Communications." In *Proceedings of the Eighth Workshop on Parallel and Distributed Simulation (PADS'94)*, 187–197. New York: ACM Press, 1994.

210. Grimmett, G. *Percolation.* Berlin: Springer-Verlag, 1989.

211. Gropengiesser, U. "The Ground-State Energy of the $\pm J$-Spin Glass—A Comparison of Various Biologically Motivated Algorithms." *J. Stat. Phys.* 79 (1995): 1005–1012.
212. Gross, L. "Hypercontractivity, Logarithmic Sobolev Inequalities and Applications: A Survey of Surveys." Preprint, 2005.
213. Gross, L. "Logarithmic Sobolev Inequalities." *Amer. J. Math.* 97 (1975): 1061–1083.
214. Grötschel, M., M. Jünger, and G. Reinelt. "Calculating Exact Ground States of Spin Glasses: A Polyhedral Approach." In *Heidelberg Colloquium on Glassy Dynamics*, ed. J. L. van Hemmen and I. Morgenstern, 325–353. Lecture Notes in Physics, vol. 275. Berlin: Springer-Verlag, 1987.
215. Grover, L. K. "Quantum Mechanics Helps in Searching for a Needle in a Haystack." *Phys. Rev. Lett.* 79 (1997): 325–328.
216. Grunbaum, B., and G. Shephard. *Tilings and Patterns*. New York: Freeman and Company, 1986.
217. Grüner, W., R. Giegerich, D. Strothmann, C. M. Reidys, J. Weber, I. L. Hofacker, P. F. Stadler, and P. K. Schuster. "Analysis of RNA Sequence Structure Maps by Exhaustive Enumeration I. Neutral Networks." *Chemical Monthly* 127 (1996): 355–374.
218. Grüner, W., R. Giegerich, D. Strothmann, C. M. Reidys, J. Weber, I. L. Hofacker, P. F. Stadler, and P. K. Schuster. "Analysis of RNA Sequence Structure Maps by Exhaustive Enumeration II. Structures of Neutral Networks and Shape Space Covering." *Chemical Monthly* 127 (1996): 375–389.
219. Gu, J., R. Puri, and B. Du. "Satisfiability Problems in VLSI Engineering." Unpublished manuscript, 1996.
220. Gu, J., P. W. Purdom, J. Franco, and B. W. Wah. "Algorithms for Satisfiability (SAT) Problem: A Survey." In *Satisfiability Problem: Theory and Applications*, ed. D. Du, J. Gu, and P. M. Pardalos, 19–151. DIMACS Series on Discrete Mathematics and Theoretical Computer Science, vol. 35. American Mathematical Society, 1997.
221. Häggström, O. "Zero-Temperature Dynamics for the Ferromagnetic Ising Model on Random Graph." *Physica A* 310 (2002): 275–284.
222. Häggström, O., G. Kalai, and E. Mossel. "A Law of Large Numbers for Weighted Majority." Discussion Paper No. 363, Center for Rationality and Interactive Decision Theory, Hebrew University, Jerusalem. http://www.ratio.huji.ac.il/dp363.pdf (accessed September 27, 2005).
223. Hajiaghayi, M., and G. B. Sorkin. "The Satisfiability Threshold of Random 3-SAT is at least 3.52." arXiv.org E-print Archive, Cornell University Library, 2003. http://arXiv.org/abs/math.CO/0310193 (accessed September 27, 2005).
224. Harel, D. "Recurring Dominos: Making Highly Undecidable Highly Understandable." *Ann. Discrete Math.* 24 (1985): 51–72.
225. Harper, L. H. "Optimal Numberings and Isoperimetric Problems on Graphs." *J. Comb. Theor.* 1 (1966): 385–393.

226. Hart, S. "A Note on the Edges of the n-Cube." *Discrete Math.* 14 (1976): 157–163.

227. Hartmanis, J., and R. Stearns. "On the Computational Complexity of Algorithms." *Trans. Am. Math. Soc.* 117 (1965): 285–306.

228. Hartmann, A. K. "Ground-State Clusters of Two-, Three-, and Four-Dimensional $\pm J$ Ising Spin Glasses." *Phys. Rev. E* 63 (2001): 016106.

229. Hartmann, A. K. "Ground-State Landscape of $\pm J$ Ising Spin Glasses." *Eur. Phys. J. B* 8 (1999): 619–626.

230. Hartmann, A. K., and H. Rieger. *Optimization Algorithms in Physics*. Berlin: Wiley-VHC Verlag, 2002.

231. Hartwig, A., F. Daske, and S. Kobe. "A Recursive Branch-and-Bound Algorithm for the Exact Ground State of Ising Spin-Glass Models." *Comp. Phys. Commun.* 32 (1984): 133–138.

232. Håstad, J. "Almost Optimal Lower Bounds for Small Depth Circuits." In *Randomness and Computation*, ed. S. Micali, 143–170. Advances in Computing Research, vol. 5. JAI Press, 1989.

233. Håstad, J. "Clique is Hard to Approximate within n to the Power $1-\epsilon$." *Acta Mathematica* 182 (1999): 105–142.

234. Håstad, J. "A Slight Sharpening of LMN." *J. Comp. Syst. Sci.* 63 (2001): 498–508.

235. Håstad, J. "Some Optimal Inapproximability Results." *J. ACM* 48 (2001): 798–859.

236. Hayes, B. "Computing Science: Can't Get No Satisfaction." *Amer. Sci.* 85(2) (1997): 108–112.

237. Hayes, B. "Computing Science: The Easiest Hard Problem." *Amer. Sci.* 90(2) (2002): 113–117.

238. Hed, G., A. K. Hartmann, D. Stauffer, and E. Domany. "Spin Domains Generate Hierarchical Ground State Structure in $J = \pm 1$ Spin Glasses." *Phys. Rev. Lett.* 86 (2001): 3148–3151.

239. Henschen, L., and L. Wos. "Unit Refutations and Horn Sets." *J. ACM* 21 (1974): 590–605.

240. Hirst, T., and D. Harel. "Taking it to the Limit: On Infinite Variants of NP-Complete Problems." *J. Comp. Syst. Sci.* 53 (1996): 180–193.

241. Hofacker, I. L., P. K. Schuster, and P. F. Stadler. "Combinatorics of RNA Secondary Structures." *Discrete Appl. Math.* 88 (1998): 207–237.

242. Hofacker, I. L., W. Fontana, L. S. Stadler, P. F. Bonhoeffer, M. Tacker, and P. K. Schuster. Vienna RNA Package. http://www.tbi.univie.ac.at/~ivo/RNA/ (accessed September 27, 2005).

243. Höfting, F., and E. Wanke. "Minimum Cost Paths in Dynamic Graphs." *SIAM J. Comp.* 24 (1995): 1051–1067.

244. Höfting, F., and E. Wanke. "Polynomial Time Analysis of Toroidal Dynamic Graphs." *J. Algorithms* 34 (2000): 14–39.

245. Höfting, F., T. Lengauer, and E. Wanke. "Processing of Hierarchically Defined Graphs and Graph Families." In *Data Structures and Efficient Algorithms*, ed.

B. Monien and T. Ottmann, 44–69. Lecture Notes in Computer Science, vol. 594. Berlin: Springer-Verlag, 1992.

246. Hogg, T. "Adiabatic Quantum Computing for Random Satisfiability Problems." *Phys. Rev. A* 67 (2003): 022314.

247. Hogg, T. "Exploiting Problem Structure as a Search Heuristic." *Intl. J. Mod. Phys. C* 9 (1998): 13–29.

248. Hogg, T. "A Framework for Structured Quantum Search." *Physica D* 120 (1998): 102–116.

249. Hogg, T. "Highly Structured Searches with Quantum Computers." *Phys. Rev. Lett.* 80 (1998): 2473–2476.

250. Hogg, T. "Quantum Search Heuristics." *Phys. Rev. A* 61 (2000): 052311.

251. Hogg, T. "Single-Step Quantum Search using Problem Structure." *Intl. J. Mod. Phys. C* 11 (2000): 739–773.

252. Hogg, T, and D. Portnov. "Quantum Optimization." *Inf. Sci.* 128 (2000): 181–197.

253. Hogg, T., and C. P. Williams. "The Hardest Constraint Problems: A Double Phase Transition." *Art. Intel.* 69 (1994): 359–377.

254. Hogg, T., B. A. Huberman, and C. Williams, eds. "Frontiers in Problem Solving: Phase Transitions and Complexity." *Art. Intel.* 81 (1996): 1–15.

255. Hogg, T., C. Mochon, E. Rieffel, and W. Polak. "Tools for Quantum Algorithms." *Intl. J. Mod. Phys. C* 10 (1999): 1347–1361.

256. Hong, H., B. J. Kim, and M. Y. Choi. "Comment on 'Ising Model on a Small World Network.'" *Phys. Rev. E* 66 (2002): 018101.

257. Hong, H., M. Y. Choi, and B. J. Kim. "Phase Ordering on Small-World Networks with Nearest-Neighbor Edges." *Phys. Rev. E* 65 (2002): 047104.

258. Hoos, H. H. "A Mixture-Model for the Behavior of SLS Algorithms for SAT." In *Proceedings of the 18th National Conference on Artificial Intelligence (AAAI'02)*, 661–667. Menlo Park, CA: AAAI Press, 2002.

259. Hoos, H. H., and T. Stützle. "Local Search Algorithms for SAT: An Empirical Evaluation." *J. Automated Reasoning* 24 (2000): 421–481.

260. Hoppe, B., and E. Tardos. "The Quickest Transshipment Problem." *Math. Oper. Res.* 25 (2000): 36–62.

261. Horvitz, E., Y. Ruan, C. P. Gomes, H. Kautz, B. Selman, and D. M. Chickering. "A Bayesian Approach to Tackling Hard Computational Problems." In *Proceedings of the 17th Conference on Uncertainty in Artificial Intelligence (UAI'01)*, ed. J. Breeze and D. Koller, 235–244. San Francisco: Morgan Kaufmann, 2001.

262. Houdayer, J., and O. C. Martin. "Hierarchical Approach for Computing Spin Glass Ground States." *Phys. Rev. E* 64 (2001): 056704.

263. Howell, J. A., T. F. Smith, and M. S. Waterman. "Computation of Generating Functions for Biological Molecules." *SIAM J. Appl. Math.* 39 (1980): 119–133.

264. Huberman, B. A., and T. Hogg. "Phase Transitions in Artificial Intelligence Systems." *Art. Intel.* 33 (1987): 155–171.

265. Huberman, B. A., R. M. Lukose, and T. Hogg. "An Economics Approach to Hard Computational Problems." *Science* 275 (1997): 51–54.

266. Hunt, H., III, M. Marathe, V. Radhakrishnan, S. Ravi, D. Rosenkrantz, and R. Stearns. "NC-approximation Schemes for NP- and PSPACE-hard Problems for Geometric Graphs." *J. Algorithms* 26 (1998): 238–274.

267. Hunt, H., III, R. Stearns, and M. Marathe. "Relational Representability, Local Reductions and the Complexity of Generalized Satisfiability Problem." Technical Report No. LA-UR-00-6108, Los Alamos National Laboratory, Los Alamos, NM, 2000.

268. Hunt, H., III, R. Stearns and M. Marathe. "Strongly Local Reductions and the Complexity/Efficient Approximability of Algebra and Optimization on Abstract Algebraic Structures." In *Proceedings of the Seventeenth International Joint Conference on Artificial Intelligence (IJCAI'01)*, ed. B. Nebel, 183–191. San Mateo, CA: Morgan Kaufmann, 2001.

269. Hunt, H., III, M. Marathe. V. Radhakrishnan, S. Ravi, D. Rosenkrantz, and R. Stearns. "Parallel Approximation Schemes for a Class of Planar and Near Planar Combinatorial Problems." *Information and Computation* 173 (2002): 40–63.

270. Istrate, G. "Computational Complexity and Phase Transitions." In *Proceedings of the 15th IEEE Annual Conference on Computational Complexity (CCC 2000)*, 104–115. IEEE Computer Society, 2000.

271. Istrate, G. "The Phase Transition in Random Horn Satisfiability and Its Algorithmic Implications." *Rand. Struct. & Algorithms* 20 (2002): 483–506.

272. Istrate, G. "On the Satisfiability of Random k-Horn Formulae." In *Graphs, Morphisms and Statistical Physics*, ed. J. Nesetril and P. Winkler, 113–136. DIMACS Series in Discrete Mathematics and Theoretical Computer Science, vol. 63. American Mathematical Society, 2004.

273. Istrate, G., S. Boettcher, and A. G. Percus. "Spines of Random Constraint Satisfaction Problems: Definition and Connection with Computational Complexity." *Ann. Math. & Art. Intel.* 44 (2004): 353–372.

274. Iwano, K., and K. Steiglitz. "Optimization of One-Bit Full Adders Embedded in Regular Structures." *IEEE Trans. Acoustics, Speech, and Signal Processing* 34 (1986): 1289-1300. Reprinted in *Computer Arithmetic*, ed. E. Swartzlander, 193–204. Los Alamitos, CA: IEEE Computer Society, 1990.

275. Iwano, K., and K. Steiglitz. "Planarity Testing of Doubly Connected Dynamic Infinite Graphs." *Networks* 18 (1988): 205–222.

276. Iwano, K., and K. Steiglitz. "Testing for Cycles in Infinite Graphs with Dynamic Structure." In *Proceedings of the 19th Annual ACM Symposium on Theory of Computing (STOC'87)*, 46–53. New York: ACM Press, 1987.

277. Janson, S. "New Versions of Suen's Correlation Inequality." *Rand. Struct. & Algorithms* 13 (1998): 467–483.

278. Janson, S., Y. C. Stamatiou, and M. Vamvakari. "Bounding the Unsatisfiability Threshold of Random 3-SAT." *Rand. Struct. & Algorithms* 17 (2000): 103–116.

279. Janson, S., T. Luczak, and A. Rucinski. *Random Graphs.* New York: John Wiley & Sons, 2000.

280. Jefferson, D. R. "Virtual Time." *ACM Trans. Prog. Lang. Syst.* 7 (1985): 404–425.

281. Johnson, D. S., C. R. Aragon, L. A. McGeoch, and C. Schevon. "Optimization by Simulated Annealing: An Experimental Evaluation; Part II, Graph Coloring and Number Partitioning." *Oper. Res.* 39 (1991): 378–406.

282. Johnson, D. S., L. A. McGeoch, and E. E. Rothberg. "Asymptotic Experimental Analysis for the Held-Karp Traveling Salesman Bound." In *Proceedings of the 7th Annual ACM-SIAM Symposium on Discrete Algorithms (SODA'96)*, 341–350. New York: ACM Press, 1996.

283. Jones, N. D., and W. T. Laaser. "Complete Problems for Deterministic Polynomial Time." *Theor. Comp. Sci.* 3 (1977): 105–117.

284. Joyce, G. F. "Directed Molecular Evolution." *Sci. Am.* 267(6) (1992): 90–97.

285. Kadanoff, L. P., W. Götze, D. Hamblen, R. Hecht, E. A. S. Lewis, V. V. Palciauskas, M. Rayl, J. Swift, D. Aspnes, and J. Kane. "Static Phenomena near Critical Points: Theory and Experiment." *Rev. Mod. Phys.* 39 (1967): 395–431.

286. Kahn, J., and G. Kalai. "A Discrete Isoperimetric Conjecture with Probabilistic Applications." Preprint (2005).

287. Kahn, J., G. Kalai, and N. Linial. "The Influence of Variables on Boolean Functions. In *Proceedings of the 29th Annual IEEE Symposium on Foundations of Computer Science (FOCS'88)*, 68–80. IEEE Computer Society, 1988.

288. Kalai, G. "A Fourier-Theoretic Perspective for the Condorcet Paradox and Arrow's Theorem." *Adv. in Appl. Math.* 29 (2002): 412–426.

289. Kalai, G. "Noise Sensitivity and Chaos in Social Choice Theory." Discussion Paper No. 399. Center for Rationality and Interactive Decision Theory, Hebrew University, Jerusalem. http://ratio.huji.ac.il/dp/dp399.pdf (accessed September 27, 2005).

290. Kalai, G. "Social Choice and Threshold Phenomena." Discussion Paper No. 279. Center for Rationality and Interactive Decision Theory, Hebrew University, Jerusalem. http://ratio.huji.ac.il/dp/dp279.pdf (accessed September 27, 2005).

291. Kalai, G. "Social Indeterminacy." *Econometrica* 72 (2004): 1565–1581.

292. Kamath, A., R. Motwani, K. Palem, and P. Spirakis. "Tail Bounds for Occupancy and the Satisfiability Threshold Conjecture." *Rand. Struct. & Algorithms* 7 (1995): 59–80.

293. Kaporis, A. C., L. M. Kirousis, Y. C. Stamatiou, M. Vamvakari, and M. Zito. "The Unsatisfiability Threshold Revisited." Paper presented at LICS 2001 Workshop on Theory and Applications of Satisfiability Testing." *Elec. Notes Discrete Math.* 9 (2001): Paper no. 7.

294. Kaporis, A. C., L. M. Kirousis, and E. G. Lalas. "The Probabilistic Analysis of a Greedy Satisfiability Algorithm." In *Proceedings of the 10th Annual Eu-*

ropean Symposium on Algorithms, ed. R. H. Möhring and R. Raman, 574–585. Lecture Notes in Computer Science, vol. 2461. Berlin: Springer-Verlag, 2002.

295. Kaporis, A. C., L. M. Kirousis, and E. G. Lalas. "Selecting Complementary Pairs of Literals." *Elec. Notes Discrete Math.* 16 (2003): 47–70.

296. Kardar, M., G. Parisi, and Y.-C. Zhang. "Dynamic Scaling of Growing Interfaces." *Phys. Rev. Lett.* 56 (1986): 889–892.

297. Karmarkar, N., and R. M. Karp. "The Differencing Method of Set Partitioning." Technical Report UCB/CSD 81/113, Computer Science Division, University of California, Berkeley, 1982.

298. Karmarkar, N., R. M. Karp, G. S. Lueker, and A. M. Odlyzko. "Probabilistic Analysis of Optimum Partitioning." *J. Appl. Prob.* 23 (1986): 626–645.

299. Karp, R. M. "Reducibility among Combinatorial Problems." In *Complexity of Computer Computations*, ed. R. E. Miller and J. W. Thatcher, 85–103. New York: Plenum Press, 1972.

300. Karp, R. M. "The Transitive Closure of a Random Digraph." *Rand. Struct. & Algorithms* 1 (1990): 73–93.

301. Karp, R. M., and J. Pearl. "Searching for an Optimal Path in a Tree with Random Costs." *Art. Intel.* 21 (1983): 99–116.

302. Karp, R. M., R. E. Miller, and S. Winograd. "The Organization of Computations for Uniform Recurrence Equations." *J. ACM* 14 (1967): 563–590.

303. Kautz, H., Y. Ruan, D. Achlioptas, C. Gomes, B. Selman, and M. Stickel. "Balance and Filtering in Structured Satisfiable Problems." In *Proceedings of the Seventeenth International Joint Conference on Artificial Intelligence (IJCAI'01)*, ed. B. Nebel, 351–358. San Mateo, CA: Morgan Kaufmann, 2001. Available at http://www.cs.cornell.edu/gomes/new-papers.htm (accessed September 27, 2005).

304. Kautz, H., E. Horvitz, Y. Ruan, C. Gomes, and B. Selman. "Dynamic Restart Policies." In *Proceedings of the 18th National Conference on Artificial Intelligence (AAAI'02)*, 674–681. Menlo Park, CA: AAAI Press, 2002.

305. Kempe, D., J. Kleinberg, and A. Kumar. "Connectivity and Inference Problems for Temporal Networks." *J. Comp. Syst. Sci.* 64 (2002): 820–842.

306. Kesten, H. "The Critical Probability of Bond Percolation on the Square Lattice Equals 1/2." *Comm. Math. Phys.* 74 (1980): 41–59.

307. Kesten, H. "Scaling Relations for 2D-Percolation." *Comm. Math. Phys.* 109 (1987): 109–156.

308. Kesten, H., and Y. Zhang. "Strict Inequalities for Some Critical Exponents in 2D-Percolation." *J. Stat. Phys.* 46 (1987): 1031–1055.

309. Khanna, S., and R. Motwani. "Towards a Syntactic Characterization of PTAS." In *Proceedings of the 28th Annual ACM Symposium on Theory of Computing (STOC'96)*, 329–337. New York: ACM Press, 1996.

310. Khanna, S., M. Sudan, L. Trevisan, and D. Williamson. "The Approximability of Constraint Satisfaction Problems." *SIAM J. Comp.* 30 (2001): 1863–1920.

311. Khintchine, A. "Über dyadische Brüche." *Math. Z.* 18 (1923): 109–116.

312. Khot, S. "On the Power of Unique 2-Prover 1-Round Games." In *Proceedings of the 34th Annual ACM Symposium on Theory of Computing (STOC'02)*, 767–775. New York: ACM Press, 2002.

313. Khot, S., and O. Regev. "Vertex Cover Might be Hard to Approximate to Within $2 - \varepsilon$." In *Proceedings of the 18th IEEE Annual Conference on Computational Complexity (CCC'03)*, 379–386. IEEE Computer Society, 2003.

314. Khot, S., and N. Vishnoi. "The Unique Games Conjecture, Integrality Gap for Cut Problems and Embeddability of Negative Type Metrics into ℓ_1." In *Proceedings of the 46th Annual IEEE Symposium on Foundations of Computer Science (FOCS'05)*, to appear. IEEE Computer Society, 2005.

315. Khot, S., G. Kindler, E. Mossel, and R. O'Donnell. "Optimal Inapproximability Results for MAX-CUT and Other 2-Variable CSPs?" In *Proceedings of the 45th Annual IEEE Symposium on Foundations of Computer Science (FOCS'04)*, 146–154. IEEE Computer Society, 2004.

316. Kim, B. J., H. Hong, P. Holme, G. S. Jeon, P. Minnhagen, and M. Y. Choi. "XY Model in Small-World Networks." *Phys. Rev. E* 64 (2001): 056135.

317. Kimura, M. *The Neutral Theory of Molecular Evolution*. Cambridge, UK: Cambridge University Press, 1983.

318. Kirkpatrick, S. "Rough Times Ahead." *Science* 299 (2003): 668–669.

319. Kirkpatrick, S., and B. Selman. "Critical Behavior in the Satisfiability of Random Boolean Expressions." *Science* 264 (1994): 1297–1301.

320. Kirkpatrick, S., C. D. Gelatt, and M. P. Vecchi. "Optimization by Simulated Annealing." *Science* 220 (1983): 671–680.

321. Kirkpatrick, S., G. Györgi, N. Tishby, and L. Troyansky. "The Statistical Mechanics of k-Satisfaction." In *Advances in Neural Information Processing Systems*, ed. J. D. Cowan, G. Tesauro, and J. Alspector, vol. 6, 439–446. San Mateo, CA: Morgan Kaufmann Publishers, 1993.

322. Kirousis, L. M., E. Kranakis, and D. Krizanc. "An Upper Bound for a Basic Hypergeometric Series." Technical Report TR-96-07, Carleton University, School of Computer Science, Canada, 1996. Available at http://www.scs.carleton.ca/research/tech_reports/1996 (accessed September 27, 2005).

323. Kirousis, L. M., E. Kranakis, and D. Krizanc. "A Better Upper Bound for the Unsatisfiability Threshold." In *Satisfiability Problem: Theory and Applications*, ed. D. Du, J. Gu, and P. M. Pardalos, 643–648. DIMACS Series in Discrete Mathematics and Theoretical Computer Science, vol. 35. American Mathematical Society, 1997.

324. Kirousis, L. M., E. Kranakis, D. Krizanc, and Y. C. Stamatiou. "Approximating the Unsatisfiability Threshold of Random Formulas." *Rand. Struct. & Algorithms* 12 (1998): 253–269.

325. Kirousis, L. M., Y. C. Stamatiou, and M. Vamvakari. "Upper Bounds and Asymptotics for the q-Binomial Coefficients." *Stud. Appl. Math.* 107 (2001): 43–62.

326. Kleinberg, J. "Navigation in a Small World." *Nature* 406 (2000): 845.

327. Klotz, T. "Zur Phasenraumstruktur in ungeordneten ±I Ising-Spinsystemen." Thesis, Technische Universität Dresden, 1996

328. Klotz, T., and S. Kobe. "Cluster Structures in the Configuration Space and Relaxation in 3d ±I Ising Spin-Glass Model." In *Hayashibara Forum '95, Int. Symp. Coherent Approaches to Fluctuations*, ed. by M. Suzuki and N. Kawashima, 192–195. Singapore: World Scientific, 1996.

329. Klotz, T., and S. Kobe. "Exact Low-Energy Landscape and Relaxation Phenomena in Ising Spin Glasses." *Acta Phys. Slovaca* 44 (1994): 347–356.

330. Klotz, T., and S. Kobe. "'Valley Structure' in the Phase Space of a Finite 3D Ising Spin Glass with ±I Interactions." *J. Phys. A: Math. Gen.* 27 (1994): L95–L100.

331. Klug, S. J., and M. Famulok. "All You Wanted to Know about SELEX." *Mol. Biol. Rep.* 20 (1994): 97–107.

332. Knuth, D. E. *Stable Marriage and its Relation to Other Combinatorial Problems: An Introduction to the Mathematical Analysis of Algorithms.* CRM Proceedings & Lecture Notes, vol. 10. American Mathematical Society, 1997. First French edition: Les Presses de l'Université de Montréal, 1976.

333. Knuth, D. E., R. Motwani, and B. Pittel. "Stable Husbands." *Rand. Struct. & Algorithms* 1 (1990): 1–14.

334. Kobe, S. "Ground State of an Ising Antiferromagnet with Dense Random Packing Structure." In *Amorphous Magnetism II*, ed. R. A. Levy and R. Hasegawa, 529–534. New York and London: Plenum Press, 1977.

335. Kobe, S., and K. Handrich. "Correlation Function and Misfit in a Computer-Simulated Two-Dimensional Amorphous Ising Antiferromagnet." *Phys. Stat. Sol.* 73(b) (1976): K65–K67.

336. Kobe, S., and A. Hartwig. "Exact Ground State of Finite Amorphous Ising Systems." *Comp. Phys. Commun.* 16 (1978): 1–4.

337. Kobe, S., and T. Klotz. "Frustration: How It Can be Measured." *Phys. Rev. E* 52 (1995): 5660–5663.

338. Kodialam, M., and J. B. Orlin. "Recognizing Strong Connectivity in Dynamic Graphs and Its Relation to Integer Programming." In *Proceedings of the 2nd Annual ACM-SIAM Symposium on Discrete Algorithms (SODA '91)*, 131–135. New York: ACM Press, 1991.

339. Kolaitis, P., and T. Raffill. "In Search of a Phase Transition in the AC-Matching Problem." In *Proceedings of the Seventh International Conference on Principles and Practice of Constraint Programming (CP 2001)*, ed. T. Walsh, 433–450. Berlin: Springer-Verlag, 2001.

340. Kolakowska, A. K., M. A. Novotny, and G. Korniss. "Algorithmic Scalability in Globally Constrained Conservative Parallel Discrete Event Simulations of Asynchronous Systems." *Phys. Rev. E* 67 (2003): 046703.

341. Korf, R. E. "A Complete Anytime Algorithm for Number Partitioning." *Art. Intel.* 106 (1998): 181–203.

342. Korniss, G., M. A. Novotny, and P. A. Rikvold. "Parallelization of a Dynamic Monte Carlo Algorithm: A Partially Rejection-Free Conservative Approach." *J. Comp. Phys.* 153 (1999): 488–508.

343. Korniss, G., Z. Toroczkai, M. A. Novotny, and P. A. Rikvold. "From Massively Parallel Algorithms and Fluctuating Time Horizons to Nonequilibrium Surface Growth." *Phys. Rev. Lett.* 84 (2000): 1351–1354.

344. Korniss, G., M. A. Novotny, Z. Toroczkai, and P. A. Rikvold. "Non-Equilibrium Surface Growth and Scalability of Parallel Algorithms for Large Asynchronous Systems." In *Computer Simulated Studies in Condensed Matter Physics XIII*, ed. D. P. Landau, S. P. Lewis and H.-B. Schüttler, 183–188. Berlin: Springer-Verlag, 2001.

345. Korniss, G., M. A. Novotny, P. A. Rikvold, H. Guclu, and Z. Toroczkai. "Going Through Rough Times: From Non-Equilibrium Surface Growth to Algorithmic Scalability." *Mat. Res. Soc. Symp. Proc.* 700 (2002): 297–308.

346. Korniss, G., M. A. Novotny, H. Guclu, Z. Toroczkai, and P. A. Rikvold. "Suppressing Roughness of Virtual Times in Parallel Discrete-Event Simulations." *Science* 299 (2003): 677–679.

347. Kosaraju, K. R., and G. F. Sullivan. "Detecting Cycles in Dynamic Graphs in Polynomial Time." In *Proceedings of the 27th Annual IEEE Symposium on Foundations of Computer Science (FOCS'88)*, 398–406. IEEE Computer Society, 1988.

348. Krauth, W., and M. Mézard. "The Cavity Method and the Travelling-Salesman Problem." *Europhys. Lett.* 8 (1989): 213–218.

349. Krawczyk, J., and S. Kobe. "Low-Temperature Dynamics of Spin Glasses: Walking in the Energy Landscape." *Physica A* 315 (2002): 302–307.

350. Krug, J., and P. Meakin. "Universal Finite-Size Effects in the Rate of Growth Processes." *J. Phys. A* 23 (1990): L987–L994.

351. Kschischang, F. R., B. J. Frey, and H.-A. Loeliger. "Factor Graphs and the Sum-Product Algorithm." *IEEE Trans. Inf. Theory* 47 (2001): 498–519.

352. Ladner, R. "On the Structure of Polynomial Time Reducibility." *J. ACM* 22 (1975): 155–171.

353. Lancaster, D. "Two Combinatorial Models with Identical Statics Yet Different Dynamics." *J. Phys. A: Math. Gen.* 37 (2003): 1125–1143. Cond-mat/0310743.

354. Land, A. H., and A. G. Doig. "An Automatic Method for Solving Discrete Programming Problems." *Econometrica* 28 (1960): 497–520.

355. Lawler, G., O. Schramm, and W. Werner. "One-Arm Exponent for Critical 2D Percolation." *Elec. J. Prob.* 7 (2002): Paper no. 2.

356. Lebrecht, W., and E. E. Vogel. "Ground-State Properties of Finite Square and Triangular Ising Lattices with Mixed Exchange Interactions." *Phys. Rev. B* 49 (1994): 6018–6027.

357. Ledoux, M. *The Concentration of Measure Phenomenon*, Mathematical Surveys and Monographs, 89. Providence, RI: American Mathematical Society, 2001.

358. Lengauer, C. "Loop Parallelization in the Polytope Model." In *Proceedings of the 4th International Conference on Concurrency Theory*, 398–416. Lecture Notes in Computer Science, vol. 715. Berlin: Springer-Verlag, 1993.

359. Leone, M., A. Vázquez, A. Vespignani, and R. Zecchina. "Ferromagnetic Ordering in Graphs with Arbitrary Degree Distribution." *Eur. Phys. J. B* 28 (2002): 191–197.

360. Levin, L. "Universal Sequential Search Problems." *Problems of Information Transmission* 9(3) (1973): 265–266.

361. Liebmann, R. *Statistical Mechanics of Periodic Frustrated Ising Systems*. Lecture Notes in Physics, vol. 251. Berlin: Springer-Verlag, 1986

362. Linial, N., Y. Mansour, and N. Nisan. "Constant Depth Circuits, Fourier Transform, and Learnability." *J. Assoc. Comp. Mach.* 40 (1993): 607–620.

363. Little, J. D. C., K. G. Murty, D. W. Sweeney, and C. Karel. "An Algorithm for the Traveling-Salesman Problem." *Oper. Res.* 11 (1963): 972–989.

364. Loomis, L., and H. Whitney. "An Inequality Related to the Isoperimetric Inequality." *Bull. Amer. Math. Soc.* 55 (1949): 961–962.

365. Lubachevsky, B. D. "Efficient Parallel Simulations of Asynchronous Cellular Arrays." *Complex Systems* 1 (1987): 1099–1123.

366. Lubachevsky, B. D. "Efficient Parallel Simulations of Dynamic Ising Spin Systems." *J. Comp. Phys.* 75 (1988): 103–122.

367. Lubachevsky, B. D. "Fast Simulation of Multicomponent Dynamic Systems." *Bell Labs Tech. J.* 5 (2000): 134–156.

368. Luby, M., and W. Ertel. "Optimal Parallelization of Las Vegas Algorithms." In *STACS '94: 11th Annual Symposium on Theoretical Aspects of Computer Science*, ed. P. Enjalbert, E. Mayr, and K.W. Wagner, 463–475. Lecture Notes in Computer Science, vol. 775. Berlin: Springer-Verlag, 1994.

369. Luby, M., A. Sinclair, and D. Zuckerman. "Optimal Speedup of Las Vegas Algorithms." *Inf. Proc. Lett.* 47 (1993): 173–180.

370. Lueker, G. S. "Exponentially Small Bounds on the Expected Optimum of the Partition and Subset Sum Problems." *Rand. Struct. & Algorithms* 12 (1998): 51–62.

371. Lynch, J. F. "On the Threshold of Chaos in Random Boolean Cellular Automata." *Rand. Struct. & Algorithms* 6 (1995): 239–260.

372. Lynch, J. F. "A Phase Transition in Random Boolean Networks." In *Artificial Life IV*, ed. Rodney A. Brooks and Pattie Maes, 236–245. Cambridge, MA: MIT Press, 1994.

373. MacLane, S., and G. Birkhoff. *Algebra*. New York: Macmillan, 1967.

374. Majumdar, S. N., and P. L. Krapivsky. "Extreme Value Statistics and Traveling Fronts: Application to Computer Science." *Phys. Rev. E* 65 (2002): 036127.

375. Makowsky, J. A. "Why Horn Formulas Matter in Computer Science: Initial Structures and Generic Examples." *J. Comp. Syst. Sci.* 34 (1987): 266–292.

376. Marathe, M.V. "Towards a Predictive Computational Complexity Theory." In *Proceedings of the 29th International Colloquium on Automata Languages*

and Programming, ed. P. Widmayer, F. T. Ruiz, R. Morales, M. Hennessy, S. Eidenbenz, and R. Conejo, 22–31. Lecture Notes in Computer Science, vol. 2380. Berlin: Springer-Verlag, 2002.

377. Marathe, M. V., H. B. Hunt III, R. E. Stearns, and V. Radhakrishnan. "A Dichotomy Theorem for Hierarchically and 1-Dimensional Periodically Specified Satisfiability Problems with Applications." Unpublished manuscript, 1996.

378. Marathe, M. V., H. B. Hunt III, R. E. Stearns, and V. Radhakrishnan. "Complexity of Hierarchically and 1-Dimensional Dynamically Specified Problems I: Hardness Results." In *Satisfiability Problem: Theory and Application*, ed. D. Du., J. Gu, and P. M. Pardalos, 225–259. DIMACS Series on Discrete Mathematics and Theoretical Computer Science, vol. 35. American Mathematical Society, 1997.

379. Marathe, M. V., H. B. Hunt III, R. E. Stearns, and V. Radhakrishnan. "Approximation Algorithms for PSPACE-Hard Hierarchically and Dynamically Specified Problems." *SIAM J. Comp.* 27 (1998): 1237–1261.

380. Marathe, M. V., H. B. Hunt III, D. J. Rosenkrantz, and R. E. Stearns. "Theory of Dynamically Specified Problems: Complexity and Approximability." In *Proceedings of the 13th IEEE Annual Conference on Computational Complexity*, 106-119. Washington, DC: IEEE Computer Society, 1998.

381. Margulis, G. "Probabilistic Characteristics of Graphs with Large Connectivity (in Russian)." *Probl. Pered. Inf.* 10 (1974): 101–108.

382. Martin, O. C., R. Monasson, and R. Zecchina. "Statistical Mechanics Methods and Phase Transitions in Optimization Problems." *Theor. Comp. Sci.* 265 (2001): 3–67.

383. Maurer, S. M., T. Hogg, and B. A. Huberman. "Portfolios of Quantum Algorithms." *Phys. Rev. Lett.* 87 (2001): 257901.

384. McAllester, D., B. Selman, and H. Kautz. "Evidence for Invariants in Local Search." In *Proceedings of the 14th National Conference on Artificial Intelligence (AAAI'97)*, 321–326. Menlo Park, CA: AAAI Press, 1997.

385. McKane, A. J., M. Droz, J. Vannimenus, and D. Wolf, eds. *Scale Invariance, Interfaces and Non-Equilibrium Dynamics*. NATO ASI Series B, vol. 344. New York: Plenum, 1995.

386. Melin, R., J. C. Angles d'Auriac, P. Chandra, and B. Douçot. "Glassy Behavior in the Ferromagnetic Ising Model on a Cayley Tree." *J. Phys. A* 29 (1996): 5773–5804.

387. Merkle, R. C., and M. E. Hellman. "Hiding Informations and Signatures in Trapdoor Knapsacks." *IEEE Trans. Inf. Theory* 24 (1978): 525–530.

388. Mertens, S. "Computational Complexity for Physicists." *Comp. Sci. & Eng.* 4(3) (2002): 31–47.

389. Mertens, S. "Phase Transition in the Number Partitioning Problem" *Phys. Rev. Lett.* 81 (1998): 4281–4284.

390. Mertens, S. "A Physicist's Approach to Number Partitioning." *Theor. Comp. Sci.* 265 (2001): 79–108.

391. Mertens, S. "Random Costs in Combinatorial Optimization." *Phys. Rev. Lett.* 84 (2000): 1347–1350.

392. Mézard, M., and G. Parisi. "The Cavity Method at Zero Temperature." *J. Stat. Phys.* 111 (2003): 1–34.

393. Mézard, M., and G. Parisi. "A Replica Analysis of the Travelling Salesman Problem." *J. Physique* 47 (1986): 1285–1296.

394. Mézard, M., and G. Parisi. "Replicas and Optimization." *J. Physique Lett.* 46 (1985): L771–L778.

395. Mézard, M., and R. Zecchina. "Random K-Satisfiability Problem: From an Analytic Solution to an Efficient Algorithm." *Phys. Rev. E* 66 (2002): 056126.

396. Mézard, M., G. Parisi, and M. A. Virasoro. *Spin Glass Theory and Beyond.* Singapore: World Scientific, 1987.

397. Mézard, M., G. Parisi, and R. Zecchina. "Analytic and Algorithmic Solutions of Random Satisfiability Problems." *Science* 297 (2002): 812–815.

398. Mézard, M., F. Ricci-Tersenghi, and R. Zecchina. "Two Solutions to Diluted p-Spin Models and XORSAT Problems." *J. Stat. Phys.* 111 (2003): 505–533.

399. Mills, D. R., R. L. Peterson, and S. Spiegelman. "An Extracellular Darwinian Experiment with a Self-Duplicating Nucleic Acid Molecule." *PNAS* 58 (1967): 217–224.

400. Mitchell, D., B. Selman, and H. Levesque. "Hard and Easy Distributions of SAT Problems." In *Proceedings of the Tenth National Conference on Artificial Intelligence (AAAI'92)*, 440–446. Menlo Park, CA: AAAI Press, 1992.

401. Molloy, M. "Models for Random Constraint Satisfaction Problems." *SIAM J. Comp.* 32 (2003): 935–949.

402. Molloy, M. Private communication, February 26, 2001.

403. Molloy, M. "Thresholds for Colourability and Satisfiability in Random Graphs and Boolean Formulae." In *Surveys in Combinatorics, 2001*, ed. J. Hirschfeld, 166–200. LMS Lecture Note Series 288. Cambridge, UK: Cambridge University Press, 2001.

404. Monasson, R. "Structural Glass Transition and the Entropy of the Metastable States." *Phys. Rev. Lett.* 75 (1995): 2847–2850.

405. Monasson, R., and R. Zecchina. "Statistical Mechanics of the Random K-Satisfiability Model." *Phys. Rev. E* 56 (1997): 1357–1370.

406. Monasson, R., R. Zecchina, S. Kirkpatrick, B. Selman, and L. Troyansky. "Determining Computational Complexity from Characteristic 'Phase Transitions'." *Nature* 400 (1999):133–137.

407. Monasson, R., R. Zecchina, S. Kirkpatrick, B. Selman, and L. Troyansky. "2+p-SAT: Relation of Typical-Case Complexity to the Nature of the Phase Transition." *Rand. Struct. & Algorithms* 15 (1999): 414–435.

408. Montanari, A., and R. Zecchina. "Optimizing Searches via Rare Events. *Phys. Rev. Lett.* 88 (2002): 178701.

409. Moore, C. Personal communication, 2003.

410. Mossel, E., R. O'Donnell, and F. Oleszkiewicz. "Noise Stability of Functions with Low Influences: Invariance and Optimality." arXiv.org E-print Archive,

Cornell University Library, 2005. http://www.arxiv.org/abs/math/0503503 (accessed September 27, 2005).

411. Motwani, R., and P. Raghavan. *Randomized Algorithms.* Cambridge, UK: Cambridge University Press, 2000.

412. Mulet, R., A. Pagnani, M. Weigt, and R. Zecchina. "Coloring Random Graphs." *Phys. Rev. Lett.* 89 (2002): 268701.

413. Nelson, E. "The Free Markov Field." *J. Functional Analysis* 12 (1973): 211–227.

414. Netcraft Ltd. "Web Server Survey." Netcraft web server surveys from 2005. http://news.netcraft.com/archives/web_server_survey.html (accessed September 27, 2005).

415. Newman, M. E. J., and D. J. Watts. "Renormalization Group Analysis of the Small-World Network Model." *Phys. Lett. A* 263 (1999): 341–346.

416. Nicol, D. M., and R. M. Fujimoto. "Parallel Simulation Today." *Ann. Oper. Res.* 53 (1994): 249–286.

417. Odlyzko, A. M. "Asymptotic Enumeration Methods." In *Handbook of Combinatorics*, ed. R. L. Graham, M. Grötschel, and L. Lovász, vol. 2, 1063–1229. Amsterdam: Elsevier Science, 1995.

418. O'Donnell, R., M. Saks, O. Schramm, and R. Servedio. "Every Decision Tree has an Influential Variable." In *Proceedings of the 46th Annual IEEE Symposium on Foundations of Computer Science (FOCS'05)*, to appear. IEEE Computer Society, 2005.

419. Orlin, J. B. "The Complexity of Dynamic/Dynamic Languages and Optimization Problems." Sloan Working paper 1679-86. Alfred P. Sloan School of Management, MIT, Cambridge, MA, July 1985. Preliminary version in *Proceedings of the 13th Annual ACM Symposium on Theory of Computing (STOC'78)*, 218–227. New York: ACM Press, 1981.

420. Orlin, J. B. "Minimum Convex Cost Dynamic Network Flows." *Math. Oper. Res.* 9 (1984): 190–207.

421. Orlin, J. B. "Some Problems on Dynamic/Dynamic Graphs." In *Progress in Combinatorial Optimization*, ed. W. R. Pullerybank, 273-293. Toronto: Academic Press, 1984.

422. Palmer, R. G., and J. Adler. "Ground States for Large Samples of Two-Dimensional Ising Spin Glasses." *Int. J. Mod. Phys. C* 10 (1999): 667–675.

423. Papadimitriou, C. H. *Computational Complexity.* Reading, MA: Addison-Wesley, 1994.

424. Papadimitriou, C. H. "On Selecting a Satisfying Truth Assignment." In *Proceedings of the 32nd Annual IEEE Symposium on Foundations of Computer Science* (1991): 163–169. IEEE Computer Society, 1991.

425. Papadimitriou, C. H., and K. Steiglitz. *Combinatorial Optimization: Algorithms and Complexity.* Englewood Cliffs, NJ: Prentice-Hall, 1982.

426. Papadimitriou, C. H., and M. Yannakakis. "A Note on Succinct Representations of Graphs." *Information and Control* 71 (1986): 181–185.

427. Parisi, G. "Constraint Optimization and Statistical Mechanics." In *The Physics of Complex Systems*, ed. F. Mallamace and H. E. Stanley, 205–228. International School of Physics Enrico Fermi, vol. 134. Amsterdam: IOS Press, 2004.

428. Parisi, G. "Some Remarks on the Survey Decimation Algorithm for K-Satisfiability." arXiv.org E-print Archive, Cornell University Library, 2003. http://arxiv.org/abs/cs/0301015 (accessed September 27, 2005).

429. Parisi, G. "On the Survey-Propagation Equations for the Random K-Satisfiability Problem." arXiv.org E-print Archive, Cornell University Library, 2002. http://arxiv.org/abs/cs.CC/0212009 (accessed September 27, 2005).

430. Parkes, A. J. "Scaling Properties of Pure Random Walk on Random 3-SAT." In *Proceedings of the Eighth International Conference on Principles and Practice of Constraint Programming (CP 2002)*, ed. P. von Hentenryek, 708–713. Lecture Notes in Computer Science, vol. 2470. Berlin: Springer-Verlag, 2002.

431. Pearl, J. *Probabilistic Reasoning in Intelligent Systems: Network of Plausible Inference*. San Francisco: Morgan Kaufmann, 1988.

432. Pemberton, J. C., and W. Zhang. "Epsilon-Transformation: Exploiting Phase Transitions to Solve Combinatorial Optimization Problems." *Art. Intel.* 81 (1996): 297–325.

433. Pennock, D. M., and Q. F. Stout. "Exploiting a Theory of Phase Transitions in Three-Satisfiability Problems." In *Proceedings of the 13th National Conference on Artificial Intelligence (AAAI'96)*, 253–258. Menlo Park, CA: AAAI Press, 1996.

434. Percus, A. G., and O. C. Martin. "The Stochastic Traveling Salesman Problem: Finite Size Scaling and the Cavity Prediction." *J. Stat. Phys.* 94 (1999): 739–758.

435. Peres, Y. "Noise Stability of Weighted Majority." arXiv.org E-print Archive, Cornell University Library, 2005. http://arxiv.org/abs/math.PR/0412377 (accessed September 27, 2005).

436. Pittel, B., J. Spencer, and N. Wormald. "Sudden Emergence of a Giant k-Core in a Random Graph." *J. Comb. Theor. B* 67 (1996): 111–151.

437. Powell, W., P. Jaillet, and A. Odoni. "Stochastic and Dynamic Networks and Routing." In *Handbook of Operations Research and Management Science: Network and Routing*, ed. M. Ball, T. Magnanti, C. Monma, and G. Nemhauser, 141–295. Amsterdam: Elsevier, 1999.

438. Raz, R. "A Parallel Repetition Theorem." *SIAM J. Comp.* 27 (1998): 763–803.

439. Raz, R., and S. Safra. "A Sub-Constant Error-Probability Low-Degree Test, and A Sub-Constant Error-Probability PCP Characterization of NP." In *Proceedings of the 29th Annual ACM Symposium on Theory of Computing (STOC'97)*, 475–484. New York: ACM Press, 1997.

440. Reidys, C. M. "Distances in Random Induced Subgraphs of Generalized n-Cubes." *Comb. Prob. & Comp.* 11 (2002): 599–605.

441. Reidys, C. M. "Random Induced Subgraphs of Generalized n-Cubes." *Adv. Appl. Math.* 19 (1997): 360–377.

442. Reidys, C. M., and P. F. Stadler. "Bio-Molecular Shapes and Algebraic Structures." *Comp. & Chem.* 20 (1996): 85–94.

443. Reidys, C. M., P. F. Stadler, and P. Schuster. "Generic Properties of Combinatory Maps: Neutral Networks of RNA Secondary Structures." *Bull. Math. Biol.* 59 (1997): 339–397.

444. Reinelt, G. *The Travelling Salesman. Computational Solutions for TSP Applications.* Lecture Notes in Computer Science, vol. 840. Berlin: Springer-Verlag, 1994.

445. Ricci-Tersenghi, F., M. Weigt, and R. Zecchina. "Simplest Random K-Satisfiability Problem." *Phys. Rev. E* 63 (2001): 026702.

446. Richardson, T., and R. Urbanke. "An Introduction to the Analysis of Iterative Coding Systems." In *Codes, Systems, and Graphical Models*, ed. B. Marcus and J. Rosenthal, 1–37. New York: Springer, 2001.

447. Robinson, C. *Dynamical Systems Stability, Symbolic Dynamics, and Chaos*, 2d ed. Boca Raton, FL: CRC Press, 1999.

448. Ruml, W., J. Ngo, J. Marks, and S. Shieber. "Easily Searched Encodings for Number Partitioning." *J. Opt. Theory Appl.* 89 (1996): 251–291.

449. Russo, L. "An Approximate Zero-One Law." *Zeitschrift für Wahrscheinlichkeitstheorie und Verwandte Gebiete* 61 (1982): 129–139.

450. Russo, L. "A Note on Percolation." *Zeitschrift für Wahrscheinlichkeitstheorie und Verwandte Gebiete* 43 (1978): 39–48.

451. Samet, Y. "Equilibria with Information Aggregation in Sharp Threshold Voting Rules." M.Sc. thesis, Hebrew University of Jerusalem, 2004.

452. Sassanfar, M., and J. W. Szostak. "An RNA Motif that Binds ATP." *Nature* 364 (1993): 550–553.

453. Sato, H., and R. Kikuchi. Dilute Antiferromagnetic Systems in FCC and BCC Lattices." In *AIP Conf. Proc. No. 18, Part 1, Magnetism and Magnetic Materials*, ed. C. D. Graham, Jr., and J. J. Rhyne, 605–609. New York: AIP, 1974.

454. Savelsberg, M., and P. van Emde Boas. "Bounded Tiling, An Alternative to SATISFIABILITY." In *Proceedings of the 2nd Frege Conference*, ed. G. Wechsung, 354–363. Berlin: Akademie Verlag, 1984.

455. Schaefer, T. "The Complexity of Satisfiability Problems." In *Proceedings of the 10th Annual ACM Symposium on Theory of Computing (STOC'78)*, 216–226. New York: ACM Press, 1978.

456. Schmitt, W. R., and M. S. Waterman. "Plane Trees and RNA Secondary Structure." *Discrete Appl. Math.* 51 (1994): 317–323.

457. Schoneveld, A. "Parallel Complex Systems Simulation." Ph.D. thesis, Universiteit van Amsterdam, 1999.

458. Schöning, U. "A Probabilistic Algorithm for k-SAT Based on Limited Local Search and Restart. *Algorithmica* 32 (2002): 615–623.

459. Schramm, O., and J. Steif. "Quantitative Noise Sensitivity and Exceptional Times for Percolation." arXiv.org E-print Archive, Cornell University Library, 2005. http://arxiv.org/abs/math/0504586 (accessed September 27, 2005).

460. Schramm, O., and B. Tsirelson. "Trees, Not Cubes: Hypercontractivity, Cosiness, and Noise Stability." *Elec. Comm. Prob.* 4 (1999): 39–49.

461. Schultes, E., and P. Bartels. "One Sequence, Two Ribozymes: Implications for the Emergence of New Ribozyme Folds." *Science* 289 (2000): 448–452.

462. Schuster, P. K. "Landscapes and Molecular Evolution." *Physica D* 107 (1997): 351–365.

463. Schuster, P. K., and P. F. Stadler. "Landscapes: Complex Optimization Problems and Biopolymer Structures." *Comp. & Chem.* 18 (1994): 295–314.

464. Schuster, P. K., W. Fontana, P. F. Stadler, and I. L. Hofacker. "From Sequences to Shapes and Back: A Case Study in RNA Secondary Structures." *Proc. Roy. Soc. Lond. B* 255 (1994): 279–284.

465. Schuster, P. K., J. Weber, W. Grüner, and C. M. Reidys. "Molecular Evolutionary Biology: From Concepts to Technology." In *Physics of Biological Systems: From Molecules to Species*, ed. H. Flyvbjerg, J. Hertz, M. H. Jensen, K. Sneppen, and O. G. Mouritsen, 283–306. Berlin: Springer, 1997.

466. Selman, B., and S. Kirkpatrick. "Critical Behavior in the Computational Cost of Satisfiability Testing." *Art. Intel.* 81 (1996): 273–295.

467. Selman, B., H. Levesque, and D. Mitchell. "A New Method for Solving Hard Satisfiability Problems." In *Proceedings of the 10th National Conference on Artificial Intelligence (AAAI'92)*, 440–446. Menlo Park, CA: AAAI Press, 1992.

468. Selman, B., H. Kautz, and B. Cohen. "Noise Strategies for Improving Local Search." In *Proceedings of the 12th National Conference on Artificial Intelligence (AAAI'94)*, 337–343. Menlo Park, CA: AAAI Press, 1994.

469. Selman, B., D. G. Mitchell, and H. J. Levesque. "Generating Hard Satisfiability Problems." *Art. Intel.* 81 (1996): 17–29.

470. Selman, B., H. Kautz, and B. Cohen. "Local Search Strategies for Satisfiability Testing." In *Cliques, Coloring, and Satisfiability: Second DIMACS Implementation Challenge*, ed. D. S. Johnson and M. A. Trick, 521–531. DIMACS Series in Discrete Mathematics and Theoretical Computer Science, vol. 26. American Mathematical Society, 1996.

471. Semerjian, G., and L. F. Cugliandolo. "Cluster Expansions in Dilute Systems: Applications to Satisfiability Problems and Spin Glasses." *Phys. Rev. E* 64 (2001): 036115.

472. Semerjian, G., and R. Monasson. "Relaxation and Metastability in a Local Search Procedure for the Random Satisfiability Problem." *Phys. Rev. E* 67 (2003): 066103.

473. SETI@home. Home Page. http://setiathome.ssl.berkeley.edu/ (accessed September 27, 2005).

474. Sherrington, D., and S. Kirkpatrick. "Solvable Model of a Spin-Glass." *Phys. Rev. Lett.* 35 (1975): 1792–1796.

475. Simon, J. C., J. Carlier, O. Dubois, and O. Moulines. "Étude statistique de l'existence de solutions de problèmes SAT, application aux systèmes-experts." *C.R. Acad. Sci. Paris. Sér. I Math.* 302 (1986): 283–286.

476. Sistla, A. P., and E. Clark. "Complexity of Linear Temporal Logics." *J. ACM* 32 (1985): 733–749.

477. Slaney, J., and T. Walsh. "Backbones in Optimization and Approximation." In *Proceedings of the Seventeenth International Joint Conference on Artificial Intelligence (IJCAI'01)*, ed. B. Nebel, 254–259. San Francisco: Morgan Kaufmann, 2001.

478. Sloot, P. M. A., B. J. Overeinder, and A. Schoneveld. "Self-Organized Criticality in Simulated Correlated Systems." *Comp. Phys. Commun.* 142 (2001): 76–81.

479. Smirnov, S. "Critical Percolation in the Plane: Conformal Invariance, Cardy's Formula, Scaling Limits." *C. R. Acad. Sci. Paris Sér. I Math.* 333 (2001): 239–244.

480. Snedecor, G. W., and W. G. Cochran. *Statistical Methods*, 6th ed. Ames, Iowa: Iowa State University Press, 1967.

481. Spielman, D. A. "The Complexity of Error-Correcting Codes." In *Proceedings of the 11th International Symposium on Fundamentals of Computation Theory (FCT 1997)*, ed. B. S. Chlebus and L. Czaja, 67–84. Lecture Notes in Computer Science, vol. 1279. Berlin: Springer-Verlag, 1997.

482. Spirin, V., P. L. Krapivsky, and S. Redner. "Freezing in Ising Ferromagnets." *Phys. Rev. E* 65 (2001): 016119.

483. Stadler, P. F., W. Hordijk, and J. F. Fontanari. "Phase Transition and Landscape Statistics of the Number Partitioning Problem." *Phys. Rev. E* 67 (2003): 056701.

484. Stauffer, D. "Frustration and Simulation." *Physics World* 23. May 1999.

485. Stauffer, D., and A. Aharony. *Introduction to Percolation Theory*. London: Taylor and Francis, 1994.

486. Steane, A. "Quantum Computing." *Rep. Prog. Phys.* 61 (1998): 117–173.

487. Stearns, R. E. "It's Time to Reconsider Time." *Comm. ACM* 37 (1994): 95–99.

488. Stearns, R. E., and H. B. Hunt III. "Power Indices and Easier Hard Problems." *Math. Syst. Theory* 23 (1990): 209–225.

489. Steffen, M., W. van Dam, T. Hogg, G. Breyta, and I. Chuang. "Experimental Implementation of an Adiabatic Quantum Optimization Algorithm." *Phys. Rev. Lett.* 90 (2003): 067903.

490. Stone, H. S., and P. Sipala. "The Average Complexity of Depth-First Search with Backtracking and Cutoff." *IBM J. Res. & Dev.* 30 (1986): 242–258.

491. Strogatz, S. H. "Exploring Complex Networks." *Nature* 410 (2001): 268–276.

492. Suen, W. C. "A Correlation Inequality and a Poisson Limit Theorem for Nonoverlapping Balanced Subgraphs of a Random Graph." *Rand. Struct. & Algorithms* 1 (1990): 231–242.

493. Svenson, P. "Freezing in Random Graph Ferromagnets." *Phys. Rev. E* 64 (2001): 036122.

494. Svenson, P., and M. G. Nordhal. "Relaxation in Graph Coloring and Satisfiability Problems." *Phys. Rev. E* 59 (1999): 3983–3999.

495. Talagrand, M. "On Boundaries and Influences." *Combinatorica* 17 (1997): 275–285.

496. Talagrand, M. "Concentration and Influences." *Israel J. Math.* 111 (1999): 275–284.

497. Talagrand, M. "Concentration of Measure and Isoperimetric Inequalities in Product Spaces." *Publ. I.H.E.S.* 81 (1995): 73–205.

498. Talagrand, M. "Isoperimetry, Logarithmic Sobolev Inequalities on the Discrete Cube, and Margulis' Graph Connectivity Theorem." *Geom. & Funct. Anal.* 3 (1993): 295–314.

499. Talagrand, M. "On Russo's Approximate Zero-One Law." *Ann. Prob.* 22 (1994): 1576–1587.

500. Tina: a Beowulf Supercomputer. Institute of Theoretical Physics, Otto-von-Guericke-Universität, Magdeburg. http://tina.nat.uni-magdeburg.de (accessed September 27, 2005).

501. Toroczkai, Z., G. Korniss, S. Das Sarma, and R. K. P. Zia. "Extremal-Point Densities of Interface Fluctuations." *Phys. Rev. E* 62 (2000): 276–294.

502. Toulouse, G. "Theory of the Frustration Effect in Spin Glasses: I." *Comm. Physics* 2 (1977): 115–119.

503. Trotter, H. F. "Approximation of Semi-Groups of Operators." *Pacific J. Math.* 8 (1958): 887–919.

504. Tsai, L.-H. "Asymptotic Analysis of an Algorithm for Balanced Parallel Processor Scheduling." *SIAM J. Comp.* 21 (1992): 59–64.

505. Tsirelson, B. "Scaling Limit, Noise, Stability." In *Lectures on Probability Theory and Statistics*, 1–106. Lecture Notes in Mathematics, 1840. Berlin: Springer, 2004.

506. Tsirelson, B., and A. Vershik. "Examples of Nonlinear Continuous Tensor Products of Measure Spaces and Non-Fock Factorizations." *Rev. Math. Phys.* 10 (1998): 81–145.

507. Tuerk, C., and L. Gold. "Systematic Evolution of Ligands by Exponential Enrichment: RNA Ligands to Bacteriophage T4 DNA Polymerase." *Science* 249 (1990): 505–510.

508. van Dam, W., M. Mosca, and U. Vazirani. "How Powerful is Adiabatic Quantum Computation?" In *Proceedings of the 42nd Annual IEEE Symposium on Foundations of Computer Science (FOCS'01)*, 279–287. IEEE Computer Society, 2001.

509. van Emde Boas, P. "Dominoes are Forever." In *Proceedings of the 1st GTI Workshop*, 76–95. Paderborn, 1983.

510. Vardi, M. Y., and P. Wolper. "An Automata-Theoretic Approach to Automatic Program Verification (preliminary report)." In *Proceedings of the 1st IEEE Symposium on Logic in Computer Science (LICS'86)*, 332–344. Washington, DC: IEEE Computer Society, 1986.

511. Vogel, E. E., J. Cartes, S. Contreras, W. Lebrecht, and J. Villegas. "Ground-State Properties of Finite Square and Triangular Ising Lattices with Mixed Exchange Interactions." *Phys. Rev. B* 49 (1994): 6018–6027.

512. Vogel, E. E., J. Cartes, P. Vargas, D. Altbir, S. Kobe, T. Klotz, and M. Nogala. "Hysteresis in $\pm J$ Ising Square Lattices." *Phys. Rev. B* 59 (1999): 3325–3328

513. Vogel, E. E., A. J. Ramirez-Pastor, and F. Nieto. "Detailed Structure of Configuration Space and Its Importance on Ergodic Separation of $\pm J$ Ising Lattices." *Physica A* 310 (2002): 384–396.

514. Walsh, T. "The Constrainedness Knife-Edge." In *Proceedings of the 15th National Conference on Artificial Intelligence (AAAI'98)*, 406–411. Menlo Park, CA: AAAI Press, 1998.

515. Wang, H. "Proving Theorems by Pattern Recognition II." *Bell System Tech. J.* 40 (1961): 1–41.

516. Wanke, E. "Paths and Cycles in Finite Dynamic Graphs." In *Proceedings of the 20th Symposium on Mathematical Foundations of Computer Science (MFCS'93)*, ed. A. M. Borzyszkowski and S. Sokolowski, 751–760. Lecture Notes in Computer Science, vol. 711. Berlin: Springer-Verlag, 1993.

517. Wannier, G. H. "Antiferromagnetism. The Triangular Ising Net." *Phys. Rev.* 79 (1950): 357–364.

518. Waterman, M. S. "Combinatorics of RNA Hairpins and Cloverleaves." *Stud. Appl. Math.* 60 (1978): 91–96.

519. Watts, D.J., and S. H. Strogatz. "Collective Dynamics of 'Small-World' Networks." *Nature* 393 (1998): 440–442.

520. Weber, J. *Dynamics on Neutral Evolution.* Ph.D. thesis, Friedrich Schiller University, Jena, 1997.

521. Weigt, M. "Dynamics of Heuristic Optimization Algorithms on Random Graphs." *Eur. Phys. J. B* 28 (2002): 369–381.

522. Weigt, M., and A. K. Hartmann. "Minimal Vertex Covers on Finite-Connectivity Random Graphs: A Hard-Sphere Lattice-Gas Picture." *Phys. Rev. E* 63 (2001): 056127.

523. Weigt, M., and A. K. Hartmann. "The Number of Guards Needed by a Museum: A Phase Transition in Vertex Covering of Random Graphs." *Phys. Rev. Lett.* 84 (2000): 6118–6121.

524. Weigt, M., and A. K. Hartmann. "Typical Solution Time for a Vertex-Covering Algorithm on Finite-Connectivity Random Graphs." *Phys. Rev. Lett.* 86 (2001): 1658–1661.

525. West, D. *Introduction to Graph Theory.* Princeton, NJ: Prentice Hall, 1994.

526. Westheimer, F. H. "Polyribonucleic Acids as Enzymes." *Nature* 319 (1986): 534–536.

527. Wilson, D. B. "On the Critical Exponents of Random k-SAT." *Rand. Struct. & Algorithms.* 21 (2002): 182–195.

528. Wolfram, S. *Theory and Applications of Cellular Automata.* Singapore: World Scientific, 1987.

529. Wormald, N. C. "Differential Equations for Random Processes and Random Graphs." *Ann. Appl. Prob.* 5 (1995): 1217–1235.

530. Wright, S. "Random Drift and the Shifting Balance Theory of Evolution." In *Mathematical Topics in Population Genetics*, ed. K. Kojima, 1–31. Berlin: Springer-Verlag, 1970.

531. Wright, S. "The Roles of Mutation, Inbreeding, Crossbreeeding and Selection in Evolution." In *International Proceedings of the Sixth International Congress on Genetics*, ed. D. F. Jones, vol. 1, 356–366. Menosha, WI: Brooklyn Botanic Garden, 1932. On-line facsimile version available from Electronic Scholarly Publishing. http://www.esp.org/books/6th-congress/facsimile (accessed September 27, 2005).

532. Yakir, B. "The Differencing Algorithm LDM for Partitioning: A Proof of a Conjecture of Karmarkar and Karp." *Math. Oper. Res.* 21 (1996): 85–99.

533. Yedidia, J. S., W. T. Freeman and Y. Weiss. "Generalized Belief Propagation." In *Advances in Neural Information Processing Systems (NIPS)*, ed. T. K. Leen, T. G. Dietterich, and V. Tresp, vol. 13, 689–695. Cambridge, MA: MIT Press, 2001.

534. Young, A. P. "Spin Glasses: A Computational Challenge for the 21st Century." *Comp. Phys. Commun.* 146 (2002): 107–112.

535. Young, H. P. "Condorcet's Theory of Voting." *Amer. Pol. Sci. Rev.* 82 (1988): 1231–1244.

536. Zecchina, R. Survey Based Algorithm for Random Satisfiability. http://www.ictp.trieste.it/~zecchina/SP (accessed September 27, 2005).

537. Zhan, Z. F., L. W. Lee, and J.-S. Wang. "A New Approach to the Study of the Ground-State Properties of 2D Ising Spin Glass." *Physica A* 285 (2000): 239–247.

538. Zito, M. "Randomised Techniques in Combinatorial Algorithmics." Ph.D. thesis, Department of Computer Science, University of Warwick, November 1999.

Index

Printed in the United States
By Bookmasters